SYSTEMS BUILDING WITH ORACLE

ORACLE

The Theory and Practice of Database Design

SYSTEMS BUILDING WITH ORACLE

The Theory and Practice of Database Design

William Smith

First published 2004 by
PALGRAVE MACMILLAN
Houndmills, Basingstoke, Hampshire RG21 6XS and
175 Fifth Avenue, New York, N. Y. 10010
Companies and representatives throughout the world

PALGRAVE MACMILLAN is the global academic imprint of the Palgrave Macmillan division of St. Martin's Press LLC and of Palgrave Macmillan Ltd. Macmillan® is a registered trademark in the United States, United Kingdom and other countries. Palgrave is a registered trademark in the European Union and other countries.

ISBN 1–4039–0169–4

This book is printed on paper suitable for recycling and made from fully managed and sustained forest sources.

A catalogue record for this book is available from the British Library.

10   9   8   7   6   5   4   3   2   1
13 12 11 10 09 08 07 06 05 04

Printed and bound in China

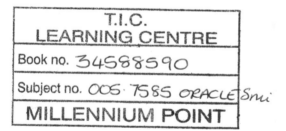

CONTENTS

I try to leave out the parts that people skip

Elmore Leonard

PREFACE

I'm not interested in developing a powerful brain. All I'm after is just a mediocre brain, something like the President of the American Telephone and Telegraph Company.

Alan Turing

This book comes from teaching introductory, intermediate and advanced level courses at undergraduate and postgraduate level. Much of the structure and content reflects support material for courses that establish the theoretical aspects of database systems, underpin practical workshops or initiate advanced, research-oriented studies.

I have included coverage of all of the central and optional database topics likely to arise during the whole of a student's undergraduate career. The material is also suitable to support students following an MSc conversion programme.

The book is divided into four parts. Part 1, *Getting Started*, offers introductory material on the development of data storage techniques, data models and databases. It also sets out the background for the Liga Utopia case study that provides most of the practical examples in the succeeding text.

The second part, *Database Systems*, contains course material for a course in database theory, typically taken as part of the second year of study for an undergraduate programme or as a major element of a conversion MSc. The volume of material in this section is aimed at a full unit within such a modular programme. Sample teaching plans, lecture slides, tutorial questions and coursework assignments are available on the support web site.

Implementing the System, the third part, deals with practical issues. This offers a guide to the problems and solutions associated with the implementation of the Liga Utopia case study. This can be used to support group workshop tasks. It also offers insights for individual project work.

The final part, *Advanced Database Issues*, reviews several topics of current research interest and delves deeper into some of the material treated in Part 2. Its aim is to introduce these areas of study in order to facilitate a research-based unit at final year level. Each chapter finishes with suggestions for project-based work in these areas.

I have included a bibliography at the back of the book. These references deal with basic concepts and the reader will see that they date from the period where this material represented the leading edge of database research. I have concentrated on providing only references to original and seminal papers for several reasons.

In the majority of cases, they express fundamental principles in clear descriptive prose without recourse to complex mathematical and logic symbology. This offers inclusive reading for the students targeted by this book.

They provide a clear portal, through citation, into subsequent publications. This enables tracking of both theoretical and practical developments.

The wide availability of full-text electronic libraries, notably from the ACM and IEEE, means that students can, and should be encouraged to, do their own research. They will obtain fresh references reflecting modern research trends beyond the publication date of this book.

The practical examples and case studies in the text are based on Oracle 9i(2). Many UK Universities use this database in their teaching programmes. My own University makes the CD installation available for students. The CDs are also available from the Oracle Technology Network or are downloadable zip files (1.5 GByte).

Borland's JBuilder is similarly widely used in Higher Education both to support the development of front-end database applications and to underpin the teaching of programming. I have used Enterprise Edition Version 7 to produce the Liga Utopia case study and the other web interface programs. All the code in the book has been cut and pasted from working programs. Any run-time difficulties will be a matter of correcting the environment configuration. I have included guidance on this with the examples.

Finally, I must acknowledge the contribution of my colleague, Mark Campbell, to this text. Mark started out on the rocky road of authorship with me but was prevented from completing the journey by ill health. Much of the material on Oracle PL/SQL and parallel databases is due to him.

William Smith

PART 1

GETTING STARTED

CHAPTER 1

A BRIEF HISTORY OF DATA

Technology is the knack of so arranging the world so that we do not experience it.

Max Frisch

1.1 NORMANS AND LYONS

When William the Conqueror invaded England in 1066 and defeated Harold's army near Hastings, his immediate task was to pacify the country. After a phase of castle building, land redistribution and military suppression of the Anglo Saxons, William ruled in relative peace. He knew that in order to rule a country he needed a stable government based on a sound income. He needed to raise taxes. In order to do this he needed **data** about the land holdings, the agricultural output and the military capacity of the population.

Therefore, he ordered an inventory. The Domesday Book was completed in 1085. In a little over 400 handwritten pages, all of the wealth of England was described.

Towards the end of the 18th century, Britain's youngest ever Prime Minister, William Pitt, was facing two similar problems. Firstly, he had an expensive war to fight against Napoleonic Europe. Secondly, his principal revenue, based on the agricultural wealth of England, held by relatively few landowners, was giving way to industrial wealth created in the burgeoning cities, centred on the new manufactories. In 1799, he changed the fiscal face of England by introducing Income Tax to tap into this wealth and pay for his war. In so doing, he multiplied the number of taxpayers by perhaps a factor of 1000 and created a new role for the Treasury in collecting and collating tax **data** on an unprecedented scale.

DATA	Recorded values describing the characteristics of a real world object or concept.

By the middle of the 20th century, not only governments but also large national corporations were dealing with huge numbers of customers, offering a wide range of products distributed through complex wholesale and retail networks. All of this activity was controlled using paper records, card indexes, thousands of clerks and mechanical office equipment that still relied on the human brain for most of its logic.

One of the first commercial computer systems to be introduced in Britain was the Lyons Electronic Office – LEO. In 1951, the LEO computer was operational and ran the world's first routine office computer jobs. It used computing equipment based on programmable computers with tape storage to calculate, among other things, the payroll for J Lyons & Co.

1.2 DEUS EX MACHINA[1]

A technological revolution was on the horizon. The new science of electronics had created a machine capable of storing complex instructions and applying them to data at a seemingly incredible speed. The first use of this type of computing machine had been in cracking German wartime codes. The instructions were defined by physically varying the connected parts of the machine using plug cables.

After the war, the machines had been improved so that the set of instructions could be varied simply by loading a 'program' encoded on a roll of punched paper tape. It was not long before it was realized that much of the logic of commercial and administrative processes could be captured as a program and applied to records stored on magnetic tape.

It is part of the physical nature of magnetic tape that the records are stored one after the other along the tape. Just as with an audio cassette, if you want to play track 6 you must fast-forward the tape to the position you need. If you then want to play track 3, you must rewind and so on.

RANDOM ORGANIZATION	Data items recorded one after the other with no implicit ordering.
SEQUENTIAL ORGANIZATION	Data items, sorted on some attribute, recorded one after the other.

The data on these early reels of tape were said to be organized **randomly** if the data items had no particular order. If the order of the data items was sorted in some way, say by surname, they were said to be organized sequentially. The access method, however, is serial whatever the organization of the tape

---

1 Spirit of the machine

The introduction of disk storage made a great difference to the way that data could be processed. The data is stored on the magnetically coated surface of a disk that rotates at high speed.

A read/write head 'flies' just above the disk and reads or writes the data using a powerful focused magnetic field to manipulate the signals recorded on the disk. The data is stored in concentric **tracks** on the disk (Figure 1.1). By moving the recording head in or out over a radius of the disk, a different track passes under it.

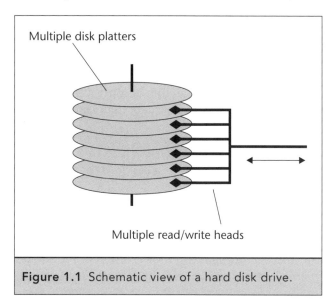

Multiple disk platters

Multiple read/write heads

Figure 1.1 Schematic view of a hard disk drive.

Moving between data items is much faster, since the head can quickly move to fly above the appropriate track and wait not more than one revolution of the disk for the data to pass under it. Multiple disks on a single spindle with a head for each surface increased the storage capacity of the disk pack. It was now possible to position the head array over track 20, say, on platter 1 and without physically moving the head to read track 20 on platter 2 simply by electronically switching the active head.

TRACK	An imaginary circle on the surface of a disk, centred on the disk hub and described by the passage of the disk under the read/write head.
CYLINDER	An imaginary 3D shape formed by the same tracks on successive disk platters.

Storing related records on the same track but on different platters of the disk pack means that a virtual **cylinder** of data is created (Figure 1.1).

This freedom of movement for the read/write head clearly has implications for processing speed. On a tape drive, the head does not move; the tape merely passes underneath it. One item of data follows another. The order of the items that are stored clearly fixes the order of reading.

DIRECT ACCESS	A method of data access where the next position is not predicated by the current position. Compare with serial access.

A disk does not have its next position prescribed for it by the storage method. It can read track 20, followed by track 6 followed by track 56. Because we cannot predict its next position from its current position, a disk is described as a **direct access** device. The operating system that is controlling the movements of the disk is free to move it to wherever the next data item is to be found.

MULTI-TASKING	An operating system feature that allows more than one active process to reside in the computer's memory. CPU time is allocated to the queued processes by a scheduler.

Additionally, more than one program at a time can make read or write requests at different positions according to their own different requirements. A direct access disk supports **multi-tasking** in a way that a serial device could never do.

1.3 FILES AND FILING SYSTEMS

By the 1960s the US Government, in collaboration with several large computer corporations agreed on a standard programming language for business applications. The COmmon Business-Oriented Language (COBOL) was soon available for most large or mainframe computers and was relatively easy to use for trained programmers. The scale of business operations that were being transferred to computers grew sharply.

RECORD	A collection of data about a single real word object. Records have attributes or fields containing values for the characteristics of that object

It became common to find banks, for example, with customer **records** numbered in the millions. Clearly, the size of the **file** that contained such data was huge and it might span several disk devices.

FILE	A collection of records about the same type of real-world object. All records in the file generally have the same structure.

The problem of efficient access to such files was shared by most applications, and COBOL was augmented with a number of standard file handling procedures. These might allow a program to step through a file, stopping at each customer record to perform a task and then moving on until encountering the end of the file. This would suit an application executed at the end of each month to print a statement for each of a bank's customers. Figure 1.2 shows how files can be organized either randomly or sequentially.

Author	Subject	Data
Grant	History	...
Hepburn	Biology	...
Wells	Anatomy	...
Tracy	Physics	...
Monroe	Medicine	...
Hayworth	Biology	...

Author File: random organization; new records are added at the end

Author	Subject	Data
Grant	History	...
Hayworth	Biology	...
Hepburn	Biology	...
Monroe	Medicine	...
Tracy	Physics	...
Wells	Anatomy	...

Author File: sequential organization; new records require a complete re-sort of the file on Author

Figure 1.2 File organization.

Another program might need to home in on a particular customer to retrieve his financial history in the process of deciding on an individual loan application. In this case, it would very inefficient to scan through the whole file, and the use of **index files** (Figure 1.3) was added to COBOL.

INDEX FILE	A secondary file associated with a main data file and sorted on one or more unique attribute values with a pointer to the occurrence of such an attribute value in the records of the main file.

An index works just like the catalogue in a library. A separate card file, sorted on some unique identifier, is kept. In a library catalogue, the reader can search on

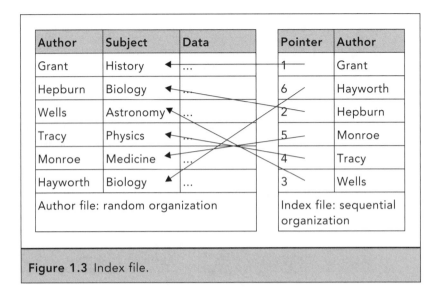

Figure 1.3 Index file.

author's surname. Since the record cards are kept in alphabetical order, it is relatively easy to find the author's card.

Searching through cards organized alphabetically, looking for the correct author, is then very simple. By looking about halfway through the file, you should find the 'M's. Knowing that the author is in the second half of the alphabet, by looking halfway between the 'M's and 'Z's you will probably find the 'S's and so on.

When the correct card is found, it contains a reference that points to the shelf where the author's books are kept. The reader goes to the shelf and retrieves the book. In this case, the unique identifier is the author's surname. Figure 1.3 shows an example of a sorted index of a small number of records, with each entry pointing to the record number of the main data item. Adding new records in the main file means reorganizing the index file.

There were several disadvantages associated with using a language like COBOL to manage large files in this way. Firstly, each program had to have a section in it that described what kind of data was being used. Since there might be many programs to perform all the processing associated with the business's needs, if the data structures changed, all the programs would need to be updated with the amended structure.

Secondly, there would have to be separate programs to create the indexes and to update them when data was added or deleted and, of course, to keep the main data file in a consistent state. These are known as maintenance tasks.

Over time, the program code for these common maintenance tasks was incorporated into code libraries that could be linked to application programs at compile time. This way of working was more efficient, but it still meant that the size of the executable program was very large and made heavy demands on the memory of the computer.

As operating systems design advanced, it became possible to enable more than one user to run a copy of each program simultaneously (Figure 1.4). This multi-user facility had two implications: there would now be multiple copies of already large

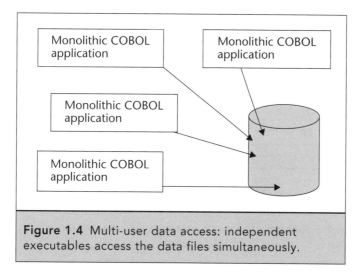

Figure 1.4 Multi-user data access: independent executables access the data files simultaneously.

executables resident in the machine's memory and the data files had to be protected from two or more users reading and updating the same data item at the same time. Adding memory to the machine could solve the first problem. The second problem needed substantial additions to the standard code libraries to allow synchronized access to data items.

The use of simple monolithic programs to undertake data processing tasks on ever-larger data stores was becoming increasingly unwieldy and needed rationalizing.

One idea was to separate the business logic from the storage and maintenance of the data. Creating a separate executable program that was responsible for storing a single image of the data structure and managing the standard maintenance functions would make it possible to strip the entire encumbrance from the user programs.

One copy of the manager program would be resident in the computer and several copies of the smaller user programs would communicate with it, requesting standard functions like searching for a particular data item, updating it free from interference from other users and storing the update reliably. The idea of the database had arrived.

1.4 DATABASE MANAGERS

A database manager is a system program available for communication with user programs (Figure 1.5). At the start of its development, database software ran on a large computer known as a mainframe. The user programs ran on the same machine. Inter-process communication between the user programs and the database manager was achieved using signals and semaphores managed by the operating system.

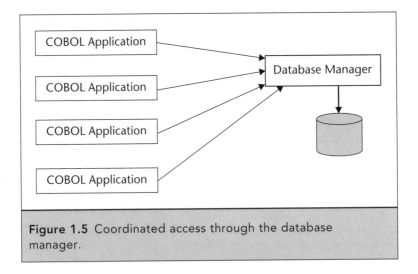

Figure 1.5 Coordinated access through the database manager.

Separation of the business logic in the user program from the common maintenance tasks in the database manager could be said to preview the later development of the *client–server* paradigm. The chief differences were the method of communication and that fact that 'client' and 'server' occupied the same memory space in the same computer.

CLIENT–SERVER	The monolithic application is divided into two. One program, the client, handles the user interface and application logic, communicating, either locally or across a network, with the server program which handles data access.
SCHEMA	Information about the record types, the relationships between them and the attributes that they contain. Stored separately in the database and used to check the data for consistency before and after each update, insertion or deletion.

In order to achieve these aims, the Database Management System (DBMS) had objectives as set out in Table 1.1. These are general specifications for a complex software engineering project.

The design brief says nothing about how the data is visualized and defined; it does not prescribe the storage method and it does not lay down a particular internal language to perform queries on the data.

The separation of logic from data enables:

● efficient and reliable data management

● reliable and safe schema management

Table 1.1 The Objectives of a DBMS.	
Schema control	Allow a specially authorized user or group of users (the database administrators – DBAs) to define the data items contained in the database and to define relationships between specified types of data item. Allow the DBA to alter these definitions and to generally manage the schema.
	Establish the DBA as the link between systems designers and application developers. Disallow these two groups direct access to schema maintenance.
	Allow the DBA to bulk load the data into the database's files, automatically checking data item structure against the current definition and automatically establishing the defined relationship between types of data item.
Security	Ensure that the only way for any user to access the database files is through authorized use of the database management functions. Allow the DBA to define which users may have access to the database and to restrict their access to specific data items and to specific functions.
	Protect the database from catastrophic events such as disk crashes and power failure.
Data control	Allow users access to the data: provide search, navigation and data insertion, amendment and deletion functions. Ensure that data changes by users end with the database continuing to obey the schema definitions set up by the DBA
	Resolve conflicts caused by users attempting simultaneous access to the same data.

- efficient and safe application development
- efficient utilization of hardware resources
- optimized performance and response

All database management software follows these guidelines and in addition will have further, more particular, definitions that allow a broad characterization of DBMSs into five groups that were developed by the major computer corporations over the 30 year period from 1965 to 1995.

1.5 HIERARCHICAL DATABASES

IBM started development work on the first database, IMS, in the mid-1960s. Early versions of the software were released in 1968. IMS was based on a view of the data that became known as *hierarchical*.

Each type of real-world object was modelled as a record type. Records describing the same type of object had the same structure and consisted of fields describing the common characteristics of the object.

Thus, there might be a record type *Customer* that would have fields for *surname*, *first name*, *date of birth* etc. If this were a banking application then there might also be a separate record type called *Account* that described the particular accounts a customer might hold. Branches in the bank would be represented as another record type and so on.

Figure 1.6 illustrates the logic of this view. The relationship is in one direction only, parent to child, and in the physical database is captured as a pointer connecting, for example, each customer to the account held. This pointer is actually the disk address of the owned record. If, as in the case of the branch/customer relationship, the branch were responsible for many customers, then the pointer would indicate the first customer and a chain of pointers would connect all the customers from the same branch.

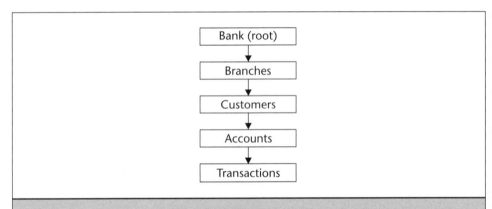

Figure 1.6 Hierarchical database: example schema. In this example, there are five record types. The pointers indicate ownership. Access to the database is through the root of the hierarchy, the Bank.

Each record has to have additional spaces to store child pointer(s) and chain pointer(s). The pointers would be disk addresses of the storage positions of the records. The central point about this data model is that the relationship between record types was expressed through *ownership*. Thus, branches might own customers who would in turn own accounts. This view is sometimes also called a *parent/child* relationship.

Searching in such a database implies following the links of the pointers. To find a particular branch we start at the bank/root and find the first branch owned by the bank.

The chain of branches is then traversed until the particular branch that meets the search criteria is found. Descending to the first customer, that chain can be traversed to find all the customers in a branch. This is known as a navigational query, where record identity and relationships are established by pointer values.

Figure 1.7 shows that Branch *Able* has Customers *567, 9348, 2894, 2849* and *8723,* which has an end pointer in the Next Customer field.

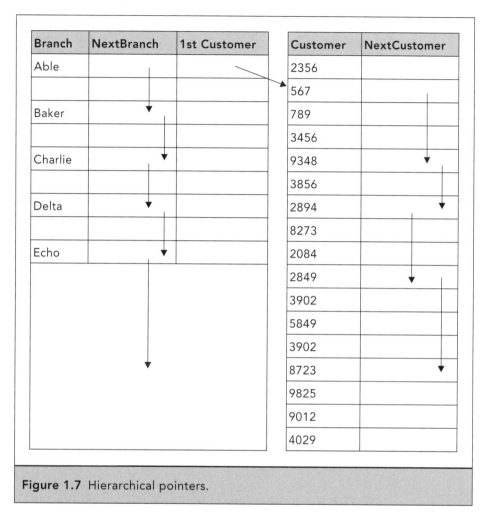

Branch	NextBranch	1st Customer		Customer	NextCustomer
Able				2356	
				567	
Baker				789	
				3456	
Charlie				9348	
				3856	
Delta				2894	
				8273	
Echo				2084	
				2849	
				3902	
				5849	
				3902	
				8723	
				9825	
				9012	
				4029	

Figure 1.7 Hierarchical pointers.

The customer records for a particular branch may not be stored together on the disk, nevertheless they can be retrieved very quickly by following the chain pointer trail in *NextBranch* and *NextCustomer*, directing the read head to the precise position indicated by the pointer value.

The definition of the hierarchical tree of relationships is established before any data is loaded. Linking the disk positions of stored data means that the schema design must be very carefully thought out. Once the data is loaded, it is not easy to vary the shape of the tree. However, this same reliance on disk position offers extremely high-performance data access. This is both because the disk head can be directed straight to a precise disk position and because related records like the list of customers for a particular branch can be stored by the database in contiguous positions on the disk.

Hierarchical databases can be characterized as having very inflexible design but offering high performance for very large collections of data. One of the very first databases, IMS, is still very much in use today, especially in the financial services industry, where the data structures and the processing logic are relatively stable but data volumes are high

1.6 CODASYL DATABASES

Starting in 1969 and working through to 1972, the Conference on Data Systems Languages (CODASYL), which had previously agreed the standard for COBOL, was developing a different data model based on the concept of a network of relationships (Figure 1.8).

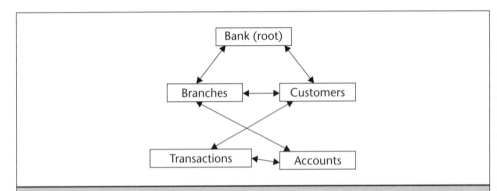

Figure 1.8 CODASYL database: example schema. The same five record types as in Figure 1.6 are present, and the pointers still indicate ownership. Access to the database is through the root of the network, the Bank. Notice that the logical relationships can be bi-directional.

Each relationship is still expressed through ownership, but the network database allows a parent record type to own more than one type of child record. Furthermore, each relationship, again expressed through disk position, is capable of being represented bi-directionally. There are now ascent and descent pointers to move between record types. Chain pointers enable a traversal of instances of a record type.

Figure 1.9 still shows that branch *Able* has customers *567, 9348, 2894, 2084* and *5849*, which has an end pointer in the *Next Customer* field. Although the customer records for a particular branch may or may not be stored together on the disk, nevertheless we can retrieve them very quickly by following the chain pointer trail.

What is new here is the ascent pointer, allowing navigation from *Able*'s last customer, *5849*, back to the *Able* branch record. From here, it is possible then to move along the branch chain pointers to inspect another Branch and its customers.

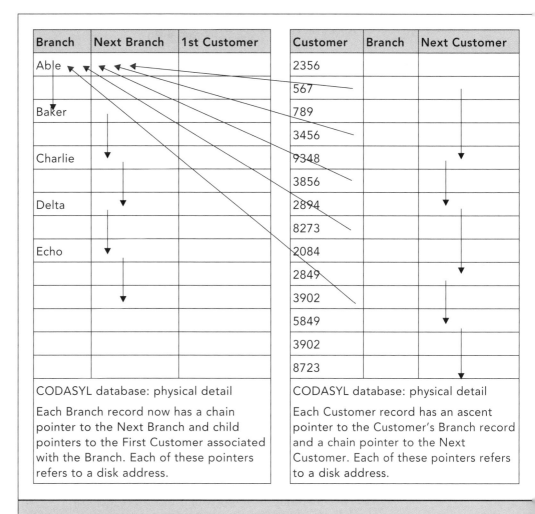

Branch	Next Branch	1st Customer
Able		
Baker		
Charlie		
Delta		
Echo		

Customer	Branch	Next Customer
2356		
567		
789		
3456		
9348		
3856		
2894		
8273		
2084		
2849		
3902		
5849		
3902		
8723		

CODASYL database: physical detail

Each Branch record now has a chain pointer to the Next Branch and child pointers to the First Customer associated with the Branch. Each of these pointers refers to a disk address.

CODASYL database: physical detail

Each Customer record has an ascent pointer to the Customer's Branch record and a chain pointer to the Next Customer. Each of these pointers refers to a disk address.

Figure 1.9 CODASYL pointers.

The increased opportunity for complexity of relationships enabled more diverse business scenarios to be modelled in the database, but brought even greater inflexibility to schema design. Performance for data access was high, and navigational concepts such as descent and traversal were still present and supplemented with the concept of ascent.

As with the hierarchical model, network databases need specialist programmers to write the user programs which use their navigational facilities. They were suitable for organizations whose data processing needs were complex but well known and stable. Large volumes of data could be manipulated very efficiently. A typical CODASYL database was IDMS, which was widely used through the early 1980s.

1.7 ∈ RELATIONAL DATABASES

Ted Codd, an IBM researcher, published a paper (Codd, 1970) that sought to apply the well-known mathematical concepts of set theory to the problems of handling large collections of data. Groups of similarly structured objects are known as relations. Applying this theory to databases gave rise to the relational data model.

In the hierarchical and network models, the connections among record types are held as physical addresses. The content of such records therefore consists of different data representations. There are the values of real world characteristics of the object being modelled such as 'Grant' or 'Hepburn' in the surname field. Then there is a child pointer with value '0185674345965', which refers not to any characteristic of the real-world object, but to the disk position of the first child of the record.

> **METADATA** Another term for the structural description or schema of a database. Used particularly to describe the stored image of the structure (*see also* Schema, Data Dictionary).

The schema or **metadata**(data about data) is stored in the database as a series of rules about two completely different types of data. One type comes from the real-world characteristics; the other is about the record position of the data.

The first data type is easy for end-users to visualize. The second needs specialist training and knowledge of programming to understand.

The relational model uses the data values themselves to express the connections in the database. Each instance in a relation is referred to as a **tuple**, a **row** or a **record**. All the tuples in a relation have the same structure or collection of attributes. No two tuples can have the same values for all their attributes, otherwise they become indistinguishable.

Each tuple is distinguished not by its position in the physical database but by the unique values of one of its attributes or some combination of its attributes (Figure 1.10). The identity of the tuple is based on value, not position. The connection between branch and customer can still be modelled by placing a unique value identifying the branch into the customer's tuple.

> **TUPLE** An abstract mathematical term for a member of a relation. More correctly used when discussing the design of relations before creating a stored instance.
>
> **ROW** A corresponding term for a tuple when physically stored in a relational database. More correctly used when discussing operational aspects of relational databases such as the formulation of queries.

Branch	Data
Able	...
Baker	...
Charlie	...
Delta	...
Echo	...

Figure 1.10 Tuples (rows) in a relation.

The data and the metadata now contain only one kind of data representation. End-users can more easily visualize both the data and the metadata. The data model for any particular application is still stored as a schema in the database, but, as far as the user is concerned, it contains no mention of how the data is physically stored. Instead, it contains only rules for connecting relations based on equality of shared data values. This data model contains only information from the real world and nothing about the physical structure of the database. It is an abstract model centred only on the data (Figure 1.11).

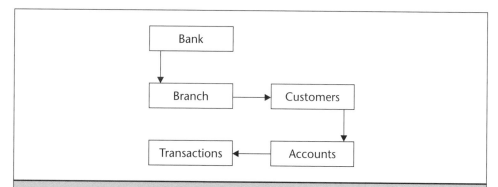

Figure 1.11 Relational database example schema. The five record types of Figures 1.6 and 1.8 now have relationships expressed through values of the characteristics of each of the types. Access to the data is through the value of any characteristic of any of the types. Notice that the logical relationships can only be uni-directional.

Because the data model was derived from formal mathematical theories, it was possible to envisage formal proofs of the systems analyst's work in defining the schema view of the real world. The relational model unified data and schema in a provably correct way.

In 1975, a major research effort was initiated at the Berkeley campus of the University of California. This was known as the Ingres project. Teams of computer scientists who worked on the Ingres project went on to join the commercial project teams responsible for products such as Oracle and Sybase. Ingres became a commercial product as well. By the early 1980s there were commercial products available ready to challenge the position of older packages like IMS and IDMS.

Relational databases are more flexible in their design aspects and it is often possible to alter the structure of relations and the definition of their interconnections without unloading and reloading the data. The data access language that became known as *SQL (Structured Query Language)* is based on a value-only view of the database, so that it is independent of physical storage or changes in the file system. *SQL* enables impromptu queries that do not rely on hard-wired navigational pointer trails. It is easier to train non-computing specialists to use the language.

The major disadvantage for relational databases is that the flexibility that comes from the abstract view may cause performance problems for the very reason that there are no well-worn navigational pointer trails to aid the speedy resolution of queries on large data (Figure 1.12).

Branch	Data...		Customer	Data...	Branch
Able			2356	...	Charlie
Baker			567	...	Able
Charlie			789	...	Baker
Delta			3456	...	Delta
Echo			9348	...	Able
			3856	...	Charlie
			2894	...	Able
			8273	...	Baker
			2084	...	Delta
			2849	...	Able
			3902	...	Baker
			5849	...	Echo
			4029	...	Echo

Figure 1.12 Branches and Customers.

However, advances in hardware performance mean that this criterion is becoming less significant in discriminating between databases founded on the relational, network and hierarchical models. Relational databases are now dominant in the market for moderately sized data, serving organizations whose needs are regularly subject to change or development.

1.8 ⊂ OBJECTION SUSTAINED

One of the driving forces behind the development of databases was the need for data abstraction: the separation of data and its storage from the application logic. This was thought desirable in order to standardize methods of storage, to offer protection to the data from multiple users and to give the data a safe environment for program developers

Throughout the same period, academics were examining ways of strengthening these aspects of programming languages.

As early as 1967, researchers introduced a new language feature called the class, which could be extended through an inheritance mechanism. These capabilities laid the groundwork for object-oriented programming.

What was good for data could also be good for logic. Another important feature of object orientation is that program code or methods could also be defined within a class (Figure 1.13). Since the class could be protected from amendment and inherited, it became one answer to the general problem of providing a safe development environment (Figure 1.14).

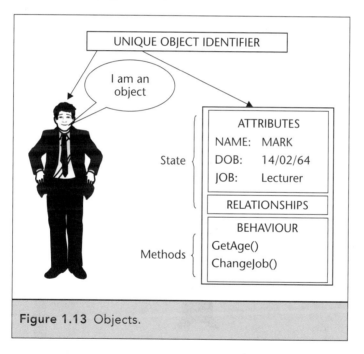

Figure 1.13 Objects.

By 1983, the Smalltalk-80 and C++ languages had been defined. These allowed the inheritance of classes, dividing the data elements and the methods (or procedural elements) into **public** and **private** sections.

Data or methods in the private sections could be accessed only through the public section. Enclosing or protecting data and method in this way is called encapsulation and is meant to ensure that programmers make use of the class only

Figure 1.14 Objects: instantiated classes.

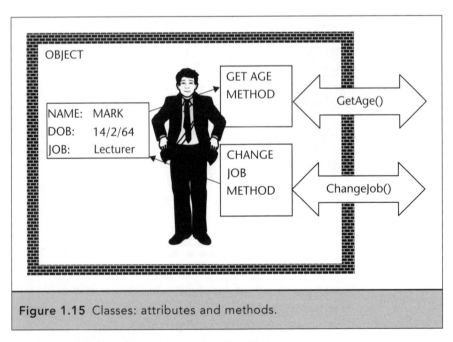

Figure 1.15 Classes: attributes and methods.

in the way that its authors intended (Figure 1.15). By incorporating standard classes into their programs, developers could hope for reliable, trustworthy, reusable class libraries.

Once a class is securely defined, it can be protected from amendment and used as a foundation for a new, more specialized class. Thus a class called *Person*, which contains attributes for *surname, forename, address, date of birth* etc., can be inherited by the class *Employee*, which also needs these same characteristics.

Additional attributes can be added outside of the inheritance to complete the *Employee* data. The *Employee* class can also be inherited by the class *Doctor* or the class *Nurse*. In each case the basic personal and employment details have been incorporated reliably and consistently into the data structure (Figure 1.16).

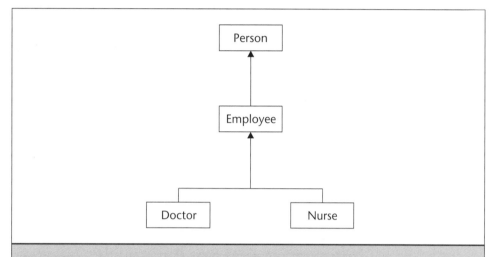

Figure 1.16 Trust Me, I'm a Person: the characteristics of the *Person* class are inherited by the *Employee* class with additional characteristics. In a hospital schema, the *Doctor* and *Nurse* classes inherit from both *Person* and *Employee* with further characteristics specific either to a doctor or to a nurse. A *Patient* class would be in a different sub-tree, inheriting directly from *Person*.

During the 1980s the idea of the class was extended to include complex definitions (Figure 1.17). Multiple inheritances meant that a class could inherit from two or more different class definitions.

Data attributes could be atomic, consisting of simple types (integer, float, string etc.) or could consist of other classes. Collections of instantiated objects referred to as lists (ordered) or sets (unordered) could form a single attribute in a class definition. One of the attributes of a car is a set of wheels (Figure 1.18).

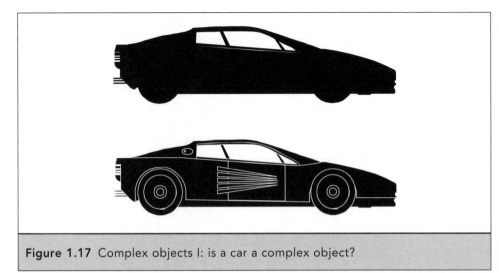

Figure 1.17 Complex objects I: is a car a complex object?

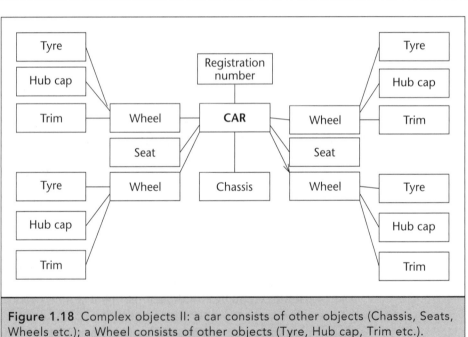

Figure 1.18 Complex objects II: a car consists of other objects (Chassis, Seats, Wheels etc.); a Wheel consists of other objects (Tyre, Hub cap, Trim etc.).

1.9 OBJECT DATABASES

When a program instantiates a class, it creates an object. That object exists in a reserved area of volatile RAM and is referenced by an object identifier that is a pointer to the beginning of the object's reserved memory. Messages may only be sent to the public data or methods through the pointer. The identity of the object is connected to the value of its pointer – its address in the memory of the computer –

not to the value of any of its attributes. If any of the object's attributes refer to other objects or to object collections such as lists or sets, then these are stored as pointers to the other objects or to the head of the list or set. When the program stops, the data is destroyed.

The lack of a consistent model for *persistent* objects was a major reason for the lack of penetration of languages like Smalltalk and C++ into the commercial arena.

The need for the development of object databases was underlined by the kind of application that objects are good at supporting. These all have a wide variety of data types and almost always include some kind of graphic or image storage and retrieval requirement (Table 1.2).

Table 1.2 Typical object database applications.
Computer-Aided Design (CAD)
Computer-Aided Manufacturing (CAM)
Computer-Aided Software Engineering (CASE)
Office Information Systems (OIS)
Multimedia systems
Digital publishing
Geographic Information Systems (GIS)
Scientific and medical systems

Unlike the relational model, the object model has no basis in mathematics; there is no consistent definition of an object. The precise definition is empirical and a decision for those who specify each of the languages that claim to be object-oriented. The development of object databases mirrored the earlier development of standard data storage functions for COBOL. Measures for storing objects were first proposed as extensions of particular object-oriented languages like Smalltalk or C++, or even specific manufacturers' versions of these languages.

However, many of the object databases share certain characteristics. The metadata or data dictionary is kept as a class hierarchy, allowing at least single inheritance. References to instantiated, stored objects are kept as pointers to disk or file locations and are relative to an arbitrary root of the data. Complex objects, which refer to other objects or to collections, are also modelled using pointers to disk or file locations. These can be single pointers to just one object or the head of a linked list to a collection. Fast access to the data is achieved using a navigational language embedded in the database software and which allows traversal of the pointer framework. This access method identifies each object by its pointer value, not by any value of its attributes (Table 1.3).

Mention of a pointer framework inevitably leads to a comparison with the CODASYL or network database model, and there are striking similarities. A complex schema where the DBMS is responsible for transparent maintenance of the pointer connections implies inflexibility of the definition but speed of access.

Table 1.3 Technology for persistent objects.

OOPL	OODBMS
Complex objects	Persistence
Object ID	Disk management
Methods and messages	Data sharing
Inheritance	Reliability
Polymorphism	Security
Extensibility	*Ad hoc* queries
Computational completeness	

The object database has the added complication of providing classes with inheritance and of storing the program code for methods both as original source and, perhaps, as target microcode for the host machine.

This hints at two major problems for the architects of an OODBMS; firstly, how should the OIDs of a complex object structure in the database map to the OIDs of the same object structure once it is retrieved into the memory of a client (Figure 1.19), and secondly where should the code for an object's methods execute?

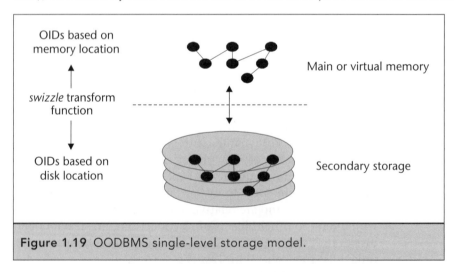

OIDs based on memory location

Main or virtual memory

swizzle transform function

OIDs based on disk location

Secondary storage

Figure 1.19 OODBMS single-level storage model.

Clearly, any user program that is designed to access an object database should be compatible with the way that objects are identified in the database. A persistent complex object consists of individual simple objects connected by persistent pointers referring to their permanent locations. Retrieving such an object into the RAM of the client machine for interrogation or update implies using a programming language whose syntax is comfortable with a mapping of persistent to transient (volatile memory) pointers. Most object database vendors provide a variant of C++ or some other language that offers such mapping transparently. A so-called *swizzle* function provides for the mapping and allows new connections and new objects to be stored persistently following a client's editing session.

The question of where method code runs raises questions of database security if the code runs in the server and of compatibility if the code is destined to run in the client. The code can either be pre-compiled and stored as microcode for the server's CPU, or the source might be delivered to the client, which must then have an appropriate compiler to generate the necessary microcode for the client CPU.

One solution is to provide a limited version of an OOPL in which method code may be written. Constructs, such as direct memory access to the server's RAM, are removed so that only *friendly* code may be generated and the method code stored on the server.

When objects are retrieved from the database, they are transferred to a page of memory in the server (Figure 1.20). That page is mirrored in the client, along with a page manager. Client application code is applied to the objects in the client page and changes are mirrored to the server page. Changes caused by trusted method code running in the server are applied to objects in the server page and mirrored immediately to the client page.

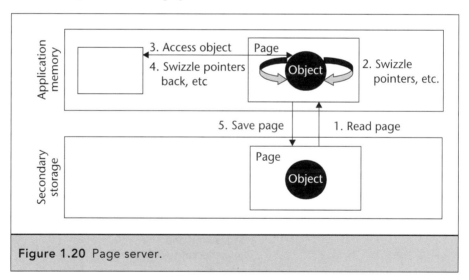

Figure 1.20 Page server.

The application code can be written in any language that can access the client page objects. Methods can be stored once in the server as compiled microcode.

Object databases are good for applications that require a rich data model and where the queries and transactions are well known in advance and can be represented in the connections between complex objects. Such queries are essentially *pre-joined* and execute with more efficiency that those under the relational model. Object databases are stretched to perform well with *ad hoc* queries, where a form of *Object SQL* often underpins such functionality. The natural retrieval mode of an OODBMS is navigational, based on the OID pointer network. Supporting queries based on the values of attributes is alien to the data model and using indexes to improve performance introduces yet more impedance into the system.

The object database shares a major disadvantage with the Codasyl databases: the inflexible schema repository. Because the connections between objects are *hard-wired*, changing the existing class hierarchy can mean unloading the data, amending the structure and then reloading the data. Schema evolution is a desirable feature if the database is to adapt to changing business needs. The relational database, because connections are expressed through equality of attribute value, has advantages in this respect over all other database types.

Of course, vendors are keen to offer as wide a range of facilities as possible in order to compete. Often this means that the natural advantages of persistent objects are compromised. Much the same could be said about the vendors of relational databases, who, for similar reasons, have taken their products away from the initial pure and provable data model to approach object orientation from the other direction.

1.10 OBJECT RELATIONAL DATABASES

The growing popularity of object orientation as a development method has led several relational database vendors to offer an object relational solution (Figure 1.21). Oracle Corporation, notably in version 9i of its relational DBMS, offers the ability to superimpose an object view on its relational structure. The DBA can define supertypes, from which relations inherit both data attributes and methods. However, the underlying data storage remains committed to the relational model;

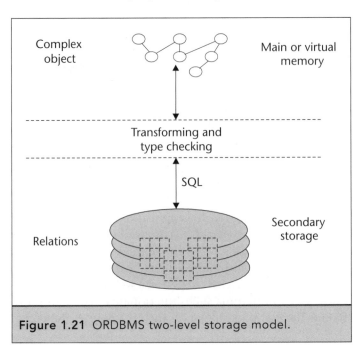

Figure 1.21 ORDBMS two-level storage model.

the principal data access method remains SQL and the product overall retains backward compatibility with previous versions of strictly relational products.

When the data model and the data access method are not based on the same view there is said to be an impedance mismatch. This applies just as much to the object database vendor who provides a special version of SQL to query or update persistent objects as the relational database vendor who provides an OO layer above a storage system based on relational concepts.

1.10.1   OBJECT TYPES

Oracle 9i is actually an object relational database, so some of the concepts about objects described in earlier sections can be used to create standard types that consist of non-atomic values. The basis of Oracle's object orientation lies in the object type. The ability for users to define object types is a central part of the extensibility requirement in *SQL:1999*. User-defined types (UDTs) serve as a template for data in the database and user-defined routines (UDRs) may be connected to the data types and stored in the database, completing the analogy with the object model.

An object type specifies the elements, called attributes, that make up a structured data unit, such as a customer bank account. Some attributes, such as the list of transactions, can be other structured data units. The object type may also specify the methods that can be performed on the data unit, such as determining the current balance of the account.

Figure 1.22 shows an example of how the bank account object can be built up in SQL by successively defining more and more complex object types. The customer definition consists only of other object types. The list of transactions accruing to an account is defined as a table of the transaction object type.

This certainly looks like an object-oriented scheme. The linkage between an account and its list of transactions will be maintained through system-generated OIDs. The underlying storage is, however, still relational. What looks like a table of transactions nested within the account type will be stored as separate tables with the generated OID links supplied by the system.

The relationship discovery mechanism is still based on that shown in Figure 1.12: referential equality. Instead of the reference being based on the value of a meaningful data attribute, it is based on equality of the abstract object identity.

In an object database, as with a CODASYL database, the relationship is discovered by navigating a pointer trail which may consist of any number of elements and which refers to position in the database. In an object relational database the relationship may only be discovered by scanning the transactions table looking for the dependent's OID, albeit with the assistance of an index.

Object relational databases offer an increase in the richness of the data model through new in-built types that can store video frames, pictures and other multimedia elements as well as the UDTs. Methods can be included as part of an object type so that the object encapsulates both data and behaviour. Simple inheritance is

```
create type person as object (
  name      varchar2(30),
  phone     varchar2(20) );

create type address as object (
road        varchar2(30),
town        varchar2(30)
county      varchar2(30)
postcode    varchar2(10));

create type customer as object(
contact     external_person,
home        address,
statement   address);

create type transaction as object (
  item_no   number,
  amount    number(12,2));

create type transaction_table as table of transaction;

create type account as object (
  account_no           number,
  cust customer,
  transactions    transaction_table,

member function
current_balance return number );
```

Figure 1.22 Oracle object types.

possible: sub-types can be derived from types. Clearly, complex objects can be modelled: object attributes can consist of other objects and even object collections.

The development of object relational databases seems to be more marketing driven than market driven. It appears more concerned with competing on a facilities manifest with object databases than responding to a genuine consumer demand. The relational model sits perfectly with the SQL processing model, both being derived from the same mathematical principles. Introducing an object view of the data places an impedance between the data model and the favoured processing model. Using a view does not reduce the existing impedance between the relational model and an object or record-based processing model since the underlying structure is unchanged.

1.11 KEY TERMS

Filing systems	Sequential and random organization; Indexes
Databases	Separation of data and logic; Functions: storage, structure management, security, query access, concurrency, recovery
Hierarchical database	Uni-directional pointers to record locations; Tree structure; Navigational queries; Inflexible schema;
CODASYL databases	Bi-directional pointers to record locations; Network structure; Navigational queries; Inflexible schema
Relational databases	Connection based on equality of attribute value; SQL set-based queries; Flexible schema
Objects	Encapsulate attributes and method; Inheritance; Polymorphism; Complex objects
Object databases	Persistent extension to OOPL; Identity through OID; OID pointer to location; Page servers; Swizzle functions; Navigational queries; Inflexible schema; OSQL: impedance mismatch
Object relational databases	Object view through object type; Nested tables; Generated OID; Flexible schema; SQL impedance mismatch

1.12 QUESTIONS

(i) Explain what is meant by an attribute. Give three examples.

(ii) Explain what is meant by a record type. Give three examples.

(iii) Illustrate how a hierarchical database schema might establish a link between customers and their credit card transactions.

(iv) Adapt your answer to Question (iii) to show how this might be achieved in a relational database.

1.13 EXERCISES

(i) Draft the principal record types for:
- A public lending library
- A national car hire company
- An insurance claims department
- A door entry/swipe card system
- A system to monitor hospital waiting lists

(ii) Search the Internet for examples of applications where the characteristics of each of the database types are considered an advantage or a disadvantage. Write a short report matching what you find with the material in this chapter.

CHAPTER 2

LIGA UTOPIA

Some people think football is a matter of life and death but I can assure them it is much more serious than that.

Bill Shankly

2.1 ∈ THE UTOPIAN FOOTBALL LEAGUE

In Utopia, the Utopian Football Association, UFA, regulates football. This body is responsible for interpreting the rules of football; for the disciplinary hearings of cases reported to it; for developing coaching programmes in the amateur game; for organizing the national team; and for keeping a register of players and coaching staff for all the leagues of professional and amateur teams in Utopia. In addition, UFA organizes a number of competitions between the clubs, notably the UFA Cup for professional sides and the UFA Urn for amateur clubs.

There are 80 professional football clubs in Utopia. They are organized and regulated by the Utopian Football League, UFL. The clubs are divided into four divisions of 20 clubs each. UFL sets the fixture list of matches between clubs at the start of each season, which lasts from August of each year to May of the following year.

Figure 2.1 shows the clubs and some of the players in the league. Each club plays all of the other clubs in its division twice: once at home and once away. UFL maintains a league table for the four divisions based on a points system of 3 points for a win and 1 point each for a drawn match. Teams with equal points scores are ordered by the difference between goals scored and goals conceded.

The UFL also keeps a record of the team sheets for each game, including substitutions of players during the game. Goal scorers are noted as well as those players who receive official cautions (yellow card) or are sent off (red card) by the match officials. Serious infringements can lead to disciplinary hearings that result in match suspensions.

1st Division clubs	Player	Club
AC Compassion	Constantine	Beauty United
Beauty United	Dickens	Beauty United
Bountiful Athletic	Diocletian	Beauty United
Nirvana City	Gregory	Beauty United
Forgiveness FC	Hegel	Beauty United
Freedom United	Kant	Beauty United
Grace Town	More	Beauty United
Honesty United	Paul	Beauty United
Knowledge City	Plato	Beauty United
Liberation United	Socrates	Beauty United
Pity City	Thackeray	Beauty United
Purity FC	Aristotle	Purity FC
Sobriety FC	Augustus	Purity FC
Steadfast United	Austen	Purity FC
Thrift City	Bacon	Purity FC
Truth FC	Erasmus	Purity FC
Valour FC	Innocent	Purity FC
Virtue Thursday	John	Purity FC
Wisdom United	Justinian	Purity FC
	Marx	Purity FC
	Shakespeare	Purity FC
	Tiberius	Purity FC

Figure 2.1 Clubs and players.

The clubs employ the players. Each played is allocated a squad number, which he wears on his shirt. This number identifies him to match officials who check the team sheets submitted by the club before each game. The squad number does not indicate the position at which the player plays. This is indicated on the team sheet and reflects his general classification, maintained by the club, as a goalkeeper, defender, midfielder or forward.

Players may play for several clubs during their careers. They have a contract with the club that indicates when they joined the club and when they left the club. Each club also has a manager as well as a specialist coaching staff, all of whom also have to be registered with the UFA. Players, managers and trainers are all subject to the UFA disciplinary code.

UFA also regulates the transfer of players between clubs in the league as well into the league from other countries and out of the league to other countries. Details of contracts are kept so that over time these records become a history of the players' careers.

The UFL currently keeps all its records on a card index filing system but wishes to computerize. The UFL Secretary has heard of a database package called Oracle and his regular golf partner has told him about a method of systems development called object orientation. Apparently, systems designed by this method can be implemented on a local area network of PCs using either the Java or Visual Basic languages.

The UFL has therefore called in a consultancy company called *Perfect Solutions Unlimited* (*PSU*) to investigate the opportunities for computerization and to produce a prototype implementation as part of an evaluation exercise before a production system is commissioned. The prototype design will look only at first division clubs and a selection of their players.

2.2 ∈ UML SPECIFICATION

The Unified Modeling Language is fast becoming a standard language for analyzing and specifying the parts of software systems. Object technology began to become available for commercial use in the early 1990s. With the technology came attempts to support object analysis and design. Each author proposed their own competing and incompatible design languages. The lack of a standard method for modelling systems based on object technology was seen as a hindrance to its penetration in the market.

Booch, Rumbaugh and Jacobson decided to join in designing a common unified language. UML 1.0 was adopted by the Object Management Group[1] as a standard in 1997. The OMG is a consortium of software vendors who, with an eye to the commercial benefits of standards, aim to promote common frameworks for systems development. As well as the UML standard, OMG are responsible for the publication of the CORBA[2] middleware specification.

Various levels of abstraction can be expressed in UML, ranging from high-level user requirements, to detailed models of object behaviour. Some UML tools can generate code from UML models. UML includes Object Constraint Language, to provide the necessary level of precise formal details for implementations. Figure 2.2 shows the hierarchy of diagrams used in UML.

Designing applications before coding gives an assurance that functionality is complete and correct, end-user requirements are met, and that scalability, robustness, security and extendability issues have been addressed before implementation.

---

1 http://www.omg.org/
2 Common Object Request Broker Architecture

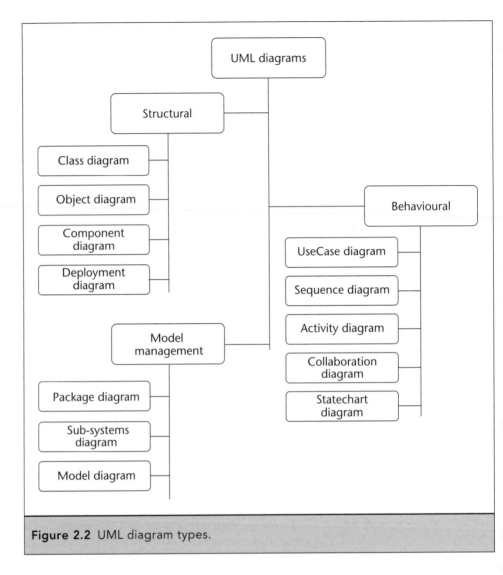

Figure 2.2 UML diagram types.

UML may be used to define systems boundaries and display major functionality from user perspectives. The data component structure may be modelled with class diagrams and the behaviour of objects (class instantiations) within the system illustrated with state transition diagrams.

This is not a book on Systems Analysis and Design so there will be no detailed discussion of UML. The next section, on UseCases, illustrates their use in determining the client requirements for the UFL system.

2.3 ⊂ UFL USECASES

A UseCase is a pattern of behaviour that the system exhibits (represented by a named oval). The name indicates that it is an example, an illustration or a case of how the system is used. Each UseCase is a dialogue between the system and the person or thing initiating a transaction or receiving information from it. In UML, the external entity (person or thing) is known as an Actor.

Actors are often people employed in the client organization. Their requirements can be determined by routine investigative techniques: observation and interviews about current work practices. Sometimes the management will have strategic aims concerned with extending or enhancing these work processes through automation. External computing resources may need to interact with the planned system. Computer systems outside the organization can be Actors.

The UseCase diagram is a picture of the system from an external viewpoint. It can be drawn to represent varying levels of detail.

Figure 2.3 shows the overview of the proposed UFL system. This shows that the only functionality is concerned with the organization's core business of maintaining a record of events directly connected with football matches. There is no requirement for a payroll system for UFL staff or for any connection to a remote computer system. All of the users will be UFL staff. The system boundary is clear and the user population is defined. The major functions are simplified into just

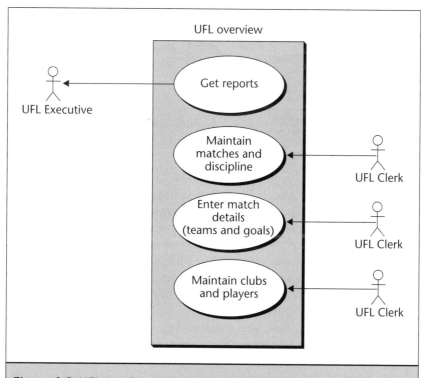

Figure 2.3 UFL UseCase overview.

four UseCases. This high-level view can be further detailed in a second-level diagram.

Figure 2.4 shows such a diagram for the matches and discipline UseCase. It is evident from this that the UseCase which occupied just one oval in the overview diagram has been decomposed into three UseCases. These offer more detailed information about the overview process.

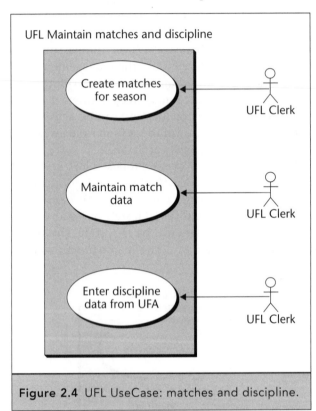

Figure 2.4 UFL UseCase: matches and discipline.

The second-level UseCase can be further decomposed, as Figure 2.5 shows. Here the Maintain Match Data use case has been broken down into its component operations. The UseCase diagram informs the discovery of processes as well as data elements within the required system.

For the sake of completeness, and also to underpin the functional design of the Java implementation of the UFL application, Figures 2.6 and 2.7 show the second-level use case diagrams derived from the overview.

At this level, the top level has been split into three functions undertaken by clerks in the organization. It may be that this is sufficient detail to conclude that the three activities will translate into three screens in the proposed system.

The reports diagram shows that there are three reports that the UFL executive finds necessary.

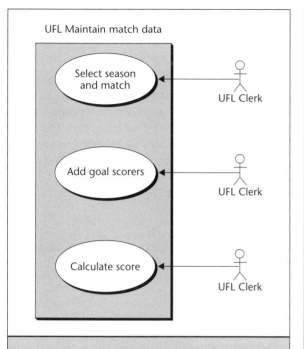

Figure 2.5 UFL UseCase: maintain match data.

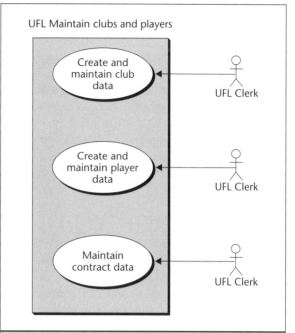

Figure 2.6 UFL UseCase: clubs and players.

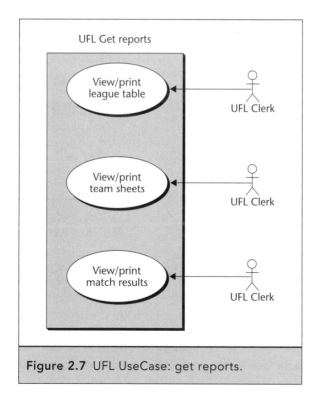

Figure 2.7 UFL UseCase: get reports.

2.4 ⊆ CLASS DIAGRAMS

When a fair representation of the business functions has been captured in the UseCase diagrams, it is time to look at the major items of data needed to perform the day-to-day processing and the other regular maintenance represented in the diagrams. A class diagram is used to do this. A class consists of data items and internal mini-programs called methods that work on the data items. To make sure the list of classes is complete, look through the UseCases to identify nouns that might lead to data items and verbs that give clues about the methods associated with the data.

2.4.1 SIMPLE CLASSES

There is a standard way of representing classes within UML and a standard way of representing the relationships that exist between them.

It is a good idea to define an Address class. Many of the other classes, such as Club, Player or Coach may have one or more addresses. If a common pattern is defined then the other classes that use it will always have the same format.

Figure 2.8 shows that the diagram for the Address class consists of a rectangle divided into two sections: at the top is the name of the class and in the second part we define the data items that will hold values when the class type is instantiated as an object. The names of these data items do not tell us very much about their purpose, so a better version would be as shown in Figure 2.9.

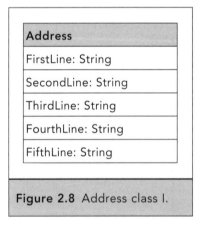

Figure 2.8 Address class I.

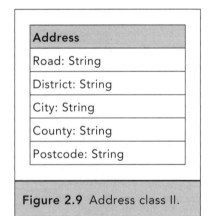

Figure 2.9 Address class II.

2.4.2 ENCAPSULATION

The class is still incomplete. Classes can have public and private data. They can also have program code or methods associated with their definition. It makes sense to protect or **encapsulate** the data items in a private section so that access to the data can be controlled and the address verified. The next version, in Figure 2.10, has private data items only and defines public and private methods.

Address
Private
Road: String
District: String
City: String
County: String
Postcode: String
Public
Address GetAddress()
Boolean SetAddress(x: Address)
Private
Boolean VerifyAddress(x: Address)

Figure 2.10 Address class III.

Three method definitions have been added in a new third section of the class. These definitions are called method signatures and they each show four types of information about the method. Firstly, two of the signatures are public and one is private. This means that the first two can be called directly by other objects sending messages to an Address object. The third method is internal and private and can only be called by one of the first two. Secondly, the names of the methods haves been defined: *GetAddress*, *SetAddress* and *VerifyAddress*.

Each of the methods has a return type. When the *GetAddress* method is invoked, an answer is sent back in the form of an address structure of five lines. When *SetAddress* is invoked, a Boolean value (True or False) is sent back, signifying whether the data was acceptable and was stored.

Input parameters for *SetAddress* and *VerifyAddress* have been defined. *SetAddress* receives an input parameter in the form of five lines of address data, which it will assign to the data items. The program code for the public method, *SetAddress,* will call the private method *VerifyAddress*, which could, for example, check whether the input parameter contains mandatory values for *Road* and *Postcode* and whether *Postcode* is in the Utopia Mail format.

It is interesting to note that here the input parameters are defined recursively as being of type Address in the midst of defining that very same address type.

The Address data consists only of simple atomic data types. They are called atomic because they are indivisible: they have no underlying structure and can be manipulated only as a whole. Atomic date types vary according to implementation language.

2.4.3 COLLECTIONS

The attributes of a class do not have to be single-valued (atomic). A collection of many instances of a different class can be assigned as a single attribute. There are two main types of collection: the set and the list. Lists are ordered and sets are unordered.

A department in a company could, for example, have an attribute, *workforce*, whose type would be a list of employees (Figure 2.11). Employee objects can be assigned to and deleted from the list as they join or leave the department.

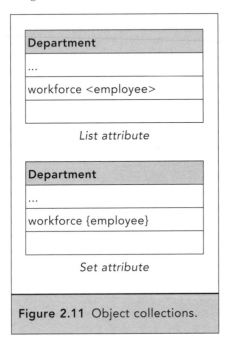

Figure 2.11 Object collections.

Collections are held as linked lists in memory. Each node of the linked list points to the next node. Inside the node is a pointer to the object that is a member of the collection. The object itself cannot be in the node, since it may be a member of several collections.

2.4.4 COMPLEX CLASSES

A complex class is one that is made up, at least in part, of other classes. Figure 2.12 is a first attempt at defining the Player class.

Figure 2.12 consists of a rectangular box divided into three sections. The top section gives the name of the class and must be unique in the eventual class diagram.

The second section lists the data items associated with the Player class. Some of them are simple atomic data types such as String or Integer; others consist of other object types such as Address that will be defined elsewhere in the class diagram.

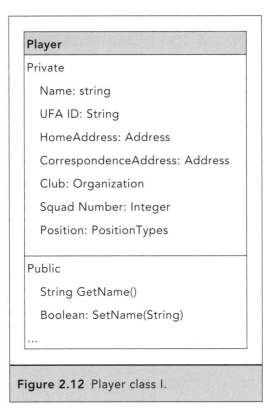

Figure 2.12 Player class I.

In the third section, the method signatures are listed. These are essentially declarations for the methods or program code associated with the Player class. All of these have return types and some of them accept input parameters. For example, *GetAddress* returns an *Address* object and has no input parameter. *SetAddress* accepts an input parameter of type *Address* and returns a Boolean value indicating success or failure of the operation.

2.4.5 INHERITANCE

Several of the object typesidentified in the UFL prototype share some common characteristics. For example, the Utopian Football Association and the Utopian Football League are both organizations. Players, managers, trainers and referees are all people and all have to be registered with the UFA.

The object-oriented approach allows the definition of general classes and then other more specialized classes that inherit the attributes of the general class. The specialized class may then have other data attributes and methods that relate to its more specialized role in the application. A general class definition may be checked for accuracy and completeness. Developers can then be assured that every subclass that inherits from it has the same accuracy and completeness. It is a good way to ensure uniformity of design and to avoid errors either in the scope of data attributes or in the program code for inherited methods.

Inheritance is shown in the class diagram by a connecting line with an arrow indicating the superclass. Figure 2.13 shows that the Player and Coach classes inherit from Person. This means that they both are automatically assigned the simple data elements *ufa_id*, *surname*, *forename* and the collection attribute *employed* from Person. They also inherit the methods *SetSurname* and *SetUfa_ID* in the same way.

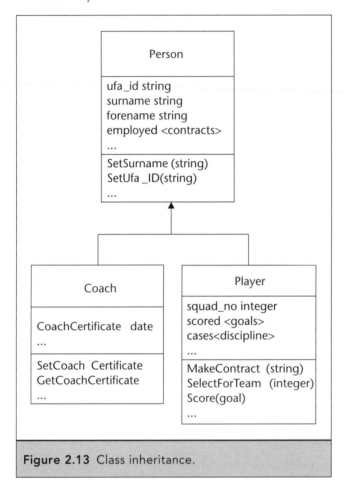

Figure 2.13 Class inheritance.

The Player class has extra data attributes, *squad_no*, *scored* and *cases*, and three methods, *MakeContract*, *SelectForTeam* and *Score*. The Coach class has a different specialized date attribute called *CoachCertificate* and two specialized methods called *GetCoachingCertificate* and *SetCoachingCertificate* (Figure 2.14).

2.4.6 POLYMORPHISM

When a subclass descends from a superclass, the inherited characteristics are subject to optional change. If an attribute or method signature is superimposed in

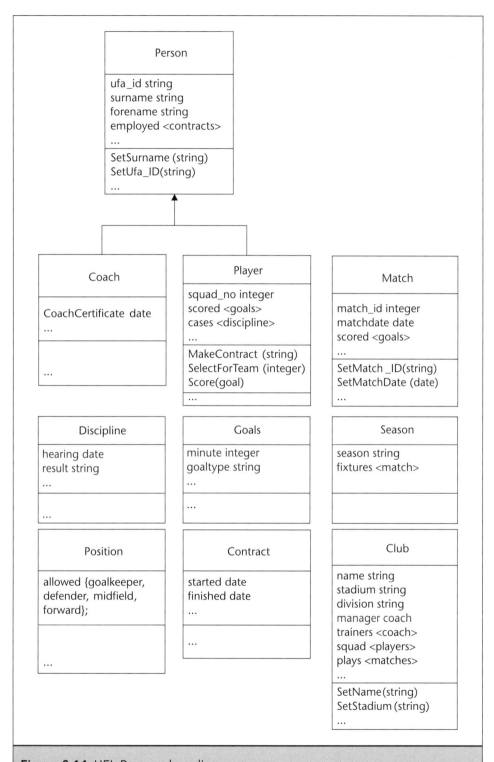

Figure 2.14 UFL Person class diagram.

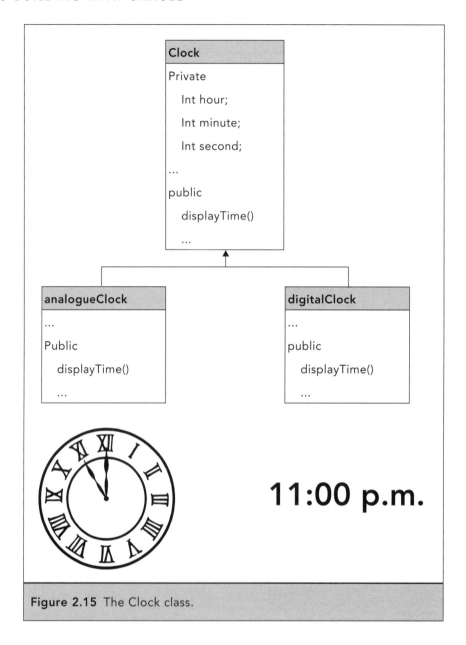

Figure 2.15 The Clock class.

the subclass it takes precedence over any inherited attribute or method with the same name when the class is instantiated as an object.

The Clock class (Figure 2.15) has a *displayTime* method that does not perform any action. The analogueClock class and the digitalClock class both inherit from the Clock class. Each of the descendants has a method, *displayTime*, which overrides the inherited method.

2.5 ⋲ KEY TERMS

UML

Use cases   Diagramming technique for capturing user requirements and overview of system behaviour; Actors perform actions in scenario cases; Higher level cases may be decomposed into low-level case detail.

OBJECTS

Encapsulation   Control access to attributes and methods by means of public and private sections in class definition

Complexity   Class attributes consist of other class or class collections

Collections   Multiple instances of objects: lists and sets

Inheritance   Subclass assumes attributes and methods of superclass

Polymorphism   Subclass overrides inherited characteristics

2.6 ⋲ QUESTIONS

(i)   Name five properties that an object model should establish.

(ii)   Explain the properties identified in Question (i).

2.7 ⋲ EXERCISE

(i)   Draft a class diagram for:
- The UFA coaching scheme
- A monitoring system for treatment outcomes in a hospital
- A children-at-risk register
- An electronic elections system

PART 2

DATABASE SYSTEMS

CHAPTER 3

DATA MODELLING

The tendency has always been strong to believe that whatever received a name must be an entity or being, having an independent existence of its own. And if no real entity answering to the name could be found, men did not for that reason suppose that none existed, but imagined that it was something peculiarly abstruse and mysterious

John Stuart Mill, *A System of Logic*

3.1 ⊨ A CLEAR PICTURE OF THE DATA

The Object Diagram derived in Section 3.4 will form the basis of the analysis for the creation of a database schema for the UFL application. Because it follows object-oriented principles, it also contains a great deal of the specifications for the processing logic of the proposed system. Each of the object definitions shows the object's data elements as well as the methods it contains.

However, the system will be implemented by storing the data in an Oracle relational database. While this product does allow for the storage of data and, to some extent, the storage of standard procedures, it is not a fully featured object database and there will have to be some compromises made as the original design progresses into reality.

The object diagram will be retained as an important systems design document. It provides an inventory of the data and processes in the developing system. It will be used to audit the database schema as well as the functionality of the Java or Visual Basic programs.

The first step is to take the data parts of the object diagram and to prepare a diagram suitable to act as a template for the schema of a relational database.

A diagram will be used because a picture can portray a lot of information – it has a high information density. A diagram is preferable because, if it conforms to a known and accepted standard, it can convey its information in an unambiguous manner.

An **entity–relationship diagram** will be developed for the UFL application. This shows the entities or record types in a system, the relationship between them and a formal description of each relationship. It is a vital planning tool for the development of a relational database schema.

A way of viewing real world objects and the data describing them will need to be determined. This view must allow a model of the data to be built which is suitable for inclusion in a relational database. A data model is a set of data structures with a collection of operations that can be applied to those data structures and a set of general **integrity rules**.

INTEGRITY RULES	Rules embedded in the database schema to ensure that structural and logical constraints are applied to data operations, preventing changes that would undermine compliance with the application requirements.

Using a data model provides the designer and the programmer with substantial advantages: the detailed data design makes use of a few building blocks, and the manipulation of data is performed in the same ways for all data structures.

The entity –relationship model was originally proposed by Peter Chen (1976) as a way to unify the network and relational database views. Subsequently there has been a proliferation of theoretical extensions and practical applications of it.

The model is used routinely for system analysis and design. Every year there is an international conference devoted to it. It is simple enough that the basic concepts can be learned readily, yet sufficiently powerful for scientific and technical applications. Entity–relationship is often abbreviated as ER. One refers therefore to the ER model.

3.1.1 ENTITIES

An **entity** is simply a person, an event, a real-world object or a concept about which data is collected. An **entity set** is a collection of similar entities. **Attributes** are the collection of characteristics that apply to all members of an entity set. No two attributes of an entity should describe the same characteristic of the real-world object.

Figure 3.1 shows part of the *Players* entity set. Each entity is described by a set of six attributes: *UFA_ID*, *Surname*, *Forename*, *Dateofbirth*, *Nationality* and *Club*. In order to be a member of the *Players* entity set, each instance must display these six attributes.

Each member of the entity set is called a **tuple** (Figure 3.2). The collection of tuples is a **relation**.

Each attribute has a permitted set of values called a **domain**. *Dateofbirth* has a domain of valid dates that might go back 35 years and come forward to seventeen

UFA_ID	Surname	Forename	Dateofbirth	Nationality	Club
UT23685	Constantine	George	02/05/1985	Utopian	Beauty United
UT236965	Dickens	Henry	23/08/1980	Utopian	Beauty United
VT432167	Diocletian	Pierre	15/06/1978	Valhallan	Beauty United
FT246517	Gregory	Alan	02/07/1976	Utopian	Beauty United
AT245876	Hegel	Brian	22/03/1984	Utopian	Beauty United
QT873456	Kant	Edward	03/11/1983	Utopian	Beauty United

Figure 3.1 Players relation.

Players is a six-tuple (v1, v2, v3, v4, v5, v6)
Each tuple consists of six values v1, v2, v3, v4, v5 and v6 where:

$v1 \in D1, v2 \in D2, v3 \in D3, v4 \in D4, v5 \in D5, v6 \in D6$[1]

Figure 3.2 Tuples and attributes.

years ago. Clearly, it cannot contain the values *Blue* or *150*. *Club* has a value within a list of the valid names of clubs. The relation *Players* has six attributes. Each attribute has a permitted range of values. Attribute names must be unique in the relation scheme and must describe *different* aspects of the entity's nature.

It is important to distinguish a **database scheme**(logical design) from a **database instance**(data in the database at a point in time). A **relation-scheme** is a list of attributes and their corresponding domains. A relation is created in the database and contains values. Its structure is based on the relation-scheme (Figure 3.3).

players-scheme = (ufa_id, surname, forename, dateofbirth, nationality, club)

Players is a relation on player-scheme:

Players (players-scheme)

Figure 3.3 Relation-schemes and relations.

---

1 v1 is a value within the domain D1, v2 is a value within the domain D2 and so on. The symbol $\in$ means 'is a member of' or 'is an element of': $1 \in \{1..9\}$

The relation-scheme can be further specified by adding domains (Figure 3.4). Domains such as *string* could be further restricted to allow only certain values such as the list of valid nationalities or valid clubs. Date domains can be restricted to allow only dates within an approved range.

---

players-scheme = (ufa_id: string, surname: string, forename: string, dateofbirth: date, nationality: string, club: string)

When the players relation is stored in the database, it consists of the tuples t1, t2 and so on. Each tuple has the values indicated

Players = {t1 (UT23685, Constantine, George, 02/05/1985, Utopian, Beauty United), t2 (UT236965Dickens, Henry, 23/08/1980, Utopian, Beauty United)...}

Figure 3.4 Domains and values.

The *Players* relation consists of tuples, and tuples are members of the *Players* relation (Figure 3.4).

Relation-schemes define the tuple structure in terms of attributes and domains. Relations are based on relation-schemes. Relations consists of tuples which contain values in conformance to the specification of the relation-scheme (Figure 3.5).

{ t1(UT23685,Constantine, George, 02/05/1985, Utopian, Beauty United) } ∈ Players

The character ∈ means 'is a member of' or 'is an element of', so this formula means that the tuple defined by the values given is an element of the relation players. The elements of a set are enclosed in {}; t1 is a member of the relation Players.

Figure 3.5 Set membership.

3.1.2 OBJECTS, EVENTS, CONCEPTS AND ENTITIES

The first step in producing the entity–relationship diagram is to identify the entities: the real-world objects, events or concepts specified in the class diagram. Certain of the classes may not have an independent existence but are included only to provide a user-defined data type. An example of this is the address class, which is used to specify a consistent compound data element within other classes. The Golden Rule to start this process is that classes will generally equate to entities (Figure 3.6).

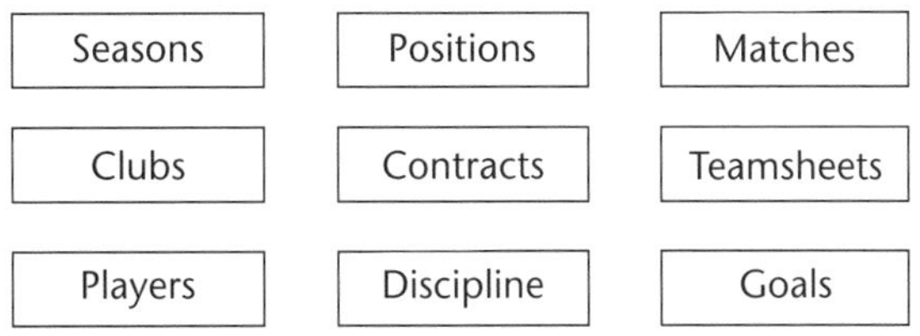

Seasons	Positions	Matches
Clubs	Contracts	Teamsheets
Players	Discipline	Goals

Figure 3.6 UFL entities. Translating the object diagram gives nine entities.

The UFL object diagram has nine major classes: *Seasons, Clubs, Players, Matches, Contract, Discipline, Positions, Teamsheets* and *Goals*.

3.2 ∈ RELATIONSHIPS

A **relationship** is an association between entities (Figure 3.7).

Players Matches relationship

   Players PLAY IN Matches is an association between Players and Matches

Players Contracts Clubs relationship

   Players HAVE Contracts WITH clubs is an association between Players, Contracts and Clubs.

Figure 3.7 Examples of relationships.

One entity may be involved in several relationships. In one instance, all the members may be involved (Figure 3.7). All players, for example, have a contract. Not all players score goals. A different subset of players receive match suspensions for disciplinary offences arising from matches. Roles can be defined in such cases (Figure 3.8).

Players ARE EMPLOYED BY clubs
Players REPRESENT clubs IN matches
Players SCORE Goals
Players RECEIVE Discipline

Figure 3.8 Players' roles.

The roles of *player* are *employee, representative, scorer* or *defendant.* This is more satisfactory than partitioning *employees, representatives, scorers* and *defenders* into four distinct non-overlapping entity sets.

Sometimes the same entity set can appear more than once in a relationship, playing different *roles* (Figure 3.9).

Person IS THE FATHER OF Person

Figure 3.9 Recursive role.

The entity set *Person* appears twice in the relationship in Figure 3.9 and plays the roles of *Father* and *Child* in the first and second occurrences respectively. Such relationships are also called **recursive**.

Dimensionality is the number of different entity sets participating in a relationship. It can be one or more, as should be clear from previous examples. A recursive relationship is **unary**. A relationship of dimensionality two is called **binary**. A relationship of dimensionality three is called **ternary**.

3.2.1 CARDINALITIES

A relationship has certain numerical characteristics that indicate the nature of the roles played by the entity sets that take part in the relationship. The minimum and maximum occurrences of each entity set in the relationship indicates its **cardinality** in the relationship.

The relationship coverage in Figure 3.10 is **total** on *matches*. Every match must have at least one player. If it is possible that one player may be selected for zero matches, the relationship coverage is **partial** on *players*. This aspect of the relationship is also called the **participation** or **ordinality**. The ordinality can only be zero or one. If the ordinality is zero the participation is optional; if it is one, the participation is mandatory.

An entity's **arity** in a relationship is the maximum number of its instances that can refer to one instance in the other entity set. It is important only to distinguish between one and many.

In the *players/matches* relationship, *players* has arity *n* and *matches* also has arity *n*. An equivalent but more concise way to express the combination of participation and arity is to define two integer numbers for every entity set in a relationship, called the minimum and maximum cardinality, abbreviated as **MinC** and **MaxC**. They represent the minimum and maximum occurrence of any member of the entity set in the relationship. They are normally written within square brackets – [MinC, MaxC] – in the relationship definition (Figure 3.10).

MinC of an entity set indicates the absolute minimum number of instances from the other entity set that **must** be assigned to every one of its members. MaxC of an

Players[0,n] PLAY IN Matches[1,n]	
Role: Player	Role: Matches
Participation: Optional Arity: *n*	Participation: Mandatory Arity: *n*
Not every player is selected to play in a match. Many players can play in one match	Every match must have at least one player. Many matches can feature the same player

Figure 3.10 Players and matches.

entity set indicates how many of its members can refer to **one** member of the other entity set.

When determining the participation in a relationship between entity set A and B, look to see how the word *every* or the phrase *at least one* can be used with an appropriate verb to describe the relationship. Alternatively, look to see how the word *zero* can be used with an appropriate verb (Figure 3.11).

Every A has at least one B	mandatory on A
Not every A has a B	optional on A
An A can have zero Bs	optional on A
An A cannot have zero Bs	mandatory on A

Figure 3.11 Recognizing participation.

When determining the arity of the relationship of A to B, look to see if the word 'many' or the phrase 'only one' can be used with an appropriate verb (Figure 3.12).

Many As can have the same B	arity of *n* on A
Many As cannot have the same B	arity of 1 on A
Only one A can have a B	arity of 1 on A

Figure 3.12 Recognizing arity.

Then do the same for the relationship of B to A (Figure 3.13).

Players[1,1] HAVE Contracts[1,*n*]	
Role: Players	Role: Contract
Participation: Mandatory Arity:1	Participation: Mandatory Arity: *n*
Every Player has at least one contract	Every contract refers to only one player
Only one player can have a particular contract	Many contracts may refer to the same player

Figure 3.13 Players have contracts: the sanity clause.

The father/child relationship in Figure 3.14 is recursive between persons. *Person* assumes the role of father on one side and child on the other. Not all persons are fathers; some are female! All children, male or female, have fathers.

Person [0,1] IS THE FATHER OF Person [1,*n*]	
Role: Father	Role: Child
Participation: Optional Arity: 1	Participation: Mandatory Arity: *n*
Not every person is a father	Every child has one father
Many persons cannot be father to the same child	Many children may have the same father

Figure 3.14 The child is father to the man.

Binary relationships can be classified as in Figure 3.15, according to the **arities** of the two entity sets they relate.

3.3 KEYS

The identity of a record in the hierarchical data model is determined by a pointer value based on the record's position on the disk, and the same applies to the network model. The important difference between the relational model and its precursors is that **the identity of a tuple is determined by the values of its attributes**. It is impossible for two tuples in a relation to have identical values for all their attributes, since there would then be no way to distinguish between them. They

Arities	Binary relationship
1:1	one-to-one
N:1	many-to-one
1:N	one-to-many
N:M	many-to-many

Relationship	Arities
Players PLAY IN Matches	N:M
Players HAVE Contracts	1:N
Person IS THE FATHER OF Person	1:N

Figure 3.15 Binary relationships.

would effectively be describing the same real-world object or concept and one of them would be redundant.

3.3.1 SUPERKEYS

All relations have one or more attributes which, when taken together, provide a unique set of values which serve to set each tuple apart from its neighbours within the entity set. Any set of attributes that serves in this way is called a **superkey**.

In the sample *Players* relation in Figure 3.1, the *Nationality* attribute on its own or even in combination with the *Club* attribute does not contain values that differentiate between the tuples shown. However, the set of attributes {*Surname, Nationality, Club*} does distinguish the rows and *for this fragment* of the relation is a superkey. Figure 3.16 shows other examples of attribute sets that are superkeys for this fragment.

[Dateofbirth]
[Surname, Dateofbirth]
[Surname, Forename, Dateofbirth]
[UFA_ID, Club]
[UFA_ID]

Figure 3.16 Player superkeys I.

However, a superkey should serve not just for this relation fragment, but also for the whole relation. *Players* will contain tuples with attribute values over the whole range of their respective domains. Clearly, there will be several players who share the same birthday, and even a pair of twins with the same surname and birthday. By taking into account the possibility of attributes displaying the range of their domain values, a more precise definition of a superkey may be offered.

SUPERKEY DEFINITION	A superkey is a proper set of one or more attributes which, taken together, allows the unique identification of an entity within an entity set.

This definition still yields many superkeys, some of which consist of attribute sets that require several facts to be known about a player before a search can be mounted in the relation. A superkey that minimizes the search information needed is clearly of interest (Figure 3.17).

[UFA_ID, Club]
[UFA_ID, Surname, Club]
[UFA_ID]
[UFA_ID, Surname, Dateofbirth, Club].
[Surname, Forename, Dateofbirth]

Figure 3.17 Player superkeys II.

The superkey [*UFA_ID*] is issued by the Utopian Football Association for each player and is based on an attribute set with one member, containing a unique identifier, in a domain where duplicates are not allowed. Three other superkeys contain this attribute in combination with other attributes. Any set of attributes that contains a superkey is also a superkey.

3.3.2   CANDIDATE KEYS.

The central interest is to pick a number of superkeys which do not contain superfluous attributes and which might serve as the principal identifier for each row when it is stored in the database. Each of these optimized superkeys has the potential to be chosen and is called a candidate key. In order to give a rule for minimizing the number and size of the superkeys, a new definition is introduced.

CANDIDATE KEYS	A candidate key is a superkey in which no proper subset of its attributes is also a superkey.

Three of the superkeys in Figure 3.17 cannot become candidate keys because they each contain the subset [*UFA_ID*], which is itself a superkey.

Figure 3.18 shows the candidate keys and either may be chosen as the unique identifier when the p*layers scheme* is defined in the database. *UFA_ID*s are known to be unique and the combination of *Surname, Forename* and *Dateofbirth* should be unique in the Utopian Football League.

[UFA_ID]
[Surname, Forename, Dateofbirth]

Figure 3.18 Candidate keys for players.

This latter, which contains an attribute set of three members, is called a **composite key**. The *UFA_ID* will generally be preferred because a search based on it will require only one fact about a player to be known, whereas the composite key requires three facts to be known before a unique identification can be constructed.

UFA_ID does not really describe a real-world characteristic of a player. People are not born with this attribute. The same goes for *National Insurance Number, Employee Number, Passport Number* and so on. These are artificial constructs, allocated to individuals when their actual characteristics cannot uniquely identify them. These **abstract keys** have the advantage of guaranteeing uniqueness.

3.3.3 PRIMARY KEYS

When one of the candidate keys is chosen by the database designer as a unique identifier for a table (relation), it becomes a **Primary key**. DBMSs allow the specification of a primary key at the time that the table is created. The DBMS will then check every insertion of a row for a unique value in the primary key attribute.

Not all entity sets, although they may have candidate keys, have a primary key chosen by the database designer. An entity set that depends on another entity set for its existence may not have a primary key specified at the time the table is created.

STRONG AND WEAK ENTITIES	An entity set which has a primary key is a strong entity set. An entity set which does not have a primary key is a weak entity set

3.3.4 FOREIGN KEYS

Clearly, a weak entity set cannot be left as a table definition without some sort of key to link it into the schema of relationships. If this were done, there would be no way to distinguish its rows. The important characteristic of a weak entity set is that is depends for its existence on its relationship with a strong entity set.

Consider the entity set *Goals*. It is clear that a goal cannot exist without a player to score it (Figure 3.19).

Players[0,1] SCORE Goals[1,n]

Figure 3.19 Strong and weak relations.

A link can be created **within** the relation *Goals* by inserting an attribute indicating the identity of the scorer. The only sure way of identifying that player is to use the primary key of the *Players* table.

Figure 3.20 shows fragments of the *Players* and *Goals* relations as they might be implemented in the database. *Players* has a primary key, [*UFA_ID*]. *Goals* has no primary key but the primary key of the player who scored each goal has been inserted into the *Goals* table.

UFA ID	Surname	Forename
UT23685	Constantine	George
UT236965	Dickens	Henry
VT432167	Diocletian	Pierre
FT246517	Gregory	Alan
Players relation		

UFA_ID	Time	Date
VT432167	16	01/02/2004
UT23685	23	07/02/2004
UT236965	34	07/02/2004
VT432167	24	07/02/2004
VT432167	57	14/02/2004
VT432167	78	14/02/2004
Goals relation		

Figure 3.20 A foreign key links goals to players.

An attribute of an entity set that is the primary key of another entity set is called a **Foreign key**. Notice that, while the [*UFA_ID*] attribute in the *Players* table has unique values, the foreign key [*UFA_ID*] attribute in the *Goals* table has duplicated values. This enables, for example, Pierre Diocletian to score three goals. The relations *Players* and *Goals* are members of the 1:*n* (one-to-many) relationship, SCORES.

In the same way, a disciplinary hearing cannot exist without a player who is accused of an offence. *Players* are quite capable of having a completely unblemished record with no disciplinary hearings. In the relationship between *Players* and *Discipline*, *Players* is the strong entity. It has a primary key. Each row in *Discipline* must contain a reference to the player who committed the offence. *Discipline* is dependent on *Players*. It is a weak entity.

Characterizing relations as strong or weak depends on the role they play in particular relationship. The answer to identifying strong and weak relations is to look at the **cardinality** of the relationship. An entity with a [0,1] role in the relationship is very definitely strong. It can exist with out being connected to any instances of the second relation. A MinC value of zero gives the clue. An entity with a cardinality of [1,N] is just as definitely weak. It must be associated with at least one row of the other relation in order to exist, and furthermore, more than one of its rows can refer to the same row in the other table. A MinC value of 1 and MaxC value of N give the clue.

Remember that the cardinality of a relation is about the role it plays in a particular relationship. An entity may display different cardinalities in different relationships. Identifying an entity as strong or weak depends on which relationship is being considered. Figure 3.21 shows two roles that *Orders* takes in two different relationships.

Customers[0,1] MAKE Orders[1,N]
Orders[1,1] CONTAIN Lineitems[1,N]

Figure 3.21 Roles for the *Person* relation.

In the first relationship, a *Customer* can exist without making any orders. *Customers* is the strong relation and *Orders* is weak. In the second, a row in *Lineitems* cannot exist without being associated with a row in *Orders*. In this relationship, *Orders* is strong. The values of MinC and MaxC determine the strong or weak status.

If the MinCs for the two relations are 0 and 1, then the relation with zero participation is strong. If both MinCs are 1, look at the MaxCs. If the MaxCs are 1 and N, Then the relation with arity 1 is strong. If both MaxCs are N then the relationship is M:N and must be decomposed before strong and weak characteristics can be determined.

Oracle allows the database designer to nominate attributes in weak entity sets as foreign keys when the table structure is created. Such nomination will imply the imposition of **integrity rules** into the schema.

Since tuples in the weak relation depend on the strong relation for their existence, if a tuple from the strong relation were deleted, any tuple in the weak relation that contained a reference to the deleted row would also have to be deleted. Deleting rows in the weak relation might then trigger further deletes in other relationships where it played a strong role.

It should also be impossible to insert a row in the dependent table unless a row in the strong relation already exists with an appropriate primary key.

These two rule examples indicate that the database is ensuring **referential integrity**. Foreign key values in a weak relation cannot exist without a counterpart in the primary key values of the strong relation.

3.4 ENTITY–RELATIONSHIP DIAGRAMS

The collection of entities, relationships and their properties is called a conceptual schema: conceptual because it exists outside of the physical implementation in a database; schema because it describes a plurality of relation schemes. An entity–relationship diagram is a graphical representation of a conceptual schema. The original form of the ER diagram, as defined by Chen (1976), featured:

- An entity set as a rectangular box with the entity set name inside.
- A relationship set as a lozenge with a line connecting it to each entity set that participates in the relationship. The arity is written by the line.

Over the years since Chen first proposed this method of diagramming a database design, a number of academics, systems analysts and writers have published their own ideas on how an ER diagram should look. This book uses what is known as the Information Engineering approach. The principal difference from Chen's original proposal is that the cardinalities in the relationships are coded into the line symbols.

The *Clubs* entity, shown in Figure 3.22, has four attributes. The primary key is *Name*. All of the entities in the UFL schema design are shown in detail in the appendix. All of the relationships are shown in the full entity–relationship diagram, given later in Figure 3.32.

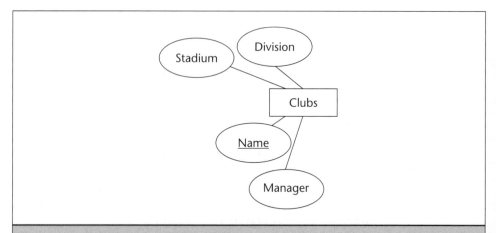

Figure 3.22 ERD entities and attributes. An entity is shown as a rectangular box with the name of the entity in it. Attributes are show as ovals connected to the entity. Keys are underlined.

Figure 3.23 shows an ERD for a typical 1:*n* relationship. Players must have at least one contract and many players cannot be referred to by one contract. The cardinality of the relationship is [1,1] on *Players* and this is shown by the double bar across the line connecting the *Players* entity to the relationship.

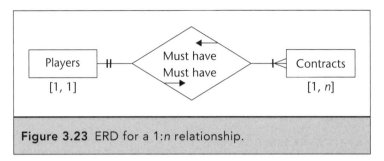

Figure 3.23 ERD for a 1:*n* relationship.

A contract refers to at least one player but many contracts can refer to the same player. The cardinality is [1,*n*] on *Contracts* and this is shown by the bar and the crow's foot on the line connecting *Contracts* to the relationship.

Figure 3.24 shows that a player may have zero discipline cases and many players cannot be defendants in one case. The cardinality of *Players* is [0,1]. The optional participation of players in the relationship is shown by the zero over the line connecting *Players* to the relationship.

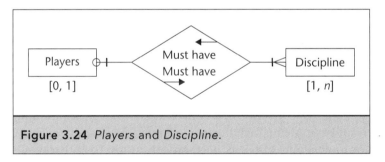

Figure 3.24 *Players* and *Discipline*.

A discipline case must involve at least one player and many cases can involve the same player. The cardinality of *Discipline* is [1,*n*] and the symbols on the connecting line show this.

When a 1:*N* relationship is proposed, the full ER diagram must show the primary key attribute of the strong entity and the foreign key attribute of the weak entity.

The participation of an entity in a relationship can only have one of two possible values, 0 or 1. The arity of an entity can have one of two possible values, 1 or *n*. The cardinality of an entity in a relationship therefore can have only four possible combinations. There are only four different line encodings to consider. Figure 3.25 shows the diagram conventions for these cardinalities.

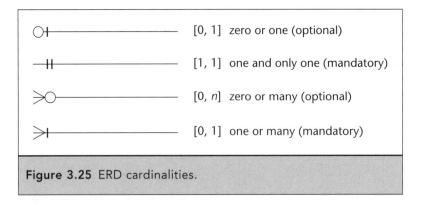

Figure 3.25 ERD cardinalities.

3.4.1 MANY-TO-MANY RELATIONSHIPS

Figure 3.26 shows an ER diagram for the players/matches relationship. In this relationship, a player plays in a minimum of 0 matches and a maximum of n matches. A match must have a minimum of 1 player and a maximum of n players.

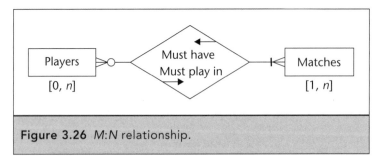

Figure 3.26 M:N relationship.

It is perfectly valid to represent *M:N* relationships in this way as far as the ER diagramming convention is concerned. However, as it stands, this relationship cannot be implemented directly in a relational database.

To understand this it is necessary not only to think about the interaction of players and matches as real-world objects but also to consider what this chapter has had to say about keys and the structure of entities.

The players relation will have a primary key, *UFA_ID* that must be unique in the players relation. Yet players may play in many matches.

In order to express this in the database, a *Players* tuple should contain a foreign key to relate it to the match in which the player appeared. Not just once, but every time the player appears in a match, another foreign key must appear. Either the *Players* tuple must be duplicated each time he appears so that the additional foreign key can be accommodated, or a *Players* tuple must contain enough space for unknown multiple occurrences of foreign keys representing each of his appearances. The same problem occurs in the matches relation, which must accommodate multiple players appearing in the same match.

Neither suggestion is either practical or possible. Duplicating tuples offends against the primary key unique property in the relation; replicating space for multiple foreign keys offends against the definition of an entity, which can only have one occurrence of each attribute in its attribute set. There appears to be a paradox.

The answer is to decompose or resolve the *M:N* relationship, creating two 1:*N* relationships and a third entity to express the foreign keys of both *Players* and *Matches* (Figure 3.27).

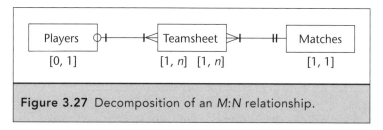

Figure 3.27 Decomposition of an *M:N* relationship.

The teamsheet entity records the players selected for a particular match and the matches in which a player appears. It must have at least two attributes: a foreign key to *Players* and a foreign key to *Matches*. Whenever decomposition is performed, the cardinalities follow the same pattern (Figure 3.28).

UFA_ID	Surname		UFA_ID	Match_id		Match_id	Matchdate
UT236965	Dickens		UT236965	1		1	04-Jan-04
VT432167	Diocletian		VT432167	1		2	28-Dec-03
FT246517	Gregory		FT246517	1		3	28-Dec-03
			VT432167	2		4	26-Dec-03
Players			Teamsheets			Matches	

Figure 3.28 Players, matches and teamsheets.

The original relations have the same participation in their new relationships as they had before. *Players* has an optional participation with *Teamsheets* and *Matches* has a mandatory participation. The arities of the original relations in their new relationship is always 1. The new relation always has mandatory participation and an arity of *n* in its relationships with each of the original relations.

Players and *Matches* are unchanged. They retain their previous primary keys and are free to participate in other relationships with other entities. *Teamsheets* depends upon the *M:N* relationship between *Players* and *Matches* for its existence. This dependency is expressed through the foreign keys it contains. It has no other attributes, so it may be termed an *abstract entity*. In the UFL application, it serves no other purpose than to link players and matches and to express their *M:N* relationship.

Diocletian appears twice in Figure 3.28, which illustrates a fragment of the *Teamsheets* relation. This records the fact that he played in match 1 and match 2 without any conflict with the primary key of *Players*. Match 1 appears three times, again without compromising the primary key of *Matches*.

Often, an entity that performs this linking function has attributes of it own as well as the two foreign keys. It represents a real-world object and carries important information for the application.

Whenever the configuration shown in Figure 3.29 appears in an ER diagram, there is an *M:N* relationship being expressed. These are regularly discovered only after the ER diagram is prepared. The linking entity has an existence of its own and appears from the start of the analysis as an important part of the application.

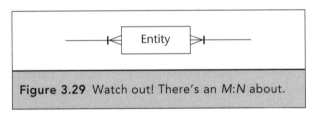

Figure 3.29 Watch out! There's an *M:N* about.

There are at least three such entities in the full UFL diagram. *Contracts* has already been mentioned in an example of a 1:*N* relationship with *Players*. However, *Contracts* needs not just a player but also a club to be complete (Figure 3.30). The *Contracts* entity has a 1:*N* relationship with *Clubs*. It also has attributes of its own: *Joined* and *Left* which show when a player joined and left a club. It tracks the player's career and the club's employer history.

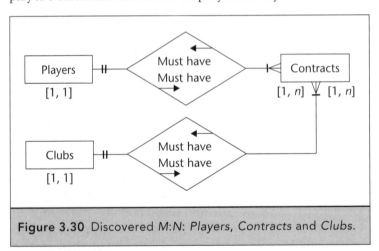

Figure 3.30 Discovered *M:N*: *Players*, *Contracts* and *Clubs*.

Recording goals is a vital part of the UFL scenario. It is not good enough just to put the final score in the match entity. Players need a record of their goals as well. This 1:*N* relation has already been shown as an example and *Goals* is part of another 1:*N* relationship with *Matches*.

But just a minute! The early part of this section was spent proving such a relation and inventing a new entity, *Teamsheets*, which services just this connection. Is there not a way in which *Goals* and *Teamsheets* could be combined? This would certainly save a lot of separate process programming and, in a real application, space.

In this case, the answer is, unfortunately no.

The reasons are to be found in Figures 3.30 and 3.31. Players, if selected, can appear only once in a match, but they can score any number of goals. In addition, if they are selected, they may not score any goals in a match. A match may not have any goals but it must have players. The participation of matches in the two *M:N* relationships is different. The two relationships, *Teamsheets* and *Goals* are describing completely different aspects of the connection between *Players* and *Matches*.

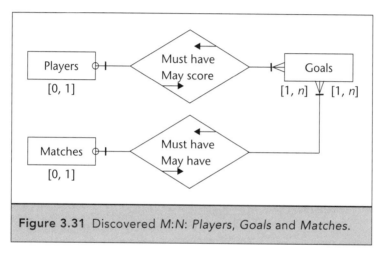

Figure 3.31 Discovered M:N: *Players, Goals* and *Matches*.

In fact, the rule that players can only be selected once for a match should be enforced by giving teamsheets a compound primary key {UFA_ID, Match_id}. This would ensure that the combination could only occur once in the *Teamsheets* relation.

This would not work for goals. The compound key would prevent the recording of more than one goal by a player in any one match. Further, *Goals* has other attributes of its own. A record is kept of the minute the goal is scored and its type – *goal, penalty, own goal. Goals* is not an abstract entity. If it could be combined with *Teamsheets*, these attributes would be wasted for most of the rows in a combined relation.

Players and *Matches* have two quite different *M:N* relationships, which, for structural and semantic reasons, require two separate resolutions into 1:*N* relationships.

3.5 ⊟   THE UFL ENTITY–RELATIONSHIP DIAGRAM

The full entity–relationship diagram for the UFL application is shown in Figure 3.32. The nine entities are present, participating in ten relationships. Each entity either has a primary key or has a foreign key to bind it into a relationship. The cardinalities are shown in the lines that connect entities with relationships.

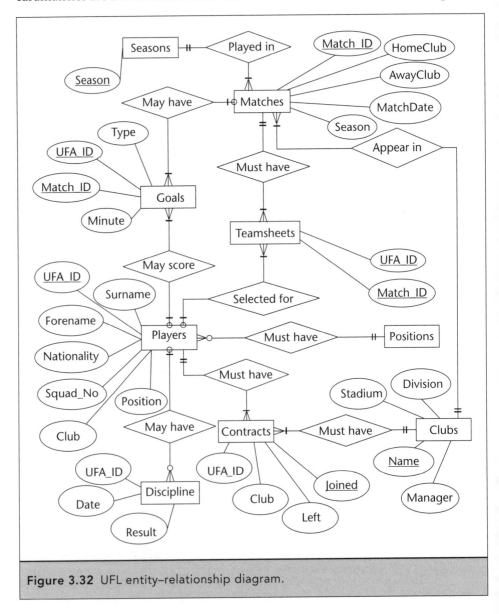

Figure 3.32 UFL entity–relationship diagram.

Some entities have more than one key. *Players* has a primary key, *UFA_ID*, which is used to express a strong relationship with *Discipline*, *Goals*, *Contracts* and

Teamsheets. It has a foreign key, *Position*, which is used to express its weak relationship with *Positions*.

Matches takes part in two relationships, with *Teamsheets* and with *Goals*, where its primary key expresses a strong relationship to these entities. It also takes a weak role with *Seasons*: a foreign key links each tuple to the permitted values for the season in which a match is played.

When an otherwise strong relation also participates as the weak side of a relationship, it is often a way of enforcing domain value restriction on an attribute.

3.6 ⊂ ERD ISSUES

There are some aspects of the UFL diagram that need clarification and explanation.

3.6.1 CALCULATED ATTRIBUTES

Players has an attribute, *Club,* which is not used in any relationship. Yet this attribute relates to the primary key of *Clubs* and shows the current club of a player. It is a calculated attribute and strictly does not belong in *Players*.

Calculated attributes can always be inferred from other values in the database. The current club of a player can be found by examining the *Contracts* relation for a player's career history. The tuple with no date value in the *Left* attribute will show to which club he is currently attached.

There is some risk in including a calculated attribute. If the player moves club, the *Left* attribute will be updated: a new *Contracts* tuple will be created and inserted into the *Contracts* relation to show the new club and the date he joined. If the calculated attribute is not updated in the same operation, there is a danger of the database becoming inconsistent. The *Players* relation will show one value for his current club and the *Contracts* relation will show another.

Calculated attributes are strictly outside the formal definitions of entities and their tuple structures. They also offend against the principals of normalization, outlined in the next chapter.

They are sometimes used in production databases, when performance issues are critical, as a way of reducing the number or complexity of queries submitted by users.

Leaving the attribute *Club* in the *Players* relation gives an opportunity later to illustrate the trigger facility of Oracle, which can be used to assure database consistency by preventing unwanted anomalies from occurring.

3.6.2 SUSPECTED *M:N*

Surely a club plays in many matches and matches must be between at least and no more than two clubs. Is there not an *M:N* relationship here that has been mistakenly characterized as 1:*N*? Moreover, are not the attributes *HomeClub* and *AwayClub* describing essentially the same characteristic of *Matches*, therefore offending against the rules for entity structure? If so, this should have been resolved into the additional relationship of Figure 3.33.

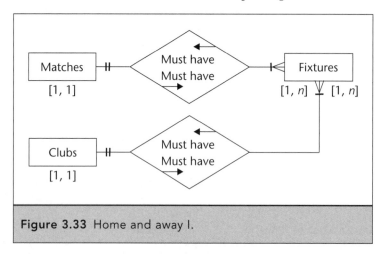

Figure 3.33 Home and away I.

If the resolution is carried out, *Fixtures* will have two attributes, for foreign keys to *Matches* and *Clubs*, and must also carry an attribute indicating whether the club is home or away in this fixture. A fixture will consist of two tuples for each match.

However, it is known that a single match will only ever be related to two clubs (i.e. n is 2). It can be argued that one match will relate to only one member of *Clubs* in the role of *Home* and to only one member of *Clubs* in the role of *Away*. The arity of clubs in the home role is 1 and in the away role is 1. Many matches can relate to one club in the home role and many matches can relate to one club in the away role. The arity of matches is n with respect to each of the roles of *Clubs*.

Matches is involved in two parallel 1:N relationships with *Clubs* (Figure 3.34). These are expressed in one foreign key to *Clubs* in the *Home* role and another foreign key to *Clubs* in the *Away* role. The attributes *HomeClub* and *AwayClub* are foreign keys for each of these two relationships respectively and offend against neither the rules of entity structure nor normalization.

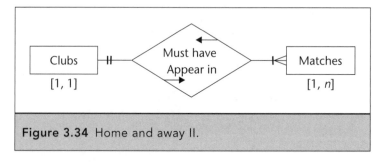

Figure 3.34 Home and away II.

3.7 ⊨ KEY TERMS

Entities	The things or concepts described by the data in a database: players, contracts, clubs.
Attributes	The characteristics of an entity: Player(surname, forename…). Translates to a column in a database table.
Tuples	An instance of an entity that consists of valid data for each of the entity's attributes. Translates to a row in a database table.
Keys	An identifier that distinguishes one instance of an entity from another.
Superkeys	A group of different attribute combinations that distinguish rows in an entity set.
Candidate keys	Those superkeys that do not contain other superkeys.
Primary key	The candidate key chosen as a unique identifier when a table is created in the database.
Foreign key	A reference to the primary key in another relation that establishes a relationship.
Relationships	A logical association between relations.
Cardinality	A measure of the role each relation plays in the relationship. Expressed as participation and arity or [MinC, MaxC].
Strong/ weak	A description of the role each relation plays in the relationship. Can be determined by inspection of the cardinalities. A strong entity has a primary key; a weak entity has a foreign key.
Entity–relationship diagram (ERD)	Diagramming tool for database design. Several different conventions for showing entities, their attributes and the cardinality of relationships. The Information Engineering method codes the cardinality into symbols on the connecting lines.

3.8 ⊨ QUESTIONS

(i) Explain what is meant by the terms *attribute*, *domain* and *tuple*.

(ii) Explain what is meant by the terms *strong relation* and *weak relation*. Explain how an entity can simultaneously be a strong and a weak relation.

(iii) Explain the terms *participation*, *arity* and *cardinality*.

(iv) Explain why an *M:N* relationship should always be decomposed in an ERD.

3.9 ∈ EXERCISES

(i) Draft an ERD for:

- A patient treatment database
- A criminal records database
- An electronic bookstore
- An equestrian studbook

CHAPTER 4

NORMALIZATION

It is often stated that of all the theories proposed in this century, the silliest is quantum theory. In fact, some say that the only thing that quantum theory has going for it is that it is unquestionably correct.

Michio Kaku, *Hyperspace*

4.1 ∈ SET THEORY AND THE ENTITY–RELATIONSHIP MODEL

E. F. Codd's first article on the application of set theory to stored data led to the development of the relational data model. Part of this application of set theory gives the definitions of entity sets participating in relationships. By using just these definitions, the entity–relationship diagram can illustrate the entity types in a database schema and the relationships that exist between these entity types.

If the entity–relationship model is derived from mathematical principles, is there a way to check our data analysis in a rigorous way to ensure its correctness? In fact, the entity–relationship model depends on this rigour at the initial stages to ensure that the query language, SQL, works properly.

The query language is based on defined ways to manipulate sets, subsets and the relationships between them. It is founded on the **relational calculus**: a series of set manipulation functions within set theory that, in turn, depend upon the sets being well formed. The sets – their attributes, the primary and foreign keys, the relationships in the schema – must conform to certain and definite rules that enable the database design to be checked for accuracy, consistency and correctness.

These rules define a series of so-called **Normal Forms** that allow the proposed entity sets and their attributes to be verified against the underlying mathematical principles of set theory and the needs of a query language based on the relational calculus.

4.2 ∈ FIRST NORMAL FORM

The first rule is that attributes of an entity should have atomic values and that each attribute should occur only once in the attribute set for each entity. Attributes describing the same characteristic of an entity must occur only once.

Version I of the *Players* relation in Figure 4.1 attempts to record the disciplinary history of each player. In the Utopian Football League, discipline is generally good and few players get more than two suspensions in their career. Disciplinary hearings are held following a referee's report and generally result in a match suspension for the player.

UFA_ID	Surname	Disciplinary hearing	
		Date	Result
UT23685	Constantine	2/4/03	1 match
UT236965	Dickens		
VT432167	Diocletian	12/11/03	1 match
FT246517	Gregory	17/2/2001	2 matches
		3/02/2003	2 matches
AT245876	Hegel		
QT873456	Kant		

Figure 4.1 Discipline relation I.

This design allows the date and result of any number of hearings to be recorded for each player. However, there are attributes that contain multiple values. If this table were to be queried for the dates of Gregory's hearings, a single string value – the concatenation of the two dates – would be retrieved.

The same thing will happen for a query on the outcomes of his hearings. Further, it is not clear what the names of the attributes are. There seems to be an attribute called *Disciplinary hearing* divided into two sub-attributes: *Date* and *Result. A*ll of this offends against the rule that attributes must be single-valued and that these values must come from one domain. Entities must have atomic attributes.

The second design (Figure 4.2) attempts to rectify this by allowing two hearings to be recorded. Each of the attributes has distinct names; the values in each are atomic and come from single domains.

This relation is in trouble already, because if Gregory is involved in another incident there will be no space to record the hearing, and for three players space is wasted because they have led blameless lives (on the pitch at least!).

UFA_ID	Surname	dh1_date	dh1_result	dh2_date	dh2_result
UT23685	Constantine	2/4/03	1 match		
UT236965	Dickens				
VT432167	Diocletian	12/11/03	1 match		
FT246517	Gregory	17/2/2001	2 matches	3/02/2003	3 matches
AT245876	Hegel				
QT873456	Kant				

Figure 4.2 Discipline relation II.

A query on this table would have to refer to what is essentially the same characteristic of a player by two different attribute names. Moreover, it can be seen that details of disciplinary hearings are not something that every player has.

Although this is a design that a relational database would accept, it has logical faults in terms of the definition of an entity. As far as the rules for the construction of an entity set are concerned, *dh1_date* and *dh2_date* are repeated attributes and may not even be attributes for some players.

The solution to this is to recognize that *Discipline* is in fact a separate entity from *Players* and has an attribute set with two members, *Date* and *Result* (Figure 4.3). It has a relationship with *Players*, expressed through a foreign key.

UFA_ID	Surname		UFA_ID	date	result
UT23685	Constantine		FT246517	3/02/03	2 matches
UT236965	Dickens		UT23685	2/04/03	1 match
VT432167	Diocletian		VT432167	12/11/03	1 match
FT246517	Gregory		FT246517	24/1/04	3 matches
AT245876	Hegel				
QT873456	Kant				

Figure 4.3 Discipline relation III.

Discipline is a weak relation, dependent on the strong relation, *Players*. The third design splits the original versions into two entities, adding a foreign key to *Discipline* that indicates the row in *Players* for whom this is a history.

```
Players[0,1] RECEIVE Discipline[1.n]
```

These are two relations in a one-to-many relationship. Gregory's next infringement will mean a row is added to *Discipline* to record the outcome. In fact, he can be as uncontrolled as he wishes; there will always be room for his full disciplinary history. Those players who do not have a disciplinary record do not appear in the new relation.

FIRST NORMAL FORM DEFINITION	A relation is in First Normal Form if each attribute is single-valued for each tuple and each attribute occurs only once in a tuple.

4.3 A IS FOR ANOMALY, AXIOM, AND ARMSTRONG

The basis of the rest of the normalization process is about the connection between key and non-key attributes in a relation. There are difficulties that can arise later when the query language is applied to an implemented relation if this connection is not well-formed.

AXIOM	A self-evident principle, accepted as true without proof.

The particular problems associated with relations that do not have a well-formed key are known as update anomalies and they can arise when tuples are inserted, deleted or modified.

Figure 4.4 shows a tentative design for the *contracts* relation that records the employment history of players. It identifies the player, shows when he joined or left a particular club, and names his manager.

UFA_ID	Surname	Club	Joined	Left	Manager
BR546732	Erasmus	Purity FC	21/6/1998	3/5/2000	Mercury
FT246517	Gregory	Forgiveness FC	26/7/1999	12/8/2002	Krishna
VT432167	Diocletian	Beauty United	12/4/2000		Thor
BR546732	Erasmus	Sobriety FC	3/5/2000	13/9/2002	Ganesh
UT23685	Constantine	Nirvana City	23/3/2001	2/5/2002	Wotan
UT23685	Constantine	Freedom United	2/5/2002	10/8/2003	Zeus
FT246517	Gregory	Beauty United	12/8/2002		Thor
BR546732	Erasmus	Purity FC	13/9/2002		Mercury
UT23685	Constantine	Beauty United	10/8/2003		Thor

Figure 4.4 Contracts relation – version I.

If a well-formed key is not chosen for this relation and for the other entities with which it has a relationship, it can exhibit all the different forms of the update anomaly.

4.3.1   INSERT ANOMALY

It may be possible to insert a new contract for a player who does not exist in the *Players* relation and assign him to club that does not exist in the *Clubs* relation.

4.3.2   DELETE ANOMALY

If a player is deleted from the *Players* relation, a side-effect may be experienced of some of the rows in the *Contracts* relation either referring to a player that does not exist or being deleted along with the row in the *Players* relation.

4.3.3   MODIFICATION ANOMALY

If the player with *UFA_ID* UT23685 leaves Beauty United, the *Left* attribute in the *Contracts* relation must be updated. If an update to the contracts relation is attempted, putting a date value into the *Left* attribute but identifying the tuple only by UFA_ID = 'UT23685', three tuples will be modified instead of just the one intended. What is worse, the data in two of the tuples will be overwritten and previous values lost.

If this same player were to change his surname, the *Player* relation would be updated. This would have no effect on the *Contracts* relation. There would then be, within the database, a *UFA_ID* referring to a player by two different surnames in two relations.

4.3.4   FUNCTIONAL DEPENDENCY

The concept of functional dependency is used to specify a formal measure of the compliance of relation designs with the underlying theory and to apply increasingly strict **normal forms** to improve that compliance. The functional dependency within a relation is a formal way of specifying the ideas developed about keys in Section 3.3 and a way of provably assuring the relation design.

Functional dependencies are *constraints* on the relation that are derived from the *meaning* and *interrelationships* of the data attributes. A functional dependency is derived by first considering a set, X, of the attributes of a relation. A second set is taken, possibly overlapping, called Y. If, in a relation instance, whenever the same combined values for X are found, the same combined values for Y are found, then it is certain that X determines Y. Another way of saying this is that Y is functionally dependent on X.

FUNCTIONAL DETERMINISM	A set of attributes X functionally determines a set of attributes Y if the value of X determines a unique value for Y.
	This is written as X → Y

If R is a relation, then r(R) is a relation instance such as the fragment in Figure 4.4. If X → Y, the set of attributes, X, functionally determines the set of attributes, Y, then whenever two tuples (t1,t2) have the same value for X, they *must have* the same value for Y.

RELATION CONSTRAINT	If t1[X] = t2[X] and t1[Y] = t2[Y] in any relation instance r(R)
	X → Y in relation R specifies a constraint on all relation instances r(R)

In the *Contracts* relation (Figure 4.4), it can be seen that if a set of attributes is considered so that X is {*UFA_ID, Club*} and a second set, Y is {*Surname, Manager*}, the same combination of *UFA_ID* and *Club* values implies the same values of *Surname* and *Manager* in combination (Figure 4.5).

Tuple 1 [BR546732, Purity FC] = Tuple 8[BR546732, Purity FC]

And

Tuple 1 [Erasmus, Mercury] = Tuple 8[Erasmus, Mercury]

So

{UFA_ID, Club} → {Surname, Manager}

Figure 4.5 Functional dependency example.

Functional dependencies must be derived from the real-world constraints on the attributes. A functional dependency is a property of the attributes in a relation schema and therefore must apply as a constraint on any instance in the database that implements the relation schema. A property of the attributes must hold true, whatever the values, in any implementation.

The two sets, X and Y, do not have to cover all of the attributes in a relation for there to be a functional dependency. However, when the LHS and the RHS of a functional dependency cover all of the attributes, we are on the track of a superkey (Figure 4.6).

UFA_ID, Joined determines Surname, Club, Left, Manager
{UFA_ID, Joined} → {Surname, Club, Left, Manager}

Figure 4.6 *Contracts* relation dependencies.

At first glance it might seem probable that the two attributes keys *UFA_ID* and *Club* would play a deterministic role in the *contracts* relation. However, looking at the career of the player Erasmus, it can be seen that he rejoined Purity FC after a spell at Sobriety FC. The same combination of attributes for *UFA_ID* and *Club* do not determine the same combined set of values for *Surname, Joined, Left* and *Manager*. Therefore there is no functional dependence between these two sets of attributes.

There may be more than one functional dependency within a relation. Remember that the definition is in terms of a set of attributes influencing another set of attributes. Just as several superkeys could be determined in a relation, more than one functional dependency can probably be found (Figure 4.7).

{UFA_ID, Left} → {Surname, Joined, Manager}
UFA_ID → {Surname}
{UFA_ID, Club} → {Surname, Manager}
{UFA_ID, Club, Joined} → {Surname, Left, Manager}
{Club} → {Manager}

Figure 4.7 Other functional dependencies for *Contracts*.

4.3.5   ARMSTRONG'S AXIOMS

Given a set of functional dependencies, F, additional functional dependencies can be *inferred* that hold whenever the functional dependencies in F hold. These are known as Armstrong's Axioms or Armstrong's Inference Rules (Armstrong, 1974).

They are used in selecting an appropriate key which does not give rise to update anomalies. The series of axioms first outlined by Armstrong is used to formalize the connection or dependency of a set of attributes in an entity on another set of attributes within the same entity.

The notion of correctness in a set of axioms is based on the concepts of soundness and completeness. Armstrong's axioms are sound because they can be proven to generate only correct functional dependencies.

They are complete because they can be shown to generate all possible functional dependencies from a given set, F, of functional dependencies. Armstrong's axioms are shown in Figure 4.8.

Reflexive rule
If Y is a subset of X, then X → Y

{Club, Left} is a subset of {UFA_ID, Club, Left}
therefore
{UFA_ID, Club, Left} → {Club, Left}

Augmentation rule
If X → Y, then XZ → YZ
(Notation: XZ stands for X → Z)

{UFA_ID, Club} → {Manager}
therefore
{UFA_ID, Club, Surname} → {Surname, Manager}

Transitive rule
If X → Y and Y → Z, then X → Z

{UFA_ID, Joined} → {Club} and {Club} → {Manager}
therefore
{UFA_ID, Joined} → {Manager}

Figure 4.8 Armstrong's axioms.

From the first three rules, it is possible to infer three more rules, shown in Figure 4.9.

Closure of a set F of functional dependencies is the set F+ of all the functional dependencies that can be inferred from F using Armstrong's inference rules. If we look at the rule examples above, then we have at least the functional dependencies of Figure 4.10).

4.4 SECOND NORMAL FORM

Second Normal Form is a check that we have chosen a key attribute or set of attributes that determines the values of all of the non-key attributes in the relation. It also specifies that the non-key attributes must be functionally dependent on the **full** key. If we have a single attribute as a superkey then that poses no problem, because if a single attribute determines all the other attributes, they must be functionally dependent on the full key. However, all the functional dependencies in the *Contracts* relation that would yield a potential candidate key involve more than one attribute.

There are several superkeys, based on functional dependencies that relate all the attributes in the relation (Figure 4.11). In all cases, not all of the non-key fields are

Decomposition rule
If X → YZ, then X → Y and X → Z

{UFA_ID, Joined} → {Surname, Club, Left}
      X   YZ
therefore
{UFA_ID, Joined} → {Surname} and {UFA_ID, Joined} → {Club, Left}
     X   Y   X   Z

Union rule
If X → Y and X → Z, then X → YZ

{UFA_ID, Joined} → {Club} and {UFA_ID, Joined} → {Left}
     X   Y   X   Z
therefore
{UFA_ID, Joined} → {Club, Left}
     X   YZ

Pseudo-transitivity rule
If X → Y and WY → Z, then WX → Z

{UFA_ID, Joined} → {Club} and {Club, Left } → {Manager}
     X   Y   WY   Z
therefore
{UFA_ID, Joined, Left } → {Manager}
    WX   Z

Figure 4.9 Rules derived from Armstrong's axioms.

{UFA_ID, Joined} → {Surname, Club, Left, Manager }
{UFA_ID, Left} → {Surname, Club, Joined, Manager }
{UFA_ID, Joined, Club} → {Surname, Left, Manager}
{UFA_ID, Joined, Left} → {Surname, Club, Manager}
{Club, Left} → {Manager}
{UFA_ID} → {Surname}

Figure 4.10 Functional dependencies in the *Contracts* relation.

fully functionally dependent on the key because of partial functional dependencies (Figure 4.12).

The compound keys, {*UFA_ID, Joined, Club*} and {*UFA_ID, Joined, Left*} must first be rejected as candidate keys because they contain a superkey as a subset. This

{UFA_ID, Joined} → {Surname, Club, Left, Manager }
{UFA_ID, Joined, Left} → {Surname, Club, Manager }
{UFA_ID, Left} → {Surname, Club, Joined, Manager }
{UFA_ID, Joined, Club} → {Surname, Left, Manager}

Figure 4.11 Functional dependencies indicating superkeys.

{UFA_ID} → {Surname}
{Club} → {Manager}

Figure 4.12 Partial key dependencies.

UFA_ID	Club	Joined	Left	Manager
BR546732	Purity FC	21/6/1998	3/5/2000	Mercury
FT246517	Forgiveness FC	26/7/1999	12/8/2002	Krishna
VT432167	Beauty United	12/4/2000		Thor
BR546732	Sobriety FC	3/5/2000	13/9/2002	Ganesh
UT23685	Nirvana City	23/3/2001	2/5/2002	Wotan
UT23685	Freedom United	2/5/2002	10/8/2003	Zeus
FT246517	Beauty United	12/8/2002		Thor
BR546732	Purity FC	13/9/2002		Mercury
UT23685	Beauty United	10/8/2003		Thor

Figure 4.13 *Contracts* relation – version II.

leaves us only two superkeys, {*UFA_ID*, *Joined*} and {*UFA_ID*, *Left*}, that might become candidate keys.

SECOND NORMAL FORM	A relation is in Second Normal Form if it is in First Normal Form and all the non-key attributes are fully functionally dependent on the key.

Neither of these superkeys can be nominated as candidate keys while the *Surname* attribute remains in the relation because it is only partially dependent on either of them. Again, the answer here is to split the relation, forming a new relation based on the dependency. In fact, in this case, the new relation will be subsumed into the *Players* relation.

The revised *Contracts* relation (Figure 4.13) has two compound candidate key, {*UFA_ID, Joined*} and {*UFA_ID, left*}. All non-key fields are fully functionally dependent on either of the keys; the original version of the *contracts* relation was in 1NF. It is now in Second Normal Form.

Removing a partial key dependency always yields two relations with a strong/weak relationship. The partial key attribute, *UFA_ID*, is a foreign key in the original relation; it is a primary key in the new relation.

4.5 ⊆ THIRD NORMAL FORM

Although a relation may be in 2NF, there may be non-key attributes that have a deterministic relationship. The second design still allows updates of the *Manager* attribute in *Contracts* without synchronizing the *Manager* attribute in *Clubs*, causing an anomaly

The revised *Contracts* relation exhibits a dependency between the non-key fields *Club* and *Manager*. The *Manager* attribute has a transitive dependency on the key (Figure 4.14).

{UFA_ID, Joined} → {Club} and {Club} → {Manager}

Figure 4.14 Transitive dependency.

The way to remove the dependency is again to leave the LHS of the transitive dependency in the relation and create a second relation based on the dependency. When this is done, it must be remembered that duplicate tuples are not allowed or the new relation will not have a candidate key.

Figure 4.15 shows the revised *Contracts* relation. The transitive key, *Club*, and its dependent attribute, *Manager,* form the basis of the *Clubs* relation. Removing a transitive dependency always yields two relations with a strong/weak relationship. The transitive attribute is a foreign key in the original relation; it is a primary key in the new relation.

| **THIRD NORMAL FORM DEFINITION** | A relation is in Third Normal Form if it is in Second Normal Form and no non-key attribute is transitively dependent on the key. |

UFA_ID	Club	Joined	Left
BR546732	Purity FC	21/6/1998	3/5/2000
FT246517	Forgiveness FC	26/7/1999	12/8/2002
VT432167	Beauty United	12/4/2000	
BR546732	Sobriety FC	3/5/2000	13/9/2002
UT23685	Nirvana City	23/3/2001	2/5/2002
UT23685	Freedom United	2/5/2002	10/8/2003
FT246517	Beauty United	12/8/2002	
BR546732	Purity FC	13/9/2002	
UT23685	Beauty United	10/8/2003	

Figure 4.15 *Contracts* relation – version III.

4.6 ⊆ BOYCE–CODD NORMAL FORM

A further constraint on the design is expressed through Boyce–Codd Normal Form(BCNF). This rule is concerned with the status of the key attributes and with the choice of a primary key.

BOYCE–CODD NORMAL FORM	A relation is in Boyce–Codd Normal Form(BCNF) if it is in Third Normal Form and all determinants are candidate keys.

This rule is important only when the candidate keys are composite and they overlap. That situation does occur in *Contracts*, but none of the parts of the candidate keys is a determinant. There is no dependency between *UFA_ID* (the overlapping attribute) and any of the other attributes.

If the player's *Position* had been included in the attributes for contracts, then the situation would be different. The candidate keys would be the same, but the overlapping attribute, *UFA_ID*, would be a determinant for *Position* (*UFA_ID* → *Position*). Since *UFA_ID* is not itself a candidate key, the relation would not be in BCNF. Not all determinants would be candidate keys. Boyce–Codd violations are rare when the removal of partial key dependencies and transitive dependencies have brought the relation to 3NF.

The BCNF rule ensures that all the non-key field are describing an aspect of the entity in question; it rules out any non-key field that describes a characteristic of a part of a composite key.

In selecting a primary key, the candidate key {*UFA_ID*, *Joined*} is preferable to {*UFA_ID*, *Left*} because the attribute *Left* can contain the null value for a player who is still with a club. This latter combination still yields a valid key, but in practical terms, and, given that there is a good alternative, {*UFA_ID*, *Left*} should be rejected because it may lead to unnecessary complications in queries on the relation if it is implemented in the database.

The candidate key, {*UFA_ID*, *Joined*} is chosen as the primary key of the *Contracts* relation (Figure 4.16). This satisfies the rule for Boyce–Codd Normal Form.

UFA_ID (prime)	Club	Joined (prime)	Left
BR546732	Purity FC	21/6/1998	3/5/2000
FT246517	Forgiveness FC	26/7/1999	12/8/2002
VT432167	Beauty United	12/4/2000	
BR546732	Sobriety FC	3/5/2000	13/9/2002
UT23685	Nirvana City	23/3/2001	2/5/2002
UT23685	Freedom United	2/5/2002	10/8/2003
FT246517	Beauty United	12/8/2002	
BR546732	Purity FC	13/9/2002	
UT23685	Beauty United	10/8/2003	

Figure 4.16 Contracts relation – version IV.

4.6.1   REALITY CHECK

The process of normalization is a formal check on the validity of a database design. Normalizing the data view is a vital stage in the development process as it ensures that the application has a sound foundation for the subsequent construction of program logic.

Often the business rules of an organization lead to complex queries linking many tables, each of which may contain many thousands, even millions, of rows. The execution of such queries may involve many hours of intensive database activity and may affect overall performance. In such circumstances, two strategies may alleviate the situation:

• Questioning the business rule that leads to such an expensive query

• Scheduling the query to a less sensitive time

It may be that neither of these options is available because the business rule is essential and because the query is so long that it cannot be rescheduled. In these circumstances, there is a temptation to use a third tactic – de-normalize the data structure to enable the query to be broken down into manageable parts.

This route is sometimes taken in large production databases, although, with increasing CPU and disk speeds, it is becoming less common. The decision to de-normalize should never be taken lightly because the database's consistency is at stake. Introducing de-normalized structures opens the database to the update anomalies reviewed at the start of this chapter. If the decision is taken and the affected tables are part of the online database, then it must be accompanied by the creation of automatic controls to protect the consistency of the data. In Oracle, these controls are known as triggers and are discussed in detail in Chapter 10.

A more secure option is to create temporary tables that hold the de-normalized data as a snapshot of the data at a certain time and which can be segregated from all other users. Such temporary tables will not contain updates made after they were created, in which case the query must be qualified as having only a temporal consistency with the main data.

4.7 ⊨ KEY TERMS

First Normal Form – 1NF	Remove repeating groups or duplicated attributes into a separate relation. Ensure all attributes have atomic values.
Functional dependency	Find all functional dependencies in the relation. Minimize the set of functional dependencies using Armstrong's Axioms, eliminating those which can be derived by any of the six rules from the other functional dependencies.
	Identify those functional dependencies that result in superkeys for the relation. Eliminate from the list of superkeys any that contain other superkeys as subsets. This is now the list of candidate keys
Second Normal Form – 2NF	Take any attributes that exhibit only partial dependency on the superkeys out of the relation to form a separate relation with the partial key. Leave the partial key in the original relation. Remove any duplicated tuples from the new relation to preserve functional dependency.
Third Normal Form – 3NF	Examine the revised relation for non-key transitive dependencies. Take any attributes that exhibit transitive dependency, copying the transitive attribute to form a separate relation with the transitive attribute as candidate key. Leave the transitive attribute in the original relation as a foreign key. Remove any duplicated tuples from the new relation to preserve functional dependency.

Boyce–Codd Normal Form – BCNF Identify candidate keys from the 3NF relation; ensure that all determinants are candidate keys. Remove any offending dependencies by extracting the dependent attribute to another relation. Choose a primary key from the candidate keys in the original relation. Base the choice on minimal attribute set membership, no null values in keys, and convenience. Assign the attributes of the primary key as prime.

4.8 EXERCISES

(i) Describe the kinds of adverse effects on database consistency resulting from creating a relation that is not in:

- First Normal Form
- Second Normal Form
- Third Normal Form
- BCNF

(ii) Design the entities for a database to serve one of the following:

- An althletics competition
- A criminal intelligence system
- A car hire company
- Show that your design has all entities in BCNF.

CHAPTER 5

THE ROOTS OF SQL

What are the roots that clutch, what branches grow

Out of this stony rubbish?

T.S. Eliot, *The Waste Land*

The relational model depends on a well-established branch of mathematics called set theory. This theory has led to the process of normalization to ensure that the entities described in the UFL design are well formed and that the relationships that exist between entities are correctly specified.

Normalization is used to prove the correctness of a database design in terms of the real-world objects that will influence the application and the model of them in the database. All of this rigour is necessary to ensure that when the data is manipulated, it will behave in accordance with the ground rules of the relational model.

The following section provides optional reading that explains briefly where SQL comes from (see Figure 5.1). There are a few mathematical concepts and some special symbols that are defined. The aim of this section is to demystify the

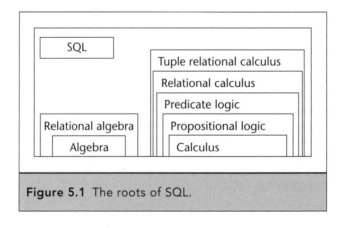

Figure 5.1 The roots of SQL.

language used in many academic journal articles so as to give students without a deep background in mathematics access to the more formal research literature.

5.1 ∈ CALCULUS

The word *calculus* has come to mean a way of calculating. Differential calculus is applied to very small differences of values. It allows a study of the relationships between quantities. When the relationship is expressed in an equation involving two or more quantities that are capable of containing values varying over a continuous range, the rate of change of values (gradient) can be determined through this method.

When the quantities may hold only one of two values, true or false, the problem becomes one of logic; other methods need to be adopted.

5.2 ∈ PROPOSITIONAL LOGIC

A proposition is simply a statement that might be true or false (Figure 5.2).

Students like course BIS101
Students don't like course BIS106

Figure 5.2 Propositions.

Propositional logic is concerned with operators that create new propositions from given ones (Figure 5.3).

Students like BIS101 and students don't like course BIS106

Figure 5.3 New proposition.

Expressions or sentences of propositional logic rely on the propositional grammar. From this grammar, sentences can be built consisting of atoms and connectives with parentheses as punctuation (Table 5.1).

Very complex sentences can be constructed, linking many atoms and connectives, but propositions can evaluate only to true or false. This depends on the interpretation given to their atoms with reference to real-world circumstances. If we have a proposition, $p := $ *students like course BIS101*, then it must be evaluated according to what is known about students and courses

Table 5.1 Propositional grammar.

Type	Symbol	Explanation
Atoms	q, p	Statements which may be true or false
Logical connectives	∨ q ∨ p	Disjunction The sentence is true if p is true OR q is true, OR both are true
	∧ q ∧ p	Conjunction The sentence is true if both p and q are true
	¬ ¬ p	Negation (applies to only one atom) If p is true then ¬ p is false If p is false then ¬ p is true
	⇒ q ⇒ p	Implication if p is true then q is true
	⇔ q ⇔ p	Equivalence p and q are either both true or both false

A sentence composed of only one atom can only have one of two values, *true* or *false*. A sentence composed of two atoms, each having two possible values, can have four states and so on. A truth table can demonstrate the semantics or meaning of expressions in propositional logic.

The two propositions, p and q, can each have two possible values; so there are four combinations. Only if both p and q are true can the sentence p ∧ q be true. The truth table that defines the basic propositional connectives is outlined in Figure 5.4.

p	q	¬ p	¬ q	p ∨ q	p ∧ q	p ⇒ q	p ⇔ q
T	T	F	F	T	T	T	T
T	F	F	T	T	F	F	F
F	T	T	F	T	F	F	F
F	F	T	T	F	F	T	T

Figure 5.4 Propositional truths.

5.3 ∈ PREDICATE LOGIC

Predicate logic is an extension of propositional logic interested both in the sentence connectives of the atomic propositions, and in the internal structure of the atomic propositions.

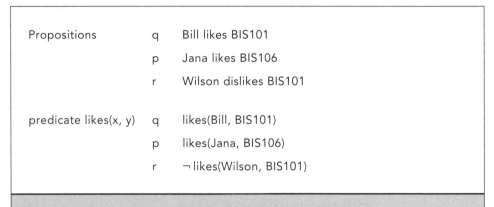

Propositions	q	Bill likes BIS101
	p	Jana likes BIS106
	r	Wilson dislikes BIS101
predicate likes(x, y)	q	likes(Bill, BIS101)
	p	likes(Jana, BIS106)
	r	¬ likes(Wilson, BIS101)

Figure 5.5 Propositions and predicate functions.

Predicates are parameterized propositions, allowing references to classes of objects. Atoms allow functions and relations on variables. Figure 5.5 shows the function *likes* applied to instances of the relation *Students* and *Courses*.

The variables may be quantified (Table 5.2). A quantified variable is said to be *bound*; an unquantified variable is said to be *free*.

Table 5.2 Predicate quantifiers.

∃	there exists
∀	for all
∀c∃ s1∃ s2(likes(s1,c) ∧ ¬ likes(s2,c))	For each course c there exists a student s1 that likes the course, and a student s2 that doesn't like it

The sentence in Table 5.2 must be capable of resolving into either a true or a false value by reference to the *Courses* relation and the likes and dislikes of the *Students*. Some more examples of predicates are given in Figure 5.6.

5.4 ∈ TUPLE RELATIONAL CALCULUS

The tuple relational calculus (TRC) formulates a query on a relation or relations to form the definition of a resultant set. TRC uses predicate logic with free (unquantified) variables as the target.

You can fool some of the people all of the time
(∃ x)(∀ t)(person(x) ∧ time(t)) ⇒ can-fool(x, t)

You can fool all of the people some of the time
(∀ x)(∃ t)(person(x) ∧ time(t)) ⇒ can-fool(x, t)

Figure 5.6 Honest Abe's political predicates.

For all courses in set c whose elements are BIS101 and BIS106, there is a student who likes all the courses in c and a student who dislikes all the courses in c. The targets of the query are the two free variables, s1 and s2; c is a quantified variable (Figure 5.7).

∀c ∈ {BIS101,BIS106}(likes(s1,c) ∧ ¬ likes(s2,c))

Figure 5.7 Predicate query.

The student set consists of {Bill, Jana, Wilson}. The values of the *likes* and *dislikes* predicates are shown in the truth table in Figure 5.8.

likes	bis101	bis106	(likes(s1,c)	¬ likes(s2,c))
Bill	true	true	T	F
Jana	true	false	F	F
Wilson	false	false	F	T

Figure 5.8 Predicate values.

Bill likes both courses so, in the s1 role, his *likes* predicate is true. The *dislikes* predicate for Bill in the s2 role is false.

The **domain** of a query consists of the tuples that may be assigned to the free variables of the formula (Figure 5.9)

	{Bill, Jana, Wilson} × {Bill, Jana, Wilson}	
role	s1	s2
	Likes both	Dislikes both

Figure 5.9 Query domain.

There is a Cartesian product between the students in two roles, s1 and s2 and it will have nine different combinations.

An assignment of values to the free variables of a formula is a tuple that provides a true or false value to the formula. The **selection** of a query is defined by the set of assignments to the free variables that satisfy the formula when the two predicates are connected by the conjunction operator.

Figure 5.8 shows the *likes* and *dislikes* values that each of the students brings individually to the s1 and s2 roles. The final evaluation in Figure 5.10 is for the conjunction operator, ∧. In order for a tuple to evaluate *true* there must be a *true* in the s1 role and a *true* in the s2 role.

s1 role	s2 role	∧
Jana F	Jana F	False
Bill T	Bill F	False
Wilson F	Wilson T	False
Jana F	Bill F	False
Jana F	Wilson T	False
Bill T	Jana F	False
Bill T	Wilson T	True
Wilson F	Jana F	False
Wilson F	Bill F	False

Figure 5.10 Conjunction truth table.

Only one tuple of the Cartesian product returns a *true* value. Therefore the selection set is as shown in Figure 5.11.

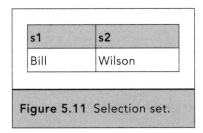

s1	s2
Bill	Wilson

Figure 5.11 Selection set.

The tuple relational calculus is simply a way of formally defining the result of a query. It has nothing to say about the mechanism by which the selection set can be achieved. Because it is composed of a specified grammar, the set can be defined unambiguously.

This would not be the case if the set were to be defined, say, in English, which is subject to international, national and even regional differences in usage.

Other forms of syntax have been developed which also rely on a specification of the resultant set. Among these is the Structured Query Language (SQL). A formal sentence in SQL is composed of three main clauses, as shown in Table 5.3.

Table 5.3 SQL clauses.

Clause	Purpose
Select ...	Define the selection set in terms of free variables
From ...	Define the domain in terms of bound variables (relations)
Where ...	Define the formula relating the bound and free variables

SQL is a variation of the relational calculus that is capable of defining the required selection set. Because it is a language derived from a formal grammar it can be translated reliably into an equivalent statement using the operations defined within the relational algebra. This provides the required base for computing SQL queries

5.5 RELATIONAL ALGEBRA

The relational algebra is defined in terms of procedural operators that can be applied to relations. Five basic operators are defined and these can be combined to form other secondary operators. The tuple relational calculus, being derived from a formal grammar, can be reliably translated into the relational algebra.

The algebraic statement can then be executed by a relational database. SQL queries, being a variant of the relational calculus, can similarly be translated into a series of database operations. Because the links are based on formal language specifications, the translations are capable of machine automation (Figure 5.12).

Figure 5.12 SQL to execution.

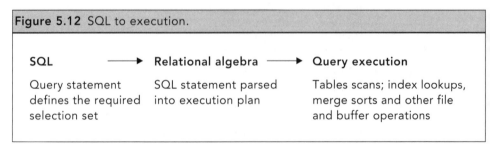

SQL	Relational algebra	Query execution
Query statement defines the required selection set	SQL statement parsed into execution plan	Tables scans; index lookups, merge sorts and other file and buffer operations

The **project** operator extracts entire attribute columns from a relation into a resultant or intermediate set. A projection may be specified on just one attribute or an attribute set. Project is applied to all the tuples of a single relation.

The **select** operator extracts entire tuples from a single relation into a resultant or intermediate relation. Tuples are extracted when they meet a selection criteria based on values in one or more attributes.

The **union** operator combines two relations, which must consist of the same attribute sets, into a single resultant or intermediate relation consisting of all of the tuples from the two original relations and with the same attribute set.

The **difference** operator compares two relations, R and S, which must also consist of the same attribute sets, and extracts all the tuples in R that do not also occur in S.

The **Cartesian product** operator combines all of the tuples in relation R with all of the tuples in relation S. The resultant set consists of the sum of the attribute sets of the contributing relations. The number of tuples in the result will be the number of tuples in R multiplied by the number of tuples in S.

PROJECT	$\Pi_{a,b}(R)$	Project attributes A and B from relation R
SELECT	$\sigma_F(R)$	Tuples from relation R based on selection criteria in F
UNION	$R \cup S$	The set of tuples either in R or S or both (no duplicates)
DIFFERENCE	$R - S$	All of the tuples in R which do not occur in S
CARTESIAN PRODUCT	$R \times S$	Combine all of the tuples in R with all of the tuples in S

The union and difference operators are drawn straight from set theory. A relation is a set of tuples, so set operations should apply. The result of combining two relations with a set operator is another relation. All of the elements of the new relation must be tuples, having the same structure, so the scope of set operators is limited to **union compatible relations.** Two relations are union compatible if both have same number of attributes, the names of the attributes are the same in both and attributes with the same name in both relations have the same domain.

From the five basic operators, a further five secondary operators can be derived. The intersection operator is also drawn from standard set theory and can only be applied against two union compatible relations.

INTERSECTION	$R \cap S R - (R - S)$
	The set of tuples in R which also occur in S

THETA JOIN	$R \bowtie_F S \; \sigma_F (R \times S)$ The select condition, F, is a conjunction of terms of the form A op B where A is an attribute in R, B is an attribute in S and op is one of $=, <, \leq, >, \geq, \neq$
EQUIJOIN	$R \bowtie_A S \; \sigma_A (R \times S)$ The select condition, A, is a conjunction of equalities
NATURAL JOIN	$R \bowtie_A S \; \sigma_A (R \times S)$ The select condition equates all and only those attributes in R and S with the same name
SEMIJOIN	$R \bowtie_F S \; \Pi_A(R \bowtie_F S)$ Project only attributes from R, left semijoin, or S, right semijoin, after making a theta join

The three set operators within the relational algebra may be illustrated by use of a Venn diagram.

There are two sets or relations R and S represented by two circles containing the tuples that are the members of each set. Some tuples may be members of both sets but within each set, there are no duplicate tuples (Figure 5.13).

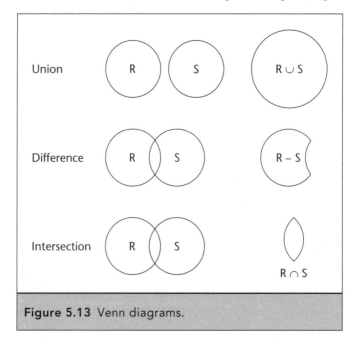

Figure 5.13 Venn diagrams.

In order to demonstrate the other primary operators, it is necessary to consider a fragment of the clubs relation (Figure 5.14).

Name (prime)	Stadium	Division	Manager
Honesty United	Arden	First	Neptune
Forgiveness FC	Balaclava	First	Krishna
Virtue Thursday	Blenheim	First	Barbarossa
Steadfast United	Brandenburg	First	Xerxes
Valour FC	Brideshead	First	Charlemagne
Purity FC	Coliseum	First	Mercury
Beauty United	Olympia	First	Thor

Figure 5.14 Clubs relation (fragment).

Projecting two columns, *Name* and *Stadium*, from *Clubs* yields a result set for each row in *Clubs*. The project operator creates vertical slices (all rows) through the relation (Figure 5.15).

Π **name, stadium(clubs)**

Name	Stadium
Honesty United	Arden
Forgiveness FC	Balaclava
Virtue Thursday	Blenheim
Steadfast United	Brandenburg
Valour FC	Brideshead
Purity FC	Coliseum
Beauty United	Olympia

Figure 5.15 Project on *Clubs*.

The selection criteria in Figure 5.16 use the Oracle operator *like* which compares the value in the stadium attribute for each row with the 'B%' string. The % symbol is a wildcard, so the term means any string beginning with a B and followed by anything. The select operator creates a result set of horizontal slices (all attributes) through the relation.

σ stadium like 'B%' (clubs)

Name (prime)	Stadium	Division	Manager
Forgiveness FC	Balaclava	First	Krishna
Virtue Thursday	Blenheim	First	Barbarossa
Steadfast United	Brandenburg	First	Xerxes
Valour FC	Brideshead	First	Charlemagne

Figure 5.16 Select on clubs.

5.6 ∈ KEY TERMS

Logic	A system of rules defining outcomes (or outcomes defining rules!)
Propositional logic	A logic system based on a propositional grammar. Atoms (statements evaluating to true or false) connected by operators for conjunction, disjunction, negation, implication or equivalence, form a sentence that evaluates to true or false
Predicate logic	A predicate is a proposition rewritten as a function which evaluates true or false. Predicates are conjoined by operators as before and quantified by *for each* and *for all*. Overall sentence evaluates true or false
Relational calculus	Extension of predicate logic applied to a relation. A tuple is selected if true. Conjunction operators as before. The result is a set of tuples that satisfy the conjoined predicates
Relational algebra	An algebra (symbolic language) of set operations. Algebraic statements can be derived from the relational calculus
Basic operators	Five basic operators: project, select, union, difference and Cartesian product
Combined operators	Combining the basic operators gives a set of secondary operators for intersection, theta join, equijoin, natural join and semijoin.

CHAPTER 6

SQL

Query: Whether the difference between a mere computer and a man of science be not, that the one computes on principles clearly conceived, and by rules evidently demonstrated, whereas the other doth not?

Bishop George Berkeley

6.1 ∈ TAKING STOCK

A method has been established whereby information about our scenario may be captured in a formal and methodical way. The object-oriented analysis methodology leads into using the Universal Modeling Language (UML), as a diagramming standard.

The UseCase diagrams help define what the UFL application will do; the class diagram enables a view of the data the application will use.

Because the Oracle database will be used, it has been necessary to convert the classes' into logical structures compatible with the relational model. That model has been defined in terms of entities and relationships and applied to create an entity–relationship diagram.

The process of normalization then gives a formal method to assure the correctness of the ER diagram. The process of transferring the design schema into reality can now begin. Oracle establishes and maintains the physical structures that will become part of the application by means of SQL.

SQL, the Structured Query Language, is a mature, powerful and versatile relational query language. The history of SQL extends back to IBM research begun in 1970.

In 1974, IBM began the System/R project and developed SEQUEL, or Structured English Query Language. System/R was implemented as an IBM prototype in 1975. It was then completely rewritten in 1976–1977 to include multi-table and multi-user features. In 1978, methodical testing commenced at customer test sites. Demonstrating both the usefulness and practicality of the system, this testing proved to be a success for IBM.

Several other software vendors accepted the rise of the relational model and announced SQL-based products. These included Oracle (who actually beat IBM to market by two years, releasing their first commercial RDBMS, in 1979), Sybase and Ingres (based on the University of California's Berkeley Ingres project).

6.1.1 SQL STANDARDS

The American National Standards Institute (ANSI) standardized SQL in 1986 and the International Organization for Standardization (ISO) standardized it in 1987. The United States government's Federal Information Processing Standard (FIPS) adopted the ANSI/ISO standard. In 1989, a revised standard known commonly as SQL89 or SQL1 was published.

Due partially to conflicting interests from commercial vendors, much of the SQL89 standard was intentionally left incomplete, and many features were labelled *implementer-defined*. In order to strengthen the standard, the ANSI committee revised its previous work with the SQL92 standard ratified in 1992 (also called SQL2).

This standard addressed several weaknesses in SQL89 and set forth conceptual SQL features which, at that time, exceeded the capabilities of any existing RDBMS implementation. In fact, the SQL92 standard was approximately six times the length of its predecessor. Because of this disparity, the authors defined three levels of SQL92 compliance: *Entry-level conformance*(only the barest improvements to SQL89), *Intermediate-level conformance* (a generally achievable set of major advancements) and *Full conformance* (total compliance with the SQL92 features).

More recently, in 1999, ANSI/ISO released the SQL:1999 standard (also called SQL3). This standard addresses some of the more advanced and previously ignored areas of modern database systems, such as object relational database concepts, call level interfaces and integrity management. SQL:1999 replaces the SQL92 levels of compliance with its own degrees of conformance: *Core SQL:1999* and *Enhanced SQL:1999*.

6.2 DATA DEFINITION LANGUAGE

SQL is divided into two main groups of commands. There are commands to define storage structures – the data definition language (DDL) – and commands to manage the stored data – the data manipulation language (DML).

The DDL consists of five principal verbs: **create**, **grant**, **revoke**, **alter** and **drop**. These form the basis of commands to create tables, indexes and other structures; to grant or revoke access to other users; to alter the internal definitions of stored structures; and to drop the structures from the data dictionary along with any data they may contain.

6.3 CREATE

The first task in implementing the UFL application is to translate the design in the ER diagram into Oracle tables. In general, each entity will equate to one table.

Each attribute has a name and is specified as being of a particular type such an integer, a string, a date and so on. These simple types are described in Table 6.1. A full list of the standard Oracle data types is given in Section 22.4.

Each of these types either has a specific size or is capable of having its size defined. Generally, if the data type has a size parameter, this must be present when a column is defined. The three most frequently used data types are strings, numbers and dates. Table 6.1 shows the Oracle data types used in the UFL application.

Table 6.1 Oracle data types used in UFL tables.	
varchar2 (size)	Variable-length character string. Maximum size is 4000, and minimum is 1
number(p, s)	Number having precision p and scale s. The precision, p, can range from 1 to 38. The scale, s, can range from –84 to 127.Precision is the total number of digits including the decimal (up to 38 digits). Scale is the number of digits to the right of the decimal point
date	Valid date range from 1 January 4712 BC to AD 31 December 9999

The number type can hold integers, fixed decimal currency or variable decimal values depending on the precision and scale definitions (Table 6.2).

Table 6.2 Oracle numbers.	
Integer	number(9) or number(9,0) e.g. 789456123
Currency	number(7,2) e.g. 1234.56
Real number	number(5,3); e.g. 3.142

Figure 6.1 shows the first attempt at creating the *Players* table using the SQL command *create table*. The command specifies the name of the table and the names of each of the columns. The columns have been assigned a data type and some definitions have been restricted to disallow null values when a row is inserted or when a value is updated. A primary key has been identified and, as a side effect of the command, an index with a system assigned name will have been created automatically. Whenever a row is inserted into the players table, the index will be maintained.

The syntax of the *create* command simply requires an indication of the type of database object to be created and its name. Here the database object is a *table* and its name is *players*. The column definitions are enclosed in brackets and each

```
create table players (ufa_id varchar2(10) primary key,
surname varchar2(25) not null,
forename varchar2(25) not null,
dateofbirth date not null,
squad_no number(2,0)
position varchar2(15),
club varchar2(30) not null);
```

Figure 6.1 Creating players I.

column definition is separated by a comma. The data type *varchar2* requires a maximum length parameter enclosed in brackets. An SQL statement is terminated by a semi-colon, which indicates that it should be executed.

Several attributes have been specified *not null*. The null is a special value, indicating that no value has been placed in the attribute. It is not the same as a zero or the empty string. It cannot be tested with the comparison operators, =, >, < etc. It can only be tested with the *is null* operator.

Attributes specified as *not null* must contain real and valid dates, strings or numbers when a row is inserted or the attribute updated.

The *create table* command is capable of very much more complexity. It has many optional clauses that can be used to specify where data will be stored, how it will be stored, how data values should be verified or validated.

The example in Figure 6.1 illustrates a greatly simplified use of the *create* command; there are some further levels of detail that are of interest.

6.3.1 CONSTRAINTS

Look at the *Club* entity in the ERD of Figure 6.2. It has four attributes. Each of these attributes has a domain of values and one of the attributes is the primary key. The *Club* entity is a strong relation and is in BCNF.

This entity translates into a table with four columns and with *Name* as the primary key.

A constraint can be specified at the time that the table is created and is a clause within the *create table* command (Figure 6.3). It has a name and its specification is stored separately from the table definition in the data dictionary. Because of this, a constraint can also be added after the table has been created and it can be dropped or altered after table creation.

Constraints offer a more flexible way of specifying the nature of a table's columns or the behaviour of the table resulting from changes in the data values in other tables that participate in a relationship.

Constraints may be defined as the *Clubs* table is created by including a constraint clause within the definition for each column. This is called a **column constraint** (Figure 6.3). In this first example, the constraint is defined in the clause relating to

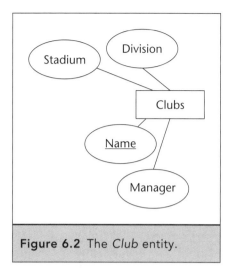

Figure 6.2 The *Club* entity.

```
create table clubs (name varchar2(25)
                    constraint pk_clubs primary key,
                    stadium varchar2(25)
                    constraint nn_stad not null,
                    division varchar2(10)
                    constraint nn_div not null,
                    manager varchar2(25)
                    constraint nn_man not null);
```

Figure 6.3 Creating table clubs with column constraints.

the specification of the *name* column of *Clubs*. The constraint is called *pk_clubs* and it defines the *name* column as a primary key. The index created will be called *pk_clubs*

The alternative is to define the constraint after defining all the columns. Adopting this syntax means that the columns involved must be indicated and a **table constraint** is created. In Figure 6.4, the alternative syntax at the end of the column definitions again indicates a constraint called *pk_clubs* and the column with which it is associated. Again, this results in the creation of an index on the *name* column; the index will be called *pk_clubs*. The other constraints require the other columns to have real and valid values set when a row is inserted or updated

Before the clubs table can be re-created using this new format, the first version must be destroyed. The **drop table** command (Figure 6.5) deletes any data in the table as well as the table structure itself. Use it with care!

The relationship that exists between clubs and players can be defined in the structure of the table *Players*. There are two ways to do this. The previously defined

```
drop table clubs
create table clubs (name varchar2(25),
                    stadium varchar2(25)
                    constraint nn_stad not null,
                    division varchar2(10)
                    constraint nn_div not null,
                    manager varchar2(25)
                    constraint nn_man not null,
                    constraint pk_clubs primary key(name));
```

name	stadium	division	manager
varchar2(25)	varchar2(25)	varchar2(10)	varchar2(25)
(Prime)	(Not null)	(Not null)	(Not null)

Figure 6.4 Creating table *Clubs* with a table constraint.

```
drop table clubs;
```

Figure 6.5 Drop the dead table.

table *Players* can be dropped and a new version created (Figure 6.6) or the table definition can be altered.

In Figure 6.6, the *Players* table is dropped. A new version of *Players* is then created, using constraints to define a primary key and disallowing null values in the other columns. A further table constraint called *fk_club*, which is associated with the *club* column, is then defined. This constrains values placed in the *Players'* column *club* to match pre-existing values in the *name* attribute of the *Clubs* table.

In other words, a foreign key has been specified in *Players* that is the basis of the 1:*N* relationship between *Players* and *Clubs*. Every time a row is inserted in the *Players* table, the database will ensure that the player is assigned to a valid club or else it will disallow the insertion.

If an attempt is made to delete a row in *Clubs* and there are players assigned to that club, the deletion will be disallowed because the result would be a value in some *Players'* rows referencing a non-existent row in *Clubs*. Notice that commas separate the table constraints.

Constraints may be used to enforce structural or referential integrity for primary and foreign keys. Other types of constraint may be used to assure behavioural integrity; that is, conformation to the business rules affecting the application. This is usually associated with checking values entered in attributes when rows are inserted or updated.

```
drop table players;

create table players (ufa_id varchar2(10),
   surname varchar2(25)
   constraint nn_sur not null,
   forename varchar2(25)
   constraint nn_fore not null,
   dateofbirth date
   constraint nn_dob not null,
   squad_no number(2,0),
   position varchar2(15),
   club varchar2(30)
   constraint nn_club not null,
   constraint pk_players primary key(ufa_id),
   constraint fk_club foreign key(club) references clubs(name));
```

Figure 6.6 Foreign key constraint.

```
drop table players;
commit;
   create table players (UFA_ID varchar2(10),
   surname varchar2(25)
   constraint sur_check check (surname=UPPER(surname))
   constraint nn_sur not null,
   forename varchar2(25)
   constraint fore_check check (forename=UPPER(forename))
   constraint nn_fore not null,
   dateofbirth date
   constraint nn_dob not null,
   squad_no number(2,0)
   constraint squad_check check squad_no<=99,
   position varchar2(15),
   nationality varchar2(20)
   constraint nn_nation not null,
   club varchar2(30)
   constraint nn_club not null,
   constraint pk_players primary key(UFA_ID),
   constraint fk_pos foreign key (position) references
     positions(allowed),
   constraint fk_club foreign key(club) references clubs(name));
```

Figure 6.7 Check constraints.

A **check constraint** can be used in applications to ensure that a salary attribute does not exceed a certain limit or that it exceeds a certain minimum or both. It can check for a minimum order quantity in the lines of an order or that the delivery date on an order is greater than the date on which the order was received.

In Figure 6.7 the check constraint has been used to ensure that *surname* and *forename* are always inserted as full upper case. Built-in functions of SQL have been used to do this. If the input string is not in upper case, an error will result. A further foreign key has been inserted so that *players.position* must reference an allowed list of positions in the *Positions* table.

6.4 ALTER

As an alternative to the current status of the constraint *fk_clubs*, it can be changed to ensure that whenever a row is deleted from *Clubs*, any related rows in *Players* are also deleted. For this, the *alter table* command is used.

This command can be used to change most of the structural definitions of a table. Columns may be dropped or added, and constraints may be dropped or added. If a column is dropped after data has been inserted, the values in all the rows for that column will be lost. If a column is added, null values are placed in that column for all existing rows, so it is not a good idea to specify a *not null* constraint for the column at the same time. Add the attribute, populate all the rows with values for that attribute and then add the *not null* constraint

Changing the *fk_club* constraint in *Players* involves dropping the constraint and adding a new constraint with the same name but containing specific instructions on how the database will react if a corresponding row in *Clubs* is deleted.

```
alter table players drop constraint fk_club;
commit;
alter table players add constraint fk_club foreign key(club)
    references clubs(name) on delete cascade;
```

Figure 6.8 Changing a constraint.

The constraint in Figure 6.8 allows a cascade delete of rows in *Players* consequent on a proposed deletion of a row in *Clubs*. In tables that have foreign key constraints based on a weak relationship to the primary key of a deleted *Players'* row, there may be collateral deletions. For example, the *Goals* table and the *Discipline* table contain a dependency on *Players*. Deleting a club could result in deleting all the players assigned to that club, all the goals scored by those players and all the disciplinary actions against those players. You can see why it is called a cascade delete. If the foreign key constraint in *Goals* does not have a cascade delete defined, then a cascade delete triggered in *Players* from *Clubs* will be aborted and the originating action cancelled.

6.5 ∈ GRANT

Access to the database is controlled by a system of rights and privileges. Every action to do with the database must be **specifically allowed** by the DBA. When a new user is created, they must be given explicit permission to connect to the database and to consume resources such as storage space and CPU time.

Rather than issue these permissions one at a time, they can be grouped into generic **roles**. Figure 6.9 shows the roles allocated to a standard user. This user has a *connect* role which allows her to connect to the database if she can supply her username and password.

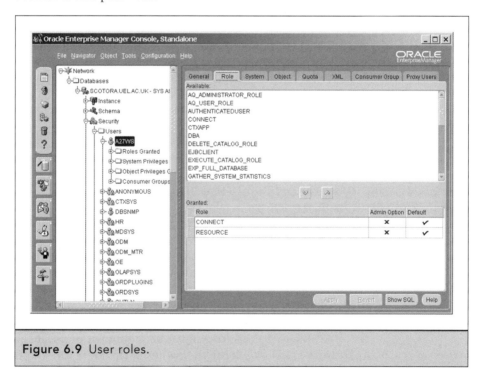

Figure 6.9 User roles.

She also has a *resource* role which enables her to create a private schema and, within that, to create tables, indexes and other data structures. She can insert rows into her tables, issue queries, update or delete rows and drop or alter structures owned by her.

In addition, this user has been granted certain system privileges by the DBA. These are shown in Figure 6.10 and include *create type, execute any type* and *unlimited tablespace*.

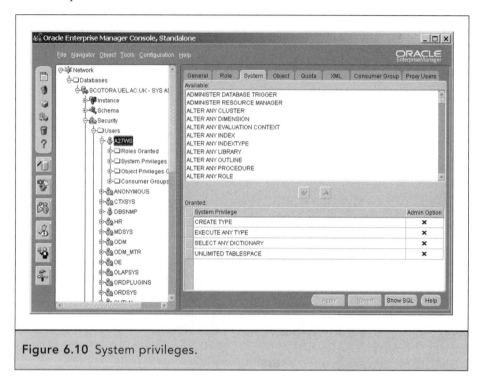

Figure 6.10 System privileges.

Privileges must generally be explicitly granted to individuals. If a role or privilege is granted with administrative rights then the user may be able to pass it on by granting it to other users. In a production database, the process of granting roles and privileges must be taken very seriously. A user with unnecessary levels of access can cause a great deal of damage, either deliberately or by accident.

When a table is created and populated with data, the table structure and its contents are private to the owner. This exclusion of access applies even to users with the *dba* role. Only a user with *sysdba* rights can access the table and view its contents. In the UFL application, a number of users will be expected to input the data and some other users will view reports taken from the data. In order for these users to be able to do this, they must be granted appropriate access.

Apart from the *sysdba*, only the owner of the table can grant access rights using the *grant* command. The command takes the form shown in Figure 6.11.

```
grant right on object to user; [with grant option]
```

Figure 6.11 *Grant.*

Myfriend may be permitted to exercise any privilege on the *Clubs* table and to pass these on to any other user (Figure 6.12).

```
grant all on clubs to myfriend with grant option;
```

Figure 6.12 *Grant option.*

The scope of access given can be restricted by specifically indicating the privileges granted. *Myfriend* can be allowed only to query and update existing rows but not insert or delete rows and not to alter or drop the table (Figure 6.13).

```
grant select, update on clubs to myfriend
```

Figure 6.13 *Grant* access modes.

The keyword *public* allows the privilege to be given to all users. The *Clubs* table can be made available to all users, allowing them to read the data but not to change it in any way (Figure 6.14).

```
grant select on clubs to public
```

Figure 6.14 *Grant* to public.

6.6 INSERT

The *insert* verb allows rows to be inserted into a table. The command must conform to any constraints on the table such as disallowed null values, unique primary keys or foreign keys referencing other tables. If there are check constraints on any column, these will also be triggered by the insertion of a row (Figure 6.15).

```
INSERT INTO table expression clause (columns) values clause
```

Figure 6.15 Insert.

Figure 6.16 shows the simplest form of the *insert* command. The table expression is a single table. All four columns have been cited in the columns section since the table was created with not null constraints for all columns

```
insert into clubs (name, stadium, division, manager )
values ('Beauty United', 'Olympia', 'First', 'Thor');
```

Figure 6.16 Inserting a row.

The *values* clause lists the string constants corresponding to the order of the *columns* section. If the *columns* section is omitted, the values must be ordered as the columns were specified in the table creation statement. Multiple *insert* statements can be grouped together as in Figure 6.17 to populate the *Positions* table.

```
create table positions (allowed varchar2(15));
insert into positions (allowed) values ('goalkeeper');
insert into positions (allowed) values ('defender');
insert into positions (allowed) values ('midfield');
insert into positions (allowed) values ('forward');
```

Figure 6.17 Inserting multiple rows.

Now there is one row in the *Clubs* table, rows can be inserted in the *Players* table (Figure 6.18). Because the *Players* table has a foreign key constraint on it, inserts will fail if there is not a corresponding club to which players may be assigned.

```
insert into players (ufa_id, surname, forename,
dateofbirth, squad_no, position, nationality, club)
values ('AK675280','BACON','ANTONIO','05-Mar-1978',
18,'defender','WONDERLAND','Purity FC');
```

Figure 6.18 Inserting a player.

Program files to create and populate the design schema are available from this book's web site.

6.7 ⊆ SELECT

The SQL *select* command is used to read the data stored in tables available to the user. It consists of three major clauses used to specify the target of the query, the domain or data source, and any criteria to be applied against the source.

The database will check that the columns in the *select* clause are to be found in the selection domain, the *from* clause. Any ambiguity, such as columns in more than one table having the same name, must be resolved with pseudonyms. If the selection predicate is left out then all the rows in the selection domain will contribute to the result set (Figure 6.19).

```
select UFA_ID, forename,          Selection set: these are the columns that
surname, dateofbirth, club        will be projected into the result

from players                      Selection domain: the source of the data

where club='Beauty United';       Selection predicate: conditions for inclusion
                                  in the selection set
```

Figure 6.19 *Select.*

The example in Figure 6.20 shows a query that demonstrates the first two clauses of a *select* statement. Firstly, the target selection set is defined as five columns from

```
select UFA_ID, forename, surname, dateofbirth as dob, club from
players;

UFA_ID          FORENAME    SURNAME     DOB         CLUB
----------------------------------------------------------
AK675280        ANTONIO     BACON       05-MAR-78   Purity FC
AN971765        PETER       AUSTEN      23-JUN-85   Purity FC
AT245876        BRIAN       HEGEL       22-MAR-84   Beauty United
BT46286         MARC        MORE        04-FEB-80   Beauty United
DX26497         EDUARDO     ERASMUS     07-FEB-84   Purity FC
ED24659         VICTOR      SOCRATES    12-JUL-80   Beauty United
EG385190        FRANCIS     JUSTINIAN   13-AUG-82   Purity FC
EH382645        PAUL        JOHN        22-MAR-84   Purity FC
FT246517        ALAN        GREGORY     02-JUL-76   Beauty United
KL23659         CHARLES     PAUL        12-MAY-81   Beauty United
...
```

Figure 6.20 A query on the *Players* table.

the *Players* table and secondly the *Players* table is confirmed as the domain or source of the query. The column *Dateofbirth* is given a pseudonym or alias. There is no selection criterion, so the whole *Players* relation contributes to the result. Twenty-two rows will be selected.

If all the attributes are required and no pseudonyms are needed then a useful shorthand is available (Figure 6.21).

```
Select * from clubs;

NAME                  STADIUM         DIVISION  MANAGER
--------------------------  ------------------------  --
Beauty United         Olympia         First     Thor
Purity FC             Coliseum        First     Mercury
Honesty United        Arden           First     Neptune
Forgiveness FC        Balaclava       First     Krishna
Virtue Thursday       Blenheim        First     Barbarossa
Steadfast United      Brandenburg     First     Xerxes
Valour FC             Brideshead      First     Charlemagne
Liberation United     Eden            First     Wellington
Nirvana City          Elysia          First     Wotan
Bountiful Athletic    Erewhon         First     Jupiter
...
```

Figure 6.21 *Select *.*

6.7.1   RESTRICTIONS

In order to introduce a restriction on the rows of players in the result, a *where* clause is used. The *where* clause in Figure 6.22 contains a selection predicate or selection criterion that all returned rows should have a value in the *Clubs* column that equals 'Beauty United'. This query returns 11 rows.

Oracle's *like* operator, illustrated in Figure 6.23, performs string comparisons between its argument and the value of *Clubs* in each row of the *Players* table. The syntax of the argument, 'B%', means that the target string should have a *B* as its first character, followed by any other characters. The % symbol is a wildcard for this operator.

More then one restriction can be included in the *where* clause by using the logical operators **and**, **or**. Care must be taken when combining these operators to ensure that they are not mutually exclusive (Figure 6.24).

A player cannot have a surname that begins with a *B* and at the same time begins with an *S*. The group of players whose surnames begin with *S* and *B* is perhaps understandable in English, but not in SQL. The selection predicate is applied to each row and must be satisfied in total if that row is to be included in the result set. In fact, this is an impossible condition.

```
select ufa_id, forename, surname, dateofbirth as dob, club
from players
where club ='Beauty United';

UFA_ID      FORENAME      SURNAME      DOB          CLUB
-----------------------------------------------------------
AT245876    BRIAN         HEGEL        22-MAR-84    Beauty United
BT46286     MARC          MORE         04-FEB-80    Beauty United
ED24659     VICTOR        SOCRATES     12-JUL-80    Beauty United
FT246517    ALAN          GREGORY      02-JUL-76    Beauty United
KL23659     CHARLES       PAUL         12-MAY-81    Beauty United
...
```

Figure 6.22 Restricted query.

```
select ufa_id, forename, surname, dateofbirth as dob, club from players
where surname like 'B%';

UFA_ID      FORENAME            SURNAME      DOB        CLUB
- ------------------------      ---------    ------------------------------
AK675280    ANTONIO             BACON                   05-MAR-78 Purity FC

1 row selected.
```

Figure 6.23 Another restriction.

```
select ufa_id, forename, surname, dateofbirth as dob, club from
players
where surname like 'B%'

and surname like 'S%';
```

Figure 6.24 Multiple restrictions I.

The correct operator is an *or* (Figure 6.25). This is the correct way of putting the question in English as well.

Comparison restrictions, using the comparison operators <, =, >, = and ? can also be applied (Figure 6.26). The comparison operators can operate on number, strings

```
select ufa_id, forename, surname, dateofbirth as dob, club from players
where surname like 'B%'
or surname like 'S%';

UFA_ID          FORENAME        SURNAME        DOB          CLUB
-----------------------------------------------------------------
AK675280        ANTONIO         BACON          05-MAR-78    Purity FC
ED24659         VICTOR          SOCRATES       12-JUL-80    Beauty United
WZ28573         LUIGI           SHAKESPEARE    10-MAY-84    Purity FC

3 rows selected.
```

Figure 6.25 Multiple restrictions II.

```
select ufa_id, forename, surname, squad_no
from players
where club like 'B%'
and squad_no<15 and squad_no>3

UFA_ID      FORENAME    SURNAME      SQUAD_NO
--------------------------------------------
ED24659     VICTOR      SOCRATES     12
FT246517    ALAN        GREGORY      9
KL23659     CHARLES     PAUL         8
QT873456    EDWARD      KANT         4
TY48429     WINSTON     PLATO        7
UT23685     GEORGE      CONSTANTINE  5
...
```

Figure 6.26 Comparison restrictions I.

or dates and the output can be sorted by one or more attributes of the selection domain, whether it is in the selection set or not (Figure 6.27).

6.8 ⊂ FORMATTING OUTPUT

An interactive session with SQL*Plus allows many formatting commands to be set in the operational environment and which enable the output from a simple SQL select to be converted into quite an acceptable report.

```
select ufa_id, forename, surname, squad_no
from players
where club > 'Beauty United'
order by dateofbirth;

UFA_ID      FORENAME  SURNAME       SQUAD_NO
--------------------------------------------
AK675280    ANTONIO   BACON         18
NH42764     NIKOS     ARISTOTLE     7
EG385190    FRANCIS   JUSTINIAN     11
QV374926    DEREK     MARX          3
DX26497     EDUARDO   ERASMUS       14
EH382645    PAUL      JOHN          10
...
```

Figure 6.27 Comparison restriction II – sorted output.

Table 6.3 shows some of the SQL*Plus formatting commands and their effects.

Table 6.3 SQL*Plus formatting.	
rem	a comment
set linesize 75	number of characters per line
set pagesize 40	number of lines on a page
set headsep |	the heading break symbol for multi-lined headings
set num 6	format numbers to 6 places
column club heading 'Club'	Renames column headings
column club format a9	sets column width to 9 characters
ttitle 'List of Players by Club'	sets the top title, centred by default
btitle left 'End of Report' right '24 Jul 2003'	set the bottom title with a string on the left and a string on the right
clear breaks	breaks are cleared
break on report on club skip 1 on position	set three breaks: at the end of the report and when the values of club and position change. The default is to print the first value of an attribute and no duplicates until the value changes
compute count label 'club count' of UFA_ID on club compute count label 'TOTAL' of UFA_ID on report	counts players by club and overall when the pre-defined breaks occur

Figure 6.28 shows a complete set of formatting statements together with an appropriate SQL statement. The formatting statements last for the entire user session. If a slightly different SQL statement is executed later, the same formatting will be applied to it.

```
rem Program: PlayersRpt.sql
rem Written by: WS
rem Description: Displays all the players by club.

set linesize 75
set pagesize 40
set headsep |
set num 6

ttitle 'List of Players by Club |================================'
BTITLE LEFT 'End of Report' RIGHT '24 Jul 2003'

clear breaks
clear computes

column club heading 'Club.'
column UFA_ID heading 'UFA Reg.'
column forename heading 'Forename.'
column surname heading 'Surname.'
column squad_no heading 'Squad|Number'
column position heading 'Position'

column club format a13
column UFA_ID format a8
column forename format a9
column surname format a11
column position format a10

break on report on club skip 1 on position
compute count label 'club count' of UFA_ID on club
compute count label 'TOTAL' of UFA_ID on report

rem The SQL query, output must be ordered for the breaks to work
select club, ufa_id, forename, surname, squad_no, position
from players
order by club, position;
```

Figure 6.28 SQL*Plus formatted report statements.

```
breaks cleared
computes cleared

Wed Jul 24                                                    page 1
                          List of Players by Club
                      ================================


                                               Squad
Club.          UFA Reg. Forename. Surname.     Number Position
-------------- -------- ---------- ----------- ------ ----------
Beauty United  BT46286  MARC       MORE            16 defender
               QT873456 EDWARD     KANT             4
               UT23685  GEORGE     CONSTANTINE      5
               FT246517 ALAN       GREGORY          9 forward
               TY48429  WINSTON    PLATO            7
               VT432167 PIERRE     DIOCLETIAN      11
               SC159647 RAMESH     THACKERAY        2 goalkeeper
               AT245876 BRIAN      HEGEL           27 midfield
               KL23659  CHARLES    PAUL             8
               ED24659  VICTOR     SOCRATES        12
               UT236965 HENRY      DICKENS          6
*************   --------                            *********
club count           11


Purity FC      AK675280 ANTONIO    BACON           18 defender
               EH382645 PAUL       JOHN            10
               EG385190 FRANCIS    JUSTINIAN       11
               DX26497  EDUARDO    ERASMUS         14 forward
               VB376512 LUCIUS     AUGUSTUS         7
               NH42764  NIKOS      ARISTOTLE        7
               PG46385  EDGAR      TIBERIUS         5 goalkeeper
               AN971765 PETER      AUSTEN          23 midfield
               SJ382901 JOHN       INNOCENT         3
               WZ28573  LUIGI      SHAKESPEARE     14
               QV374926 DEREK      MARX             3
*************   --------                            *********
club count           11


               --------
TOTAL                22

End of Report                                            24 Jul 2003
```

Figure 6.29 Report output.

Figure 6.29 (p. 117) shows the SQL*Plus output after the formatting statements have been applied and the SQL statement executed.

6.9 ⊆ CREATE WITH *SELECT*

The *create* command allows a table to be created and populated with data as a result of a *select* statement. Essentially this command is copying data from one table to another, creating the second table as part of the same query.

```
create table purity_players as select forename||' '||surname as
fullname from players
where club='Purity FC';

select * from purity_players;

FULLNAME
-------------------
ANTONIO BACON
PETER AUSTEN
EDUARDO ERASMUS
FRANCIS JUSTINIAN
PAUL JOHN
NIKOS ARISTOTLE
EDGAR TIBERIUS
DEREK MARX
JOHN INNOCENT
LUCIUS AUGUSTUS
LUIGI SHAKESPEARE

11 rows selected.
```

Figure 6.30 *Create as.*

Figure 6.30 shows a simple example. Data from the *Players* table is extracted with the select statement, which concatenates the forename and surname attributes of *Players* and populates *purity_players*. The new table has one attribute, *fullname*.

Columns take the same name and data type as in the selection set. The select clause can contain any SQL function, join, sub-query, union or other clause permitted for a standalone select. Column constraints on the target table may be added afterwards with an *alter table* statement.

6.10 ⊨ INSERT WITH SELECT

The *insert* command also allows data to be copied from one table to another pre-existing table by using a *select* statement in place of the *values* clause. If the columns for insertion are included in the *insert* clause, values from the selection set must match for data type, but do not have to have the same name.

Figure 6.31 shows an *insert* statement into *purity_players* that adds just the forename column of all players. The second select statement yields 33 rows: the 11 original rows and the 22 just inserted.

```
insert into purity_players (fullname)
       select forename from players;
select * from purity_players;

FULLNAME
--------------------------------------------------------
ANTONIO BACON
PETER AUSTEN
EDUARDO ERASMUS
FRANCIS JUSTINIAN
PAUL JOHN
NIKOS ARISTOTLE
EDGAR TIBERIUS
DEREK MARX
JOHN INNOCENT
LUCIUS AUGUSTUS
LUIGI SHAKESPEARE
ANTONIO        ⎫
PETER          ⎪
BRIAN          ⎬  inserted rows
MARC           ⎪
EDUARDO        ⎭
...
```

Figure 6.31 Inserting rows into *purity_players*.

6.11 ⊨ SEQUENCES

Oracle provides a method of generating numbers for abstract keys, which are guaranteed to be unique in a multi-user environment. A sequence is a *pseudotable* with two *pseudocolumns*: *currval* and *nextval*.

A sequence to generate, say, student IDs can be created much in the same way as a table (Figure 6.32). The starting number and the increment may be specified. The defaults are 1 and 1. Because a sequence is a pseudotable, it is subject to the same concurrency control as normal tables. Only one user at a time can update its value.

```
Create sequence newstudent start with 1000000 increment by 1;
Select newstudent.nextval from dual;

   NEXTVAL
----------
   1000000

1 row selected.

Select newstudent.currval from dual;

   CURRVAL
----------
   1000000

1 row selected.

Select newstudent.nextval from dual;

   NEXTVAL
----------
   1000001

1 row selected.
```

Figure 6.32 Sequences.

Selecting the value of *nextval* updates it and returns the new value. Selecting the value of *currval* returns its current value without any update. *Currval* is not available until after the first selection of *nextval,* which initializes the sequence.

The *dual* table used in the examples in Figure 6.32 is provided as part of the Oracle installation and, by convention, is used whenever a *select* does not otherwise have a legitimate table to include in its *from* clause. *Newstudent* is a sequence (a pseudotable), not a table, and so cannot appear in this clause.

A sequence can be used in an *insert* or *create* statement as part of the *select* clause. Figure 6.33 shows first the creation of a sequence called *newperson,* starting at 5000 and incrementing by 5. This sequence is included in the *select* clause of a *create* command with a pseudonym of *identity.* The *Players* table contributes *forename* and *surname* to the *random_people* table.

```
Create sequence newperson start with 5000 increment by 5;

Create table random_people as
select newperson.nextval as identity, forename, surname
from players
where club='Beauty United';

select * from random_people;

   IDENTITY FORENAME                      SURNAME
 ---------- ----------------------------- -------------------------
       5000 BRIAN                         HEGEL
       5005 MARC                          MORE
       5010 VICTOR                        SOCRATES
       5015 ALAN                          GREGORY
       5020 CHARLES                       PAUL
       5025 EDWARD                        KANT
       5030 RAMESH                        THACKERAY
       5035 WINSTON                       PLATO
       5040 GEORGE                        CONSTANTINE
       5045 HENRY                         DICKENS
       5050 PIERRE                        DIOCLETIAN

11 rows selected.
```

Figure 6.33 Using a sequence in *create as*.

An unrestricted select on this table reveals that each row has been given a unique number in the *identity* attribute, starting at 5000 and incrementing by 5.

6.12 ⊂ UPDATE

The *update* command can be used to change the value of a single attribute in a single row or many attributes in many rows. It takes a similar form to the *select* statement except for the order of clauses (Table 6.4).

Table 6.4 SQL update.

Update players	Query domain: usually one table
set dateofbirth = '09-Mar-1979'	Selection set: specifies attribute and new value
where UFA_ID ='AT245876';	Query predicate: specifies which rows to update

The selection predicate can be as complex as needed to identify the rows to be updated. It can contain all the restriction operators that can be used with a *select*, including sub-query joins and unions.

If an *update* statement offends against a constraint on the table or one of the columns, it will fail and be rolled back. This applies whether the statement is updating one or many rows. Oracle constraint checking is done at the statement level, but the checks are not performed until just before the end of the statement operations (Figure 6.34).

```
update players
set club='Dingbat United'
where ufa_id='AT245876';

update players
*
ERROR at line 1:
ORA-02291: integrity constraint (A27WS.FK_CLUB) violated - parent key
not found
```

Figure 6.34 Updates cannot violate constraints.

If a single statement is due to update 50,000 rows and the violation occurs at the first row it will not be discovered until just before the statement enters its pre-commit state. All 50,000 write operations will have to be rolled back.

6.13 ⊆ DELETE

The *delete* statement is very similar to the *update* statement. Deletions are carried out at the row level. Rows are selected for deletion according to a selection predicate applied against a selection domain (Table 6.5).

Table 6.5 SQL delete.

Delete from players	Selection domain: usually one table
where UFA_ID ='AT245876';	Selection predicate: specifies which rows to delete

If a *delete* statement offends against a constraint on the table or one of the columns, it will fail and be rolled back. Again, Oracle constraint checking at the statement level leads to the same vulnerability to rollback as updates.

In practice, wholesale deletes are rare. When they are required, it may be more efficient to transfer the not-to-be-deleted rows to a temporary table, drop the original table along with all remaining rows, re-create the table and re-populate it from the temporary table.

6.14 ⊆ KEY TERMS

DDL	Data Definition Language: SQL verbs to manipulate the structural elements of the data dictionary. *create, drop, alter, grant*
Create	Define table structure and create empty table
Primary key constraint	Specify primary key attribute(s). Duplicate values will be disallowed
Foreign key constraint	Specify foreign key relating to primary key of another table. Referential integrity will be imposed
Check constraints	Specify domain values that will be accepted for an attribute. Insertions will be disallowed if attribute values do not conform to the domain
Drop table A	Table A and all its contents deleted
Alter	Structure or permissions can be changed
Grant	User roles or privileges can be granted
DML	Data Manipulation Language: SQL verbs the value contents of storage object, notably tables. *Select, insert, update, delete*
Select From Where	Clauses of an SQL select statement defining the selection set (what is wanted), the selection domain (where it comes from) and the selection predicate (how to choose tuples)
Create as (Select...)	DDL variation: table is created with structure of selection set and populated with retrieved tuples
Insert into A(a, b, c) Values(1, 2, 3)	Row inserted into table with attribute values specified in statement
Insert into A(a, b, c) (select d, e, f) from B ...)	Rows in selection set from B inserted into table A, data types a, d; b, e; and c, f must be compatible
Update A Set a= ... Where ...	Rows selected from A, according the *where* predicate...; will have attribute *a* set to value...

Delete	Rows from specified table deleted if they conform to *where*
From	predicate
Where	

6.15 QUESTIONS

Write SQL statements to satisfy the following requirements:

(i) Select everything from the clubs table.

(ii) Select the players in surname order.

(iii) Select all the players who play for Purity FC.

(iv) List the surname and club of all midfield players.

(v) List the surname and position of all the goalkeepers and defenders.

(vi) List the surname and position of all the players who are not goalkeepers or defenders.

(vii) List all the players who are over 21.

(viii) List all the players who are under 19.

(ix) List all the players who are over 17 and younger than 25.

(x) Find all the players who are Taureans (21 April–21 May).

(xi) Find all the players who are not Taureans.

6.16 EXERCISES

(i) Create a table called, *Beautylist*, which consists of all the players who play for *Beauty United*.

(ii) Practise updates and deletions in *Beautylist*.

CHAPTER 7

MORE SQL

Then join you with them, like a rib of steel,

To make strength stronger

William Shakespeare, *Henry IV Part 2*

7.1 ⊨ JOINS AND JOIN CONDITIONS

A join takes place when more than one table is cited in the *from* clause of a *select* statement or in a sub-query associated with an *insert*, *update* or *delete* command.

The relational algebra has only one basic operator that can be applied to two tables and that is the Cartesian product. Joining two tables in this way is very expensive in terms of operational resources because the result will be a relation with all the attributes of both tables and with every row of the first table combined with every row of the second.

Performing a Cartesian product on a table with 6 attributes and 200 rows and another table with 4 attributes and 1000 rows will yield a table with 10 attributes and 200,000 rows!

Repeated operations like this would clearly fill the allocated tablespaces and put a huge strain on memory and even CPU time. The output table would also be very little use in terms of information value.

While the Cartesian product is the theoretical basis of the join operation, the goal is never to use it. More efficient and analytic join methods can be derived, using the *select* and *project* constructs to limit the processing time for a join and to render the output useful in terms of the application it is serving.

There are at least four secondary algebraic operators derived from the Cartesian product: the theta join, the equijoin, the natural join and the semijoin (Table 7.1).

Table 7.1 Join types.

Theta join	=, <, ≤, >, ≥, ≠	General purpose join; uses any comparison operator in the join condition
Equijoin	=	Tests for equality. Attributes can have any name but must have same data type
Natural join	=	Test for equality. Join attributes have same name and data type
Semijoin	=, <, ≤, >, ≥, ≠	Like a theta join, but project attributes only from left or right side of join: right semijoin or left semijoin

7.1.1   INNER JOINS

Joins take place in *select* statements. The selection set can take any attribute from the tables in the selection domain; the join condition, together with any other restrictions, is placed in the *where* clause or selection predicate.

More than two tables may be specified in the *from* clause. A join can only be applied between two tables at a time, since the join is a binary operator. The query is processed by joining first two tables, using the join condition that links them, to give an intermediate relation. Sufficient attributes are projected into this intermediary to apply the next join condition, and so on (Figures 7.1 and 7.2).

`Select forename, surname, dateofbirth, manager`	Selection set: these columns will be projected in the result
`From players, clubs`	Selection domain: these tables participate in the join
`Where players.club=clubs.name and players.dateofbirth<'01-Jan-82';`	Selection predicate: the join condition and any other restriction (see Figure 7.2)

Figure 7.1 SQL join.

It is important to ensure that there are enough join conditions to avoid a Cartesian product in the result. The minimum number of join conditions is one less than the number of tables in the *from* clause (Figure 7.3).

Any rows not meeting the selection predicate do not occur in the resulting relation. All players have clubs, but only those players who have scored a goal will appear in the output of the query in Figure 7.3. In fact, those players who have scored two goals will occur twice in the output, any with three goals will appear three times and so on. In this case, that is what is wanted: a list of players who have

```
Select forename, surname, dateofbirth DoB, manager
From players, clubs
Where players.club=clubs.name
And players.dateofbirth<'01-Jan-82';

FORENAME                SURNAME              DOB        MANAGER
-----  -----------------------  ---------  ------------------------

PIERRE                  DIOCLETIAN           15-JUN-78 Thor
HENRY                   DICKENS              23-AUG-80 Thor
WINSTON                 PLATO                30-DEC-79 Thor
CHARLES                 PAUL                 12-MAY-81 Thor
ALAN                    GREGORY              02-JUL-76 Thor
VICTOR                  SOCRATES             12-JUL-80 Thor
MARC                    MORE                 04-FEB-80 Thor
LUCIUS                  AUGUSTUS             24-OCT-78 Mercury
JOHN                    INNOCENT             03-SEP-79 Mercury
EDGAR                   TIBERIUS             15-APR-80 Mercury
NIKOS                   ARISTOTLE            03-SEP-80 Mercury
ANTONIO                 BACON                05-MAR-78 Mercury

12 rows selected.
```

Figure 7.2 Equijoin on clubs and players.

`select surname, name, minute, type from players, clubs, goals`	Three tables
`where players.club=clubs.name and players.ufa_id =goals.ufa_id`	Two join conditions
`and match_id=1`	Further restriction
`order by name, minute;`	Order the goals for each club

```
SURNAME              NAME             MINUTE TYPE
--------------------  ----------------  ----------

DIOCLETIAN           Beauty United     14     goal
CONSTANTINE          Beauty United     56     own goal
PLATO                Beauty United     87     goal
AUGUSTUS             Purity FC         28     penalty
AUGUSTUS             Purity FC         36     goal
INNOCENT             Purity FC         63     goal

6 rows selected.
```

Figure 7.3 Join example.

```
column club format a14;
column surname format a15;
column age format 99.9;
column service format 99.9;

select a.ufa_id, surname, a.club, months_between (sysdate,
dateofbirth)/12 as age, months_between (sysdate, joined)/12 as service
from players a,contracts b
where a.ufa_id=b.ufa_id
and left is null;

UFA_ID      SURNAME          CLUB              AGE SERVICE
----------  ---------------  ---------------  ----- -------
AK675280    BACON            Purity FC         24.4     1.1
AN971765    AUSTEN           Purity FC         17.1      .4
AT245876    HEGEL            Beauty United     18.4     2.8
BT46286     MORE             Beauty United     22.5     4.2
DX26497     ERASMUS          Purity FC         18.5     -.5
ED24659     SOCRATES         Beauty United     22.1     2.3
EG385190    JUSTINIAN        Purity FC         20.0      .9
EH382645    JOHN             Purity FC         18.4     1.4
...
```

Figure 7.4 SQL join with dates and nulls (natural join).

scored goals with a note of the minute in the match when they scored each goal. This match report shows that six goals were scored and that Purity FC won 4–2.

Another report showing a list of players, their age and length of service with their current club demonstrates a join between the *Players* and *contracts* tables. The query in Figure 7.4 shows this join. The output is formatted with SQL*Plus commands and the query makes use of date arithmetic as well as dealing with the null value.

Ages can be calculated by comparing *sysdate*(today's date and time now) and *dateofbirth* for each player. The SQL function *months_between* returns the number of months between two dates; dividing by 12 gives years. Length of service is given by applying *months_between* to *sysdate* and the *joined* attribute of *Contracts*. Each player may have had several contracts with various clubs. Their current contract has a null value in the *left* attribute of *contracts*.

Both *Players* and *Contracts* have identically named attributes. To avoid ambiguity a pseudonym is given to these tables in the *from* clause. These pseudonyms are used in the selection set and in the selection predicate.

The queries in Figures 7.3 and 7.4 are examples of inner joins. Inner joins only give results where the full join conditions are met. Rows not meeting the join conditions are excluded from the intermediate and final output relations. This exclusion at the intermediate stage will affect the results of later joins if there are any. However the query optimizer orders the joins, the result will be the same. It is desirable that exclusions take place early in the execution phase, so that subsequent joins are made between smaller intermediate relations.

7.1.2   OUTER JOINS

The manager of Beauty United needs a list of all his players showing which ones have scored goals. In order to get the goalscorers, a join of *Players* with *Goals* is needed. However, a simple inner join will exclude the players who have not scored. In this case, an outer join is used (Figure 7.5).

```
select forename, surname, minute, type
from players, goals
where players.ufa_id = goals.ufa_id(+)
and club='Beauty United'
order by surname;

FORENAME            SURNAME               MINUTE TYPE
------------------- --------------------- ---------- ----------
GEORGE              CONSTANTINE               56 own goal
HENRY               DICKENS
PIERRE              DIOCLETIAN                14 goal
PIERRE              DIOCLETIAN                73 goal
PIERRE              DIOCLETIAN                60 goal
PIERRE              DIOCLETIAN                 9 penalty
PIERRE              DIOCLETIAN                57 penalty
ALAN                GREGORY
BRIAN               HEGEL
EDWARD              KANT                      23 goal
MARC                MORE
CHARLES             PAUL                      27 goal
WINSTON             PLATO                     87 goal
WINSTON             PLATO                     48 goal
VICTOR              SOCRATES
RAMESH              THACKERAY

16 rows selected.
```

Figure 7.5 Outer join.

The (+) symbol next to the join condition for *goals.ufa_id* indicates an outer join. For *Players* who have matching *ufa_id* attributes in goals, the attributes *minute* and *type* are projected into the intermediate relation as normal. Players with no match are added to the intermediate relation with pseudo-columns for *minute* and *type*, which contain null values. These rows show up with blank spaces in the final output.

Oracle allows only one outer join in a query. The *or* logical operator and the *in* set operator are disallowed in the selection predicate.

7.1.3 SUB-QUERIES

Perhaps the most complex select restrictions are the comparison operators *in*, *any*, *all* and *exists* and their negations *not in*, *not exists*, which test for membership of a set. The set can be composed of constants or it can be the result of a query within the query. In the latter case, it is called a sub-query. If the sub-query is guaranteed to return only one row then the comparison operators can be used as well as the set membership operators.

The first example in Figure 7.6 constructs an intermediate set composed of two string constants. The value of the *club* attribute in *Players* is tested for equality with

```
select ufa_id as ufa_reg, forename, surname, squad_no from players
where club in ('Beauty United', 'West Ham')
order by surname ;

UFA_REG      FORENAME        SURNAME                   SQUAD_NO
----------   ---------------  -------------------------  ----------
UT23685      GEORGE          CONSTANTINE               5
UT236965     HENRY           DICKENS                   6
VT432167     PIERRE          DIOCLETIAN                11
FT246517     ALAN            GREGORY                   9


select ufa_id as ufa_reg, forename, surname, squad_no from players
where club in (select name from clubs
               where manager='Mercury')
order by surname ;

UFA_REG      FORENAME        SURNAME                   SQUAD_NO
----------   ----------------------------------------   ----------
NH42764      NIKOS           ARISTOTLE                 7
VB376512     LUCIUS          AUGUSTUS                  9
AN971765     PETER           AUSTEN                    23
AK675280     ANTONIO         BACON                     18
```

Figure 7.6 Restriction sub-queries.

```
Select surname, name From players, clubs        Two tables

Where players.club=clubs.name                   One join conditions

And players.ufa_id IN                           Second join condition

(select ufa_id from goals where match_id=1);    Third table as sub-query


SURNAME              NAME
------------------------- -----
DIOCLETIAN           Beauty United
CONSTANTINE          Beauty United
PLATO                Beauty United
AUGUSTUS             Purity FC
INNOCENT             Purity FC

5 rows selected.
```

Figure 7.7 Skinning a cat I.

any member of this constructed set. The overall query yields 11 rows, the players of Beauty United.

The second example constructs a comparison set from a select statement applied against the clubs table. The intermediate set will have one member with a single attribute having the value *Purity FC,* managed by *Mercury.* Again, the value of the club attribute in players is tested for equality with any member of this intermediate set. The overall query yields 11 rows: the players of *Purity FC.*

If a list of all players was required with an indication of who had scored at least one goal, the selection criteria would need to be changed. In this case, just the existence of a player's *ufa_id* in the goals table would indicate that he had scored at least once.

A sub-query with the *in* set operator gives the answer required, as shown in Figure 7.7. Again, only rows for which there is a full correspondence in the join conditions will appear in the result.

The example in Figure 7.8 provides a list of all players showing who has scored, who has been disciplined and who has had a relatively blameless, if uneventful, career. The illustration of the outer join above showed how to achieve such a report when only one outer join was required. Here, two outer joins are needed and Oracle will only allow one inside each query.

The important word there is 'query'. It would be possible to write two outer join selects: on *Players* with *Goals* and on *Players* with *Discipline* and then combine them with a union operator.

This logic will not produce the required report. There are players who have scored but who have not been disciplined and there are players who have been disciplined but who have never scored a goal. Such players would appear in the null-padded list of one of the outer joins as well as appearing either as a goal scorer

```
(Select forename, surname, position, type    Pseudonym for type attribute
as note

from players a, goals b where                Inner join condition
a.ufa_id=b.ufa_id

union

Select forename, surname, position, result   Pseudonym for result attribute
as note from players a, discipline b

where a.ufa_id=b.ufa_id                       Inner join condition

union

Select forename, surname, position, '     '  Same pseudonym, this time for
as note from players                          a string constant

where ufa_id not in (select ufa_id from       Same pseudonym, this time for
goals)                                        a string constant –

and ufa_id not in (select ufa_id from         Conjoint (ANDed) sub-queries
discipline))

order by surname;                             Combined output sorted
```

```
FORENAME              SURNAME              POSITION        NOTE
---------------       ---------------      ---------       ---------------  --
NIKOS                 ARISTOTLE            forward         goal
LUCIUS                AUGUSTUS             forward         1 match suspension
LUCIUS                AUGUSTUS             forward         2 match suspension
LUCIUS                AUGUSTUS             forward         goal
LUCIUS                AUGUSTUS             forward         penalty
PETER                 AUSTEN               midfield        1 match suspension
ANTONIO               BACON                defender        1 match suspension
GEORGE                CONSTANTINE          defender        own goal
HENRY                 DICKENS              midfield
PIERRE                DIOCLETIAN           forward         1 match suspension
PIERRE                DIOCLETIAN           forward         goal
PIERRE                DIOCLETIAN           forward         penalty
EDUARDO               ERASMUS              forward
ALAN                  GREGORY              forward
MARC                  MORE                 defender        1 match suspension
```

Figure 7.8 Skinning a cat II: union selects.

or as having had a disciplinary penalty. Players who have neither scored nor been disciplined would appear in both null-padded lists.

The answer is three *select* statements, none of which is an outer join. These are then combined using the union operator to form the final list. First, an inner join on *Players* and *Goals* reveals the goal scorers. Secondly, an inner join on *Players* and *Discipline* lists those who have been disciplined. Thirdly, an inner join with conjoined sub-queries lists those who have neither scored nor been disciplined.

The union operator is a set operator and requires its operands to be union compatible. That is, each must consist of the same attributes. This is achieved by using a pseudonym called *note*.

7.2 ∈ QUERY OPTIMIZATION

The time required to process any query is a combination of interpretation, access and processing time.

Interpretation time is the time the DBMS requires to translate the query and arrive at an execution plan. Access time is the time to read the disk and retrieve the data. Processing time is required to perform comparisons, restrictions or sort operations in buffers on the retrieved data. There may then be further access time if amended values are written back to the database. The interpretation of queries follows a sequence of steps outlined in Figure 7.9.

7.2.1 QUERY EXECUTION PLAN

The DBMS must determine how best to retrieve the data, basing its decision on the table structure and the presence or not of an appropriate index. When a query is started that requires data to be retrieved from multiple tables, the DBMS must also decide in which order to access and join the individual tables. This decision is helped if statistical information is available on the tables that need to be accessed.

By knowing the likely number of entries matching a particular query, the DBMS can make informed estimates of the number of rows resulting from a particular table access and restriction. This information is important when deciding how best to bring the tables together.

Oracle introduced this method of determination, which it refers to as *cost-based*, from version 7. Before that, the optimizer relied on built-in rules regarding tables and indexes. The query execution plan cost estimates reflect what the database knows about gathered statistics on unique and duplicated value attributes.

The revised relational algebraic formulations will reflect what is known about foreign key relationships, primary key constraints and other structural rules embedded in the schema (Figure 7.9).

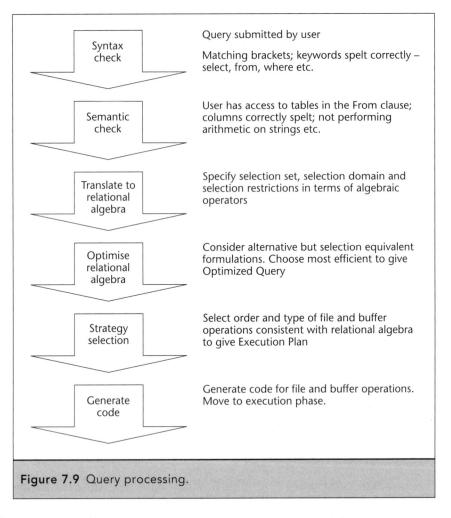

Figure 7.9 Query processing.

7.3 ⋲ EXPLAIN PLAN

Oracle reveals its query execution plan through the *explain plan* mechanism. The first step is to create a table called *plan_table* into which rows will be inserted when *explain plan* is invoked on a query. The script *ultxplan.sql* is found in the *ora92/ rdbms/admin* directory and automates the creation of this special table. Cost-based plans cannot be prepared unless statistics have been gathered about the tables in the query. The *analyze* command takes care of this (figure 7.10)

A plan is created and *plan_table* is populated by prefixing the query with *explain plan for* (Figure 7.11).

The last script, in Figure 7.11, *utlxpls*, calls a routine that is stored in the database during installation. This performs a query on the table *plan _table* and outputs the formatted result as shown in Figure 7.12.

The plan in Figure 7.13 is read bottom-up. The first operation reads all rows from the players table into a local memory buffer. Oracle has correctly estimated that

```
@utlxplan                          Oracle supplied script to create plan_table.
                                   This only needs to be done once

analyze table players compute      Collect statistics on players and clubs
statistics;                        tables

analyze table a27ws.clubs
compute statistics;
```

Figure 7.10 Preparing to explain.

```
explain plan for select surname, club    Populate plan _table with the
from players where club in (select name   query plan for the select state-
from clubs where manager='Mercury');      ment given

@utlxpls                                  Oracle supplied script to query
                                          plan_table
```

Figure 7.11 Explain plan I.

```
-------------------------------------------------------------------
| Id  | Operation             | Name    | Rows  | Bytes | Cost  |
-------------------------------------------------------------------
|   0 | SELECT STATEMENT      |         |    11 |   385 |     5 |
|*  1 |  HASH JOIN            |         |    11 |   385 |     5 |
|*  2 |   TABLE ACCESS FULL   | CLUBS   |     1 |    17 |     2 |
|   3 |   TABLE ACCESS FULL   | PLAYERS |    22 |   396 |     2 |
-------------------------------------------------------------------

Predicate Information (identified by operation id):
---------------------------------------------------
1 - access('PLAYERS'."CLUB"="CLUBS"."NAME")
2 - filter ("CLUBS"."MANAGER"='Mercury')

Note: cpu costing is off

17 rows selected.
```

Figure 7.12 Explain plan output.

this will result in an intermediate buffered relation of 22 rows (✓). Larger tables might be paged out to disk by the virtual memory system.

Next, rows from the *Clubs* table that conform to predicate 2 are read into a buffer. Oracle has correctly estimated that this will amount to 1 row (✓).

Oracle has decided that a hash join on *players.clubs* and *clubs.name* in the unsorted buffers is the cheapest way of implementing the *in* operator and the sub-query. The estimate for the intermediate relation is 11 rows (✓). The last operation is to project the required attributes into the final selection set, estimated at 11 rows (✓).

Alternative and more costly strategies are illustrated in Figures 7.13 and 7.14.

```
Read all players (22 rows)
Read all clubs (19 rows)
Perform Cartesian product (418 rows)
Restrict on clubs.manager = 'Mercury' (22 rows)
Restrict on clubs.name = players.club (11)
```

Figure 7.13 Alternative I.

```
Read all players (22 rows)
Read clubs, restrict on clubs.manager = 'Mercury' (1 row)
Sort players on players.club (22 rows)
Perform merge sort on players.club=clubs.name (11 rows)
```

Figure 7.14 Alternative II.

In Figure 7.15, Oracle plans first to make a selection on goals, estimating 2 rows will be returned on predicate 5 (*"GOALS"."MATCH_ID"=1*). This is an underestimate, but it is based on the average number of rows in the *Goals* table for different *match_ids*.

Next, a hash join is performed on predicate 2 between *Players* and *Clubs*. Because of the foreign key constraint, Oracle can determine that every player will be in the joined relation, which will therefore have 22 rows.

Finally, this intermediate relation is joined with the restricted *Goals* intermediate. Because no attributes are projected from *Goals*, a left semijoin can be carried out. Oracle is slightly underestimating the final result at 3 rows.

```
Explain plan for
Select surname, name
From players, clubs
Where players.club=clubs.name
And players.ufa_id IN
(select ufa_id from goals
where match_id=1);

@utlxpls;

-----------------------------------------------------------------
| Id  | Operation            |Name      | Rows | Bytes | Cost|
-----------------------------------------------------------------
|   0 | SELECT STATEMENT     |          |   3  |  171  |  8  |
|*  1 |  HASH JOIN SEMI      |          |   3  |  171  |  8  |
|*  2 |   HASH JOIN          |          |  22  | 1034  |  5  |
|   3 |    TABLE ACCESS FULL | CLUBS    |  19  |  399  |  2  |
|   4 |    TABLE ACCESS FULL | PLAYERS  |  22  |  572  |  2  |
|*  5 |    TABLE ACCESS FULL | GOALS    |   2  |   20  |  2  |
-----------------------------------------------------------------

Predicate Information (identified by operation id):
---------------------------------------------------

1 - access("PLAYERS"."UFA_ID"="GOALS"."UFA_ID")
2 - access("PLAYERS"."CLUB"="CLUBS"."NAME")
5 - filter ("GOALS"."MATCH_ID"=1)
```

Figure 7.15 Explain plan II.

7.4 ∈ KEY TERMS

Joins	Binary operation to join two relations; multi-table joins executed as a series, using intermediate result sets
Cartesian product	Basic relational algebra ic operator. All rows of relation R joined with all rows of relation S. All attributes of R and S in result
Restricted joins	Reduce the result set with join condition base on attribute values: theta joins, natural joins, equijoins and semijoins specify which kind of attributes and result projection

Outer joins	Include those rows failing the join condition with dummy attributes in the selection set. One outer join per SQL statement. Oracle (+) operator
Unions	Basic operator. Accumulation of two result sets into one. Sets must have the same attributes (name and type)
Query optimization	Translate the relational algebra into file and buffer operations; chose most efficient (lowest cost) execution plan. Cost usually expressed in disk I/Os and CPU time
Explain plan	Reveal the execution plan and estimates for cost of operations

7.5 QUESTIONS

Write SQL statements to provide the following:

(i) A list of players, their manager and home stadium.

(ii) A list of players who have scored goals in a match and the home and away sides in that match.

(iii) A list of all players with an indication of whether they have scored a goal or not.

(iv) A list of all players with an indication of whether they have been disciplined or not.

(v) A list of players who have scored goals, but not listing those who have been disciplined.

7.6 EXERCISES

(i) Store the result of the queries in Questions (i)–(vi) (above) in suitable temporary tables.

(ii) Determine the execution strategy for each of the queries above.

CHAPTER 8

DATA SECURITY

Security gives way to conspiracy.

William Shakespeare, *Julius Caesar*

Information kept in databases underpins the viability of almost every governmental and commercial organization.

Often the value of the data is written into the balance sheets of corporations as a critical asset with as much importance as manufacturing plant. The ability of national and local governments to raise revenue and provide services depends upon information stored in databases. Safety-critical control systems for transport or health care could not function without databases.

Clearly, there are serious and fundamental requirements for DBMS vendors to provide products that match expectations for the reliability and availability of the stored information. Any measures to secure the data must cope with situations where there may be many millions of updates in a working day; where network or telephone connections may be subject to disruption; and where the computer hosting the database software may experience mechanical or electrical failure.

As with any large-scale, complex problem, the best approach is to try to divide it into manageable areas and to come up with non-conflicting solutions for each difficulty.

8.1 TRANSACTIONS

The database software checks an SQL statement for basic conformity with the structural rules constructed by the DBA. These will include ensuring that the user has access rights; that a proposed update is permissible in terms of the domain ranges of attributes; and so on.

However, an SQL statement that results in the update of a single row in a table, because of the complexity of its restriction criteria, may have to be translated into many database operations in order to achieve that aim. It is also possible that a block of SQL *insert* or *update* statements, each logically dependent on the success of its predecessors or successors, may be submitted.

A systems failure such as a power cut may interrupt a database file operation of any of these multiple statements. One of them may contain a syntax error and fail after several have succeeded. It may be that the partial success of the block, with some updates completed and others incomplete, offends against the business rules of the organization.

There may be several independent SQL program blocks submitted simultaneously by different users and any one of them might be trying to read or write data already updated by another user.

There are four problems here:

- What is the unit of work for a user submitted job? Is it a single database file operation? Is it a single SQL statement or is it a block of interdependent SQL statements?

- If a block of statements is the job unit and it fails midway, how can already successful updates, which depend on subsequent failed updates, be prevented from compromising the adherence of the database to its business rules? If a single SQL statement is the job unit, how does the system cope with a single statement which is designed to update 25,000 rows, and which fails after updating 24,999 rows, leaving the last row out of step with the others?

- How can a temporary update from one SQL statement be protected from being overwritten by a conflicting update to the same row from another user's statement?

- Even if different users' updates are segregated in a temporary filespace, how do we reliably transfer their potentially conflicting contents into the database proper at the end of a job?

The answer to these problems is the transaction. A transaction is a concept having four critical properties that lead to a solution to the complexities of data security (Table 8.1).

8.2 ⊨ ATOMICITY

A transaction may consist of just one SQL statement or it may involve multiple statements that are logically dependent on each other and that must be all be successfully completed. A transaction cannot be defined simply as any particular number of SQL statements, since it has a variable length.

In order to achieve a clear definition of the transaction as a unit of work, it is necessary to define precisely when that work is completed. For this, a new SQL command is needed: the **commit** statement. Issuing the *commit* command finally

Table 8.1 Transaction properties (ACID).	
Atomicity	A transaction is the unit of work. As far as changes to the database are concerned, it is indivisible. Either all the components of a transaction succeed or they all fail. A transaction can consist of one or more SQL statements
Consistency	A transaction starts with the database in a consistent state and finishes with the database in a consistent state. That is, consistent with the structural, behavioural and business rules embedded by the DBA.
Isolation	The intermediate steps of a transaction are hidden from the view of other users until the transaction finishes.
Durability	The results of a transaction are permanently and securely stored in the database when the transaction finishes

and irrevocably ends the transaction. Until that time, the work is not permanently saved in the database.

A transaction can be defined as any number of SQL statements contained within two *commit* statements. The first marks the end of the previous transaction and the start of a new work unit. The second marks the end of that new work.

ATOMIC TRANSACTIONS	A transaction starts implicitly either when a user connects to the database or when a commit or rollback statement is issued against a previous transaction.
	A transaction ends when a commit or rollback statement is issued against it.

If a transaction is defined as indivisible then there must be a method of recovery. Any changes made as part of a single SQL statement or any partly completed block of SQL statements must be reversible. In the event of failure, the whole transaction must be aborted and the partial updates reverted to their previous states.

In order to deal with this situation, a second SQL command is used: the ***rollback*** statement. A *rollback* statement also marks the end of a transaction.

During its lifetime, a transaction may move between certain fixed states. The transaction starts in the active state and is in it while it is executing. After the final statement has been successfully executed, it moves to the pre-commit state. When the *commit* command is issued and the transaction is successfully completed, it moves to the committed state.

If an error occurs and execution can no longer continue, the transaction moves from the active state to the failed state. If the transaction has been rolled back and the database restored to its condition prior to the start of the transaction, the transaction moves to the aborted state (Figure 8.1).

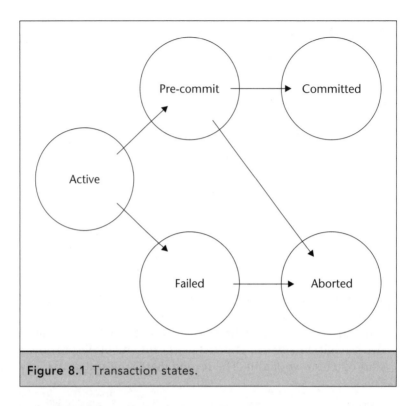

Figure 8.1 Transaction states.

The transaction may also move from the pre-commit to the aborted state if a *rollback* command is issued instead of a *commit*.

Try the sequence of SQL statements in Figure 8.2 in terms of transactions. There are three transactions. The first has just one statement before the *commit*. The second transaction has three SQL statements: a *select*, an *update* and another *select*.

This second *select* includes a mistaken update that does not offend against any database constraint, but is then manually reversed by the *rollback*; the last *select* (in a third transaction, not yet ended) shows the reverted value.

Before the *rollback* is issued, the mistaken update can only be seen within the transaction and only by the user executing it. Other users cannot read this intermediate result.

8.3 CONSISTENCY

A single SQL statement can still contain instructions to update, insert or delete rows in a way that would offend against the business policies of an organization.

Before the database prepares a statement for execution, it is checked for **syntactic validity**: unmatched or missing brackets, misspelled keywords and so on. In other words, does the statement conform to the defined grammar?

Update players set dateofbirth = '09-Mar-1979' where UFA_ID ='AT245876';	Brian Hegel's date of birth is corrected
commit;	The change is stored
Select * from players;	Listing the players confirms that the change has been made
Update players set dateofbirth = '24-Apr-2001' where UFA_ID ='BT46286';	Marc More's date of birth is mistakenly corrected
select * from players;	The mistaken correction appears to have been made
rollback;	
Select * from players;	The previous value for Marc More's date of birth has been restored. The correction was not permanently stored.

Figure 8.2 Commit and rollback: *Players* table exercise.

If it does, then it is checked for **semantic validity**. Does the user have access to the items in the *from* clause; do they exist; are the names of columns misspelled?

After semantic checking, the statement is passed for execution. At the end of this phase, the statement is checked for conformity with constraints imposed by the DBA: has the statement changed or deleted a primary key, leaving foreign keys unreferenced; does an update exceed the percentage increase allowed on this row? If these checks find a constraint violation, the statement will fail.

If the statement passes all these checks, it will execute and enter the pre-commit stage. Choosing to commit the statement will take the database to a state which is consistent with the syntactic, semantic and constraint rules embedded in its schema. Choosing to roll back the statement will take the database back to a state that was already consistent with these rules.

An SQL statement is therefore guaranteed to preserve consistency of the database by virtue of the syntactic, semantic and constraint checks imposed upon it. The serial execution of multiple SQL statements must similarly be guaranteed to preserve consistency. If they are grouped within an atomic transaction, then either *all* the statements succeed and are committed or one fails and causes the *whole* transaction to be rolled back.

If transactions from different users are executed serially so that each one does not start until the previous one is committed, then they also guarantee consistency. However, this is an impractical proposal since many non-conflicting transactions would be queued. It is far better idea to allow concurrent execution of transactions and to provide a mechanism to segregate their intermediate results.

8.4 ⊆ ISOLATION

Multiple transactions are allowed to run concurrently in the system in order to increase processor and disk utilization. This leads to better transaction throughput: one transaction can be using the CPU while another is reading from or writing to the disk. The average response time for transactions is reduced.

Concurrency control schemes are implemented to achieve isolation, to control the interaction among the concurrent transactions in order to prevent them from destroying the integrity of their own or other transactions, and to preserve consistency in the database.

If the serial ordering (queuing) of transactions is inefficient, perhaps there is a way of ordering the individual database operations of two or more conflicting transactions so that the overall effect is the same as if they had been queued. This is the concept of **serializability**.

8.4.1 SERIALIZABILITY

A schedule is the sequence that indicates the chronological order in which instructions of concurrent transactions are executed. A schedule for a set of transactions must consist of all instructions of those transactions and must preserve the order in which the instructions appear in each individual transaction.

Only read and write instructions are considered because generally only these operations give rise to conflict between transactions. In between reads and writes, transactions may perform calculations or other manipulations in local buffers without conflict.

A bank example illustrates the scheduling problem. A customer has a current account and a savings account. He telephones his branch, asking for £50 to be transferred from his current account to his savings. On the same day, he decides to transfer another £40 from the current account to the savings account. Figure 8.3 shows the two transactions, T_1 and T_2.

The two transactions are not concurrent and do not interfere. At the close of business his current account is –£90 and his savings account is +£90.

Figure 8.4 shows a serialized schedule in which the instructions of T_1 and T_2 are concurrent and which preserves the consistency of the database: the sum of A and B remains the same.

Figure 8.5 shows a concurrent transaction that does not preserve the sum of A and B. T_1's write operation on A is based in the original value of A but takes place after T_2 has updated it. T_2's £40 debit update will be overwritten by T_1's £50 debit and lost.

Both transactions base their calculation of B's update on the same original value of B. T_2's update takes place after T_1's, overwriting it. The £50 deposit is lost.

At the end of the two transactions the current account balance is –£50 and the savings account is +£40. Not only did the customer fail to transfer the full £90, but he lost £10 in the process!

	Transaction 1 – T_1	Transaction 2 – T_2
read	Read (A)	
buffer	A = A − 50	
write	Write(A)	
read	Read (B)	
buffer	B = B + 50	
write	Write(B)	
read		Read (A)
buffer		A = A − 40
write		Write(A)
read		Read (B)
buffer		B = B + 40
write		Write(B)

Figure 8.3 Serial transactions.

	T_1	T_2
read	Read (A)	
buffer	A = A − 50	
write	Write(A)	
read		Read (A)
buffer		A = A − 40
write		Write(A)
read	Read (B)	
buffer	B = B + 50	
write	Write(B)	
read		Read (B)
buffer		B = B + 40
write		Write(B)

Figure 8.4 Serialized transactions.

	T_1	T_2
read	read(A)	
buffer	A = A – 50	
read		read(A)
buffer		A = A – 40
write		write(A)
read		read(B)
write	write(A)	
read	read(B)	
buffer	B = B + 50	
write	write(B)	
buffer		B = B + 40
write		write(B)

Figure 8.5 Inconsistent schedule.

Serial execution of a set of transactions preserves database consistency. A concurrent schedule is **serializable** if it is equivalent to a serial (queued) schedule and preserves database consistency

Different forms of schedule equivalence give rise to the notions of:

● conflict serializability
● view serializability

Instructions I_1 and I_2 of two transactions conflict **if and only if** there exists some item accessed by both **and** at least one of these instructions writes to it (Figure 8.6).

T_1	T_2	Conflict status
I_1 = read (A)	I_2 = read (A)	I_1 and I_2 do not conflict
I_1 = read (A)	I_2 = write (A)	They conflict
I_1 = write (A)	I_2 = read (A)	They conflict
I_1 = write (A)	I_2 = write (A)	They conflict

Figure 8.6 Transaction conflict conditions.

A conflict between two instructions forces a (logical) temporal order between them in any proposed schedule. If two instructions are consecutive in a schedule and they do not conflict, their results will remain the same even if they are temporally interchanged in the schedule.

If a schedule S can be transformed into a schedule S′ by a series of temporal interchanges of non-conflicting instructions, S and S′ are **conflict equivalent**. A schedule S is **conflict serializable** if it is conflict equivalent to a serial schedule

In Figure 8.7 there are no non-conflicting pairs of instructions from T_3 and T_4. Therefore no temporal interchanges can be made to obtain either the serial schedule <T_3, T_4> or the serial schedule <T_4, T_3>.

T_3	T_4
read (A)	
	write (A)
write (A)	

Figure 8.7 Not serializable.

The serialized schedule in Figure 8.8 can be rewritten because there are two pairs of non-conflicting instructions that can be temporally interchanged to achieve a serial schedule:

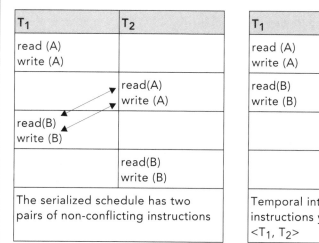

T_1	T_2	T_1	T_2
read (A) write (A)		read (A) write (A)	
	read(A) write (A)	read(B) write (B)	
read(B) write (B)			read(A) write (A)
	read(B) write (B)		read(B) write (B)
The serialized schedule has two pairs of non-conflicting instructions		Temporal interchange of these instructions yields a serial schedule <T_1, T_2>	

Figure 8.8 View equivalence.

If S and S' are two schedules with the same set of transactions, S and S' are **view equivalent** if three conditions are met:

- For each data item, if transaction T_i reads its initial value in schedule S, then transaction T_i must also read its initial value in schedule S'.

- For each data item, if transaction T_i executes a read on it in schedule S, and that value was produced by transaction T_j (if any), then, in schedule S', transaction T_i must also read the value of it that was produced by transaction T_j.

- For each data item, the transaction (if any) that performs the final write operation on it in schedule S must perform the final write operation on it in schedule S'.

A schedule S is view serializable if it is view equivalent to a serial schedule. Every conflict serializable schedule is also view serializable.

Figure 8.9 shows a schedule that is view serializable but not conflict serializable. Any view serializable schedule that is not also conflict serializable must contain blind writes (writing an item without reading it first).

T_1	T_2	T_3
read (A)		
	write (A)	
write (A)		
		write (B)

Figure 8.9 View serializable.

When considering the schedules of concurrent transactions, it is important to remember that uncommitted data is being read in the conflicting instruction streams. If a transaction should fail this will have implications for other transaction with which it shared updated data items. The schedule itself must be **recoverable** for the database to retain consistency.

If a transaction T_1 reads a data item previously written by a transaction T_2, the commit operation of T_1 must appear before the commit operation of T_2.

The schedule in Figure 8.10 is not recoverable if T_2 commits immediately after the read.

If T_1 should then abort, T_2 would have read an inconsistent database state. The database must ensure that schedules are recoverable. There is a need to address the effect of transaction failures on concurrently running transactions. In a cascading rollback a single transaction failure leads to a series of other transaction rollbacks.

Figure 8.11 shows a schedule of three uncommitted transactions. For the schedule to be recoverable, if T_1 fails, T_2 and T_3 must also be rolled back. This can lead to the undoing of a significant amount of work.

T₁	T₂
read (A) write (A)	
	read(A)
read(B)	

Figure 8.10 Unrecoverable schedule.

T₁	T₂	T₃
read (A) read(B) write (A)		
	read(A) write (A)	
		read(A)

Figure 8.11 Cascading rollback.

With **cascadeless schedules** cascading rollbacks cannot occur. A schedule is cascadeless if, for each pair of transactions T_i and T_j where T_j reads a data item previously written by T_i, the commit operation of T_i appears before the read operation of T_j

Every cascadeless schedule is also recoverable. From the point of view of avoiding the unnecessary loss of work, it is desirable to restrict the schedules to those that are cascadeless.

Serializability can be shown through precedence graphs. This is a directed graph where the nodes are the transactions. An edge is drawn between two nodes if conflict over a data item arises. The direction of the edge shows which transaction accessed the disputed data item first. The edge is labelled with the data item causing the conflict (Figure 8.12).

The schedule in Figure 8.13 shows several conflicts arising between four concurrent transactions. The conflicts can be first listed and then translated into a precedence graph (Figure 8.14).

A schedule is conflict serializable if and only if its precedence graph is acyclic (the edge vectors do not form a circle). If the precedence graph is acyclic, the serializability order can be obtained by a topological sorting of the graph. For

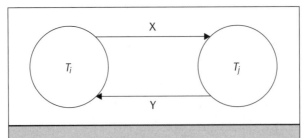

Figure 8.12 Precedence graph.

T₁	T₂	T₃	T₄
	read (A)		
read (B)			
read (C)			
	read (B)		
	write (B)	write (C)	read (B)
			write (B)
read (D)			read (C)

T1 conflicts with T2 over item B; T1 accessed B first

T2 conflicts with T4 over item B; T2 accessed B first

T3 conflicts with T4 over item C; T3 accessed C first

T1 conflicts with T3 over item C; T1 accessed C first

Figure 8.13 Example schedule.

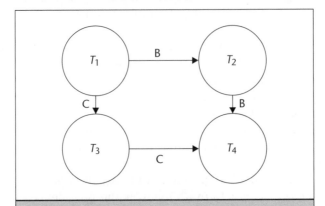

Figure 8.14 Precedence graph from Figure 8.13.

example, a serializability order for the schedule in Figure 8.14 would be $T_1 \to T_3 \to T_2 \to T_4$.

The goal is to develop concurrency control protocols that will assure serializability. They will generally not examine the precedence graph as it is being created. Instead, a protocol will impose a discipline that avoids non-serializable schedules. Tests for serializability help demonstrate the correctness of a concurrency control protocol.

8.5 DURABILITY

Once a transaction commits, the system must guarantee that the results of its operations will never be lost, in spite of subsequent failures. This same condition must also hold true if the transaction aborts.

The same database component that assures atomicity also provides durability assurance: the recovery manager guarantees commit and rollback.

During a transaction, there may be many temporary updates of the data. In order to preserve recoverability the previous values of the affected rows must be kept until the transaction ends. This guarantees the possibility of rollback. Tracking the progress of updates to the data during a transaction is called **logging** and implies the use of a separate tablespace used for this purpose.

In order to protect against catastrophic system failure like a disk crash, it is a wise strategy to store the log tablespace on a second disk away from the user's database tables. This brings performance benefits as well as improving security; disk I/O to the log and to the database can take place in parallel (Table 8.2).

Table 8.2 Implementing acid transactions.	
Property	Responsibility
Atomicity	Recovery Manager
Consistency	SQL parser Access controller Execution monitor
Isolation	Concurrency controller
Durability	Recovery Manager

8.6 CONCURRENCY CONTROL

The concurrency control mechanism of a database is the means of enforcing the transaction isolation principle. Views of two or more transactions in a schedule show the ordering of reads, writes and, sometimes, other operations that cause conflict and must be separated in time. For the schedule to proceed to the pre-commit state for each of the transactions in it there must be some kind of mechanism to guarantee the schedule.

There are two principal types of concurrency control approaches for resolving conflict. Either, when two operations conflict, the second is made to wait until the first has completed or the operations conflict is noted and resolved at the pre-commit stage.

The first approach assumes that there will often be conflict and that all operations need protection to be put immediately in place on their first access of a data item in case a subsequent operation causes conflict. That second operation will be put into a wait state. This approach leads a group of concurrency measures that are known as **pessimistic**.

Optimistic measures are those that assume that conflict will be relatively rare and avoid all the overhead of providing immediate protection to database operations. Instead, they determine if conflict has occurred at the pre-commit stage and, if it has, roll back the conflicting transactions and possibly restart them. If the savings in resource utilization, gained from avoiding immediate protection, outweigh the work lost in rollbacks, then optimism in concurrency control can offer greater throughput of work and still guarantee database consistency.

8.6.1 LOCKING

The simplest pessimistic scheme of concurrency control uses some kind of locking system. Locks indicate conflict and are blocking in that they cause wait states. A database will lock data at the row, page or table level and use at least two kinds of locks to indicate what kind of operation caused the lock: a read lock or a write lock.

A read operation within an SQL statement cannot access the data until it has requested and acquired a read lock on the target row and the same condition applies for a write operation. Conflicts only occur when one of the competing transactions, T_1 or T_2 wishes to initiate a write. The lock manager arbitrates lock requests using the rules of Table 8.3.

Table 8.3 Lock requests.

T_1	T_2	Lock manager
Read lock on (A) acquired	Request read lock on (A)	Granted
Read lock on (A) acquired	Request write lock on (A)	Not granted, wait for lock
Write lock on (A) acquired	Request read lock on (A)	Not granted, wait for lock
Write lock on (A) acquired	Request write lock on (A)	Not granted, wait for lock

A transaction may request an escalation of a read lock to a write lock based on conditions for the write being met by the information received in earlier read operations. A transaction may request a *read-intending-write* lock on a number of data items. So far as this simplified scheme is concerned, these are treated as write lock requests.

Lock systems are under the control of the lock manager, which uses a data structure called a lock table to store existing locks. Information in the lock tables is used to make decisions on lock requests.

The lock rules may be represented as a lock compatibility matrix. Table 8.4 shows the simplest example, where the lock manager provides only read or write locks. The matrix can be expanded on either edge to allow for additional lock types.

Table 8.4 Lock compatibility matrix.

	Lock request by T_2	
Lock held by T_1	Read	Write
Read	No conflict	Conflict
Write	Conflict	Conflict

The normal **granularity** of a lock is at the row level. If a transaction accumulates thousands of row locks during its processing, the lock manager may initiate an escalation of these locks to only several hundred page locks or just one table lock. Fewer numbers of locks would be easier to manage.

Escalation can cause conflict. Table 8.5 shows that two transactions can happily acquire multiple row level write locks in the same table. Providing they all refer to different rows, there is no conflict. If the lock managers attempt to escalate one transaction's holding to a single table lock then it must wait until the other

Table 8.5 Escalations.

T_1	T_2	Lock manager
Write lock on (A)	read lock on (D)	Granted
Write lock on (B)	read lock on (E)	Granted
Write lock on (C)	read lock on (F)	Granted
	read lock on (G)	Granted
	read lock on (H)	Granted
	read lock on (J)	Granted
	REQUEST TABLE READ LOCK	Not granted, wait for lock

transaction releases its locks for the escalation to proceed. The exclusive table lock cannot be granted while another transaction is holding a single row level lock.

8.6.2 DEADLOCKS

Mutually exclusive lock systems can also give rises to deadlocks. The four conditions for deadlock are set out in Table 8.6. A deadlock will continue forever if it is not detected and one of the conditions removed. Most databases resolve deadlock by arbitrarily aborting one of the transactions, causing a rollback and then restarting it. That is, pre-emption is introduced, removing one of the deadlock conditions.

Table 8.6 Deadlock: the deadly embrace.	
Mutual exclusion	Read and write locks are designed to mutually exclude access
No pre-emption	No mechanism for arbitrarily rolling back one transaction and releasing its locks
A wait-for state exists	Lock manager puts transactions in a wait-for state when lock cannot be granted
Circular wait	T_1 holds locks wanted by T_2. T_2 holds locks wanted by T_1

Deadlock can be detected using a wait-for graph that plots the state of all transactions in a wait state. Each transaction is a node in the graph and directed edges indicate the holder of the sought-for resource. A cyclic graph indicates that deadlock has occurred (Figure 8.15).

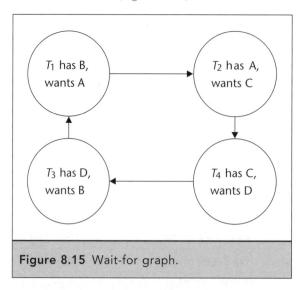

Figure 8.15 Wait-for graph.

8.6.3   OPTIMISTIC METHODS

Conflict resolution through locks is known as a pessimistic method. Conflict is expected, so prepare to resolve it immediately it occurs: at the point of request. The overhead to database operations through the lock manager process is high, but this a price most vendors are prepared to pay.

In situations where conflict is low, might it not be more efficient to allow all read and write requests as they are made and to resolve any conflict that threatens database consistency at the end of the transaction, before it is finally committed? This is the so-called optimistic approach. Optimistic concurrency control may be implemented through non-exclusive locks or timestamps or by other protocols, but they all share a common operational structure. Because there is no mutual exclusion or wait states, deadlocks cannot occur.

OPTIMISTIC TRANSACTIONS	All optimistic transactions consist of three phases: Read: all writes are to private storage (shadow copies). Validation: make sure no conflicts have occurred. Write: if validation was successful, make writes public. If not, rollback and restart).

The goal of the validation phase is to guarantee that only serializable schedules remain. The technique is actually to find an equivalent serializable schedule.

Each transaction is assigned a sequential Transaction Number (TN) during execution. If the transactions are run in the order of TNs then an equivalent serial schedule is obtained.

Each transaction has a ReadSet (RS) – the items it reads – and a WriteSet (WS) – the items it writes. Tracking the transaction and maintaining its WriteSet and ReadSet can put on a lot of overhead for transactions that perform a lot of full table scans or row updates. The transaction is validated on the basis of the three conditions in Table 8.7.

Table 8.7 Optimistic serializability conditions.
1. T_i completes its write phase before T_j starts its read phase.
2. $WS(T_i)$ intersect $RS(T_j)$ = emptyset and T_i completes its write phase before T_j starts its write phase.
3. $WS(T_i)$ intersect $RS(T_j)$ = $WS(T_i)$ intersect $WS(T_j)$ = emptyset and T_i completes its read phase before T_j completes its read phase.

Consider two transactions, T_i and T_j, where $T_i < T_j$. If any one of the three serializability conditions in Table 8.7 is true, then T_i is serializable.

There are three possible classes of conflict: W–R, R–W and W–W and two possible orderings of the transactions: i before j or j before i. Therefore there are six (3 × 2) possible conflict orderings to consider. Each condition guarantees that the transaction go in one order only: i before j.

For condition 1 all conflicts are ordered i before j (true serial execution).

For condition 2, there are no W_i–R_j or R_j–W_i conflicts since T_i's WriteSet does not insect with T_js ReadSet. There are no W_j–R_i or W_j–W_i conflicts since the write phase (and hence the read phase) of T_i precedes the write phase of T_j.

This leaves the possibility of R_i–W_j and W_i–W_j, both of which are ordered i before j.

For condition 3, there are no W_i–R_j or R_j–W_i conflicts since T_i's WriteSet does not intersect with T_j's ReadSet. There are no W_i–W_j or W_j–W_i conflicts since T_i's WriteSet does not intersect with T_j's WriteSet. W_j–R_i is not possible since the read phase of T_i precedes the write phase of T_j. This leaves only the possibility of R_i–W_j, which again is ordered i before j.

Satisfaction of any of these rules proves either a true serial execution or a serializable execution for T_i, which can then be validated and proceed to commit. If none of the conditions holds true because, for example, T_i's WriteSet does intersect with T_j's ReadSet and the two write phases overlap, then T_i must be rolled back and restarted.

Assigning TNs at the beginning of transactions is not completely optimistic, since a transaction would immediately be certain to fail the validation test if its predecessor transactions were still running. Instead, TNs are assigned at the end of the read phase. Note that this guarantees the satisfaction of the second half of condition 3.

8.6.4 TIME STAMPING

Using timestamps for concurrency control involves marking each data item with the time it was last written and the time it was last read.

Every transaction gets a unique timestamp (TS) at startup. The transaction may read a data item if its timestamp is greater than the item's Write TS. If the transaction's timestamp is greater than the item's existing Read TS, then the transaction's TS replaces the item's Read TS.

The transaction may write to an item if its timestamp is greater than either the item's Write TS or the item's Read TS. In this case, the transaction's TS replaces the item's Write TS.

If either of two cases are not true, the transaction is aborted and restarted. Forcing timestamp order imposes a much tighter restriction than other concurrency schemes and may lead to cascading aborts. The rolling back of a failed transaction, undoing the revised item timestamps, may cause other transactions to abort. There is also a price to be paid for the constant updating of timestamps that is necessary even for a read-only transaction.

Multi-version timestamping techniques involve keeping versions of the same data items distinguished by their timestamps. Transactions are again allocated a timestamp as they start. Read requests result in the appropriate version being delivered. Write requests, creating a new version, can only succeed if there are no reads between the new version and the creation of a new version (a write from another transaction). Timestamping is not a popular protocol and is not offered in any of the major vendor products. For the time being, it remains an object of interest to researchers.

8.7 ⊨ RECOVERY

In order to service the recoverability of transactions a database will keep some kind of log that records not only all uncommitted changes to the database, but in certain cases, the previous values of updated rows.

The log information can be used by the database to determine the new and previous values of data items and these values may be supplied to read operations, according to their position in a schedule.

Logging is a means of ensuring that the database is protected against catastrophic failure; it aids the isolation of transactions and guarantees durability. Logs are recorded in a separate tablespace from the normal data. A prudent DBA will place it on a separate disk with, perhaps, a second mirrored copy.

As they start, transactions are issued with a numerical or timestamp identifier. As a transaction proceeds, any write operation to update, insert or delete a row leads to the creation of a log entry. These log entries may be interspersed with the records of other transactions but not for the same rows. Concurrency control sees to that.

The log file is normally viewed as having a circular organization. It has a fixed length and records are overwritten on top of the records of already committed transactions. When the end of the file is encountered, the logging process recycles to the beginning of the file and continues to overwrite the records of committed transactions. This method of work is known as incremental logging.

Two strategies can be adopted in a logging process. The differences lie in the form of the log entry and where the update is stored pending the end of the transaction.

The **deferred update** strategy means that the database remains unchanged until commit. An *after image* of any updated and, so far, uncommitted values is kept in the log. When the transaction is committed, all of the updates are copied from the log to the database. If the transaction should be aborted, the log entries are very easily marked as complete and available for overwriting; nothing needs doing to the database proper.

While it is active, a transaction can read the results of its own updates from the *after images* in the log. If concurrency control allows it, other transactions read the original values directly from the database

This strategy means that updates are stored and accumulated in the log very quickly and the query reaches the pre-commit stage faster. The commit process is, however, much longer and therefore involves a greater risk of failure during this critical stage.

INCREMENTAL LOG: DEFERRED UPDATES	Transaction operations are recorded in a log file. The updates are not immediately written to the database. The log entries are used to update the database at commit time.
	In the event of a failure, Any transaction not completed is ignored. Any committed transaction is re-done. After a successful commit, the transaction entries are marked for reuse. Checkpoints (compressed, non-usable copies of the database) are used to limit the amount of re-working.

The *immediate update* strategy means that the updated and, so far, uncommitted values of a row are written straight into the database. It is essential that a *before image* and an *after image* of each updated row should be stored in the log.

A transaction may read its own updates directly from the database; other transactions may read the original values from the *before images* in the log, if concurrency control allows it.

INCREMENTAL LOG WITH IMMEDIATE UPDATES	Transaction writes (uncommitted) are recorded immediately in the database as well as the log. The transaction record contains both the old and the new values. When the log record is safely written, the database can be updated.
	In the event of failure, transactions not completed are undone – *before images* are written back to the database. If updates from committed transactions were buffered and lost in the failure, *after images* can be written to the database.

After commit, the log entries are marked as complete and available for overwrite. Locks are released on the already updated rows in the database. A rollback takes much longer in this case, as the before images have to be copied back to the database. In practice, there are more commits than rollbacks in most production databases, so the second strategy is generally preferred.

8.7.1 JOURNALS

In order to give a second level of defence against system failure, most databases offer the option of journaling log entries and row updates. A separate tablespace is made available on a different disk and every change to any row and every log entry is recorded. The recording is generally made in terms of update vectors rather than image copies in order to conserve space. An update vector simply records the actual change instruction that was applied to the row or log entry.

From time to time, backup copies of the database may be taken. Large data files might be copied to tape or CD and the full database might occupy several tape spools or CDs. If the backup is taken when there are no active transactions, then the journal can also be backed up and cleared.

A systems administrator would be well advised to ensure that data log and journal files are kept on separate disks to minimize the damage done by a system crash. Many corporations for whom the database is a critical survival factor keep logs and journals mirrored at remote sites (Table 8.8).

Table 8.8 Restoring the system.

Database file corrupt or destroyed	Make physical repairs. Restore database from tape. Apply all committed transactions from the journal from backup time until crash time.
Log file corrupt or destroyed	Reconstruct the log file from the journal. Reapply committed transactions if necessary. Apply rollbacks for uncommitted transactions.
Journal file corrupt or destroyed	Back up the database to tape. Restart with fresh journal.

8.8 SQL92 TRANSACTIONS

The ANSI/ISO SQL standard defines three undesirable phenomena that may be experienced by a database (Table 8.9).

Table 8.9 Operational conflicts.

Dirty read	A transaction reads data written by a concurrent uncommitted transaction.
Non-repeatable read	A transaction re-reads data it has previously read and finds that data has been modified by another transaction (that committed after the initial read).
Phantom read	A transaction re-executes a query that returned a set of rows that previously satisfied a search condition and finds that the set of rows satisfying the condition has changed due to another more recently committed transaction.

It then goes on to define four levels of transaction isolation in terms of these phenomena (Table 8.10). Three of these levels are less rigorous that the strict ACID properties outlined above. SQL92 adopts a more optimistic view of transaction conflict and strikes a compromise between operational throughput and the strict enforcement of lock conflicts always entailing wait states.

Table 8.10 SQL92 isolation levels.

Isolation level	Dirty read	Non-repeatable read	Phantom read
Read uncommitted	Possible	Possible	Possible
Read committed	Not possible	Possible	Possible
Repeatable read	Not possible	Not possible	Possible
Serializable	Not possible	Not possible	Not possible

Oracle offers only two levels of transaction isolation: *read committed* and *serializable*.

8.8.1 READ COMMITTED ISOLATION LEVEL

When a transaction runs at the *read committed* isolation level, a query statement sees only data committed before the query began; it never sees either uncommitted data or changes committed during query execution by concurrent transactions. (However, the query does see the effects of previous updates executed within its own transaction, even though they are not yet committed.)

This is a system known generally as Multi-version Concurrency Control. In effect, a query sees a snapshot of the database as of the instant that it begins to run. Serial queries may see different data, even though they are within a single transaction, if other transactions commit changes during execution of the earlier queries.

As they start, Oracle queries are given a numerical identifier, the System Change Number (SCN). The increasing numbers also indicate the order of start time. Information maintained in Oracle's rollback segments is used to provide statement level read consistency. The rollback segments contain the old values of data that have been changed by uncommitted or recently committed transactions. Figure 8.17 shows how Oracle provides statement-level read consistency using data in rollback segments.

Referring to Figure 8.17, it can be seen that as the statement with SCN 100023 proceeds, it reads blocks written with SCNs lower than 100023, confident that these must be the result of statements that committed before it began.

When it encounters a block labelled SCN 100024, this indicates a result from a statement that started after 100023 began and which may or may not have committed. Because Oracle uses an immediate update log method, the *before image* will be in the rollback segment. Statement 100023 now turns to the rollback

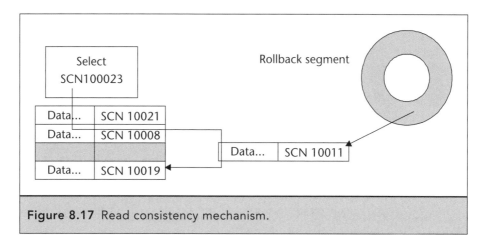

Figure 8.17 Read consistency mechanism.

segment and reconstitutes the previous version of the row, written by SCN 10011 before returning to the data block committed by SCN 10019. All of the data read by 100023 is committed although there may be a pending update on one of the data blocks it bypassed.

Since, in *read committed* mode, each new query statement starts with a new snapshot that includes all transactions committed up to that instant, subsequent queries in the same transaction may see the effects of newly committed concurrent transactions. Unrepeatable reads and phantoms in a transaction are possible at this level of isolation. Only within a single query is an absolutely consistent view of the database seen.

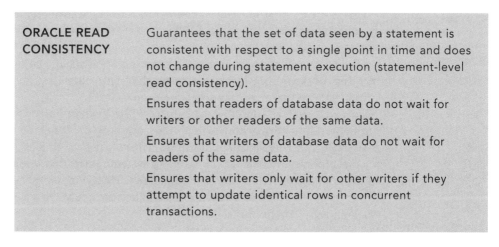

ORACLE READ CONSISTENCY	Guarantees that the set of data seen by a statement is consistent with respect to a single point in time and does not change during statement execution (statement-level read consistency).
	Ensures that readers of database data do not wait for writers or other readers of the same data.
	Ensures that writers of database data do not wait for readers of the same data.
	Ensures that writers only wait for other writers if they attempt to update identical rows in concurrent transactions.

It may be easier to view Oracle's implementation of read consistency as each query operating on a private but compatible copy of the database; hence the *multi-version consistency* model.

Updating statements can include implicit queries that select a list of rows for update. This list will reflect committed data at the time the statement began. An attempt may be made to change data that other transactions have already changed

Read committed transactions will wait if they try to change a row updated by an uncommitted concurrent transaction. The second transaction that tries to update a given row waits for the other transaction to commit or roll back and release its lock on the row. If that other transaction rolls back, the waiting transaction can proceed to change the previously locked row as if the other transaction had not existed.

However, if the other transaction commits and releases its locks, a read committed transaction proceeds with its intended update. Lost updates may therefore occur in read committed mode.

The partial transaction isolation provided by *read committed* mode is adequate for many applications, and this mode is fast and simple to use. However, for applications that do complex queries and updates, it may be necessary to guarantee a more rigorously consistent view of the database than the *read committed* mode provides.

8.8.2 SERIALIZABLE ISOLATION LEVEL

Serializable is Oracle's strictest transaction isolation. This level emulates serial transaction execution, as if transactions had been executed one after another, serially, rather than concurrently. However, applications using this level must be prepared to retry transactions due to serialization failures.

When a transaction is at the serializable level, a query sees only data committed before the transaction began; it never sees either uncommitted data or changes committed by concurrent transactions. (The query does see the effects of previous updates executed within its own transaction, even though they are not yet committed.)

This is different from *read committed* in that the query sees a snapshot as of the start of the transaction, not as of the start of the current query within the transaction. Successive queries within a single transaction always see the same data.

All query verbs, *select*, *update*, *delete* and *select for update*, behave in the same way in terms of searching for target rows: they will only find target rows that were committed as of the transaction start time.

However, such a target row may already have been updated (or deleted or marked for update) by another concurrent transaction by the time it is found. In this case, the serializable transaction will wait for the competing updating transaction either to commit or to roll back (if it is still in progress). If the first updater rolls back, then its effects are negated and the serializable transaction can proceed with updating the originally found row. The update will be consistent with the snapshot taken at the beginning of the transaction.

If the first updater commits (and actually updates or deletes the row) then the serializable transaction will be rolled back because a serializable transaction cannot modify rows changed by other transactions after it began. Such updates would be consistent with the snapshot taken at the start of the transaction, but would be inconsistent with the current committed data.

The transaction can then be restarted after rollback. The second time through, the transaction sees the committed changes from other transactions as part of its initial view of the database, so there is no logical conflict in using the new version of the row as the starting point for the new transaction.

Note that only updating transactions may need to be retried – read-only transactions will never have serialization conflicts.

The *serializable* mode provides a rigorous guarantee that each transaction sees the same wholly consistent view of the database. However, the application has to be prepared to retry transactions when concurrent updates make it impossible to sustain the illusion of serial execution. Most commonly, *serializable* mode is necessary when a transaction performs several successive queries that must see identical views of the database.

8.9 ∈ ORACLE CONCURRENCY AND RECOVERY

Oracle provides data concurrency and integrity between transactions using locking mechanisms. The normal policy adopted by the lock manager is to lock data at the lowest level of restriction that guarantees data integrity while allowing the highest degree of data concurrency.

All locks acquired by statements within a transaction are held for the duration of the transaction, preventing destructive interference (including dirty reads and lost updates) from concurrent transactions. Any changes made by one transaction become visible only to other transactions that start *after* the first transaction is committed and its locks are released.

Oracle does not use read locks. Because of multi-version concurrency control, read operations do not interfere with writes. A simple select query reads unlocked data in the database and uses the rollback segment to discover the previous values of locked, updated rows.

DML operations (*select for update*, *insert*, *update* and *delete*), which lead to write operations, acquire data locks at two different levels: for specific rows and for entire tables.

8.9.1 ORACLE ROW LOCKS

A transaction containing write operations will acquire exclusive row-level locks. The transaction must acquire each lock just prior to updating the row. If it cannot acquire the lock, it enters a wait state. There is no limit to the number of row locks held by a statement or transaction. Row locking provides the finest grain locking possible and thus the best possible concurrency and throughput.

The combination of multi-version concurrency control and row-level locking means that users contend for data only when attempting write access to the same rows.

A modified row is always locked exclusively so that other users cannot modify the row until the transaction holding the lock is committed or rolled back. If a transaction obtains a row lock for a row, the transaction also acquires a non-exclusive table lock for the corresponding table.

8.9.2 ORACLE TABLE LOCKS

A transaction acquires a table lock whenever a row lock in that table is acquired. This is necessary to reserve DML access to the table on behalf of the transaction and to prevent DDL operations that would conflict with the transaction.

A table lock will be automatically requested and acquired by DML statements and will be one of two types: row share (RS) or row exclusive (RX). Other modes are available for manual programming using the *lock table* command.

A row share table lock (RS) acquired by a *select for update* statement indicates that it holds row locks (TX) in the table preparatory to updating, but the updates will be performed by a subsequent statement in the same transaction. When the subsequent statement begins it will use the already acquired TX locks and the table lock is converted to a row exclusive table lock A row share table lock held by a transaction prevents other transactions, such as those containing DDL statements, from acquiring exclusive write access to the whole table.

A row exclusive table lock (RX) generally indicates that the transaction holding the lock is holding TX locks for one or more updates to rows in the table. These probably result from *inserts, updates* or *deletes*. A row exclusive table lock prevents more types of whole table locks being acquired by DDL transactions.

An RX lock held by a transaction allows other transactions to acquire an RX lock in order to insert, update, delete or lock rows concurrently in the same table. The TX locks resolve any conflicting row writes. Clearly, only one transaction at a time can hold a TX lock on a single row.

Select queries are least likely to interfere with other SQL statements because they only read data. *Insert, update* and *delete* statements can have implicit queries as part of the statement.

A *select* query acquires no data locks. Other transactions can update a table being queried by a *select* statement, including the specific rows being queried. Such queries are often referred to as non-blocking queries. A query does not have to wait for any data locks to be released; it can always proceed.

Implicit queries in *update, insert* or *delete* statements usually return an intermediate relation consisting of *ROWID*s to be updated, copied as inserts or deleted. Only when the statement starts its write phase does it start to acquire TX and RX locks.

8.9.3 DEADLOCK IN ORACLE

Lock escalation sometimes occurs when numerous locks are held at one level of granularity (rows) and a database raises the locks to a higher level of granularity (page or table). If a single user locks many rows in a table, some database products will automatically escalate the user's row locks to a single table lock. The number of locks is reduced, but the restrictiveness of what is being locked is increased.

Oracle has no mechanism to escalate locks. Lock escalation greatly increases the likelihood of deadlocks. Oracle automatically detects deadlock situations and resolves them by rolling back one of the statements involved in the deadlock, thereby releasing one set of the conflicting row locks. This introduction of pre-emption destroys the basis for the deadlock continuing.

Multi-table deadlocks can usually be avoided if transactions accessing the same tables lock those tables in the same order, either through implicit or explicit locks. For example, all application developers might follow the rule that when both a master and detail table are updated, the master table is locked first and then the detail table. If such rules are properly designed and then followed in all applications, deadlocks are very unlikely to occur.

8.9.4 ORACLE LOGS AND LOGGING

Oracle keeps its transaction log in a **rollback segment**. The old values of updated rows are written in the log, identified by a transaction identifier, pending a commit or rollback. The updated values are written straight to the database.

When a row is updated or deleted during a transaction, data blocks in the user tablespace and in the rollback segment are changed. Oracle records all changes to data blocks, including rollback entries, in the **redo log**. The redo log is essentially a journal mechanism.

This second recording of the rollback information is very important for active transactions (not yet committed or rolled back) at the time of a system crash. If a system crash occurs, Oracle automatically restores the rollback segment information, including the rollback entries for active transactions, as part of instance or media recovery. Once the recovery is complete, Oracle performs the actual rollbacks of transactions that had been neither committed nor rolled back at the time of the system crash.

Redo entries record data that can be used to reconstruct all changes made to the database, including the rollback segments. The online redo log also protects rollback data. When the database is recovered using redo data, Oracle reads the change vectors in the redo records and applies the changes to the relevant rollback segment or data tablespace.

8.10 ⊂ KEY TERMS

Transactions	A unit of work in a database
Atomicity	Either the whole transaction commits or the whole transaction rolls back
Consistency	Transaction moves the database from one consistent state to another consistent state
Isolation	Transactions proceed through serializable schedules. Conflict is managed by concurrency control. Locking: pessimistic. Timestamping: optimistic

Durability	Committed updates are guaranteed to be saved to the database
Locking	Mechanism for mutual exclusion based on lock conflict matrix
Deadlock	Caused by: mutual exclusion; non pre-emption; wait-for states; circular wait-for. Oracle resolves deadlock by pre-emptive rollback
Recovery	Mechanisms to protect the transaction integrity in case of failure
Logs	Deferred or immediate update strategies; Logs protect durability of transactions and may be used to enable transactions to re-read their own updates or to allow other transactions to read original pre-updated values
Journals	Records all data updates and log entries. May be used to restore database or log from a previously saved version
SQL:1999 transactions	Relaxed conditions for transaction isolation. More throughput may mean inconsistencies. Oracle uses read consistent and serializable levels

8.11 ⋲ QUESTIONS

(i) Describe in detail, giving examples, the kinds of events that a transaction manager is meant to prevent.

(ii) Show in each case which property or properties of a transaction offer a specific remedy.

(iii) Explain the necessary conditions for deadlock. Illustrate what methods can be used to resolve deadlock and what condition they eliminate.

(iv) Explain why it is that optimistic concurrency control methods, which might offer better throughput statistics, are not more used by database vendors.

8.12 ⋲ EXERCISES

(i) Research the Oracle concurrency control system and write brief notes on all the types of locks at its disposal.

(ii) The aim of a transaction management system is to provide data safety while not over-burdening the server and compromising performance. Starting with the material in this chapter and researching reliable sources on the Internet, write a short report, evaluating Oracle against other vendors in this regard.

CHAPTER 9

FURTHER SQL

Science means simply the aggregate of all the recipes that are always successful;
the rest is literature.

Paul Valéry, *Moralités*

9.1 ⊂ AGGREGATE FUNCTIONS

Up until now, retrievals have been concerned with information exactly as it was entered into the database. Often, elements of this data have been chosen for the selection set through restrictions and projections (via SQL *select* statements). However, the selection set has always been a subset of the tuples held in the relation.

There are, however, a set of problems for which such a strategy is inappropriate. For example, if it is necessary to know how many players play for each Liga Utopia club the method of selection is limited to the SQL statement in Figure 9.1. This results in an ordered list, with duplicates, of clubs. To answer the question asked, a manual count of each repetition of each club has to be carried out. This is hardly a convenient solution.

At this juncture, SQL needs to move beyond the confines of the relational algebra and allow for the aggregation (summarization) of tuples. This is achieved using the *group by* clause in the select statement (Figure 9.2).

In essence, the *group by* clause is instructing the DBMS to produce a single summary tuple for each set of players that play for a particular club. In this example, only one tuple is produced per club, regardless of how many players play for that club. This still does not answer the question. To find out how many players play for each club, aggregate rows produced by the *group by* clause need to be queried with what is known as an **aggregate function**.

```
select club
from players
order by club;

CLUB
-------------------------------
Beauty United
Beauty United
Beauty United
Beauty United
Beauty United
Beauty United
Beauty United
Beauty United
Beauty United
Beauty United
Beauty United
Purity FC
Purity FC
Purity FC
...
```

Figure 9.1 Making the data count.

```
select club
from contracts
group by club;

CLUB
----------------
Beauty United
Purity FC

2 rows selected.
```

Figure 9.2 *Group by.*

There are a number of such functions specified in SQL. Some of the most commonly used *aggregate functions* are listed in Table 9.1.

Figure 9.3 shows the **count** function in use. Like each of the other aggregate functions, *count* performs a calculation on an attribute(s) of the underlying tuples for

Table 9.1 Built-in aggregate functions.	
Count (attribute)	Counts the number of occurrences of the named attribute in the underlying tuples associated with each aggregate row
Avg (attribute)	Calculates the average value of the named, numeric, attribute in the underlying tuples associated with each aggregate row
Max (attribute)	Calculates the maximum value of the named, numeric, attribute in the underlying tuples associated with each aggregate row
Min (attribute)	Calculates the minimum value of the named, numeric, attribute in the underlying tuples associated with each aggregate row
Sum (attribute)	Calculates the sum of the named, numeric, attribute in the underlying tuples associated with each aggregate row

```
select club, count (*)
from contracts
group by club
order by club;


CLUB                         COUNT(*)
------------------------    ----------
Beauty United                   11
Purity FC                       11

2 rows selected.
```

Figure 9.3 Counting players.

each aggregated row. In this example, the use of a specific attribute is spurious – the use of any attribute, or all attributes (*), will result in the same count. The other functions in Table 9.1 are not so forgiving and require a numeric attribute to be specified as the basis of their calculation.

The *group by* clause in the Figure 9.3 statement means that, as before, only two rows will be returned by the query. The *count* function meanwhile has kept a tally of how many underlying tuples have contributed to each aggregated row in the final output.

Each of the common functions can be included in the selection set to calculate not only the number of players associated with each club, but also the club's total salary bill for their players, as well as the average, minimum and maximum salaries for such players (Figure 9.4).

It should be noted, somewhat counter-intuitively, that each of these aggregate functions could be used across a set of non-aggregated tuples! The total number of players in the league, their total salary bill and the average, minimum, and

```
select club, count (*), sum (salary), avg (salary), min (salary),
max (salary)
from contracts
group by club;

CLUB          COUNT(*) SUM(SALARY) AVG(SALARY) MIN(SALARY) MAX(SALARY)
---------    --------- ----------- ----------- ----------- -----------
Beauty United    11    9973000      906636.36    365000     2300000
Purity FC        11    14331000     1302818.18   375000     3670000

2 rows selected.
```

Figure 9.4 Counting the cost I.

```
select count (*), sum (salary), avg (salary), min (salary),
max (salary)
from contracts
where left is null;

COUNT(*)   SUM(SALARY) AVG(SALARY)  MIN(SALARY)   MAX(SALARY)
------------------------------------------------------------
22          24304000    1104727.27     365000       3670000

1 row selected.
```

Figure 9.5 Counting the cost II.

maximum salaries for all players, would be produced via the statement in Figure 9.5.

This is because once an aggregate function has been used on the *select* line, an implicit aggregation of all of the selected tuples into a 'single group' row will occur. *Only* aggregate functions are allowed in the selection set of such a statement. Any non-aggregated attributes in the selection set *must* appear in a *group by* clause. The statement in Figure 9.6 therefore results in an error.

Aggregate functions can be nested in the selection set as in Figure 9.7. Care must be taken to ensure that the query evaluates to a single group only for the outermost function.

Without a *group by* clause, the *max* function performs an implicit aggregation across the whole table, leaving nothing for the *count* function to aggregate.

```
select club, count(*)
from players;

select club, count(*)
      *
ERROR at line 1:
ORA-00937: not a single-group group function
```

Figure 9.6 Ouch!

```
Select count(max(salary))
From contracts;

ERROR at line 1:
ORA-00978: nested group function without GROUP BY
```

Figure 9.7 Ouch! again.

Inserting the *group by* clause in Figure 9.8 means that the *max* function will return two aggregated rows, one for each club, leaving the *count* function to return a single value aggregated across the whole table. Because only one *group by* is allowed within a query, this is the maximum level of function nesting permitted. Any further analysis must be done with a sub-query, as in Figure 9.9.

Here the selection domain is itself an aggregated sub-query that returns eight rows (there are four position values for each club). Each row consists of the club

```
select count(max(salary))
from players, contracts
where contracts.ufa_id=players.ufa_id
and left is null
group by players.club;
COUNT(MAX(SALARY))
------------------
2
1 row selected.
```

Figure 9.8 Nested aggregates.

```
select count(max(salary))
from (
  select players.club, avg(salary) as salary from players, contracts
  where contracts.ufa_id=players.ufa_id
  and left is null
  group by players.club, position)
group by club;
```

Figure 9.9 *Group* in a sub-query.

name and an average salary for each position type. These rows are then aggregated into two rows by the *max* function grouped by club and finally counted. When using a sub-query it is important to match return column names and types with the main query's usage.

9.2 ⊆ HAVING

It is possible to use a *where* clause as well as a *group by* clause in a single *select* statement. However, the *where* clause operates as a restriction on the base tuples, *not* on the aggregated rows produced by the *group by* clause. For instance, the SQL statement in Figure 9.10 generates an error.

```
select club, count(*)
from contracts
group by club
where salary > 500000;

where salary > 500000
*
ERROR at line 4:
ORA-00933: SQL command not properly ended
```

Figure 9.10 *Where* before *group* please.

This is because the DBMS is attempting to issue a restriction against an aggregated attribute that does not exist! To successfully use a *where* clause in an aggregation, it has to appear **before** the *group by* clause in the *select* statement (Figure 9.11).

What if it is necessary to place a restriction on the aggregated attribute? For example, if only those clubs with 10 or more players each earning more than €500,000 were required, a first attempt at restricting the *count(*)* attribute might look like Figure 9.12.

```
select club, count (*)
from contracts
where salary > 500000
group by club;

CLUB                          COUNT(*)
------------------------------------
Beauty United                        8
Purity FC                           10

2 rows selected.
```

Figure 9.11 Thank you.

```
select club, count(*)
from contracts
where salary>500000
group by club
where count(*) > 9;

where count(*) > 9
*
ERROR at line 5:
ORA-00933: SQL command not properly ended
```

Figure 9.12 Only one *where* please.

```
select club, count (*)
from contracts
where salary>500000
and left is null
group by club
having count (*) > 9;

CLUB                          COUNT(*)
------------------------- ----------
Purity FC                           10

1 row selected.
```

Figure 9.13 Counting the haves and the have nots.

```
select club, count(*)
from contracts
where salary > 500000
group by club, salary
having salary<avg(salary);

no rows selected
```

Figure 9.14 All the players are average.

The problem with this syntax is that there are two *where* clauses in the same statement: one for the base tuples and one for the aggregated rows. This would be both difficult to interpret and easy to get wrong! In any event, the Oracle syntax checker will refuse to allow this query.

The solution is the introduction of the **having** clause to act as an alias for the aggregate *where* clause.

This new clause allows both base and aggregate restrictions in the same SQL statement. The statement in Figure 9.13 will exclude players with a salary of less

```
select club, salary, count (*), avg (salary)
from contracts
where salary > 500000
group by club, salary;

CLUB                        SALARY   COUNT(*) AVG(SALARY)
------------------------- ---------- ---------- -----------
Purity FC                   750000        2       750000
Purity FC                   527000        1       527000
Purity FC                   574000        1       574000
Purity FC                   835000        1       835000
Purity FC                  1250000        1      1250000
Purity FC                  1450000        1      1450000
Purity FC                  1650000        1      1650000
Purity FC                  2500000        1      2500000
Purity FC                  3670000        1      3670000
Beauty United               650000        1       650000
Beauty United               750000        1       750000
Beauty United               548000        1       548000
Beauty United               625000        1       625000
...
```

Figure 9.15 Each group has an average.

than €500,000 from being aggregated into the count for their club. Further, once aggregation has taken place, any club with fewer than ten well-paid players is restricted from appearing in the final output.

Some care in formulating queries is still needed and an appreciation of how the query is implemented assists in this. The query in Figure 9.14 is syntactically correct but yields no rows. The aim was to count those players who earn more than €500,000 euros but less for the average salary for their club. Some players fit into this category, but the query is not finding them. Why?

The answer is in the *group by* clause. The base rows are being grouped on *salary* so that *salary* can appear in the *having* clause. This satisfies a first-level syntax rule: all base attributes must be grouped in an aggregate query.

The *avg(salary)* aggregate is therefore being calculated for each set of players in the same club *and* with the same salary. Since no one earns more than the average in such circumstances, the query returns no rows.

The *having* clause is applied only when the preceding parts of the statement have produced an intermediate relation. If the first part of the query is applied separately, then Figure 9.15 shows that 18 players have salaries over €500000. Two, who play for Purity FC, have been grouped on salary to give an average of their identical

```
select a.club, salary, average, count (*)
from contracts a, (select club, avg (salary) as average from contracts
 group by club) b
where a.club=b.club
and salary > 500000
group by a.club, salary, average
having salary<average;


CLUB                            SALARY    AVERAGE   COUNT(*)
------------------------------  --------  --------  --------
Purity FC                        750000 1302818.18         2
Purity FC                        527000 1302818.18         1
Purity FC                        574000 1302818.18         1
Purity FC                        835000 1302818.18         1
Purity FC                       1250000 1302818.18         1
Beauty United                    650000 906636.364         1
Beauty United                    750000 906636.364         1
Beauty United                    548000 906636.364         1
Beauty United                    625000 906636.364         1
Beauty United                    825000 906636.364         1

10 rows selected.
```

Figure 9.16 Some players are below average.

```
explain plan for
select a.club, salary, average, count (*)
from contracts a, (select club, avg (salary) as average from
contracts group by club) b
where a.club=b.club
and salary > 500000
group by a.club ,salary, average
having salary<average;

@utlxpls

plan _table OUTPUT
-----------------------------------------------------------------------
| Id  | Operation               | Name     | Rows | Bytes | Cost |
-----------------------------------------------------------------------
|   0 | SELECT STATEMENT        |          |    2 |    58 |    9 |
|*  1 |  FILTER                 |          |      |       |      |
|   2 |   SORT GROUP BY         |          |    2 |    58 |    9 |
|   3 |    VIEW                 |          |   36 |  1044 |    7 |
|   4 |     SORT GROUP BY       |          |   36 |  1260 |    7 |
|*  5 |      HASH JOIN          |          |  232 |  8120 |    5 |
|*  6 |       TABLE ACCESS FULL | CONTRACTS|   21 |   441 |    2 |
|   7 |       TABLE ACCESS FULL | CONTRACTS|   22 |   308 |    2 |
-----------------------------------------------------------------------
Predicate Information (identified by operation id):

   1 - filter ("$vm_view "."SALARY"<"$vm_view"."AVERAGE")
   5 - access("A"."CLUB"="B"."CLUB")
   6 - filter ("A"."SALARY">500000)
```

Figure 9.17 Under the hood.

salaries of €750000. In all cases, because of the grouping the player's salary is equal to the average salary of that group. Notice that the *count(*)* aggregate is similarly counting only players with the same salary who play for the same club.

When the *having* clause is applied to this intermediate relation, not unsurprisingly, it yields no rows.

The answer, as with many problems in computing, is to divide the query into its component parts. First, find the average salary for each club in a sub-query and, using roles, join that intermediate relation with the full *contracts* relation and perform the restricted count

Figure 9.16 shows the result for this strategy. The contracts relation has role *a* and the intermediate result of the sub-query has role *b*. This intermediate relation

```
select club, sum (countstar)
from
(select a.club, salary, average, count (*) as countstar
from contracts a, (select club, avg (salary) as average from
contracts group by club) b
where a.club=b.club
and salary > 500000
group by a.club ,salary, average
having salary<average)
group by club;


CLUB                          SUM(COUNTSTAR)
------------------------- -------------
Beauty United                            5
Purity FC                                6

2 rows selected.
```

Figure 9.18 Who's got the most below average players?

is itself the result of an aggregation and has two columns: *club* and *average*(an alias for *avg(salary)*.

A join between *a* (restricted on *salary>500000*) and *b*, predicated on equality of the *club* attribute, yields a further intermediate relation. This is then aggregated in the *group by* clause and further restricted in the *having* clause. These operations can clearly be seen (reading upwards) in the explain plan output for this query shown in Figure 9.17.

However, the original question has not been fully answered. The query in Figure 9.16 needs further summarization to yield a report similar to that in Figure 9.11. In Figure 9.18, the query from Figure 9.16 has been embedded in another query. The *count(*)* has been aliased and the new encapsulating query is now using the result of the previous statement as an intermediate relation in its selection domain.

9.3 SQL 3 (SQL:1999)

Ever since its standardization by the American National Standards Institute (ANSI) in 1986, and its adoption as an international standard by the International Organization for Standardization (ISO) in 1987, SQL has continued to evolve as a database language.

This evolution has taken the form of named, standardized, formal revisions of the language. The first of these was SQL89 (released in 1989), which introduced, among other minor changes, the concept of declared integrity constraints. It is this version of SQL that is often mistakenly referred to as SQL1.

The next revision of the SQL standard was released in 1992 and is formally known as SQL92, more commonly referred to as SQL2. This was a major update to the standard, adding some 600 pages to the formal specification. These additions included enhanced schema manipulation and dynamic creation and execution of SQL statements, as well as network environment features for connection and session management. It is this version of SQL that is invariably referred to as *standard SQL* and which has, to different degrees, been implemented by the major relational database vendors.

It is important to note that each release of the specification has had as one of its major goals complete upward compatibility with all previous releases of the standard. For example, a database application developed using an SQL89-based product should still function correctly if transferred to an SQL92-based environment.

The current release of SQL is formally referred to as SQL:1999. It is more commonly referred to as SQL3. This is by far the most major revision, not only of the language, but also of the underlying data model upon which the language is based. This is reflected in the fact that SQL3 was in development for the best part of a decade prior to its official release as SQL:1999, and development of parts of its

Table 9.2 SQL:1999.

Part	Title	Published
1	Framework	1999, 2002
2	Foundation	1986, 1989, 1992, 1999, 2002
3	Call-Level Interface (CLI)	1995, 1999, 2002
4	Persistent Stored Modules (PSM)	1996, 1999, 2002
5	Host Language Bindings	1992, 1999, withdrawn in 2002
6	(unused part number)	
7	Temporal	–
8	(unused part number)	
9	Management of External Data (MED)	2000/2001, 2002
10	Object Language Bindings (OLB) (embedded SQL for Java)	2000, 2002
11	Schemata	2002
12	Replication	–
13	Java routines and types	–
14	XML	–

Table 9.3 SQL:1999 Foundation.

1. Data definition and manipulation	New built-in data types User-defined data types Create table ... like ... Sensitive cursors, with hold cursors
2. Functions and operators	User-defined routines Recursive table expressions Enhanced view updatability New quantifiers *similar* condition *distinct* condition Cross tabulation (*rollup*, *cube*)
3. Object support	Table definitions based on structured types Sub-tables (single inheritance) System-generated keys (object reference values, or OIDs) via ref data types Dereferencing operators
4. Integrity	Referential action restrict Trigger
5. Security	User-defined 'roles' Column-specific select privileges
6. Transactions	Transaction savepoints

Table 9.4 SQL3 core.

Basic Object Support

Enhanced Object Support

OLAP facilities (CUBE etc.)

Active database support (triggers)

Enhanced datetime facilities

Enhanced integrity management

PSM

CLI

original specification has been postponed until a future release of the standard (Table 9.2).

The reason for the delay lies in the fact that SQL:1999 has transformed SQL from a relational data language into an object relational data language applied to an object relational data model. The principal sections of the SQL:1999 Foundation, sometimes known as Core SQL:1999, are shown in Table 9.3. The full document, in

PDF form, can be obtained from the American National Standards Institute (ANSI)[1].

Most major vendors claim compliance with the SQL3 Core (Table 9.4). This group underpins relational database interoperability; the object technology offers the advantage of a standard in the face of competition from object database vendors, as does the OLAP section with respect to proprietary multi-dimensional database vendors.

9.4 ⊨ VIEWS

SQL views are the logical external realizations of a database's schema from the perspective of an end-user.

A good relational database implementation will usually be normalized to at least BCNF. However, although this reduces data inconsistencies, it does so at the cost of increased DML complexity. Normalization generally replaces a small number of large tables with a large number of small tables. Therefore, SQL data extraction and modification of normalized tables is complicated by the common necessity to join small tables together in order to retrieve data with some inherent relationship.

An SQL view enables the construction of a virtual table that emulates the structure of an un-normalized table. This may be done in order to simplify query access, without breaking the underlying relational schema upon which it is based.

As SQL views are logical abstractions on top of a relational schema, they are most often used to limit the *view* of the underlying schema to that deemed appropriate for each set of end-users. Rather than allow access to the complete *Players* table, only the *player_v* view of it, described in Figure 9.19, would be accessible to Beauty United's management. Such restrictions on access need to be enforced through the setting of explicit security groups, with associated access rights, for each set of users.

The single table view of Figure 9.19 provides a logical subset of the *Players* SQL table that only contains the row details of those currently playing for Beauty United. Figure 9.20 shows the result of selecting all elements of this SQL view.

Figure 9.21 shows a logical view constructed over the join of two fully normalized relational tables: *Players* and *Contracts*. Again, this example view is limited to those players currently playing for Beauty United.

In the example above it is necessary to view only the current contract details of each Beauty United player. Therefore, the predicate *contracts.left IS NULL* has to evaluate to true, i.e. the contract is currently open-ended. As there is a 1:*M* relationship between *Players* and *Contracts*, without this restriction there would be a separate view-row created for each past contract (regardless of club) that exists for each current Beauty United player. This would result in the mistaken creation of

---

1 http://www.ansi.org/

```
CREATE OR REPLACE VIEW player_v
AS
  SELECT *
  FROM Players P
  WHERE P.club = 'Beauty United';
```

Figure 9.19 Creating a single table view.

```
SELECT * FROM player_v;

UFA_ID    SURNAME     FNAME    DOB       NO  POSITION    NATION     CLUB
--------  ----------  -------  --------  --  ----------  ---------  -------------
AT245876  HEGEL       BRIAN    22-MAR-84 27  midfield    UTOPIA     Beauty United
BT46286   MORE        MARC     04-FEB-80 16  defender    ELDORADO   Beauty United
ED24659   SOCRATES    VICTOR   12-JUL-80 12  midfield    LILLIPUT   Beauty United
FT246517  GREGORY     ALAN     02-JUL-76 9   forward     UTOPIA     Beauty United
KL23659   PAUL        CHARLES  12-MAY-81 8   midfield    WONDERLAND Beauty United
QT873456  KANT        EDWARD   03-NOV-83 4   defender    UTOPIA     Beauty United
SC159647  THACKERAY   RAMESH   01-APR-84 2   goalkeeper  VALHALLA   Beauty United
TY48429   PLATO       WINSTON  30-DEC-79 7   forward     ELDORADO   Beauty United
UT23685   CONSTANTINE GEORGE   02-MAY-85 5   defender    UTOPIA     Beauty United
UT236965  DICKENS     HENRY    23-AUG-80 6   midfield    UTOPIA     Beauty United
VT432167  DIOCLETIAN  PIERRE   15-JUN-78 11  forward     VALHALLA   Beauty United

11 rows selected.
```

Figure 9.20 Querying a single table view.

```
CREATE OR REPLACE VIEW players_v
AS
SELECT P.ufa_id, P.surname, P.forename, P.dateofbirth, P.squad_no,
 P.position, P.nationality, P.club, C.joined, C.left, C.salary
  FROM Players P, Contracts C
  WHERE P.ufa_id = C.ufa_id
  AND P.club = 'Beauty United'
  AND C.left IS NULL;
```

Figure 9.21 Creating a joined table view.

multiple rows of information for a single player. Figure 9.22 shows the result of selecting player details from such a syntactically correct but logically incorrect view.

Views are, under certain conditions, updatable as well as selectable. In effect, the end-user updates the logical view, and the database server updates the appropriate underlying table. Figure 9.23 shows the result of an update operation on the SQL view, *players_v*, of Figure 9.21. As can be seen, only the relevant row of the *Contracts* table has had its salary attribute altered by the update operation.

A potential problem with an updatable SQL view is that an attribute used in the view's defining expression could itself be updated. The updated row(s) may then no longer satisfy the view's definition and would therefore be *dropped* from the view. Figure 9.24 shows an example of this *row migration*. To avoid this situation a *with check option* clause can be used in a view definition.

```
CREATE OR REPLACE VIEW players_v
AS
SELECT P.ufa_id, P.surname, P.forename, P.dateofbirth, P.squad_no,
  P.position, P.nationality, P.club, C.joined, C.left, C.salary
  FROM Players P, Contracts C
  WHERE P.ufa_id = C.ufa_id
  AND P.club = 'Beauty United';

SELECT ufa_id, surname, forename, joined, salary
FROM players_v;

UFA_ID     SURNAME      FORENAME     JOINED      LEFT      SALARY
---------  -----------  -----------  ---------   -------   --------
AT245876   HEGEL        BRIAN        24-OCT-99             450000
BT46286    MORE         MARC         10-MAY-98             625000
ED24659    SOCRATES     VICTOR       06-APR-00             375000
FT246517   GREGORY      ALAN         02-AUG-99             985000
KL23659    PAUL         CHARLES      05-JUN-97             365000
QT873456   KANT         EDWARD       19-DEC-02             750000
SC159647   THACKERAY    RAMESH       05-OCT-02             2100000
TY48429    PLATO        WINSTON      03-FEB-02             2300000
UT23685    CONSTANTINE  GEORGE       09-MAR-96             8250000
UT236965   DICKENS      HENRY        13-SEP-98             548000
VT432167   DIOCLETIAN   PIERRE       01-AUG-03             650000
VT432167   DIOCLETIAN   PIERRE       01-AUG-01   31-JUL-02 200000
VT432167   DIOCLETIAN   PIERRE       01-AUG-99   31-JUL-01 50000

13 rows selected.
```

Figure 9.22 Incorrect SQL gives incorrect view.

```
UPDATE players_v
SET salary = salary*1.1
WHERE ufa_id = 'VT432167';


1 row updated.


SELECT ufa_id, surname, forename, joined, salary
FROM players_v
WHERE ufa_id = 'VT432167';


UFA_ID      SURNAME      FORENAME      JOINED        SALARY
---------   -----------  ------------  ---------     --------
VT432167    DIOCLETIAN   PIERRE        01-AUG-03     715000


1 row selected.


SELECT * FROM Contracts
WHERE ufa_id = 'VT432167';


UFA_ID      CLUB                        JOINED      LEFT        SALARY
----------  --------------------------  ---------   ---------   ----------
VT432167    Beauty United               01-AUG-03               715000
VT432167    Purity FC                   01-AUG-01 31-JUL-02     200000
VT432167    Beauty United               01-AUG-99 31-JUL-01      50000


3 rows selected.
```

Figure 9.23 Updating a joined table view.

Figure 9.25 shows an example of the *check option* in operation. This optional clause restricts view updates to prevent the removal of a row from the view that has not been removed from the view's base table(s). The clause therefore acts as an additional data integrity, and security, guarantee.

In order for a view to allow updatable operations, it cannot be based on a *select* statement that contains any of the following:

- *SET* operations
- *DISTINCT* operators
- aggregate or analytical functions
- grouping or sorting operations
- collection or sub-query selection expressions

```
CREATE OR REPLACE VIEW player_v
AS
   SELECT *
   FROM Players P
   WHERE P.club = 'Beauty United';

UPDATE player_v
SET club = 'Purity FC';

11 rows updated.

SELECT * FROM players_v;

no rows selected
```

Figure 9.24 Row migration.

```
CREATE OR REPLACE VIEW player_v
AS
   SELECT *
   FROM Players P
   WHERE P.club = 'Beauty United'
WITH CHECK OPTION;

UPDATE player_v
SET club = 'Purity FC';

UPDATE player_v
          *

ERROR at line 1:
ORA-01402: view WITH CHECK OPTION where-clause violation
```

Figure 9.25 Check option in operation.

Joined-table views are further update-restricted to only those operations that affect a single, *key-preserved*, base table.

A base table of a view is *key-preserved* if a row in the base table can only relate to a single corresponding row in the view. In such a situation, a change to a row in the view would result in an appropriate change to a single row in the base table. If a base table were not *key-preserved*, and multi-row updates were allowed via the view, data inconsistencies could occur.

In the joined-table view of Figure 9.21, the relationship between the two base tables, *Players* and *Contracts*, is 1:M: each player could have many contracts over a period of time, even though logically only one of those contracts could ever be current. However, as the primary key of the *Contracts* table is a composite of *ufa_id* and *joined*, such a logical restriction is not enforced and, it is therefore technically feasible to have more than one current contract for any particular player. This implies that a change to a single row of the *Players* base table cannot be guaranteed to affect only a single row in the *players_v* view.

Conversely, a change to the values of a *Player's* attributes within a single row of the view should not be allowed as there could be an indirect relationship with other view rows based on the same underlying base row, and inconsistency would result if only one of those related view rows was altered. For example, it would be perfectly possible to insert the two rows of Figure 9.26 into the *Contracts* table.

UFA_ID	CLUB	JOINED	LEFT	SALARY
VT432167	Beauty United	01-AUG-99	NULL	50000
VT432167	Beauty United	01-AUG-03	NULL	650000

Figure 9.26 Multiple open contracts.

This would result in the two rows of Figure 9.27 being *logically inserted* into the *players_v* view of Figure 9.21. However, both of these view rows would relate to a single row in the *Players* table.

```
select ufa_id, surname dob, club joined, left salary
from players_v
where ufa_id='VT432167';
```

UFA_ID	SURNAME	DOB	CLUB	JOINED	LEFT	SALARY
VT432167	DIOCLETIAN	15-JUN-78	Beauty United	**01-AUG-03**	**NULL**	**650000**
VT432167	DIOCLETIAN	15-JUN-78	Beauty United	**01-AUG-99**	**NULL**	**50000**

Figure 9.27 Joined table view (1:M join).

If any attempt were then made to update a *Players*-based attribute of either of those two view rows, the single underlying *Players* row would be altered accordingly, but would then be inconsistent with the remaining unaltered view row.

In order to guarantee that such inconsistencies are prevented, only the table on the *child* (weak) side of a 1:*M* joined-table view is deemed to be *key-preserved*. Updates to any attributes of the *parent* table of such a join-table view are always disallowed. Figure 9.28 documents an attempt to perform such an *illegal* update.

```
UPDATE players_v SET squad_no = 14
WHERE ufa_id = 'ED24659';

SET squad_no = 14
    *
ERROR at line 2:
ORA-01779: cannot modify a column which maps to a non key-preserved
table
```

Figure 9.28 Illegal view update.

In order to determine quickly which attributes of a view are updatable, Oracle provides *sys.user_updatable _columns*, a joined-table view in the data dictionary that contains the details of which attributes of any view are updatable. Figure 9.29

```
SELECT column_name, updatable
FROM USER_UPDATABLE_COLUMNS
WHERE table_name = 'PLAYERS_V';

COLUMN_NAME                        UPDATABLE
------------------------------     ---
UFA_ID                             NO
SURNAME                            NO
FORENAME                           NO
DATEOFBIRTH                        NO
SQUAD_NO                           NO
POSITION                           NO
NATIONALITY                        NO
CLUB                               NO
JOINED                             YES
LEFT                               YES
SALARY                             YES

11 rows selected.
```

Figure 9.29 Updatable view columns.

shows the corrected query and the result of querying the *players_v* view of Figure 9.21.

For view columns that are not directly updatable, Oracle provides *instead of* triggers that perform a user-defined procedure in place of an intercepted DML operation. Such procedures usually update the view's relevant underlying base table(s). Section 13.5.1 describes, and gives examples of, these PL/SQL triggers.

9.5 ⊏ KEY TERMS

Aggregations	Summarization of base tuples with an aggregation function: *count, sum, avg, min* and *max* are the simple examples
Group by	Aggregations need a *group by* clause to indicate the range of summary
Having	The *having* clause restricts values from the aggregation
SQL:1999	ANSI/ISO standard for SQL; most importantly, introduced object relational model. Vendors aim for conformance to Core standard as a minimum
Views	Virtual table created from restriction and/or join on base tables. Used for security purposes or to simplify queries
View updates	Updates are generally allowed to a single table view. Join view updates allowed to key preserved (weak) base tables

9.6 ⊏ QUESTIONS

Write SQL join queries to answer the following questions:

- **(i)** List the surnames of players with at least one disciplinary hearing.
- **(ii)** Who was the last player to have a disciplinary hearing?
- **(iii)** Who was the first?
- **(iv)** Who was the last player to join Beauty United?
- **(v)** Who has the longest continuous service with Beauty United
- **(vi)** Who has spent the most time playing for Beauty United? (This is not the same thing as having the longest continuous service.)
- **(vii)** What is the goal average per match for Purity FC players?
- **(viii)** Who is above that average and who is below it?

9.7 ⊏ EXERCISE

(i) Create views to support the SQL queries from this chapter. Test the performance of the queries using the tables directly compared with the view queries. Explain plan will reveal the plans, which should give an indication of performance.

CHAPTER 10

SERVER-SIDE PROGRAMMING

You pull the trigger and after that you do not understand anything that happens.

Jean-Paul Sartre, *Dirty Hands*, Act 5, Scene 2

SQL is a declarative language, not procedural or imperative. The art of writing SQL instructions is based on the ability to define clearly what is required, rather than programming a set of instructions to meet such requirements.

```
Select name
From players
Where salary > 1000000;
```

Figure 10.1 Defining a requirement.

The question, *which players earn over €1,000,000,* is translated into an SQL query. This unambiguously states that the requirement is to see the names of all players earning over €1,000,000 (Figure 10.1). At no point is there any attempt to show how these names would be picked from the physical files that make up the database.

In a relational database, it is the role of the query parser and optimizer to translate the defined requirement into the most efficient query plan and to decide the appropriate execution strategy of file access and buffer sorts and merges to provide the answer to such a query. Because the SQL language is based on a formal grammar connected to the relational calculus, it is capable of provably correct machine translation into discrete operations.

As early as the 1930s, Alan Turing proved mathematically that all problems of programming logic and computation could be accommodated by the combination of just three types of statements: sequences, selections and iterations. A computing language that provides these constructs is said to be computationally complete. SQL does not have these elements and is therefore computationally incomplete (Figure 10.2).

```
Print multiples of 5 between 1 and 100

for (x=1;x<=100; x++){                              iteration statement
   if (x mod 5 ==0){                                selection statement
      printf("%d is a multiple of 5", x);}          sequence statement
}
```

Figure 10.2 Statement types.

An SQL query, no matter how complex, provides a single answer to a single question. If a set of questions requires answering, it would be perfectly possible to issue a series of SQL queries, one per question, and record the answer to each. However, if the asking of the second question was dependent on the outcome of the first, the specifics of the third question varied according to the answer to the second, and the fourth question was repeated for each of the items given in the answer to the third, this could not be automated using SQL alone.

In such a situation, each of the questions could be considered as a single instruction, with each instruction being related to other instructions through sequence, selection and iteration operations. In essence, this would result in a set of declarative statements being woven together through a procedural language.

The requirement to bind various queries together through a procedural programming language is a very common one, and various mechanisms have been built to facilitate this. These can be classified as either server-side or client-side programming mechanisms.

The client-side mechanisms can be subdivided into the embedding of SQL statements into programming languages (using SQLJ to embed SQL into Java), or the use of middleware to translate native programming language instructions into SQL instructions (using JDBC to connect a Java program to a relational database. Chapter 12 contains a thorough discussion of client–server models and the use of JDBC.

This chapter concentrates on server-side programming mechanisms that allow for the procedural programming of sets of queries. It is important to note that, in the context of database servers, to run a program server-side implies that it will execute internally within the DBMS itself, rather than just share the DBMS's physical host.

10.1 PL/SQL

The server-side procedural programming mechanism used within Oracle database servers is known as PL/SQL, which stands for Procedural Language extensions to SQL.

Oracle introduced PL/SQL in 1991 as part of Oracle 6.0, and has continued to develop and extend it since. Procedural language extensions to SQL are not unique to Oracle. Microsoft's SQL Server and the Sybase DBMS run a set of procedural extensions known as Transact-SQL. Indeed, SQL:1999 allows for the development of server-side programs through its PSM (Persistent Stored Module) specification. However, PL/SQL is the dominant database procedural language in the market-place, and large sections of the SQL:1999 PSM specification are based upon it.

PL/SQL is a computationally complete procedural programming language. This means that it has constructs for sequence, selection and iteration, it allows for the definition, assignment and manipulation of memory-based variables, and has definable exception (error) handling. Most importantly, PL/SQL allows for the transparent integration of declarative SQL statements within the constructs of a procedural programming language. PL/SQL is also *transaction aware*, and provides the ability to checkpoint, roll back and commit transactions.

The PL/SQL programming language is block structured. This allows for a program to be broken down into logical blocks of code, and for the embedding of inner blocks within an outer block, as shown in Figure 10.3.

A PL/SQL block is subdivided into three sections: declaration, execution and exception (errors and warnings in PL/SQL are called exceptions), of which only the execution section is mandatory. Variables declared within the declaration section of a block are local to that block. For example, a variable declared within an inner block can only be referenced within that block, whereas a variable declared within an outer block could be used in the outer block and within any inner block.

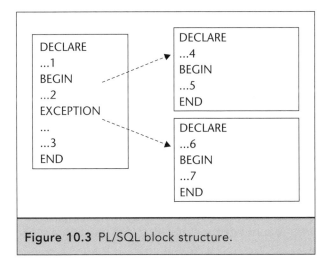

Figure 10.3 PL/SQL block structure.

This allows for the definition, should they be required, of local and global variables. Figure 10.3 shows this block structure. Variables declared in section 1 can be used anywhere in the program. The main execution block (2), contains a nested declaration and execution block as does the main exception block (3). Variables declared in (4) are scoped only for (5) and variables declared in (6) are scoped only for (7).

PL/SQL allows for the creation of five specific programming constructs: *anonymous block*, *stored procedure*, *stored function*, *package* and *trigger*, each of which will be described in this chapter.

Each PL/SQL program has development, compilation, deployment, execution and removal phases. Development consists of the creation of the procedural logic source code; compilation verifies the source code, binds any declared variables, and translates it into suitable executable object code (known as *p-code*); deployment places the executable code in the database (accessible via the data dictionary); execution implements the executable code; and removal expunges the executable code from the database.

An anonymous block is so called because it is a block of code without a permanent identifier, and differs from the other constructs in that it is immediately executed upon successful compilation and therefore does not have separate deployment and removal phases. All other PL/SQL programs have an identifier and, once successfully compiled, are stored in the database awaiting execution, and will remain there until explicitly removed.

In essence, an anonymous block is an encapsulated set of procedural instructions that are compiled for immediate execution. Since it is not stored permanently in the database, the source code is lost at the end of the session that created it. Otherwise, it may be kept in an external text file and loaded into the client tool when needed. In this respect, and, in terms of its compilation and immediate execution, its behaviour and status are equivalent to an SQL batch file or an interactive SQL query.

The PL/SQL compiler and execution component, known as the PL/SQL engine, is integrated within the Oracle database server, as well as in various client-side tools such as Oracle Forms, and Oracle Reports. Its role is to compile and execute the procedural logic statements in the PL/SQL program, and to pass all SQL statements to the SQL query executive, also located within the database server, for action. Figure 10.4 shows the architecture of the PL/SQL engine.

As an illustration of the need for procedural constructs and an example of the development of a PL/SQL program, consider the requirement for Liga Utopia to calculate each club's total points for a particular season. The calculation will involve selecting each match that a club played in that season, determining whether the club won, drew or lost the match, allocating three points for a win and one for a draw, and then adding those points to the season's total for the club. This calculation will then need to be repeated for all other clubs in the league.

Figure 10.5 provides the basic pseudo-code for such a calculation. This involves all three basic programming constructs – sequence, selection and iteration – and is therefore a prime candidate for expressing in a procedural programming language such as PL/SQL.

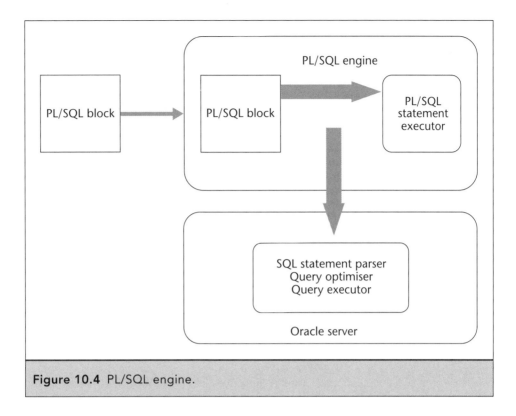

Figure 10.4 PL/SQL engine.

```
Calculate each club's total points

Input season
Fetch club until no more clubs
   Set club-total-points = 0
   Fetch club's matches for season until no more matches
      If club won match
         Add 3 to club-total-points
      Else
      If club drew match
         Add 1 to club-total-points
   Repeat for next match
Repeat for next club
```

Figure 10.5 Pseudo-code.

Figure 10.6 adds further detail to the pseudo-code through the inclusion of specific SQL statements and a set of local variables. This highlights a major inconsistency between the declarative set-based nature of SQL and the procedural record-based approach of PL/SQL.

That discrepancy is known as an *impedance mismatch*, and it is evidenced by the fact that an SQL statement, such as *select name from clubs;* will return an unknown

```
Calculate a club's total points

v_season = input;
LOOP (until no more Clubs)
   Select name from Clubs into v_club;
   v_total_points = 0;
   LOOP (until no more Matches for v_club, for v_season)
      Select match_id from Matches
              where homeclub = v_club or awayclub = v_club
              and season = v_season
      into v_match_id;
      v_goals_for = 0;
      v_goals_against = 0;
      LOOP (until no more Goals for specific match)
         Select Players.club, Goals.type
                 from Goals, Players
                 where Goals.ufa_id = Players.ufa_id
                 and match_id = v_match_id
              into v_players_club, v_goals_type;
         IF (v_club = v_players_club AND
               v_goals_type <> 'own goal')
               OR (v_club <> v_players_club AND
               v_goals_type = 'own goal'
            v_goals_for = v_goals_for + 1
         ELSE
            v_goals_against = v_goals_against + 1;
         END IF
      END LOOP (Goals)
      IF v_goals_for > v_goals_against
         v_total_points = v_total_points + 3
      ELSE IF v_goals_for = v_goals_against
         v_total_points = v_total_points + 1;
      END IF
   END LOOP (Matches)
END LOOP (Clubs)
```

Figure 10.6 Detailed pseudo-code.

number of rows, whereas PL/SQL, like any procedural language, can only work with a single row or record at a time. The *cursor* mechanism handles such a mismatch. This permits a program, having issued a potentially multi-row *select* statement, to examine each row in the returned result on a row-by-row basis.

10.2 ⊂ ANONYMOUS BLOCKS AND CURSORS

To translate the detailed pseudo-code of Figure 10.6 into workable code, it is necessary to define the local variables used in the **declaration section** of a block. The standard syntax for variable declarations is given in Figure 10.7.

```
DECLARE
    variable_name1      Oracle data type;
    variable_name2      Oracle data type;
    ...
    variable_nameN      Oracle data type;
```

Figure 10.7 Declaring PL/SQL variables I.

In the case of the pseudo-code of Figure 10.6, the variable declarations would be as shown in Figure 10.8.

```
DECLARE
    v_season           VARCHAR2(8);
    v_club             VARCHAR2(25);
    v_total_points     NUMBER(3);
    v_match_id         NUMBER;
    v_goals_for        NUMBER(2);
    v_goals_against    NUMBER(2);
    v_players_club     VARCHAR2(25);
    v_goals_type       VARCHAR2(10);
```

Figure 10.8 Declaring PL/SQL variables II.

However, certain of the variables defined in Figure 10.8 are required to hold the contents of columns belonging to tables defined in the Liga Utopia database. It would be preferable to link the variable definition explicitly to the equivalent database attribute definition. Doing this will keep the PL/SQL code synchronized with any changes to the table definition. Figure 10.9 demonstrates how to link PL/SQL variables to their database equivalents. Such declarations are referred to as **anchored declarations**.

```
DECLARE
    v_season          Matches.Season%TYPE;
    v_club            Clubs.Name%TYPE;
    v_total_points    NUMBER(3);
    v_match_id        Matches.Match_id%TYPE;
    v_goals_for       NUMBER(2);
    v_goals_against   NUMBER(2);
    v_players_club    Clubs.Name%TYPE;
    v_goals_type      Goals.Type%TYPE:
```

Figure 10.9 PL/SQL: anchored declarations.

The declaration specifies the name of the database table, followed by the name of the column in the table. The *%TYPE* instruction causes a call to the data dictionary to fetch the type definition used to define the column in the table's *create* statement. This is then used to define the PL/SQL variable.

Changing the data type of a table attribute may require changes to the source code. If, for example, an attribute is changed from a character string to a number, some of the operators applied to it in the program may no longer be appropriate. The declaration block remains constant; the execution block may need amendment. This will be determined by recompiling the PL/SQL source code and debugging any compilation errors.

If, as in the case of the *season–points–club* problem, there is a requirement to process the results of a *select* statement iteratively, a temporary holding area for the result set will need to be declared in the PL/SQL declaration section. This type of variable is referred to as a **cursor**, and its declaration syntax is shown in Figure 10.10.

```
CURSOR <cursor_name> [RETURN <return-type>] IS
    <select-statement>;
```

Figure 10.10 PL/SQL: cursor declaration I.

Cursor_name is the name of the PL/SQL variable that will be created to contain the result set produced by the execution of the specified *select* statement. The *return-type* is an optional specification that defines the structure for each of the individually referenced rows. Figure 10.11 shows the three cursors that are required for the ongoing *season–points–club* problem.

```
CURSOR c_club IS
   select name from club;

CURSOR c_match IS
   select match_id from match
   where (homeclub = v_club or awayclub = v_club)
   and season = v_season;

CURSOR c_goals RETURN v_cursor _rec_type IS
   select players.club, goals.type from goals, players
   where goals.ufa_id = players.ufa_id
   and match_id = v_match_id;
```

Figure 10.11 PL/SQL: cursor declarations II.

Note that it is permissible, indeed often necessary, to place variables in the *select* statement of a cursor definition. These variables will be type checked at compile-time, but not evaluated until run-time. Neither of the first two cursors has a return type specified. This is common practice when a cursor returns rows that always consist of a single atomic value, i.e. one column only. Return types are used to enforce type checking when fetching cursor rows, and they are particularly helpful in situations where each row returned consists of attributes with different data types.

Defining the return type of a cursor can be done in one of two ways. If the query is simple and selects all the columns from just one table then the *%ROWTYPE* attribute can be used. If the *select* statement is more complex and does not select all columns, uses operators applied to columns or involves more than one table, then the programmer must define a special return type for the cursor and for the structure to receive the cursor's returned rows.

The *%ROWTYPE* of Figure 10.12 is another example of an *anchored declaration*. In this case, it relates the type of row returned from the cursor to the attribute definitions for the *Players* table. *Players%ROWTYPE* is an example of a structured data definition, in that the type can be broken down into a set of constituent attribute types, one for each named column in the *Players* table. Figure 10.13 shows the analysis of this structured data definition.

```
CURSOR c_player RETURN players%ROWTYPE IS
   select * from players;
```

Figure 10.12 PL/SQL: cursor return type.

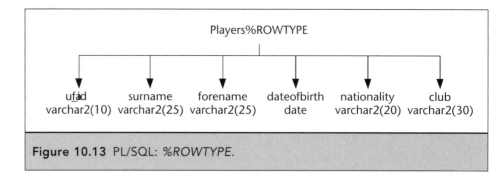

Figure 10.13 PL/SQL: *%ROWTYPE.*

If a variable of type *players%ROWTYPE* is declared, and it is assigned a row returned from the relevant cursor's select statement, it is possible to reference each of that row's attributes. Figure 10.14 shows such a declaration and gives an example of opening the cursor, retrieving the first row selected and referencing a particular attribute of interest.

```
DECLARE
    v_surname          Players.surname%TYPE;
    v_player_record    Players%ROWTYPE;

    CURSOR c_player RETURN Players%ROWTYPE IS
        select * from players;

BEGIN
    OPEN c_player;
    FETCH c_player INTO v_player_record;
    v_surname := v_player_record.surname;
    ...
END
```

Figure 10.14 PL/SQL: cursor records.

The ***open*** cursor instruction causes the cursor's defined *select* statement to be executed (in the database server), and the result set to be placed in the declared cursor variable *c_player*. The ***fetch*** statement retrieves the next data row (starting at the first) from the cursor variable, *c_player* and places it into the structured variable, *v_player_record*. The name and type of each element of *v_player_record* matches the name and type of each attribute defined in the *Players* table. The ***begin*** and ***end*** statements delimit the **execution section** of the block.

Returning to the *season–points–club* example, the third cursor defined in Figure 10.11 uses a user-defined cursor return type. The record returned from each cursor fetch is not anchored to a row in a database table. It illustrates a constructed variable record type that will have been defined in the PL/SQL block's *declaration section*. Figure 10.15 shows that the cursor will fetch each selected data row into a variable of type *v_cursor_rec_type*, the *v_goals* variable defined in the example. The two parts of a *v_cursor_rec_type* record (*players_club* and *goals_type*) can then be referenced as *v_goals.players_club* and *v_goals.goals_type*.

```
TYPE v_cursor_rec_type IS RECORD
   (players_club Clubs.Name%TYPE,
   goals_type    Goals.Type%TYPE);

v_goal v_cursor_rec_type;

CURSOR c_goals RETURN v_cursor_rec_type IS
   select players.club, goals.type from goals, players
   where goals.ufa_id = players.ufa_id
   and match_id = v_match_id;
```

Figure 10.15 PL/SQL: record types.

The local variables defined in Figure 10.9, the cursor declarations of Figure 10.11 and the cursor record definition of Figure 10.15 form the declaration section of the implementation given in Figure 10.16.

The declaration section of any block is immediately followed by the keyword **begin**. This indicates the beginning of the compulsory execution section of the block, and implicitly signifies the end of the declaration section.

Figure 10.17 gives a first-cut implementation of the execution section of the *season–points–club* example. This implementation is a direct translation from the pseudo-code of Figure 10.6, and needs to be amended in order to handle a number of omissions that are not immediately obvious.

Cursors are dynamic in that they are evaluated at run-time, and can use variables as part of their *select* statement. The advantage of this is demonstrated in the code. Such *run-time binding* allows the cursors to be evaluated multiple times within an iterative structure, each time with a new value in the predicate clause of the associated *select* statement. When the cursor, *c_match* is opened, causing its *select* statement to be executed for the first time, it will create a result set containing all the matches (for the input season) of the first in a list of clubs. When *c_match* is opened for the second time, it will result in a result set containing all the matches (for the input season) of the second in the list of clubs, and so on. In order to reallocate the memory space used to contain the result set of *c_match* it is necessary to remove the previous contents of its result set from memory. This is achieved by using the **close** statement to delete the contents of the cursor prior to reopening it with new values in the predicate clause of its *select* statement.

PL/SQL uses a colon in front of the equals sign to differentiate the assignment operator from the comparison operator, and uses <> to denote a not equal condition. Iteration is achieved within a **loop...end loop** construct, all operations within

```
DECLARE

v_season         Matches.Season%TYPE;
v_club           Clubs.Name%TYPE;
v_total_points   NUMBER(3);
v_match_id       Matches.Match_id%TYPE;
v_goals_for      NUMBER(2);
v_goals_against  NUMBER(2);

TYPE v_cursor_rec_type IS RECORD
   (players_club Clubs.Name%TYPE,
    goals_type   Goals.Type%TYPE);

v_goals       v_cursor_rec_type;

CURSOR c_club IS
   select name from club;

CURSOR c_match IS
   select match_id from match
   where (homeclub = v_club or awayclub = v_club)
   and season = v_season;

CURSOR c_goals RETURN v_cursor_rec_type IS
   select players.club from goals, players
   where goals.ufa_id = players.ufa_id
   and match_id = v_match_id;
```

Figure 10.16 PL/SQL: declaration section.

it being repeated until the loop is explicitly terminated. Selection is decided upon through the *if...then...elsif...else...end if* statement. The *elsif* and *else* clauses are both optional, as demonstrated in Figure 10.17.

The weaknesses exhibited in the first-cut solution are as follows:

- The input source for the setting of the v_season variable has not been established.

- There is no mechanism in place to exit the *loop...end loop* statements once any of the cursor result sets have been fully processed.

- Once the total club points for the season have been calculated, they are overwritten by those of the next club, prior to being reported to the client initiating the program.

```
BEGIN
   v_season := input;
   OPEN c_club;
   LOOP
      FETCH c_club INTO v_club;
      v_total_points := 0;
      OPEN c_match;
      LOOP
         FETCH c_match INTO v_match_id;
         v_goals_for := 0;
         v_goals_against := 0;
         OPEN c_goals;
         LOOP
            FETCH c_goals INTO v_goals;
            IF (v_club = v_goals.players_club AND
               v_goals.goals_type <> 'own goal') OR
               (v_club <> v_goal.players_club AND
               v_goals.goals_type = 'own goal') THEN
                  v_goals_for := v_goals_for + 1;
            ELSE
               v_goals_against := v_goals_against + 1;
            END IF;
         END LOOP;
         CLOSE c_goals;
         IF v_goals_for > v_goals_against THEN
            v_total_points := v_total_points + 3;
         ELSIF v_goals_for = v_goals_against THEN
            v_total_points := v_total_points + 1;
         END IF;
      END LOOP;
      CLOSE c_match;
   END LOOP;
   CLOSE c_club;
END;
/
```

Figure 10.17 PL/SQL: block – execution section I.

The first problem, establishing an input source for the variable *v_season*, is solved through a **substitution variable** that prompts the user to enter a value for it at run-time. Figure 10.18 demonstrates a very simple six line anonymous block that takes input via a *substitution variable* identified as *&input*. Figure 10.19 shows the output generated by the execution of this block. It should be noted that '*old 4:*' and '*new 4:*' relate to the contents of line four of the block pre- and post-variable substitution.

```
DECLARE
    v_number number;
BEGIN
v_number := &input;
END;
/
```

Figure 10.18 PL/SQL: a substitution variable.

```
Enter value for input: 2
old    4: v_number := &input;
new    4: v_number := 2;

PL/SQL procedure successfully completed
```

Figure 10.19 PL/SQL: substitution variables.

The second problem, concerning the exiting of the *loop* statement once the cursor records have all been processed, is resolved through the checking of a special cursor attribute after each *fetch* operation. A forced **exit** (Figure 10.20) from within the loop is performed if the *%NOTFOUND* attribute returns a value of true. The *exit* is contained in a separate statement from the *fetch*. Its effect is to perform a jump to the first statement after the next *end loop* if its condition is evaluated as true.

```
LOOP
FETCH c_cursor INTO v_cursor;
      EXIT WHEN c_cursor %NOTFOUND;
...
END LOOP;
```

Figure 10.20 PL/SQL: exiting a loop.

Each declared cursor has four attributes associated with it. These are explained in Table 10.1. Three of these attributes contain a Boolean value (true or false) and may be used directly in the condition of an *if* statement or in the exit condition of a loop. The *%ROWCOUNT* attribute may be used in the end condition of a *for* loop or in any other situation where the number of rows *fetched* from the cursor needs to be known.

Table 10.1 PL/SQL: cursor attributes.

%FOUND	Returns true if a row is successfully fetched from the cursor; otherwise it will return false.
%NOTFOUND	Returns true if a row is not fetched from the cursor; otherwise false.
%ISOPEN	This attribute indicates whether the associated cursor is currently open, i.e. its select statement has been executed and the result is still in buffer memory.
%ROWCOUNT	This attribute contains the total number of rows fetched from an open cursor. The variable is zeroed when the cursor is opened and incremented after each successful fetch.

A client program might well dynamically reconfigure a user interface, determining the number of returned rows to resize a grid displaying the entire row data associated with a query.

The third weakness of the first-cut solution was the lack of reporting of the calculated total points associated with each club. This can be resolved with an Oracle-supplied output mechanism that involves the use of a PL/SQL package called *dbms_output*. This contains the procedure *put_line*. Packages will be fully described later, but for the present discussion, it is only necessary to understand that the procedure *put_line* is called as *dbms_output.put_line(output)*, where *output* represents the information that is to be displayed on the user's console. In order to utilize this package from an SQL*PLUS session, the environment variable, *serveroutput* must be set *on* (Figure 10.21).

```
SQL*PLUS> set serveroutput on
```

Figure 10.21 SQL*PLUS.

With the three weaknesses of the first-cut solution to the *season–points–club* problem addressed, it is now possible to produce a more comprehensive anonymous block solution to that problem. This is detailed in Figure 10.22.

To compile and execute a PL/SQL anonymous block it is necessary to pass it to a PL/SQL engine. The most common way in which this is achieved is with a client-side interactive tool such as SQL*Plus.

SQL*Plus will consider a PL/SQL block of code as a single unit-of-work and forward it, via a single network call, to the server-side PL/SQL engine located within the database server.

Upon receipt, the PL/SQL engine will attempt to compile the block into executable object code. If successful, the object code will be executed. If the compilation fails, for whatever reason, an appropriate error message will be returned to the SQL*Plus client. The code (source or compiled) of a PL/SQL anonymous block is not stored at the database server, even if it has been successfully compiled and executed.

```
Set serveroutput on          // sets SQL*Plus environment variable
DECLARE
   v_season          Matches.Season%TYPE;
   v_club            Clubs.Name%TYPE;
   v_total_points    NUMBER(3);
   v_match_id        Matches.Match_id%TYPE;
   v_goals_for       NUMBER(2);
   v_goals_against   NUMBER(2);
   TYPE v_cursor_rec_type IS RECORD
      (players_club Clubs.Name%TYPE, goals_type Goals.Type%TYPE);
   v_goals           v_cursor_rec_type;
   CURSOR c_club IS   select name from clubs;
   CURSOR c_match IS  select match_id from matches
      where (homeclub = v_club or awayclub = v_club)
      and season = v_season;
   CURSOR c_goals RETURN v_cursor_rec_type IS
      select players.club, goals.type from goals, players
      where goals.ufa_id = players.ufa_id
      and match_id = v_match_id;

BEGIN
   v_season := &input;
   OPEN c_club;
   LOOP
      FETCH c_club INTO v_club;
      EXIT WHEN c_club%NOTFOUND;
      v_total_points := 0;
      OPEN c_match;
      LOOP
         FETCH c_match INTO v_match_id;
         EXIT WHEN c_match%NOTFOUND;
         v_goals_for := 0;
         v_goals_against := 0;
         OPEN c_goals;
         LOOP
            FETCH c_goals INTO v_goals;
            EXIT WHEN c_goals%NOTFOUND;
            IF (v_club = v_goals.players_club AND
               v_goals.goals_type <> 'own goal' ) OR
               (v_club <> v_goals.players_club AND
               v_goals.goals_type = 'own goal') THEN
```

Figure 10.22 PL/SQL: anonymous block II.

```
                        v_goals_for := v_goals_for + 1;
                ELSE
                    v_goals_against := v_goals_against + 1;
                END IF;
            END LOOP;
            CLOSE c_goals;
            IF  v_goals_for > v_goals_against THEN
                v_total_points := v_total_points + 3;
            ELSIF v_goals_for = v_goals_against THEN
                v_total_points := v_total_points + 1;
            END IF;
        END LOOP;
        CLOSE c_match;
        DBMS_OUTPUT.PUT_LINE(v_club || ' ' || v_total_points);
    END LOOP;
    CLOSE c_club;
END;
/
```

Figure 10.22 (continued)

A particular benefit of using PL/SQL, even in an anonymous block, is the reduction in network traffic between a client application and the database server. All the code (including the three *select* statements) in the anonymous block of Figure 10.22 would be transmitted to the database server as a single network call. If the three select statements were issued directly from SQL*Plus, there would need to be a minimum of three network calls before considering the effect of their iteration (Figure 10.23).

Compiling and executing the *season–points–club* block results in the output shown in Figure 10.24. The input for *v_season* must be quoted; otherwise, the result of dividing 2003 by 4 will be substituted.

10.3 ∈ PL/SQL EXCEPTIONS

Although the solution provided in Figure 10.22 fully answers the *season–points–club* problem, there are often potential run-time issues that need to be addressed when designing a PL/SQL program. For example, Figure 10.25 shows a very simple anonymous block used to display the surname of a player whose *ufa_id* is input.

The *select* statement will, at most, return one row of data (*ufa_id* is the unique primary key of the table) so there is no need to use a cursor to handle a possible multiple row result set. However, there is a possibility of an incorrect *ufa_id* being

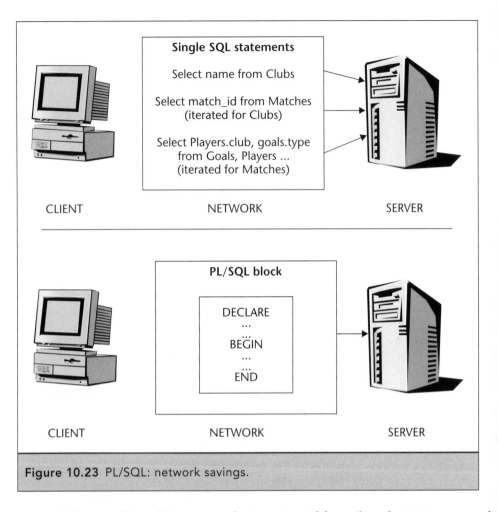

Figure 10.23 PL/SQL: network savings.

entered. This would result in no rows being returned from the *select* statement and the forcing of a *NO_DATA_FOUND* error condition (Figure 10.26).

To provide the programmer with control in situations such as this, where potential errors can be anticipated, PL/SQL provides the optional Exception Section. This section is located between the last Execution Section statement and the block's terminating *end* statement. Incorporating an exception handler in this section allows the error condition to be anticipated and dealt with inside the program. Figure 10.27 demonstrates how the *NO_DATA_FOUND* error condition can be trapped and handled so that the program fails gracefully.

Figure 10.28 demonstrates this program in operation. The *NO_DATA_FOUND* exception is one of Oracle's predefined error conditions that is included with every Oracle installation. Other pre-defined exceptions are listed in Table A.4.

As well as predefined error conditions, there are two other groups of error conditions that can be handled in PL/SQL: non-predefined database exceptions, and user-defined exceptions.

A non-predefined database exception is an existing Oracle error condition that does not posses a pre-defined exception name. For example, Oracle has a error code

```
Enter value for input: old  21:    v_season := &input;
new  21:   v_season := '2003/04';
AC Compassion        0
Beauty United        12
Bountiful Athletic   0
Forgiveness FC       0
Freedom United       0
Grace Town           0
Honesty United       0
Knowledge City       0
Liberation United    0
Nirvana City         0
Pity City            0
Purity FC            15
Sobriety FC          0
Steadfast United     0
Thrift City          0
Truth FC             0
Valour FC            0
Virtue Thursday      0
Wisdom United        0

PL/SQL procedure successfully completed.
```

Figure 10.24 PL/SQL: sample output.

```
DECLARE
v_ufa_id   varchar2(10);
v_name     varchar2(25);
BEGIN
v_ufa_id := &ufa_id;
select surname into v_name from players
        where ufa_id = v_ufa_id;
dbms_output.put_line('Player ' || v_ufa_id || ' is ' || v_name);
END;
/
```

Figure 10.25 PL/SQL: singleton select.

```
Enter value for ufa_id: 'VT432167'          Correct keyboard
old    5: v_ufa_id := &ufa_id;                entry
new    5: v_ufa_id := 'VT432167';
Player VT432167 surname is DIOCLETIAN

PL/SQL procedure successfully completed.

Enter value for ufa_id: 'VT432666'          Incorrect
old    5: v_ufa_id := &ufa_id;               keyboard entry
new    5: v_ufa_id := 'VT432666';
declare
*
ERROR at line 1:
ORA-01403: no data found
ORA-06512: at line 6
```

Figure 10.26 PL/SQL: exceptions.

```
DECLARE
v_ufa_id     varchar2(10);
v_name       varchar2(25);
BEGIN
v_ufa_id := &ufa_id;
select surname into v_name from players
        where ufa_id = v_ufa_id;
dbms_output.put_line('Player ' || v_ufa_id || ' surname is ' ||
v_name);

EXCEPTION
WHEN NO_DATA_FOUND THEN
dbms_output.put_line('Player ' || v_ufa_id || ' does not exist!');
END;
/
```

Figure 10.27 Exception handled.

(ORA-02291) that helps in handling referential integrity. If an attempt is made to insert a new row in a *detail* table, and there is not a corresponding row in the *master* table, then the ORA-02291 error condition will be raised.

Attempting to insert a row in the *Matches* table that references a non-existent club results in the error message of Figure 10.29.

```
Enter value for ufa_id: 'VT432167'
old    5: v_ufa_id := &ufa_id;
new    5: v_ufa_id := 'VT432167';
Player VT432167 surname is DIOCLETIAN

PL/SQL procedure successfully completed.

-----------------------------------------

Enter value for ufa_id: 'VT432666'
old    5: v_ufa_id := &ufa_id;
new    5: v_ufa_id := 'VT432666';
Player VT432666 does not exist!

PL/SQL procedure successfully completed.
```

Figure 10.28 PL/SQL: exception handling.

There are two alternate ways to handling such an error condition in a PL/SQL program. Firstly, it is possible to use the catch-all exception handling clause *WHEN OTHERS* in the exception section. This will handle any Oracle error condition that is not already being specifically handled. The main problem with this approach is that it is too general to distinguish between different types of error. It therefore does not allow different responses from the program when faced with varying error conditions. It is most often used as a final check to ensure that a PL/SQL program exits cleanly when an unanticipated error is encountered.

```
ORA-02291: integrity constraint (SB.FK_HOME) violated — parent key
not found
```

Figure 10.29 Oracle error code.

The second way to handle an error condition is to define it as a specific error condition to be handled. This is achieved through an error condition definition statement in the declaration section of a PL/SQL Block. Both methods are shown in the example given in Figure 10.30.

An exception variable is defined through the use of an *exception* type. Once defined it is associated with a specific Oracle error condition through a *pragma exception_init* expression. A pragma is a pseudo-instruction that acts as a compiler directive. In this case, its effect is to associate the Oracle error code, –2291, with the declared exception, *invalid_match_club*. *SQLERRM* is a predefined function that

```
DECLARE
   v_season       varchar2(10);
   v_home_club    varchar2(25);
   v_away_club    varchar2(25);

   invalid_match_club      EXCEPTION;
   PRAGMA EXCEPTION_INIT (invalid_match_club, -2291);
BEGIN
   v_season := &season;
   v_home_club := &hometeam;
   v_away_club := &awayclub;
   insert into matches values
           (newmatch.nextval, v_home_club, v_away_club, SYSDATE, v_season);
   dbms_output.put_line('Match: ' || v_home_club || ' V ' || v_away_club || 'inserted
OK');
EXCEPTION
   WHEN invalid_match_club THEN
      dbms_output.put_line('Error: club does not exist!');
   WHEN OTHERS THEN
   dbms_output.put_line('Error: (' || SQLERRM || ') TRAPPED');
END;
/
```

Figure 10.30 PL/SQL: defined exceptions I.

returns an error message associated with the most recent Oracle error (Figure 10.31).

Exceptions are evaluated top-to-bottom, so the generic *WHEN OTHERS* clause appears last in the exception section of a PL/SQL block.

A user-defined error condition is declared in a similar way as a non-predefined database error.

There is no need for the pragma association as the error is not directly related to an Oracle error condition.

The error condition is user-specific, i.e. related to the business logic of the program, as opposed to the data logic of the database server, so the raising of the error condition also has to be user-defined. Figure 10.32 gives an example of the raising of such an error condition when the number of players in a given club is less than eleven.

10.4 STORED PROGRAMS

Anonymous PL/SQL blocks are perfectly acceptable for interactive queries that require an element of procedural processing, such as the example used in the

```
Enter value for season: '2002/03'
old   8: v_season := &season;
new   8: v_season := '2002/03';
Enter value for hometeam: 'Beauty United'
old   9: v_home_club := &hometeam;
new   9: v_home_club := 'Beauty United';
Enter value for awayclub: 'Purity CF'
old  10: v_away_club := &awayclub;
new  10: v_away_club := 'Purity CF';
Error: club does not exist!

PL/SQL procedure successfully completed.


-----------------------------------------


Enter value for season: '2002/03/2003'
old   8:          v_season := &season;
new   8:          v_season := '2002/03/2003';
Enter value for hometeam: 'Beauty United'
old   9:          v_home_club := &hometeam;
new   9:          v_home_club := 'Beauty United';
Enter value for awayclub: 'Purity FC'
old  10:          v_away_club := &awayclub;
new  10:          v_away_club := 'Purity CF';
Error: (ORA-06502: PL/SQL: numeric or value error:
character string buffer too small) TRAPPED

PL/SQL procedure successfully completed.
```

Figure 10.31 PL/SQL: defined exceptions II.

previous section. There are a number of overheads and limitations associated with the use of PL/SQL anonymous blocks that require addressing.

The first of these problem areas concerns the cost associated with compiling the PL/SQL block of code each time it requires processing. If the code is to be processed rarely this is an acceptable overhead. However, if the code is to be processed often, and is unlikely to be subject to change between executions, then the cost of the second and subsequent compilations is an unnecessary overhead to the user.

The second problem lies in the fact that an anonymous block has to be available at the client for transmission to a PL/SQL engine for compilation and execution.

If there is only one client then there is no problem. However, each subsequent client will have to gain access to a copy of the code. This could be resolved by placing the source code in a file on a central repository from which it can be loaded to individual clients. This, unfortunately, introduces problems of its own in terms

```
DECLARE
v_ club          varchar2(25);
v_player_count   number(2);
insufficient_players EXCEPTION;

BEGIN
   v_club := &clubname;
   select count(*) into v_player_count
      from players where club = v_club;
   IF v_player_count < 11 THEN RAISE insufficient_players;
   END IF;

EXCEPTION
   WHEN insufficient_players THEN
      dbms_output.put_line
         ('Club ' || v_club || ' only has ' || v_player_count ||
         'players!' );
   WHEN OTHERS THEN
      dbms_output.put_line('Error: (' || SQLERRM || ') TRAPPED');
END;
/
```

Figure 10.32 PL/SQL: user-defined exception handling.

of increases in network traffic (to obtain the source code), and potential inconsistencies between the code at different clients if the source code at the repository is subject to change over time. It also probable that the database operators will find loading such files troublesome and error-prone.

The solution to both of these problems is thankfully the same. Rather than store the source code at a central repository, store the compiled code at the database server and allow it to be executed from the client. This avoids unnecessary compilation each time the code needs processing, and allows any client (with sufficient security clearance) to initiate such processing without first having to access the source code.

PL/SQL provides such a solution in the form of PL/SQL stored programs, of which there are two specific categories: **stored procedures** and **stored functions**.

10.5 STORED PROCEDURES

From a programming point of view there is very little additional coding required to change an anonymous block into a stored procedure. Indeed, it could be argued that the act of giving an anonymous block a name is all that is required to convert it. However, apart from an identifier, a stored procedure has one other major programming advantage over an anonymous block: the ability to accept input parameters.

Figure 10.33 shows how a procedure is given an identity, taking the source code from the *season–points–club* example. A block header is created that contains the name of the procedure, and the *DECLARE* statement is replaced by the *IS* keyword. Stored programs allow for input, output and input–output parameters. The *v_season* substitution variable is replaced by the input parameter *i_season*. The

```
CREATE OR REPLACE PROCEDURE club_points
(i_season IN Matches.Season%TYPE)
IS
v_club            Clubs.Name%TYPE;
v_total_points    NUMBER(3);
v_match_id        Matches.Match_id%TYPE;
v_goals_for       NUMBER(2);
v_goals_against   NUMBER(2);

TYPE v_cursor_rec_type IS RECORD
     (players_club Clubs.Name%TYPE,
      goals_type   Goals.Type%TYPE);

  v_goal          v_cursor_rec_type;

CURSOR c_club IS
     select name from clubs;

CURSOR c_match IS
     select match_id from matches
     where (homeclub = v_club or awayclub = v_club)
     and season = i_season;

CURSOR c_goals RETURN v_cursor_rec_type IS
     select players.club from goals, players
     where goals.ufa_id = players.ufa_id
     and match_id = v_match_id;
BEGIN
...
END;
/
```

Figure 10.33 PL/SQ: stored procedure.

remainder of the code is identical to that of the previous *season–points–club* anonymous block.

The intention of using a procedure is to decouple code compilation from execution. It follows that two separate operations will now have to be carried out by the database programmer in order to use such a program: compiling the code and executing the code.

To compile a procedure, its source code, as with an anonymous block, is passed to a PL/SQL engine for compilation. However, as such code has now been declared with a name, once successfully compiled, rather than being immediately executed, the compiled code is stored at the database server awaiting execution requests.

Assuming that the source code for the procedure in Figure 10.33 is stored in a script file called c:\points.sql, then the SQL*Plus operation detailed in Figure 10.34 could be used to compile that source code and place the resulting execution code in the database server.

```
SQL*PLUS> @c:\points.sql

Procedure created.
```

Figure 10.34 Batch compilation.

Once the procedure has been successfully compiled, it is available for execution. Such execution is initiated via a client request either through a client process such as SQL*Plus, or from another program already executing within the database server. The form of a procedure request from a separate client process is given in Figure 10.35.

```
SQL*PLUS> EXECUTE procedure_name (input_parameters)
```

Figure 10.35 Interactive procedure execution.

The form of a procedure request made from within an executing PL/SQL process is given in Figure 10.36.

```
procedure_name (input_parameters);
```

Figure 10.36 Procedure call.

Figure 10.37 shows the procedure call from SQL*Plus and the resulting output.

```
set serveroutput on
SQL*PLUS> execute club_points ('2003/04')

AC Compassion          0
Beauty United          12
Bountiful Athletic     0
Forgiveness FC         0
Freedom United         0
Grace Town             0
Honesty United         0
Knowledge City         0
Liberation United      0
Nirvana City           0
...


PL/SQL procedure successfully completed.
```

Figure 10.37 *Club_points* execution.

If the procedure is called incorrectly, through the omission of required parameters or the inclusion of superfluous parameters, then an appropriate error message will be generated and execution halted (Figures 10.38 and 10.39).

```
set serveroutput on

execute club_points
BEGIN club_points; END;


    *
ERROR at line 1:
ORA-06550: line 1, column 7:
PLS-00306: wrong number or types of arguments in call to 'CLUB_POINTS'
ORA-06550: line 1, column 7:
PL/SQL: Statement ignored
```

Figure 10.38 Execution errors I.

```
execute club_points ('2003/04', 'Beauty United')
BEGIN club_points ('2003/04', 'Beauty United'); END;

    *

ERROR at line 1:
ORA-06550: line 1, column 7:
PLS-00306: wrong number or types of arguments in call to 'CLUB_POINTS'
ORA-06550: line 1, column 7:
PL/SQL: Statement ignored
```

Figure 10.39 Execution errors II.

As well as allowing the use of input parameters, procedures can also use output and input–output parameters. Such parameters, when combined with the block-structured nature of PL/SQL, enable dynamic interchange of variables between calling and receiving PL/SQL programs.

The *match_goals* procedure to find the number of goals scored for, and against, a particular club, in a particular match (Figure 10.40), is called from a separate *club_points* procedure that calculates the total points scored for each club in a particular season (Figure 10.41). The output resulting from such an interaction is shown in Figure 10.42. In essence, this example takes the earlier procedure of Figure 10.33 and splits its functionality across two new procedures.

Note that the logic of the new procedure has been suitably altered to ensure that the club the player was playing for at the time of the match is credited with any goals scored by that player, rather than, as mistakenly calculated in our earlier examples, the club for which the player is currently playing. Hence the difference in output values!

Load and compile *match_goals* before *club_points*. If *match_goals* does not exist when *club_points* is compiled, the call to *match_goals* in it will cause a compilation error.

Input–output (*IN OUT*) parameters, such as those used in *match_goals*, allow variables to be passed from calling programs to receiving programs, for the receiving program to alter their values accordingly, and for the updated values to be passed back to the calling program for further calculation. Figure 10.42 shows a section of the output produced by the execution of the *club_points* procedure. This demonstrates the changed values of the *io_goals_for* and *io_goals_against* input–output variables before and after each call to *match_goals*. Input variables are read-only, whereas output variables are write-only, in that they can only be assigned values from within the called procedure.

```
CREATE OR REPLACE PROCEDURE club_points
(i_season IN Matches.Season%TYPE)
IS
   v_club            Clubs.Name%TYPE;
   v_total_points    NUMBER(3);
   v_match_id        Matches.Match_id%TYPE;
   v_goals_for       NUMBER(2);
   v_goals_against   NUMBER(2);
   CURSOR c_club IS
      select name from clubs;
   CURSOR c_match IS
      select match_id from matches
      where (homeclub = v_club or awayclub = v_club)
      and season = i_season;

BEGIN
   OPEN c_club;
   LOOP
      FETCH c_club INTO v_club;
      EXIT WHEN c_club%NOTFOUND;
      v_total_points := 0;
      OPEN c_match;
      LOOP
         FETCH c_match INTO v_match_id;
         EXIT WHEN c_match%NOTFOUND;
         v_goals_for := 0;
         v_goals_against := 0;
DBMS_OUTPUT.PUT_LINE ('Execute match_goals( ' || v_club || ',' ||
                  v_match_id || ',' || v_goals_for || ',' ||
                  v_goals_against || ' )');
   match_goals(v_club, v_match_id, v_goals_for, v_goals_against);

DBMS_OUTPUT.PUT_LINE ('Return match_goals( ' || v_club || ',' ||
                  v_match_id || ',' || v_goals_for || ',' ||
                  v_goals_against || ' )');
         IF v_goals_for > v_goals_against THEN
            v_total_points := v_total_points + 3;
         ELSIF v_goals_for = v_goals_against THEN
            v_total_points := v_total_points + 1;
         END IF;
      END LOOP;
```

Figure 10.40 Procedure *club_points* calls *match_goals* (*continued overleaf*).

```
            CLOSE c_match;
            DBMS_OUTPUT.PUT_LINE
                  (v_club || ' ' || v_total_points);
         END LOOP;
         CLOSE c_club;
      END club_points;
      /
```

Figure 10.40 (*Continued*)

```
CREATE OR REPLACE PROCEDURE match_goals
(i_club IN Clubs.name%TYPE,
 i_match IN Matches.match_id%TYPE,
 io_goals_for IN OUT NUMBER,
 io_goals_against IN OUT NUMBER)
IS
   TYPE v_cursor_rec_type IS RECORD
      (players_club Clubs.Name%TYPE,
       goals_type    Goals.Type%TYPE);

   v_goal_rec         v_cursor_rec_type;

   CURSOR c_goals RETURN v_cursor_rec_type IS
   select clubs.name, goals.type
        from goals, clubs, contracts, matches
      where goals.ufa_id = contracts.ufa_id
      and clubs.name = contracts.club
      and matches.match_id = goals.match_id
      and goals.match_id = i_match
      and matches.matchdate between contracts.joined
      and NVL(contracts.left,'31-DEC-9999');
BEGIN
   OPEN c_goals;
   LOOP
      FETCH c_goals INTO v_goal_rec;
      EXIT WHEN c_goals%NOTFOUND;
      IF (i_club = v_goal_rec.players_club AND
      v_goal_rec.goals_type <> 'own goal' ) OR
```

Figure 10.41 Procedure *match_goals* called by *club_points* (*continued opposite*).

```
            (i_club <> v_goal_rec.players_club AND
        v_goal_rec.goals_type = 'own goal') THEN
            io_goals_for := io_goals_for + 1;
        ELSE
            io_goals_against := io_goals_against + 1;
        END IF;
    END LOOP;
    CLOSE c_goals;
END match_goals;
```

Figure 10.41 (*Continued*)

```
SQL*PLUS> execute club_points ('2003/04')

Execute match_goals( AC Compassion,4,0,0 )
Return  match_goals( AC Compassion,4,0,1 )
Execute match_goals( AC Compassion,8,0,0 )
Return  match_goals( AC Compassion,8,0,2 )
AC Compassion 0
Execute match_goals( Beauty United,1,0,0 )
Return  match_goals( Beauty United,1,2,4 )
Execute match_goals( Beauty United,2,0,0 )
Return  match_goals( Beauty United,2,3,0 )
Execute match_goals( Beauty United,4,0,0 )
Return  match_goals( Beauty United,4,1,0 )
Execute match_goals( Beauty United,5,0,0 )
Return  match_goals( Beauty United,5,2,0 )
Execute match_goals( Beauty United,7,0,0 )
Return  match_goals( Beauty United,7,1,0 )
Beauty United 12
Bountiful Athletic 0
Forgiveness FC 0
Freedom United 0
...
PL/SQL procedure successfully completed.
```

Figure 10.42 Executing *club_points*.

10.6 ⊜ PL/SQL STORED FUNCTIONS

A function always returns a result, even if only a null, to its calling point. A PL/SQL function is like a function in any other programming language. It is called, as part of an assignment operation, to carry out a predetermined calculation, often with run-time input parameters, and returns the calculated result to an assignment variable. An example of a function call is in Figure 10.43, which calculates the total salary of all players currently contracted to play for a particular club:

```
v_club_salary := club_sal(i_club);
```

Figure 10.43 Calling a stored function.

The name of the function is *club_sal*, and the name of the club whose salary bill is to be calculated is represented by the input parameter *i_club*. When this assignment expression is executed (generally from within another block), *club_sal* is called with the current value of the *i_club* variable substituted as its input parameter. The value returned from the *club_sal* function is then assigned to the *v_club_salary* variable.

A PL/SQL function evaluates to an assignable value, and as such is inextricably tied to an assignment operation. To achieve the same result with *club_sal* as a procedure would require *v_club_salary* to be declared within *club_sal* as an output parameter.

Procedures can only pass back values through out or in–out parameters. Functions pass back values intrinsically as their return type. Functions can accept out and in–out parameters, but their use is considered a side-effect and is poor programming practice.

One of the main advantages of using a function rather than a procedure is that a function can be used in the selection set of a *select* statement. The *club_sal* function can easily be called for each club in the league (Figure 10.44).

```
SELECT Clubs.name, club_sal(Clubs.name)
FROM Clubs;
```

Figure 10.44 PL/SQL function in an SQL statement.

The coding of a function is almost identical to that of a procedure save for its declaration name type and return type, and the need for a return expression within the execution section. Figure 10.45 shows the code for the *club_sal* function.

```
CREATE OR REPLACE FUNCTION club_sal
(i_club IN Clubs.name%TYPE)
   RETURN NUMBER
IS
   v_club_salary NUMBER;
BEGIN
   SELECT sum(salary)
       INTO v_club_salary
       FROM Players, Contracts
       WHERE Players.ufa_id = Contracts.ufa_id
       AND Contracts.left IS NULL
       AND Players.club = i_club;
   RETURN v_club_salary;
END club_sal;
/
```

Figure 10.45 Function *club_sal*.

10.7 PL/SQL STORED PACKAGES

It is often the case that a number of procedures and functions are created for specific application areas, to provide a set of related functionality. In such cases, it would be convenient to group the related programs within a common framework. It is precisely this role that is provided by PL/SQL packages.

It is not only procedures and functions that can be contained within a package. It is also possible to include any combination of the following PL/SQL constructs:

- variables
- cursors
- constants
- exceptions
- PL/SQL tables

All such elements fall within the *scope*, or *context*, of the package that declares them, and as such can be considered as 'global variables' accessible by any of that package's programs.

A particular advantage of using packages to collect related functions and procedures is one of performance improvement over the use of standalone functions and procedures. In a standalone situation every program is loaded into process memory the first time it is called from a client process. If there are three standalone functions, all of which are called from a single procedure, there will be four separate loads of compiled p-code from disk to memory (one for the procedure and one for each of the functions). This is potentially a very inefficient mechanism, and it is far better to load all of the related programs in one operation. As soon as an element of a package is referenced, all elements of that package are loaded into process memory. This is a much more efficient mechanism, provided that only related items are included in any particular package.

A package is somewhat similar to the concept of an object in an object-oriented programming language. An object has a set of attributes and a set of methods that can act upon the attributes. Each method within the object can call any other method belonging to that object. Any other object can call a method of the given object provided it has sufficient privileges and knows the *signature* of the particular method it is interested in. The call must use the fully scoped name of the object's method and supply any required parameters (Figures 10.46 and 10.47).

```
object_name.method_name(input_parameters);
```

Figure 10.46 Object method call.

```
SQL*PLUS> execute package_name.procedure_name (input_parameters);

My_variable =package_name.function_name (input_parameters);

select package_name.function_name (input_parameters) from my_table;
```

Figure 10.47 Calls to packaged programs.

Within the context of the package specification, an *object_name* is replaced by a *package_name*, and a *method_name* is replaced by the name of a program. Therefore, a fully scoped call to a procedure or function stored within a package can be made interactively from a client such as SQL*PLUS, from another stored program or, for functions only, from within an SQL statement.

Each package separates the interface of its functions and procedures from the implementation details of those functions and procedures. A package therefore consists of a public interface, the *package header*, and a private implementation, the *package body*. Through such a mechanism, PL/SQL offers partial encapsulation. Unlike an object-oriented language, all the global variables (attributes) of a PL/SQL package are directly accessible from outside the package, provided their fully scoped names are used (Figure 10.48).

A private global variable for use only within the package must be declared within the package body, not within the package header.

```
CREATE OR REPLACE PACKAGE clubstat IS
   PROCEDURE club_points(i_season IN Matches.Season%TYPE);
   PROCEDURE match_goals(i_club IN Clubs.name%TYPE,
                i_match IN Matches.match_id%TYPE,
                io_goals_for IN OUT NUMBER,
                io_goals_against IN OUT NUMBER);
   FUNCTION club_sal(i_club IN Clubs.name%TYPE)
                RETURN NUMBER;
END clubstat;
/
```

Figure 10.48 Package header.

```
CREATE OR REPLACE PACKAGE BODY clubstat IS
PROCEDURE club_points(i_season IN Matches.Season%TYPE)IS
      v_club          Clubs.Name%TYPE;
      v_total_points  NUMBER(3);
      v_match_id      Matches.Match_id%TYPE;
      v_goals_for     NUMBER(2);
      v_goals_against NUMBER(2);
      CURSOR c_club IS
            select name from clubs;
      CURSOR c_match IS
         select match_id from matches
         where (homeclub = v_club or awayclub = v_club)
         and season = i_season;
BEGIN
. . .


END club_points;

   PROCEDURE match_goals(i_club IN Clubs.name%TYPE,
                i_match IN Matches.match_id%TYPE,
                io_goals_for IN OUT NUMBER,
                io_goals_against IN OUT NUMBER)IS
      TYPE v_cursor_rec_type IS RECORD
            (players_club Clubs.Name%TYPE,
             goals_type Goals.Type%TYPE);
```

Figure 10.49 Package body (*continued overleaf*).

```
        v_goal_rec          v_cursor_rec_type;
        CURSOR c_goals RETURN v_cursor_rec_type IS
            select clubs.name, goals.type from goals,
                        clubs, contracts, matches
            where goals.ufa_id = contracts.ufa_id
            and clubs.name = contracts.club
            and matches.match_id = goals.match_id
            and goals.match_id = i_match
            and matches.matchdate between contracts.joined
            and NVL(contracts.left,'31-DEC-9999');
    BEGIN
        ...
    END match_goals;

    FUNCTION club_sal(i_club IN Clubs.name%TYPE) RETURN NUMBER IS
        v_club_salary  NUMBER;
    BEGIN
        ...
    END club_sal;

END clubstat;
```

Figure 10.49 (*Continued*)

Figure 10.49 shows a section of the body of the PL/SQL package for club related statistics. In this example, the only variables defined are the named procedures and function. A package body is required only when its specification includes functions, procedures or cursors.

Figure 10.50 shows a standalone package specification that requires no package body. The user-defined exceptions declared in the package are available to any PL/SQL module, provided their fully scoped names are used.

```
CREATE OR REPLACE PACKAGE ligaerror IS
    invalid_match_club    EXCEPTION;
    club_not_found        EXCEPTION;
    no_salaries_found     EXCEPTION;
END ligaerror;
```

Figure 10.50 Standalone package.

Figure 10.51 shows an anonymous block that makes use of the one of the packaged exceptions and provides action code for it. User response to the *input* statement results in the exception being raised.

```
DECLARE
    v_sal NUMBER;
    v_club Clubs.name%TYPE;
BEGIN
    v_club := &club;
    v_sal := clubstat.club_sal(v_club);
    dbms_output.put_line(v_sal);
    if v_sal is NULL then raise ligaerror.no_salaries_found;
    end if;
EXCEPTION
    when ligaerror.no_salaries_found then
        dbms_output.put_line
('No salaries assigned to club ' || v_club);
END;

Enter value for club: 'Marks Club'
old    5:   v_club := &club;
new    5:   v_club := 'Marks Club';
No salaries assigned to club Marks Club

PL/SQL procedure successfully completed.
```

Figure 10.51 Using the packaged exceptions.

A particularly useful type of variable that is commonly used in a package is the PL/SQL table. Such a variable is used to hold an indexed set of elements in memory that can be retrieved, appended, deleted or updated by a program.

A table first needs to have its structure defined with its own *type* declaration statement. This statement defines both the structure of the table's elements and the table's indexing mechanism. The structure may be thought of as a dynamic two-dimensional array. It consists of just one column, but it can have a virtually unlimited number of rows. The column can be defined as any of the Oracle scalar types: *char*, *date* or *number*. Having defined its column structure, the table can hold any number of rows; its depth expands and contracts as rows are appended or deleted.

Figure 10.52 shows a declaration of a table with just one column of type *date* that is used to hold all the match dates for a season.

The *matchdates_table* can only be accessed from within the *matchdates* procedure that defines it. Such a limited 'scope' may be over-prescriptive in some situations.

```
CREATE OR REPLACE PROCEDURE matchdates
   (i_date IN DATE)
IS
   TYPE dates_table_type IS TABLE OF DATE
   INDEX BY BINARY_INTEGER;
   matchdates_table dates_table_type;
   v_date DATE;
BEGIN
   v_date := i_date;
   FOR v_week IN 1..38 LOOP
      matchdates_table(v_week) := v_date;
      v_date := v_date + 7;
   END LOOP;
END matchdates;
```

Figure 10.52 PL/SQL table.

It may be useful to be able to access a populated table from an anonymous block that lists all of the match dates still to play.

If *matchdates_table* has been declared within a procedure, rather than as a package variable, the anonymous block detailed in Figure 10.53 would produce the error condition shown.

```
BEGIN
   FOR v_week IN 1..38 LOOP
      IF matchdates.matchdates_table(v_week) >= SYSDATE THEN
         dbms_output.put_line
            (matchdates.matchdates_table(v_week));
      END IF;
   END LOOP;
END;


ERROR at line 4:
ORA-06550: line 4, column 44:
PLS-00225: subprogram or cursor 'MATCHDATES' reference is out of scope
ORA-06550: line 3, column 3:
PL/SQL: Statement ignored
```

Figure 10.53 Table reference out of scope.

A package declaration gives its variables global scope; the package description shown in Figure 10.54 would enable the anonymous block to reference *matchdates_table* successfully.

```
CREATE OR REPLACE PACKAGE clubspkg IS
   TYPE dates_table_type IS TABLE OF DATE
   INDEX BY BINARY_INTEGER;
   matchdates_table dates_table_type;
   PROCEDURE matchdates (i_date IN DATE);
END clubspkg;

CREATE OR REPLACE PACKAGE BODY clubspkg IS
   PROCEDURE matchdates(i_date IN DATE)
   IS
      v_date DATE;
   BEGIN
      v_date := i_date;
      FOR v_week IN 1..38 LOOP
         matchdates_table (v_week) := v_date;
         dbms_output.put_line('Week ' || v_week || ' - ' ||
            matchdates_table(v_week));
         v_date := v_date + 7;
      END LOOP;
   END matchdates;
END clubspkg;
```

Figure 10.54 Packaged table with global scope.

The table's fully scoped package name, *clubspkg.matchdates_table*, is now required for the anonymous block to successfully call it. Figure 10.55 shows the call required to create the table and to populate it, the code for a suitably amended anonymous block and a section of the output created by executing the anonymous block.

If the table contents were only to be available to the program elements within the package, then it would have to be declared as a *private*, or *local*, package variable. This is achieved by placing the table declaration within the package body, as shown in Figure 10.56, rather than within the package header.

Packages are an important object-oriented and modular approach to writing and deploying PL/SQL programs and are used extensively within many Oracle-based enterprise level application systems. Many of the standard functions and procedures built into the Oracle DBMS are contained within standard PL/SQL package libraries. One of the most commonly used is the *DBMS_OUTPUT* package used in several of this chapter's examples.

```
set serveroutput on
execute clubspkg.matchdates('14-AUG-2003')

Week 1 - 14-AUG-03
Week 2 - 21-AUG-03
...
Week 38 - 29-APR-04
PL/SQL procedure successfully completed.

SQL> BEGIN
  2    FOR v_week IN 1..38 LOOP
  3      IF clubspkg.matchdates_table(v_week) >= SYSDATE THEN
  4          dbms_output.put_line
  5          (clubspkg.matchdates_table(v_week));
  6      END IF;
  7    END LOOP;
  8  END;

14-AUG-03
21-AUG-03
...
29-APR-04
PL/SQL procedure successfully completed.
```

Figure 10.55

10.8 ⊂ PL/SQL TRIGGERS

PL/SQL anonymous blocks, procedures, functions and packages share a common invocation mechanism in that they all have to be explicitly run from a client process. The nature of the invocation syntax may vary, but all are executed as a response to client requests. This client-led approach is an example of a *pull* technology. A client process *pulls* information from a server process.

The *push* mechanism is a newer interaction paradigm that is *server-led*, rather than *client-driven*. In such a mechanism, a client process *registers* interest in a set of *events* that may occur at a server. The server process *advertises* the event types that it can raise, and then *notifies* registered clients (or *listeners*) when such events take place. The server process therefore *pushes* information to its clients for processing.

```
CREATE OR REPLACE PACKAGE clubspkg IS
   PROCEDURE matchdates (i_date IN DATE);
END clubspkg;

CREATE OR REPLACE PACKAGE BODY clubspkg IS
TYPE dates_table_type IS TABLE OF DATE
   INDEX BY BINARY_INTEGER;
   matchdates_table dates_table_type;

   PROCEDURE matchdates(i_date IN DATE)
   IS
      ---
   END matchdates;
END clubspkg;
```

Figure 10.56 Keeping the table declaration private.

Push technology is commonly used in applications like web-based financial news services, where users register interest in events such as movement in the value of a particular company's stocks and shares. On receiving news (an *event*) affecting the stocks or shares of a company that has registered client interest, the financial news service will send a notification message outlining the details of the event (e.g. stock price down twenty points) to all registered users.

The notification method itself could take many forms – for example, a simple text message or an automated phone call. The response to such an *event notification* is entirely user-dependent. Some may decide to buy shares if the price falls below a particular value; others may decide to jump out of the window on receiving the same news!

The events of interest within a database application are generally those that have an effect on the data content. From a DBMS perspective, the generic event types that may have interest registered in them are the SQL statements *insert*, *update* and *delete*, when applied to a particular SQL table of interest. For example, from an audit perspective, it would be helpful to record the details of any changes made to a player's salary.

Such details would likely need to include the date and time of the salary alteration took place, the previous salary, the new salary and the name of the person making the change. The event of interest is an update operation on the salary attribute of the *contracts* table, and the response to receiving a notification of such an event should be to perform an insert operation into an audit table. PL/SQL provides a mechanism for registering interest in, and programming a response to, such DML type events and their notification. This mechanism is known as a PL/SQL trigger.

PL/SQL triggers are blocks of code that contain the details of DML event notifications that the block will respond to, as well as the programmed response to such a notification being received. Figure 10.57 shows the general structure and syntax of a trigger.

```
CREATE OR REPLACE TRIGGER <trigger name>
<events of interest> [OF <attribute>] ON <table name>
[FOR EACH ROW]
[<filtering applied>]
BEGIN
  <processing after event notification>
END;
```

Figure 10.57 PL/SQL trigger syntax.

The first line of a PL/SQL trigger registers the unique name by which it will be called and executed. Note, however, that PL/SQL triggers operate within a different namespace than other named blocks, and it is the programmer's responsibility to ensure that the same name is not also used for a procedure, function or package.

The second line of the trigger registers interest in the events to which the trigger (acting as an event *consumer*) wishes to be notified, and the SQL table to which those events will apply. The registration syntax also indicates whether events of interest are those that are associated with DML operations that *have already* taken place or are associated with DML operations that are *about to* take place.

For instance, if the operation of interest was an insert into a particular table, the event of interest is either that an *insert* has taken place or that an *insert* is about to take place. The *after* keyword is used to indicate that interest is in those operations that have taken place, and the keyword *before* is used to indicate that interest is in those operations that are about to take place.

Because a before-trigger occurs prior to the execution of the DML operation that initiated or *fired* it, it is possible for the trigger's processing to alter the data contents of that DML operation. This is a very powerful mechanism, and is most often used to add transparently derived column values to inserted table rows. The cost of using a *before*-trigger that alters the data contents of the SQL operation upon which it is based is the need for an additional logical read of the (possibly updated) data once the trigger has completed and before the data is written to disk.

The *for each row* optional expression indicates the granularity of event notification. With this expression, an event notification will be raised for each and every row affected by the DML statement of interest. Without such an expression a single notification will be raised regardless of the number of rows affected. The decision as to the appropriate level of granularity to adopt is, of course, a matter for the database programmer, based on the specification requirement she or he is working on.

If the event of interest was an SQL update operation that altered the salary of players, would an event notification, and its associated processing, be required for each player affected, or would a single notification, regardless of the number of players affected, suffice?

Where it is decided that each row affected will generate an event notification, the *for each row* expression will be required. This type of trigger is known as a *row-level* trigger. If a single notification will do, then the *for each row* expression is omitted. This type of trigger is known as a *statement-level* trigger.

Another optional part of a trigger is client-based filtering of notifications received. Using the previous example of changes to the salaries of players, an appropriate filter might be to discard all notifications that concerned players from a particular club. The syntax used for such a filter is the keyword *when*, followed by a Boolean evaluation expression in parentheses, as shown in Figure 10.58.

```
CREATE OR REPLACE TRIGGER contracts_au_trigger
AFTER UPDATE ON Contracts
FOR EACH ROW
        WHEN (NEW.Club != 'Beauty United')
BEGIN
  <processing after event notification>
END;
/
```

Figure 10.58 Notification filtering syntax.

All notifications that are received which contain data values that do not evaluate to *true* in the filter will simply be discarded and thus avoid any unnecessary calls to the trigger's execution section. Because notification filtering is row-oriented, a *when* clause can only be used with a row-level trigger.

A row-level trigger has access to the before-image and after-image of each data row affected by the triggering event. This information is passed to the trigger as part of the event notification that *fires* it. If the triggering event is an update operation, then both a before-image and after-image will be populated, and will respectively contain the attribute values before the update took place and the attribute values once the update takes place. With a before-trigger these after-image values are subject to change prior to the after-image being applied to the database.

An insert trigger only has after-image data available, and a delete trigger only has before-image data available. After-image attributes are identified with the prefix **NEW**, and before-image attributes with the prefix **OLD**. In Figure 10.58, the notification filter is based on the value of the *club* attribute once the update that caused the trigger to fire has been processed.

The PL/SQL trigger in Figure 10.59 is a typical example of a row-level trigger used for audit purposes. The trigger responds to a notification that an update has been made to the *contracts* table by inserting a row into the audit table.

```
CREATE OR REPLACE TRIGGER contracts_au_trigger
AFTER UPDATE OF salary ON Contracts
FOR EACH ROW

DECLARE
v_log_details  VARCHAR2(100);

BEGIN
   v_log_details :=
      (OLD.UFA_ID || ' Old Salary: '                        ||
:OLD.salary || ' New Salary: ' || :NEW.salary);
   INSERT INTO AuditLog (datetime, user_id, details)
        VALUES (LOCALTIMESTAMP, USER, v_log_details);
END contracts_au_trigger;
```

Figure 10.59 PL/SQL trigger.

The SQL statement for creating the audit table is given in Figure 10.60. Note the use of the Oracle 9i data type *TIMESTAMP*. This is used because it acts as a more precise measure of time than the more familiar *DATE* type. The *TIMESTAMP* data type measures time intervals in hundredths of seconds rather than in full seconds, as with the *DATE* type. The PL/SQL function *LOCALTIMESTAMP* in Figure 10.59 returns the current date and time based on the geographical location in the database configuration. If this is set to GMT, it will return the date and time in the UK and automatically adjust for British Summer Time.

```
CREATE TABLE AuditLog
   datetime TIMESTAMP NOT NULL
   user_id VARCHAR2(20) NOT NULL
   details VARCHAR2(100) NOT NULL)
```

Figure 10.60 Auditlog table.

When a trigger is compiled, its generated *p-code* is saved in the database and is only loaded and invoked when the DBMS generates a suitable event notification following an operation of interest. Such invocation is implicit from the perspective of the trigger developer and completely transparent from the perspective of the database client. It is this transparency that makes PL/SQL triggers an ideal mechanism for auditing purposes.

The user issuing the DML operations is unaware that their actions are being monitored, and, if necessary, recorded. The user who issues the *update* operation shown in Figure 10.61 is completely oblivious to the fact that this operation gives rise to a series of event notifications, each of which initiates the row-level trigger *contracts_au_trigger*.

```
UPDATE contracts
SET salary=salary*1.10
WHERE club = 'Beauty United'
AND left IS NULL;
```

Figure 10.61 SQL triggering statement.

Such a user is completely unaware that the before and after details of each row affected by the update operation, together with the identity of the user initiating the change, and the date and time of each update, are recorded and held in an audit log. Figure 10.62 demonstrates the contents of such an audit log following the update operation of Figure 10.61.

```
select datetime, user_id as user, details from auditlog;

datetime                  user     details
------------------------- -------  ---------
06-DEC-02 21.39.43.751000 SB    AT245876 Old Salary: 825000 New Salary: 907500
06-DEC-02 21.39.43.771000 SB    BT46286  Old Salary: 825000 New Salary: 907500
06-DEC-02 21.39.43.771000 SB    ED24659  Old Salary: 825000 New Salary: 907500
06-DEC-02 21.39.43.771000 SB    FT246517 Old Salary: 825000 New Salary: 907500
06-DEC-02 21.39.43.771000 SB    KL23659  Old Salary: 825000 New Salary: 907500
06-DEC-02 21.39.43.771000 SB    QT873456 Old Salary: 825000 New Salary: 907500
06-DEC-02 21.39.43.771000 SB    SC159647 Old Salary: 825000 New Salary: 907500
06-DEC-02 21.39.43.771000 SB    TY48429  Old Salary: 825000 New Salary: 907500
06-DEC-02 21.39.43.771000 SB    UT23685  Old Salary: 825000 New Salary: 907500
06-DEC-02 21.39.43.771000 SB    UT236965 Old Salary: 825000 New Salary: 907500
06-DEC-02 21.39.43.771000 SB    VT432167 Old Salary: 825000 New Salary: 907500

11 rows selected.
```

Figure 10.62 Implicit PL/SQL *insert* statements affect the auditlog table.

A trigger can respond to more than one type of event notification. However, it is only possible for a trigger to be associated with events that affect one specific SQL table.

In order to distinguish which DML operation is responsible for firing a PL/SQL trigger, an event identifying function, a type of conditional predicate, is provided for each of the three DML types. *Updating* is set to *true* if an *update* operation has been executed. *Inserting* is set to *true* if an *insert* operation has been executed. *Deleting* is set to *TRUE* if an *delete* operation has been executed (Figure 10.63).

```
CREATE OR REPLACE TRIGGER contracts_aiud_trigger
AFTER INSERT OR UPDATE OR DELETE ON Contracts
FOR EACH ROW

DECLARE
v_log_details   VARCHAR2(100);

BEGIN
   IF UPDATING THEN
      v_log_details :=
       ('U Original Record: ' || :OLD.UFA_ID || :OLD.CLUB ||
 :OLD.JOINED || :OLD.LEFT || :OLD.SALARY ||
       ' Updated Record: ' || :NEW.UFA_ID || :NEW.CLUB ||
 :NEW.JOINED || :NEW.LEFT || :NEW.SALARY );
   ELSIF INSERTING THEN
      v_log_details :=
       ('I Inserted Record: ' || :NEW.UFA_ID || :NEW.CLUB ||
 :NEW.JOINED || :NEW.LEFT || :NEW.SALARY);
   ELSE
      v_log_details :=
       ('D Deleted Record: ' || :OLD.UFA_ID || :OLD.CLUB ||
 :OLD.JOINED || :OLD.LEFT || :OLD.SALARY);
   END IF;
   INSERT INTO AuditLog (datetime, user_id, details)
       VALUES (LOCALTIMESTAMP, USER, v_log_details);
END contracts_aiud_trigger;
/
```

Figure 10.63 Handling multiple notifications.

Additionally, the *UPDATING* conditional predicate can be refined to evaluate to *TRUE* only if a particular attribute has been updated. The syntax for this is shown in Figure 10.64.

Statement-level triggers are unable to reference before-images and after-images, as such information is related to specific table rows. However, statement-level

```
IF UPDATING (attribute_name) THEN
     <update related processing>
END IF;
```

Figure 10.64 Checking for updates.

triggers are a useful mechanism where the details of the rows affected by a DML event are not of interest, but the event itself is.

The creation of a single record per DML operation that records the user, time of operation and nature of operation may be all that is required from an audit trigger. Another example would be to use a before-statement-level trigger to ensure that certain users are only allowed to carry out DML operations on a particular table at specific times during the day. Such a trigger would abort those operations attempted by that set of users outside of those times.

It is possible to apply multiple triggers to a single DML operation. For instance, it is perfectly acceptable to have a *before insert* row-level trigger, an *after insert* row-level trigger, a *before insert* statement-level trigger, and an *after insert* statement-level trigger, all associated with insert operations to the same SQL table. In essence, each PL/SQL trigger registers interest in the same event, and will be notified when such an event takes place. However, the notifications of that event will arrive in a pre-defined order, thus ensuring that the triggers themselves are *fired* in sequence. Table 10.2 documents that sequence.

Table 10.2 Trigger firing sequence.
1 Before statement-level trigger
2 Before row-level trigger
3 After row-level trigger
4 After statement-level trigger

A single SQL table can potentially have 12 separate trigger types defined upon it, four for each of the three DML operation types: *insert*, *update* and *delete*. Moreover, multiple instances of each specific type (with distinguishing names) can be created and fired. It would be perfectly possible to have two, or more, *before update* row-level triggers, each interested in a separate attribute of the same SQL table.

Such multiple instances of same-type triggers have no pre-defined order of execution. In order to minimize unnecessary programming complexity they are probably best avoided. Indeed, there are only a limited number of circumstances where it would be useful to have more than one trigger for any particular DML operation.

10.9 ⊟ KEY TERMS

PL/SQL	Built-in, computationally complete, programming language for Oracle
Anonymous block	PL/SQL program with no identifier. Not stored in the database. Code is entered interactively or loaded from file; compiled and executed in one operation
Cursor	PL/SQL construct, associated with a select statement. Allows multi-row result set to be used one row at a time by procedures or functions
Procedure	Stored program; can take input parameters; private variables defined in procedure
Function	Stored program; can take input parameters; returns a value; private variables, cursors etc. defined in function. Can be used in the selection set or the predicate of an SQL statement
Package	Wrapper for related procedures and functions; can define public procedure and function signatures, variables, cursors, constants, etc. in the package header; private procedures, functions, variables etc. defined in the package body are only accessible from inside the package
Trigger	Registers interest in one or more events connected with a single schema object. Notification can be fired before or after the event. Granularity can be row-level or table-level. Provides action code that is executed when event notification received

10.10 ⊟ EXERCISE

(i) Implement the *season–points–club* example in this chapter. Extend the functionality to provide a sorted league table with points and goals for and against.

CHAPTER 11

DATABASE ARCHITECTURE

For the structure that we raise,

Time is with materials filled;

Our todays and yesterdays

Are the blocks with which we build.

Henry Wadsworth Longfellow, *The Builders*

An Oracle database is a logical storage unit. It has a name and its data is stored in several physical files, spread across the host machine's disks. The files are used for user data, for data recovery and to store control information. The files have a different internal format according to their purpose and they belong exclusively to the named database.

A database manager like Oracle is not just a single piece of software. It consists of a number of different programs, which run as separate processes on the host machine. Each process has a specific function within the general objectives of efficiently storing and presenting the data, securing and protecting transactions and ensuring reliability and availability

Most Oracle installations run in a client–server configuration: programs running on client machines communicate with the database host through a network. Providing an interface for remote access to the data management functions and hence to the data itself is a vital component of the overall package. The interface should be able to deal with any number of different hardware choices and network standards and provide a seamless entrance for user programs.

11.1 TABLES

The data area of an Oracle installation may consist of one or more physical files on the disk. The sizes of these files are set in the installation parameters. As the data grows, further physical files can be added. Oracle views each of the physical files as belonging to a **tablespace**. A tablespace consists of one or more physical files and can span one or more disks. There will be a tablespace for system use and a tablespace for user data (Figure 11.1).

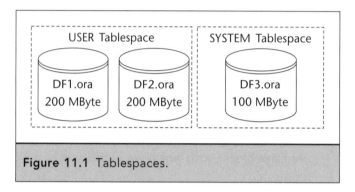

Figure 11.1 Tablespaces.

Within a tablespace there is a logical division known as a segment. There are four kinds of segment, each with different internal organization. Tables are held in a data segment. Indexes are stored in an index segment. Within the system tablespace, Oracle uses a rollback segment for data security. A temporary segment may be created to hold intermediate structures during a query. Segments can span physical files within the same tablespace.

A segment consists of extents. An extent is a contiguous allocation of data blocks: the fundamental unit of storage. The block size in bytes is specified in the installation parameters. Once established, it is constant.

When a table is created, a logical segment is created for it. An initial extent, consisting of a number of data blocks, is allocated to the segment. Rows in the table are stored in a data block. The block size may be large enough to contain several rows, or the row may be large and span two or more neighbouring blocks.

As the number of rows in the table grows, further extents are allocated to the table segment. Eventually an extent consisting of blocks from another physical file within the tablespace may be allocated. Segments can span files on different disks within the same logical tablespace.

Because rows are not necessarily inserted into a table in one operation, the extents that make up a segment may not be contiguous on the disk. The segment maintains a map of its extents. Each extent contains a map of its contiguous data blocks (Figure 11.2).

When a table is created in Oracle, initial space is allocated for the storage of a number of rows. Each row occupies the same number of bytes, which approximates to the sum of the sizes of each of its attributes. The initial storage space is allocated by default, but may be set in the *create* command. When the number of rows

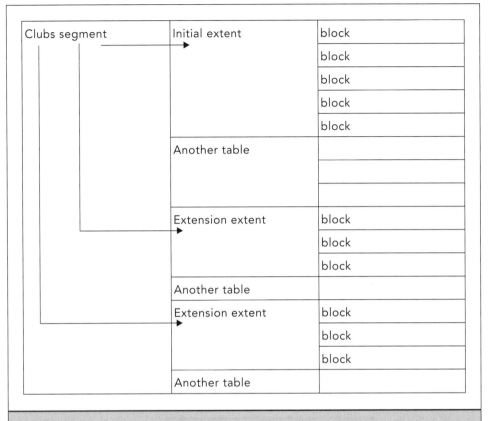

Figure 11.2 Tablespace allocations.

increases to fill the initial space, an extension extent is allocated to the segment. The size of the extension extent is set by default, but again may be varied in the *create* command. Further extension space will be allocated as the table grows until the entire tablespace is occupied. At this time, an additional physical file must be added to the tablespace by the DBA.

The Oracle system keeps track of space allocation for each user table and maps the allocated space so that the table may be viewed by the user as a logical block of data, even if the table spans several physical files. The space allocated for the initial and extension extents is configurable. Bigger sizes mean fewer extents in the table segment and less mapping work when performing queries; it may also mean wasted space for small tables.

11.2 INDEXES

When a table is created with a primary key, Oracle automatically creates an index for the table in an index segment. The index, like any user object, occupies an initial extent, and if its size is large may need extension extents to be added. Oracle uses indexes based on binary tree structures.

The index makes use of a special pseudocolumn, *ROWID*, that Oracle maintains for every table. This indicates the row number of each table row mapped over the entire table's space allocation (Figure 11.3).

Name	ROWID
AC Compassion	16
Beauty United	1
Bountiful Athletic	10
Forgiveness FC	4
Freedom United	14
Grace Town	19
Honesty United	3
Knowledge City	17
Liberation United	8
Nirvana City	9
...	...

Figure 11.3 Clubs index.

A binary tree is a data structure used for sorting and searching. Each data item occupies a node in a tree. A node has two pointers, left and right, pointing to two sub-trees. Any data item that contains a value less than a higher node in the tree is placed in the left sub-tree. A data item containing a higher value is placed in the right sub-tree. The shape of the tree reflects the order of insertion and may have asymmetrical sub-trees.

The root of the tree in Figure 11.4 is occupied by the key data item *Liberation United*. Searching for *Grace Town,* go left at *Liberation* and right at *Forgiveness*. The direction is determined by a comparison of the search data and the node data. Follow the left pointer if the search data is less than the node data; follow the right pointer if it is greater.

This tree has four levels between its root and the leaf nodes. Any node can be found by a maximum of four comparisons. Knowing the depth of the tree and therefore the work involved in finding a key is important in estimating optimal strategies for queries.

Figure 11.5 shows how a binary tree could be implemented in an index structure. The index consists of rows and columns like a table. The first column is the *ROWID* of the index rows, the second is the key value and the third is a value for the *ROWID*

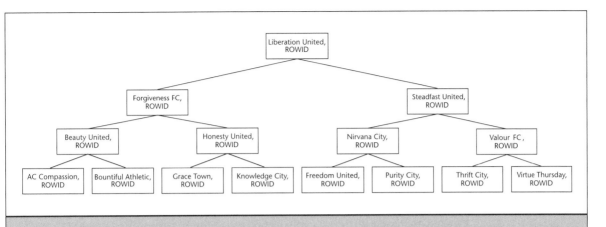

Figure 11.4 Binary tree.

Index ROWID	Name	Clubs ROWID	Left	Right
1	AC Compassion	16	0	0
2	Beauty United	1	1	3
3	Bountiful Athletic	10	0	0
4	Forgiveness FC	4	2	5
5	Freedom United	14	0	0
6	Grace Town	19	5	7
7	Honesty United	3	0	0
8	Knowledge City	17	0	0
9	Liberation United	8	4	14
10	Nirvana City	9	0	0
11	Pity City	12		
12	Purity FC	2	0	0
13	Sobriety FC	13		
14	Steadfast United	6	10	17
15	Thrift City	18	0	0
16	Truth FC	15		
17	Valour FC	7	15	18
18	Virtue Thursday	5	0	0

Figure 11.5 Binary tree logic.

in the base table, *Clubs*. Two further columns, *Left* and *Right*, contain *ROWID*s to other rows in the index.

Starting at the root, *Liberation United*, follow the *Left* value (4) to *Foriveness FC*. Then follow the *Right* value (6) to *Grace Town*. This has a *Right* value of (7), pointing to *Honesty United*, which has zeros in *Left* and *Right* and must be a leaf node. Several clubs have values for *Left* and *Right*, indictaing that they have not yet been placed in the tree. Inserting those clubs will create a new level in the tree and the existing zeros of some leaf nodes will change.

In addition to the automatic creation of an index following the designation of the *Name* attribute of the *Clubs* relation as a primary key, other indexes can be manually created on other attributes or sets of attributes. Any such indexes will be automatically maintained as new rows are added and if any key attribute values are amended.

The creation of additional indexes will aid some of the queries needed in the UFL application, but they will add to the maintenance overhead of the application. Users may not query or use indexes directly. That is open only to the Oracle query optimizer mechanism.

The tree in this example is a simple binary tree. A balanced binary tree, a B*-tree, has symmetrical sub-trees. A B*-tree is more efficient for searching. Branch nodes in a B*-tree show only a key range, indicating the contents of the two sub-trees. The actual key values and corresponding ROWIDs are kept in the leaf nodes. Because the sub-trees are symmetric, all leaf nodes are at the same level below the root. All searches involve the same number of comparisons and cost the same number of disk I/Os. See Section 15.1.1 for a further discussion of B*-tree indexes.

11.3 ⊂ METADATA

The distinguishing feature of relational databases from their predecessors was the unity of metadata with data. The hierarchical and Codasyl databases keep structural information about the record and its position in terms of direct disk addresses. Relational databases keep this information in a data dictionary, using the same table structures as the data to which it refers.

Although the metadata or data dictionary schema is complex, it is understandable in terms of the relational model. Oracle keeps information about the existence of tables in a table called *Tables* and of the columns of user tables in a table called *Columns*.

These data dictionary tables are stored in the same physical files as user tables but in a segment of the file reserved for system use. Unless the DBA designates them publicly searchable, they are not normally visible to users.

Figure 11.6 shows that user *smithw* has created a table called *Clubs* with four attributes. User *markc* has also created a table called *Clubs*, but the attributes do not have the same names and do not have precisely the same types.

There is not a problem; the two tables are stored quite separately and, because the two users' objects are completely segregated by Oracle's security mechanisms, the two tables do not interfere with each other. *smithw*'s updates will be applied only to the table owned by him and *markc* cannot access tables not owned by him.

Table	Owner	Data
Clubs	smithw	...
Players	smithw	...
Goals	smithw	...
Clubs	markc	...
Players	markc	...
Goals	markc	...

The Tables relation (simplified). The primary key is compound because different users can create a table with the same name

Table	Owner	Column	Type
Clubs	smithw	Name	Varchar2 (30)
Players	smithw	UFA_ID	Varchar2 (10)
Clubs	smithw	Manager	Varchar2 (20)
Players	smithw	DoB	Date
Goals	smithw	Scorer	Varchar2 (10)
Clubs	smithw	Stadium	Varchar2 (25)
Players	markc	UFA_ID	Varchar2 (12
Clubs	markc	Name	Varchar2 (28)
Clubs	markc	Ground	Varchar2 (25)
Clubs	smithw	Division	Varchar2 (8)

The Columns relation (simplified). The compound foreign key links each attribute specification to the table with which it is associated

Figure 11.6 *Tables* and *Columns*.

Indexes are recorded in a table called *Indexes*. This also has a compound foreign key linking its tuples to the base user table.

Figure 11.7 shows that user *smithw* has created an index called *Clubs_PK*, based on the primary key (*Name* attribute) of his *Clubs* table. He has created similar primary key indexes for the tables *Players* and *Goals*. He has also created an index called *StadMan* based on the *Clubs* table but with a compound key of *Stadium* and *Manager* in that order.

Table	Owner	Index	Column	Order
Club	smithw	Clubs_PK	Name	1
Players	smithw	Player_PK	UFA_ID	1
Club	smithw	StadMan	Stadium	1
Players	smithw	DoBIDX	DoB	1
Goals	smithw	Goals_PK	Scorer	1
Club	smithw	StadMan	Manager	2

Figure 11.7 *Indexes* table (simplified).

11.4 ⊝ ORACLE DATA

Within a tablespace, there will be data segments for each table, index segments for each index and a rollback segment where the database manager stores recovery data during transactions. The rollback segment is used to provide read consistent data for transactions and to re-establish a consistent database for failed transactions.

Figure 11.8 shows the physical files that go to make up an Oracle database. Each database is logically divided into one or more tablespaces. One or more datafiles are explicitly created for each tablespace. The combined size of a tablespace's datafiles is the total storage capacity of the tablespace. SYSTEM tablespace has 100 MByte storage capacity, while USER tablespace has 400 MByte. The combined storage capacity of the database in this example is the total storage capacity of the tablespaces – 500 Mbyte.

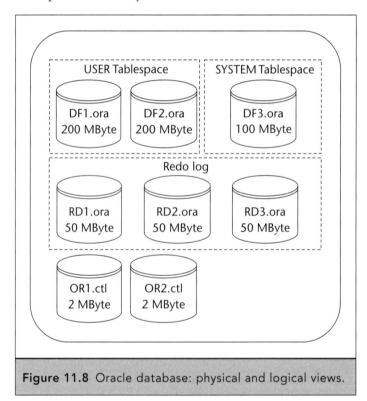

Figure 11.8 Oracle database: physical and logical views.

If user data segments and index segments fill the whole 400 MByte then further physical files will need to be created and added to the USER tablespace.

The most effective way of organizing these files is to place them all on separate disks each with their own I/O controller. This allows a degree of parallelism for a single job if a large table can be stored within the same tablespace, spread across several disks and reduces contention if several jobs require access to tables stored on different disks. This will enhance performance. Security for the database is also improved if the tablespaces and the redo log are segregated. Mirroring the redo log provides an additional level of protection.

11.4.1   PHYSICAL STRUCTURES

Every Oracle database has one or more physical datafiles. A datafile can be associated with only one database. A database's datafiles contain all the database data. The data in a datafile is read, as needed, during normal database operation and stored in memory caches or buffers.

An Oracle database has a set of two or more redo log files. The set of redo log files for a database is known as the redo log. A redo log is made up of redo entries, each of which is a group of change vectors describing a single transaction applied to the database. The primary function of the redo log is to record all changes made to the data and to the rollback segment. If data modifications cannot be permanently stored because of a disk failure, the changes can be obtained later from the redo log and work is never lost.

Every Oracle database has a control file. A control file contains entries that specify the physical structure of the database. It contains the database name and the names and locations of the datafiles and redo log files.

Every time an instance of an Oracle database is started, its control file is used to identify the database and redo log files that must be opened for database operation to proceed. If the physical makeup of the database is altered, the database's control file is automatically modified by Oracle to reflect the change.

11.5   THE ORACLE INSTANCE

When an Oracle instance is started, a large segment of shared memory is reserved for its use. This is the System Global Area (SGA). This is used for inter-process communication, as a data cache and for temporary sort space.

Oracle also launches a set of *background processes* for each instance. These relieve the server process, allowing it to concentrate on providing user service. The background processes increase parallelism for better performance and reliability.

Modified or new data is not necessarily written to a datafile immediately. To reduce the amount of disk access and increase performance, changed or new data is kept in the database buffers and written to the appropriate datafiles at irregular intervals. When the server updates a buffer, it does not have to wait for the changes to be permanently stored.

Instead of being blocked, it moves on to its next operation, leaving the database writer process to manage the buffered data. Because there is a time delay between the buffer update and the actual write operation, this is called asynchronous I/O.

The shared pool is a portion of the system global area (SGA) that contains memory constructs such as shared SQL areas. An SQL area is required to process every unique SQL statement submitted to a database. It holds information such as the parse tree and execution plan for the corresponding statement. Multiple user processes that issue identical SQL statements share a single parse tree and execution plan, leaving more shared memory for other uses.

The SGA and the set of Oracle background processes (Table 11.1) constitute an Oracle instance. At this point, no database is associated with these memory structures and processes.

Table 11.1 Oracle instance processes.	
Database Writer	Writes modified blocks from the database buffer cache to the datafiles. Writes occur only when more data needs to be read into the SGA and too few database buffers are free.
Log Writer	Redo log entries are generated in the redo log buffer of the SGA, and written sequentially into the online redo log file.
Checkpoint	A checkpoint writes all pending modifications in the SGA to the datafiles. This process signals the database writer at checkpoints and updates the control files to show the most recent checkpoint.
System Monitor	Performs crash recovery when a failed instance restarts. Also coalesces free extents within the tablespaces to make free space contiguous and easier to allocate.
Process Monitor	Performs process recovery when a user process fails, cleaning the cache and freeing any locked resources.
Dispatcher	Present when a multi-threaded server is used. Each dispatcher routes requests from connected user processes to the shared servers and returns responses.

Mounting a database associates the database with that instance. The instance finds the database control files and opens them. The control files are read to get the names of the database's datafiles and redo log files.

Opening a mounted database makes it available for normal database operations. Oracle opens the online datafiles and the online redo log files. The database is now available for any valid user to connect and to issue SQL statements (Figure 11.9).

11.6 ⊂ THE ORACLE SERVER

Server processes are created, once an instance is established, to handle requests from user processes. A server process interacts with the stored data to carry out requests of the associated user process. For example, if a user queries some data that is not

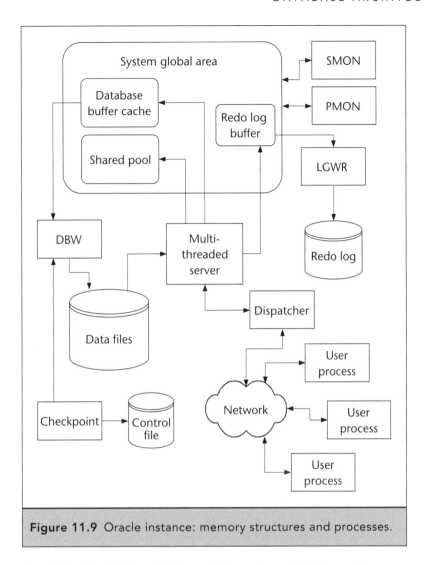

Figure 11.9 Oracle instance: memory structures and processes.

already in the database buffers of the system global area, the server reads the data blocks from the datafiles into the SGA and returns the results to the user process.

Oracle can be configured to vary the number of user processes per server. In a dedicated server configuration, a server process handles requests for a single user process. A new server is launched as each new user process connects.

A multi-threaded server configuration allows many users to share a single server, minimizing the number of server processes and maximizing the utilization of available system resources. When a multi-threaded server is configured, a dispatcher is launched as a separate background process.

The dispatcher is specific to the network protocols of the user process. It multiplexes the communication channels with connected users across the network, performs any necessary data type conversion and manages the connect status of the user processes. The dispatcher works at the presentation and session levels of the OSI network model. (For a discussion on the multi-threaded mechanism, see Section 12.1.1.)

11.6.1 HOW ORACLE WORKS

The following example illustrates an Oracle configuration where the user and associated server process are on separate machines (connected via a network).

1. A client workstation runs an application as a user process. The client application attempts to establish a connection to the Oracle server using a network driver.

2. A listener detects the connection request from the application and identifies it as using TCP/IP. The request is routed to the TCP/IP dispatcher, which takes over the communication channel with the user process. The listener reverts to listening for new requests. The dispatcher requests the creation of a user thread in the server which checks that the user, authenticated by a password, has a *CONNECT* role. The thread request is approved and the dispatcher registers the user communication channel with the thread.

3. The user executes a SQL statement and commits the transaction. For example, the user changes a value in a row of a table.

4. The server process receives the statement and checks the shared pool for any shared SQL area that contains an identical SQL statement. If a shared SQL area is found, it is used to process the statement; if not, a new shared SQL area is allocated for the statement so that it can be parsed and processed. More detailed descriptions of instance activity are shown in Table 11.2.

5. The server process retrieves the necessary row data from the actual table or, if possible, those cached in the SGA.

6. Because this is an update request, the server modifies data and rollback buffers and creates redo log entries in the SGA. The database writer stores modified blocks permanently to disk when doing so is efficient. Because the transaction committed, the log writer immediately records the transaction in the online redo log file.

7. If the transaction is successful, the server process sends a message via the dispatcher to the application. If it is not successful, an appropriate error message is transmitted and a rollback sequence is initiated.

8. Throughout this entire procedure, the other background processes run, watching for conditions that require intervention. In addition, the server manages other users' threads carrying out their transactions and prevents contention between transactions that request the same data.

Access Control	Determine whether user who issued this statement has authorization to access the schema objects in the query
Syntactic Checks	Check that the query conforms to SQL syntax. Are the clauses well-formed and are SQL functions correctly spelt
Semantic Integrity Control	Confirm the existence of elements referred to in the selection set, the join or restriction conditions. Ensure that the query will not offend against integrity rules
Query Decomposition and Optimization	Construct alternative algebraic expressions that will render the required result and choose the most efficient plan
Access Plan Management	Store the plan, map table reads, index usage, temporary tables, buffer sorts, merges and writes to action the preferred plan.
Execution Control	Perform the query, checking for consistency violations caused by updates, insertions and deletions
Concurrency Control	Engage control structures (locks and lock lists) for transaction isolation. Preserve read consistency or serializable transaction mode
Logging	For write operations, maintain the database buffers, the rollback buffers and the redo log buffers

Table 11.2 Server functions.

11.7 ⊱ SYSTEMS CONFIGURATION

The basic client–server architecture requires a host machine offering a service to be connected to a client machine through a network.

Client–server applications are independent of the precise nature of the network hardware since the networking software hides this from both the client and the server. The hardware may be configured as a local area network (LAN), a gateway onto the Internet or as two local networks connected through a secure channel across the Internet.

The *de facto* standard for network software is TCP/IP, and although this does provide transparency for the client–server connection, there are differences in performance and security ratings for the three configurations illustrated in Figure 11.10.

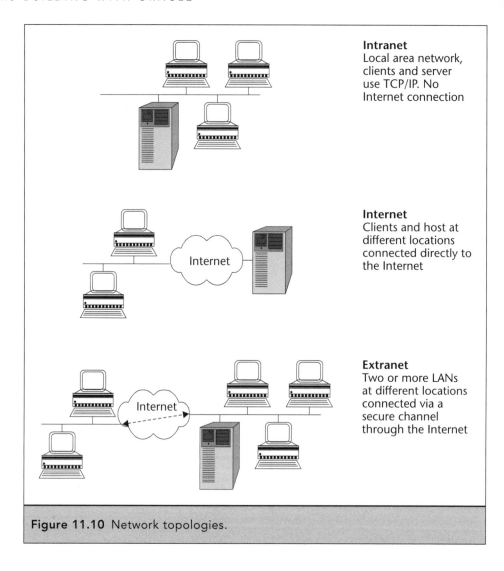

Intranet
Local area network, clients and server use TCP/IP. No Internet connection

Internet
Clients and host at different locations connected directly to the Internet

Extranet
Two or more LANs at different locations connected via a secure channel through the Internet

Figure 11.10 Network topologies.

11.8 ⊂ NETWORK SOFTWARE

The seven layers of the OSI network model provide a conceptual framework for communications across a network. Each node on a network must provide within its networking software the functionality contained within the OSI stack if communications are to be established and run reliably.

TCP/IP is overwhelming the protocol of choice for open systems networking. Where a mixture of hardware platforms and different operating systems must communicate transparently across networks constructed from different physical media, TCP/IP has the advantage of being independent of equipment and software vendors.

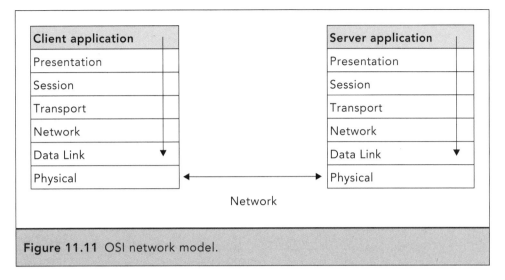

Figure 11.11 OSI network model.

Figure 11.11 shows the OSI/ISO seven layer model for network services. TCP/IP provides standard services that approximate to the transport and network layers. Network equipment manufacturers are generally responsible for compliance with international standards operating below IP. These might be LAN specifications such as Ethernet or Token Ring, which regulate packet structures and the physical interfaces that connect nodes and interconnect networks. Often, their software, which provides a link between IP and the network media, is bundled with operating systems like Windows XP or Linux.

Application vendors are responsible for ensuring that the functionality of the presentation and session layers above TCP, are provided by their products (Figure 11.12). Oracle has developed software which is positioned between the application and the network stack and which provides presentation and session layer services.

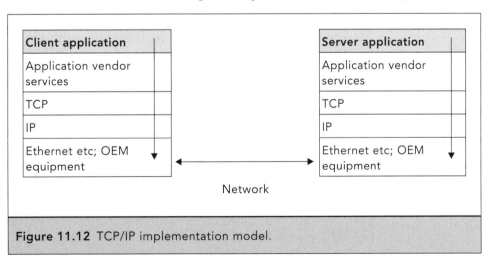

Figure 11.12 TCP/IP implementation model.

11.8.1   THE PROGRAM INTERFACE

A user process communicates with a server process through the *program interface*. The interface provides presentation and session services for both the client and the server.

On the client side, the software may be bound to the application when it is compiled and standard Oracle libraries are linked to the executable. Alternatively, it may be present in external drivers (libraries) such as ODBC or in Oracle-provided Java classes such as JDBC. On the server side, separate processes receive client requests and route them to the appropriate server process (Figure 11.13).

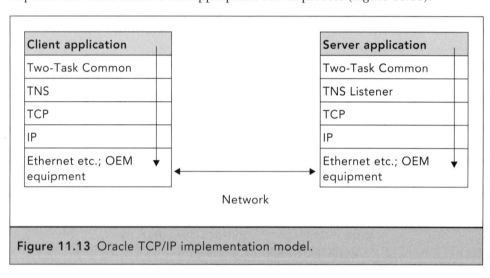

Figure 11.13 Oracle TCP/IP implementation model.

Presentation services are provided through Two-Task Common. This enables character set and data type conversion between different formats on the client and server. For example between ASCII and Unicode or between 32 bit integers on one side and 64 bit on the other. When a connection is initiated, Two-Task Common evaluates the needs for conversion based on information exchanged between the client and the server sides.

Session layer functionality is provided through Oracle's *transparent network substrate* (TNS). This is implemented as a separate process on the server host. This process is called a **listener**. When an Oracle instance is started, it registers its service name with the listener. More than one Oracle instance may run on a single machine, in which case the listener will hold multiple service registrations. The listener also registers dispatchers if a multi-threaded server (MTS) is configured as part of the instance.

Clients have a configuration file, tnsnames.ora, which defines a net service name. This contains the network location of a listener, the network protocol to use and the service to which it will connect. Client connection requests are received first by the listener, which routes the connection request to the appropriate service.

Alternatively, if the client is a Java/JDBC program, this information may be embedded in the program as a comment string.

If a multi-threaded server is running, the request is forwarded to its dispatcher. If the instance is configured for dedicated servers, the listener will already have spawned a number of server processes to deal with client requests. If one of these is idle, the request is passed to it. If they are all active (dealing with other clients) it spawns a new server process to deal with the new client's request. Such a spawned server exists only for the lifetime of the connect session.

In either case, once the request has been routed, the client and the dispatcher or the client and the dedicated server communicate directly (Figure 11.14).

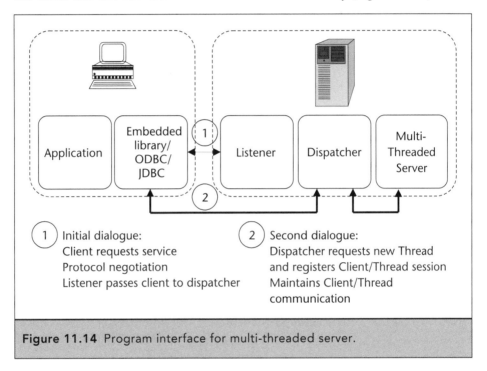

Figure 11.14 Program interface for multi-threaded server.

11.9 ⊢ KEY TERMS

Storage objects	Files; tablespaces for user and system objects
Tables	Extents: blocks
Indexes	Logical storage: B*-trees
Metadata	Table and index structural information stored in tables

Oracle instance	Memory resident processes
Server	Queries: syntactic and semantic checker; Optimizer. Transaction Manager; Lock Manager
Other processes	Co-resident. DB Writer; Log Writer; Dispatcher; Listener. Relieve server of work

11.10 ⊏ EXERCISES

(i) Investigate structures other than B-trees that can be used for indexes. Write a report which discusses their advantages or disadvantages over B-trees.

(ii) Write a program to load data items from a file into a simple B-tree. Investigate the various orders these data can be output using a tree walk.

PART 3

IMPLEMENTING THE SYSTEM

CHAPTER 12

CLIENT–SERVER MODELS

A client is to me a mere unit, a factor in a problem.

Sherlock Holmes, in *The Sign of Four* (Sir Arthur Conan Doyle)

12.1 ∈ MULTI-TASKING, MULTI-THREADED

The first section of this book introduced the idea of separating the common functions for data storage and retrieval from the interface and business logic functions. This results in smaller application programs communicating with a database manager and requesting data access services.

This raises two questions: how do the applications communicate their requests to the DBMS and how does the DBMS handle requests arriving simultaneously from the applications?

12.1.1 LOCAL ACCESS FOR MULTIPLE REQUESTS

Early solutions to these two interlinked problems relied on the architecture of second-generation operating systems running on very large capacity machines, known as mainframes. From about 1960, operating systems began to be developed with facilities to enable more than one process to be resident in the main memory of the computer. These processes or jobs were controlled by the operating system scheduler (Figure 12.1).

Detailed information about the running state of each process is kept in queue structures that enable the scheduler to allocate CPU time to each job in turn, giving more or fewer CPU cycles to each according to its relative priority. Jobs that request services from the I/O controllers are placed in a 'blocked' queue because, until the requested input or output is delivered, there is no point in allocating the process any CPU time. Jobs that are dormant, waiting perhaps for user input, are placed in a

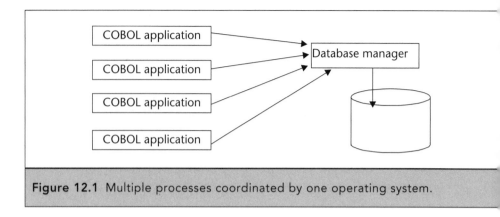

Figure 12.1 Multiple processes coordinated by one operating system.

'suspended' or 'wait' queue. Jobs that are ready to run are kept in the 'run' queue from where they are given their time slot on the CPU.

The information needed to allow a process to be stopped and restarted is called the process **context**. The queues are made up of **process context blocks** that describe the current state of the process. A PCB contains the code segment – the memory address or addresses where the program is loaded, an instruction counter showing which instruction is next to be loaded to the CPU, the addresses of the program's data segments and so on. The scheduler runs on the CPU every time a process is 'stopped' in order to perform queue management. Allocating CPU time to a process consists of loading the process context into the registers of the CPU and passing control to the next instruction in the process context. This is called a **context switch**. The scheduler manages the queues, moving jobs between queues and from the run queue to the CPU according to the scheduling algorithm (Figure 12.2).

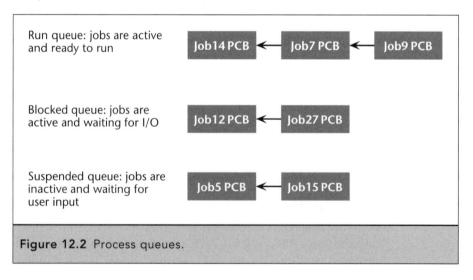

Figure 12.2 Process queues.

Inter-Process Communication (IPC) is conducted through a reserved segment of main memory. Applications can leave messages here; the DBMS can pick them up, act on them and place results back in the reserved segment for the application to pick up. The memory segment acts like a letterbox, enabling a dialogue between an application and the DBMS.

Clearly, each such dialogue can either take place in separate segments or else access to a shared segment has to be controlled so that one application's request does not interfere with another's returned results. The use of **semaphores** and **monitor** functions in operating systems allows shared segments of memory to be managed efficiently and safely.

The operating system scheduler maintains a *run queue* of distinct processes using a linked list of *process context blocks*. By analogy, it should be possible for a single process, required to handle concurrent service requests, to maintain a similar internal queue structure consisting of the contexts of each of the service requests within the single process. Within a process, each of these service contexts is called a **thread of control**.

The **thread contexts** are managed internally by the process, much as the scheduler manages the process queues. Within the CPU time slice allocated by the operating system, a **dispatcher** thread allocates time to each of the user threads that it is currently managing. There will be at least one thread for every concurrent service request, together with the manager thread (dispatcher). Each of the thread contexts will contain information about the process's common data areas, the addresses of any thread specific data and a program counter showing which instruction within the process is to be loaded next. Processes capable of handling multiple service requests by this method are said to be **multi-threaded**.

It can now be seen how the DBMS software and many copies of the user application can be resident in the same machine; the applications and the DBMS communicate and the DBMS can handle multiple concurrent requests from the applications. Until the early 1980s, all of these processes would have been resident in the same mainframe. Although the mainframe had plenty of memory to accommodate the processes, a single CPU still had to run all the applications as well as the DBMS.

The development of cheap personal computers and of faster and more reliable network standards led system architects to consider removing the user applications to individual PCs and to communicate requests remotely to a dedicated high-performance machine where the DBMS would not have to share CPU time directly with users.

12.2 REMOTE PROCEDURE CALL

In the 1980s the key phrase **client–server** came into vogue. This simply meant that the server software is positioned on one machine and multiple clients on several other machines. The client software is responsible for the user interface and for most of the business logic. It communicates with the server through a network. The server, based on a multi-threaded architecture, receives service requests from each of the client machines and responds to the client through the network[1]. The key difference is that the server machine's CPU is relieved of the work now associated with the client processes. As the PC gained power, it became able to support a graphical user interface (GUI). Machines hosting the server software can have special I/O devices: fast channel hard drives, large memory caches, designed to augment their performance in meeting client requests.

Clearly, a new mechanism was required to facilitate communication between the client and the server. The first solution was the Remote Procedure Call (RPC). In order to understand how the remote procedure call works, consider Figure 12.3.

```
#include <stdio.h>

int add (int x, int y){
return (x + y);
}
void main(){
int sum, a, b ;
a=2;
b=3;
sum =add(a, b);
printf("sum is %d", sum);
}
```

Figure 12.3 Local program.

This simple program has a *main* function that receives control when the program executes. It has a function, *add()*, which is called in the *main* function. The function *add()* takes two integer parameters and returns a single integer, the result of adding the two input integers. Compiling this program will end not just in the transformation of the simple statements to machine code.

A mechanism is inserted by the compiler to enable the line of control to jump to the address of the subroutine, retaining access to the two input parameters as well as information on how to return to the calling position (Figure 12.4).

The program makes use of a stack structure to communicate between the *main* function and the *add()* function. The data is *marshalled* to enable the procedure call.

Making a remote procedure call uses this same principle but there are two additional problems. The *addresses* of variables cannot be passed, since the client program and the server program are running on two machines with different and

---

1   Bruce Nelson originated the idea of the Remote Procedure Call (RPC) in his PhD thesis in 1981. He later co-authored a paper on the subject: Birrell and Nelson (1984).

```
main function starts;
allocate address for variables a, b and sum;
value 2 allocated to a;
value 3 allocated to b;
prepare to call add() function:
    push address of a onto stack
    push address of b onto stack
    push address of current instruction onto stack
jump to address of add() function
allocate addresses to variables x and y
prepare to accept parameters:
    pop return address from stack
    pop address of b, allocate contents to variable y
    pop address of a, allocate contents to variable x
add x and y, push result onto stack
jump back to return address \* we are now back at the calling
instruction
pop return value from the stack, assign to variable sum
print variable sum
```

Figure 12.4 Local procedure call.

autonomous memory spaces. Allowance must be made for the fact that the two machines may have different processors with different data representations. An integer on one may occupy 64 bits, while on the other it may occupy 128 bits.

The marshalling for a remote procedure call makes use of a standard data type called external data representation (XDR). Parameters are passed as values rather than addresses and are converted to XDR before transmission across the network. There is a defined protocol within RPC of call and response so that a simple dialogue where the *add()* function is part of the server might look like the exchange illustrated in Figure 12.5.

It should be noted that in this exchange the client, having sent the request, waits for the server response. The client is said to have made a **blocking** call. This is a **synchronous** mode of operation.

When the client does not need to wait for a response but moves on, leaving the server to complete the request or when the client is itself multi-threaded and spawns a thread to make the call while the main line of control moves on, the call is **non-blocking** and the mode of operation is **asynchronous**.

Most UNIX or Linux systems feature a tool call *Rpcgen* that takes a specification for server functions written in a syntax similar to the C language. It produces headers and C program source for a simple client and for a lightweight (multi-threaded) server. The specification file used by Rpcgen can be thought of as an interface definition for the client and the server.

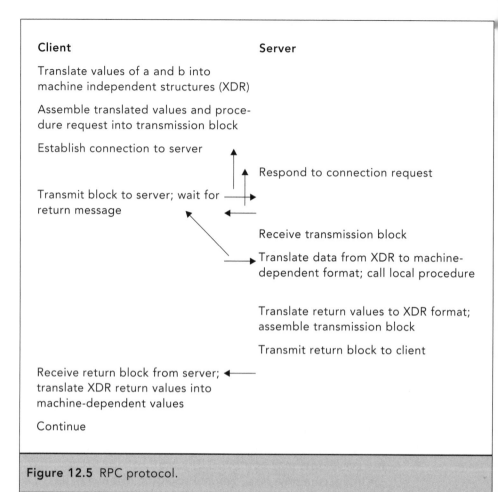

Figure 12.5 RPC protocol.

The programmer then completes the client logic and the code for the actual server functions. A sample client–server program written in C can be found on the web site associated with this book

12.3 REMOTE METHOD INVOCATION

When the client and the server are both Java programs, a variation of the RPC is used. This is called Remote Method Invocation (RMI) and it is specific to the Java language.

The RMI architecture is more complex than RPC because of the nature of Java as an interpreted language and because of the Java object model.

When designing a client and server that will use RMI[2], the first stage is again a definition of the interface: the methods that will be called from the client. Method signatures (declarations) are specified in Java in an interface file. This is compiled using the RMI compiler (rmic) which produces a stub class and a skeleton class (Figure 12.6).

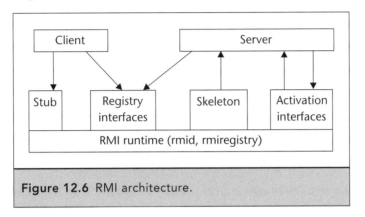

Figure 12.6 RMI architecture.

The stub and skeleton provide methods for marshalling the data and for establishing a communications channel across a network. There is no need for data type conversion since all Java programs use the same basic types, but there is a need for objects identified by memory pointers to be dereferenced from one memory space to the other and for complex structures to be serialized for transmission across the network as byte streams.

The client classes and the server classes are written in Java with references to the stub or skeleton classes as appropriate and compiled with the Java compiler, javac. Each Java class actually runs in a **Java Virtual Machine** (JVM). The JVM is the active process recognized by the operating system. Network communication can only be made between processes. The client JVM cannot call to the server JVM directly. The client class will be trying to invoke a method within a server class that is hidden from the operating system within the server JVM.

An additional process is therefore needed to identify the specific JVM (there could be several in a multi-user machine) in which the requested method resides. A process called the **RMI registry** runs on the server machine. It is assigned a specific port number and listens for requests on that port.

When a server class starts up, it registers its presence with the local RMI registry. The client invokes a method request via the registry process (using the machine address and the registry port number). The request is then passed on to the appropriate JVM process that registered the method. The skeleton class associated with the server class then establishes a network channel with the stub class associated with the calling client.

---

2 A sample client and activatable server example can be found at `http://java.sun.com/j2se/1.3/docs/guide/rmi/getstart.doc.html` (July 2003).

From then on, the dialogue is similar to the RPC protocol. The server class receives the request along with associated parameters, acts on it and responds with a result. If the request is successful, this may be a return value or a stream of values. If the request causes an error, the response will be an **exception** message that must be handled by the client.

This way of invoking a remote method depends on the server class registering the method at it starts up. If the server has not already started, it may be started automatically through a procedure known as **activation**.

The client needs no changes in order to use activation. The server class is made **activatable** so that if it not already instantiated and registered it may be started when a request is received.

An additional process, the RMI daemon (*rmid*) must be running as well as the RMI registry. The *rmid* provides a JVM from which other JVM instances may be spawned.

A special setup class is written for each activatable class on the server. The setup class creates all the information necessary to instantiate the activatable class, without actually creating an instance of the remote object. The setup class passes information about the activatable class to *rmid*, registers a remote reference and a name with the *rmi registry*, and then exits.

The client makes the request in the normal way. The *rmi registry* has an activation entry for the requested method so passes it to the *rmid*, which starts up a new JVM invoking the server class with it. A communication channel between the client and the newly activated class is opened through the stub and the skeleton classes as before.

12.4 ⊂ DATA ACCESS MECHANISMS

When a client application makes a service request of an Oracle server, it is generally for the execution of an SQL statement and often for the return of data rows associated with that query. Requests of this nature are in the application layer of the OSI model and were originally enabled, using RPC calls made from purpose-written third-generation language applications: C or C++, Fortran, COBOL etc.

The server interface was therefore designed to respond to function calls using an RPC interface. The submission of a single SQL statement and the associated return of data could involve as many as twenty or thirty distinct function calls, often requiring complex data structures submitted as parameters.

Most database vendors provided pre-compilers that would automatically convert SQL statements into these function calls. The program was then compiled and linked with standard libraries as well as special libraries provided by the vendor. It was then ready to be run as a client, communicate with the database server, make RPC requests and receive responses (Figure 12.7).

Not every vendor provided an interface at the server side that offered the same functionality or even referred to its various services by the same name. The same client program would have to be pre-compiled separately for each target database

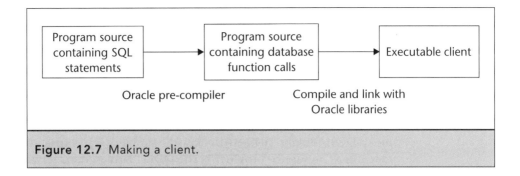

Figure 12.7 Making a client.

and would even need code modifications in order to work properly with that database software. This became quite a problem for third-party software houses whose accounting, personnel, purchase order or CAD systems were expected to use Oracle, Ingres, Sybase or SQL Server according to their customers' preferences.

Eventually the database vendors agreed on a standard, issued as the X/OPEN Call Level Interface and eventually confirmed in SQL:1999. CLI is primarily aimed at a distributed transaction processing (DTP) environment with data sources resident in a variety of database systems. The aim of CLI is that it should comply with the functionality defined within SQL92. Further revisions to the standard will bring it up to compliance with SQL:1999. OCLI is a minimum standard. Many database vendors have additional functions that extend CLI functionality (Figure 12.8).

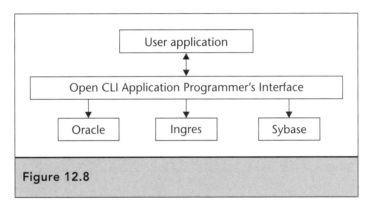

Figure 12.8

It is possible to write a program that accesses a database at the Call Level but such an application, despite the X/OPEN standard, will probably still need to be separately complied and linked with vendor-specific libraries. The CLI standard has reduced the necessary modifications (if any) in adapting an application to use different products.

Alternatively, a higher level of functionality, at some intermediate stage between SQL and the Call Level, can be defined as an API. The client is written to comply with this and a run-time service is provided to translate the intermediate level to the Call Level. This the concept behind ODBC and JDBC.

12.5 ⊂ OPEN DATABASE CONNECTIVITY – ODBC

ODBC is a standard developed by Microsoft that allows client applications to connect to relational database and to make queries. The application is mainly restricted to running in a Windows environment.

The ODBC standard is defined in terms of an Application Program Interface (API). The client application is written (or generated within an Integrated Development Environment (IDE) to make API function calls to a service on the same machine. The service provider is the ODBC Driver Manager and an ODBC driver specific to the remote database (Figure 12.9).

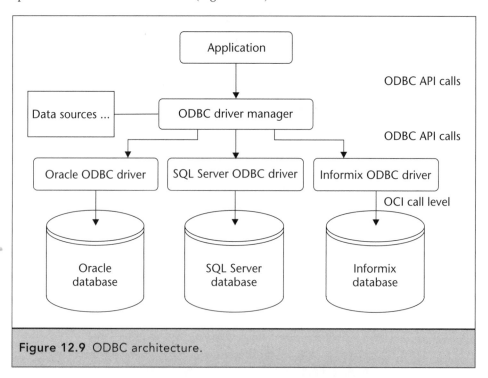

Figure 12.9 ODBC architecture.

This architecture means that the application does not need to be changed in order to access Oracle, Informix or SQL Server. Access is achieved using the correct ODBC driver that translates the ODBC calls it receives from the client application into Call Level (RPC) functions specific to the remote database for which it was written.

12.5.1 THE DRIVER MANAGER

The Driver Manager is a dynamic link library (DLL) that manages communication between applications and drivers. It maintains a list of data source names that correspond to the different databases to which applications on the client machine might connect. These names indicate the type of database, its connection details and which driver to load for applications requesting connection to the datasource.

The application needs only to be linked to the Driver Manager and calls ODBC functions in the Driver Manager, not the driver. The application identifies the data source name in making such calls and the Driver Managers loads the correct driver into memory on the client machine.

12.5.2   THE ODBC DRIVER

The Driver Manager passes ODBC calls from the application to the driver. Drivers are also dynamic link libraries that implement the functions in the ODBC API. Each driver is specific to a particular database management system. A driver for Oracle cannot directly access data in an Informix DBMS.

The driver translates ODBC calls passed to it from the application into OCI functions and forwards them to the database. Returned data or messages are packaged as the returns of ODBC functions and forwarded to the application. As far as the database server is concerned, it is receiving OCI calls with appropriate parameters. The translation process and the actual nature of the client application are hidden from it.

Multiple drivers can coexist, which allows the application simultaneous access to more than one data source. This makes ODBC a potential vehicle for implementing a heterogeneous distributed database. The application uses ODBC in such a manner that the application is not tied to any one DBMS, although it might be tied to a limited number of DBMSs that provide similar functionality (Table 12.1).

Table 12.1 ODBC: common tasks.
Selecting and connecting to a data source
Submitting SQL for execution
Retrieving results
Processing errors
Committing or rolling back transactions
Disconnecting from the data source

In addition to the tasks performed at the application level the ODBC driver undertakes data conversion between the client and the server and maintains the connect session with the DBMS. It thus provides presentation and session level services above a network stack such as TCP /IP.

Using ODBC requires the Driver Manager and the vendor specific driver to be present on the client machine. The driver manager is distributed with most Windows variants. The vendor is usually responsible for providing the driver.

12.6 JAVA DATABASE CONNECTIVITY – JDBC

JDBC is another example of an attempt to provide an alternative to direct CLI programming. Because, as its name suggests, it is specific to the Java language, it benefits from superior portability compared with ODBC. Applications using JDBC will run unchanged on any client machine that has a Java Virtual Machine installed on it. Changing the target database has minimal effect for the program code. If the database is supplied by a different vendor, the driver manger must be changed and the new database location updated; otherwise, the program and its API calls remain the same.

The Java language is defined and maintained by Sun Microsystems. JDBC is defined as a series of extension classes distributed with the language in the Java Developer Kit (JDK)[3]. These classes enable the developer to request database operations at a considerably higher level than the CLI.

12.6.1 JDBC DRIVERS

In the end though, the database can only receive CLI requests. Sun defines four types of driver that can provide the translation between the high-level JDBC request and the database. These are described in Table 12.2.

Software vendors like Borland, who offer the JBuilder Java developer tool, include a type 1 JDBC –ODBC bridge with their package. This has the advantage of compatibility with a Windows environment that includes the ODBC driver

Table 12.2 JDBC driver types.	
Type 1	JDBC is implemented as a mapping to another data access API, such as ODBC. Drivers of this type generally require a machine or operating system dependent library, which limits their portability.
Type 2	Written partly in Java and partly in machine or o/s dependent code, these drivers use a client library specific to the database to which they connect. Because of the native code, their portability is limited.
Type 3	Drivers that use a pure Java client and communicate with a middleware server using a database-independent protocol. The middleware server then communicates the client's requests to the database.
Type 4	Drivers that are pure Java and implement the network protocol for a specific database. The client connects directly to the database server through the JDBC classes.

---

3 The JDK Version 2.0 Enterprise Edition (J2EE) is available from http://java.sun.com/j2ee/docs.html (July 2003).

manager. When the application is deployed, a specific ODBC driver must also be installed on the client machines and the datasource names separately administered.

Oracle and other database vendors offer type 2 JDBC–OCI drivers. When the application is deployed, these have a complex installation requirement for special libraries and networking software. The number of communications phases involved in using this type of driver can have performance implications, but the speed of the native code library usually compensates for this (Figure 12.10).

Type 3 drivers are generally written by the client development team for specific circumstances that prevent the use of other types of driver. A type 3 driver communicates with an external server, possibly on a remote machine using a protocol such as RMI or IIOP[4]. This server then performs the database access or may even forward the request to another process to perform the access. Because of their complexity and the need to write bespoke software, type 3 drivers have not achieved significant usage.

Type 4 drivers are written in pure Java and specific versions are supplied by each database vendor. Figure 12.10 shows that this driver type has the simplest

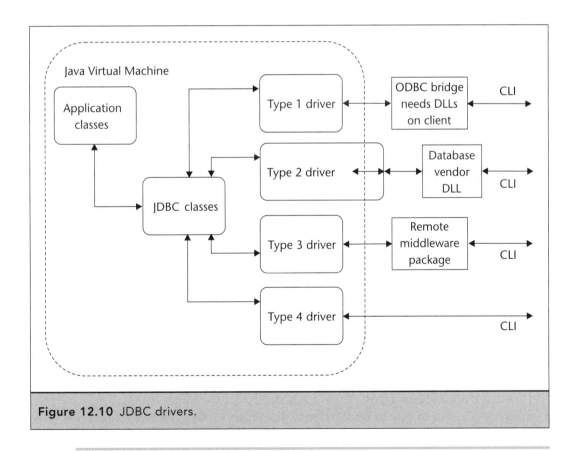

Figure 12.10 JDBC drivers.

---

4 Internet InterOperability Protocol: used by CORBA-compliant object request brokers.

configuration. Presentation and session layer services are included within the driver as well as the translation facility for CLI calls. This may account for their relative popularity. There are doubts about performance for Java-only drivers, although advances in price/performance ratios for client workstations make this factor increasingly less significant. The driver software libraries must be included as part of the deployment package with the application.

The ability to interface a Java application with more than one vendor database makes JDBC a simple vehicle for the construction of a distributed database. In a situation where the databases are owned and maintained by separate organizations, there may be situations where the pooling of information would be advantageous (Figure 12.11).

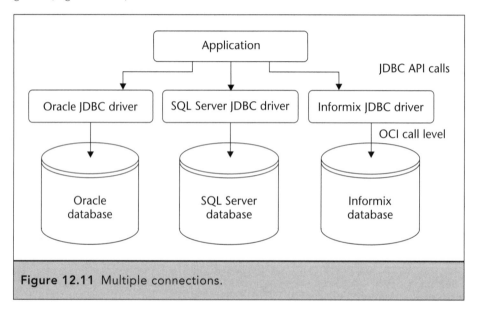

Figure 12.11 Multiple connections.

For example, the motor insurance industry exchanges data about claims in order to combat fraud. If a central association were given limited access to each member's database, then a relatively simple Java application could summarize claims information. This would enable queries to show all the claims involving the same vehicle, regardless of underwriter.

12.6.2   JDBC CLASSES AND DRIVERS

JDBC is implemented as a group of extension classes to the standard Java language and is distributed as the *java.sql* package. The classes and their methods enable functions for connecting to a database, performing queries and receiving the returned data. The data dictionary of the target database may be queried and the structure of returned data determined within the program (Table 12.3).

Each database vendor supplies a driver manager with the drivers it distributes, so there is a general driver manager for Oracle drivers. The driver manager selects the

Table 12.3 JDBC classes.

Connection	Establishes database connection; maintain session may have multiple statement objects associated with it
Statement	Contains a standard SQL statement as a string constant
Prepared Statement	Contains a parameterized SQL statement; the parameters can be given values at run-time
Callable Statement	Contains a reference to a stored code on the database server; may be used to call a PL/SQL program in Oracle
DB Meta Data	Examine the data dictionary of the target database
ResultSet	A flexible data structure that is dynamically configured for the columns, types and number of rows of the returned data
RS Meta Data	Examine the structure of a ResultSet

Table 12.4 Driver managers.

JDBC–ODBC bridge	sun.jdbc.odbc.JdbcOdbcDriver
Oracle database	oracle.jdbc.driver.OracleDriver

appropriate type of driver according to the parameters of the connection (Table 12.4).

A connection object may be instantiated once the driver manager has been selected. The connection constructor takes at least a single parameter in the form of a URL (Uniform Resource Locator). This describes the driver type, the location of the database and may include the address of a listener process; login details may be added if necessary. Figure 12.12 shows some JDBC URLs: the ODBC example

```
jdbc:<subprotocol>:<subname>
jdbc:odbc:MyAccessDatabase

jdbc:<subprotocol>:<<host>:<port>:<sub-subname>>
jdbc:oracle:thin:@orion.uel.ac.uk:1521:bisora
```

Figure 12.12 JDBC URLs.

depends on *MyAccessDatabase* having been previously defined as a datasource name in the ODBC manager; the Oracle URL is remote and requires the host address, the port number of the listener and name of the database. The sections of the URL are colon-separated.

Figure 12.13 shows a program fragment illustrating the construction of a connection object. First, all classes in the *javax.sql* package are imported. The driver manager is instantiated using the general class constructor, *Class.forName*. The *ClassNotFoundException* is raised if the driver is not present.

```
import javax.sql.*;

public class JDBCConnection {

public JDBCConnection()
  throws SQLException, ClassNotFoundException {

  Class.forName("oracle.jdbc.driver.OracleDriver");

  Connection conn = DriverManager.getConnection
   ("jdbc:oracle:thin:@orion.uel.ac.uk:1521:bisora",
    "scott", "tiger");

  Statement stmt = conn.createStatement();
  }
}
```

Figure 12.13 JDBC connection.

The driver manager has a method for constructing a connection, thus ensuring that the connection is associated with a particular driver. The URL supplied as the first parameter tells the *getConnection* method what type of driver to use, the location of the database host, the port number of the listener and the database name. Additional parameters give the username and password. Statements are associated with a connection so the connection class has a method, *createStatement* that calls a statement constructor.

12.6.3 STATEMENTS AND RESULTS

A statement, once created can be executed by calling its *executeQuery()* method. This method takes a simple string parameter containing an SQL statement that may return zero or more rows. Figure 12.14 shows how a *ResultSet* object is constructed and assigned to the returned data of the SQL in one program line.

```
...
Connection conn = DriverManager.getConnection
                ("jdbc:oracle:thin:@orion.uel.ac.uk:
                1521:bisora",    "scott", "tiger");
Statement stmt = conn.createStatement();

ResultSet rs = stmt.executeQuery("SELECT id, type FROM PARTS");
while (rs.next()) {
  int partId = rs.getInt(1);
  String partType = rs.getString(2);
  System.out.println(partId + ", " + partType);
}
rs.close();
stmt.close();
conn.close();
```

Figure 12.14 JDBC multi-row retrieval.

The *ResultSet* class provide a flexible structure, similar to an array but with several important differences. Firstly, the *ResultSet* is dynamically configured on assignment with the same column names and data types as the columns in the returned data. The columns in the *ResultSet* may be referred to by name or by an index: 1, 2, 3 etc.

Secondly, although the *ResultSet* can contain as many rows as are returned by the query, access to the data by the program is limited to one row at a time. The *ResultSet* is the mechanism for overcoming the impedance between set-oriented SQL and the record-oriented programming language.

The *ResultSet* may have different mechanisms for moving through the returned rows. These are determined by properties of the statement to which the *ResultSet* is assigned. The default behaviour is to use the concept of a cursor indicating the current row. Immediately following the query execution the cursor may be validated by calling *ResultSet.next()*. This returns a Boolean, indicating whether the operation was successful (the query returned at least one row) and, if it was, establishes a cursor pointing at the first row.

The contents of this current row may now be accessed in the program. Calls to *ResultSet.next()* move the cursor forward, enabling program access to the subsequent rows. When the cursor is moved beyond the last row, it returns *false*. By default, the cursor only moves forward. The alternative is to make the cursor *scrollable*, in which case it may be moved forwards and backwards.

Unless specified, the data returned by the query is treated as a snapshot taken at execution time. Any subsequent changes caused by other users updating or inserting rows will not be reflected in the *ResultSet*. The *ResultSet* may be made sensitive to concurrent changes in the database. These changes will reflect committed transactions by other users and uncommitted changes made in the running program. The *ResultSet* can also be configured to make non-SQL updates or to be read only.

Figure 12.15 shows how the options are implemented through the statement. Both examples will make the *ResultSet* scrollable when it is constructed. In the first fragment, the *ResultSet* is made insensitive to concurrent changes and read-only, disallowing non-SQL updates. In the second example, it will reflect concurrent changes and non-SQL updates are enabled.

```
...
Statement stmt = conn.createStatement(
                            ResultSet.TYPE_SCROLL_INSENSITIVE,
                            ResultSet.CONCUR_READ_ONLY);
ResultSet rs = stmt.executeQuery("SELECT id, type FROM PARTS");
...

...
Statement stmt = conn.createStatement(
                            ResultSet.TYPE_SCROLL_SENSITIVE,
                            ResultSet.CONCUR_UPDATABLE);
ResultSet rs = stmt.executeQuery("SELECT id, type FROM PARTS");
...
```

Figure 12.15 *ResultSet* options.

JDBC 2.0 thus gives two ways to make updates in the database: a standard SQL statement and a *ResultSet* update.

Figure 12.16 shows both alternatives. The first consists of a single program line and can clearly contain SQL to change just one row, as shown, or many thousands of rows. The second method involves several program lines and may be adapted to

```
stmt.executeUpdate("update parts set qty = 10 where id=1");

Statement stmt = conn.createStatement(
                            ResultSet.TYPE_SCROLL_SENSITIVE,
                            ResultSet.CONCUR_UPDATABLE);
ResultSet rs = stmt.executeQuery("select id, qty from parts where id
=1");
rs.next();              //validates the cursor
rs.updateInt("qty",10); //updates the integer-type qty attribute
rs.updateRow();         //saves the current row to the database
```

Figure 12.16 JDBC updates.

support a graphical user interface where multiple rows are retrieved and data in the *ResultSet* underlies a grid display, allowing the user to browse the rows and interactively update values in individual cells of the grid.

12.6.4 PREPARED STATEMENTS

Often the values of attributes in a query are not known before run-time. These values may be set interactively by the user, who may not have the necessary skills or permissions to supply the full statement. In such a case, the query may be prepared with placeholders inserted where the interactive values should be introduced. The example in Figure 12.17 shows the construction of a JDBC prepared statement with two placeholders (the question marks). The actual values are then inserted using the statement's type sensitive methods. The first of these assigns the contents of *part_Id* to the first placeholder as an integer; the second assigns the contents of *partType* to the second placeholder as a string. Although, in this case, the values are embedded in the program code, they could just as easily have come from user input through the program's GUI.

```
Connection conn = DriverManager.getConnection(
"jdbc:oracle:thin:@orion.uel.ac.uk:1521:bisora","scott","tiger");

int partId = 123;
String partType = "PART-TYPE-1";

PreparedStatement stmt = conn.prepareStatement
  ("INSERT INTO PARTS (id, type) VALUES (?, ?)");
stmt.setInt(1, partId);
stmt.setString(2, partType);

stmt.execute();
stmt.close();
conn.close();
```

Figure 12.17 JDBC row insert.

Once the statement is executed, the statement and the connection are closed. This is good programming practice. Although the JVM's garbage collection routines will usually recover the unassigned remnants of a finished program, explicit recovery is generally quicker and more reliable.

12.6.5 CALLABLE STATEMENTS

Most database systems allow procedural code to be stored in the database itself. The PL/SQL language is used by Oracle and may be stored as a procedure or function body within a package. The performance experiment in Section 17.6 uses a package called *makeCustomer* that contains one function and one procedure.

Each time it is called, the procedure *fillCustomer* will create 50,000 rows in the customer table and associate these with 200,000 orders and 2,000,000 rows in the *lineitems* table.

The fragment of Java code in Figure 12.18 uses the *cs.execute()* method because the procedure contains multiple SQL statements, both queries and inserts. None of the queries returns any data to the caller, so there is no need to associate the statement with a *ResultSet*.

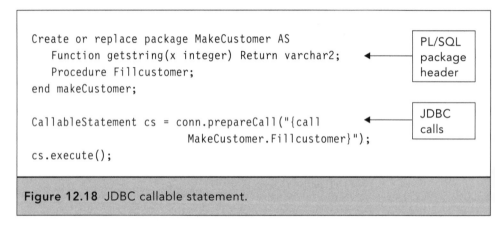

```
Create or replace package MakeCustomer AS
    Function getstring(x integer) Return varchar2;        PL/SQL
    Procedure Fillcustomer;                               package
end makeCustomer;                                         header

CallableStatement cs = conn.prepareCall("{call           JDBC
                MakeCustomer.Fillcustomer}");             calls
cs.execute();
```

Figure 12.18 JDBC callable statement.

12.7 ⊖ SUMMARY

Operating systems offer multi-tasking through a scheduling program that manages queues of processes. Jobs in the run queue are allocated time on the CPU through a context switch. The context information is moved between the run, wait and suspended queues by the scheduler.

Using the context queue analogy, a process may establish threads to service simultaneous user requests. A dispatcher thread manages the thread contexts. A single process can thus offer multi-threaded, multi-user facilities.

The various mechanisms discussed in this chapter – RPC, RMI, ODBC and JDBC – provide support for remote access from a client program to a server.

RPC and RMI allow communication with any kind of server that is able to receive the protocol messages. Server applications as varied as a time clock, a central rendering service for multimedia or a network authentication service can be built within this generalized framework. Database servers use RPC as the basis of their service functions.

ODBC and JDBC offer specific services for connection to a database and translate local program calls to their specialized and proprietary APIs into remote CLI calls to the database.

ODBC can be considered as specific to a Windows environment which, given the spread of Microsoft desktop systems, may not be much of a limiting factor. However, Windows is available for different CPU architectures, and client programs that use ODBC must be rewritten and recompiled for those CPUs.

JDBC is only applicable to Java clients. Any machine with a JVM will run the unamended client. Using a type 4 JDBC driver with such a client will ensure complete portability. Doubts about the performance of an interpreted language such as Java are being dispelled by advances in moderately priced hardware.

12.8 KEY TERMS

Multi-tasking	More than one user process resident in main memory. Access to CPU managed by OS scheduler using process contexts
Multi-threading	Time allocated to process is itself split into servicing threads. Dispatcher, internal to the process, uses thread context switching
Remote Procedure Call	Mechanism for calling a service on a remote host; Service requests and any paramenters are marshalled and de-marshalled to the XDR format. Basis of client–server architecture
Remote Method Invocation	Similar in concept to RPC, but Java-only. Made more complex because Java is an interpreted language
ODBC	Microsoft standard API. Converts API calls in the client to CLI format. Transported to server as RPC calls
JDBC	Sun standard; same principle as ODBC. JDBC calling client translated to CLI. More portable because linked to Java
Connection	JDBC construct to preserve client session with a server
Statements	Associated with connection. Statements can be simple SQL strings, parameterized strings or calls to PL/SQL packages
ResultSet	Flexible container for returned rows of statement. Automatically adjusts to the number of columns and number of rows.

(i)   Write a simple Java program to produce the following:

- A list of players for *Purity FC*
- The number of goals scored by *Diocletian*
- The number of disciplinary cases against *Constantine*

(ii) Write two packaged PL/SQL functions which will perform the last two tasks in Question (i), but with the player's *ufa_id* sent as a parameter. Write a Java program to call these functions with appropriate parameters.

CHAPTER 13

FURTHER PL/SQL

Something further may follow of this Masquerade.

Herman Melville, *The Confidence-Man*

The discussion on PL/SQL was left at the end of Chapter 10, having introduced the block structure of the language and the various forms this structure may take. The simplest form is the *anonymous block* that has no name and is not stored on the server, although, for convenience, the client may store it in an external file.

Stored procedures and *stored functions* do have names and are stored as data items in a schema of the database. A *package* is also named and retained within the database. It generally consists of several procedures, functions, declared variables and cursors that share a related purpose and that may be referenced from within the package according to the scoping rules.

Triggers are always stored; because their activation relies on database events, it is essential that they are permanently available whenever the event occurs.

This chapter completes the survey of PL/SQL programming structures and techniques, illustrating more complex use of the language elements and introducing further constructs which give the seasoned programmer full control over the database operation.

All of the PL/SQL introduced here and in the previous discussion may be written, tested and stored in the database to create a library of standard routines. These are accessible by the front-end applications developer and offer an economic, reliable and powerful bank of reusable code.

13.1 MUTATING TABLES

One particular situation in which multiple trigger types are essential is in avoiding the so-called *mutating table problem*. This problem generally occurs when a row-level trigger attempts to reference a data item in the trigger's related SQL table through a *select* statement rather than from the before-image or after-image of the current row.

A row-trigger is created to assure a complex legal contract drawn up between a club and its leading goal scorer. It ensures that he continues to be the league's highest paid player whenever the salary of any other league player is increased, or any new player is registered in the league. This causes a *mutating table problem* to occur. The update or insertion of other rows in the *contracts* table fire the trigger but the trigger seeks to update the leading goal scorer's contract salary not the player's contract responsible for the event. An example of such a trigger is given in Figure 13.1. Its associated output, following an appropriate update request, is demonstrated in Figure 13.2.

```
CREATE OR REPLACE TRIGGER contracts_biu_trigger
BEFORE INSERT OR UPDATE OF Salary ON Contracts
FOR EACH ROW

DECLARE
v_max_sal   NUMBER;
v_ufa_id    CHAR(8);

BEGIN
  SELECT ufa_id, salary INTO v_ufa_id, v_max_sal
  FROM Contracts
  WHERE salary = (SELECT MAX(salary) FROM Contracts
                  WHERE Contracts.left IS NULL);
IF :NEW.salary >= v_max_sal THEN
      DBMS_OUTPUT.PUT_LINE('Player ' || v_ufa_id ||
         ' requires a salary in excess of ' || :NEW.salary ||
         ' to ensure his contractual advantage!');
END IF;
END contracts_biu_trigger;
```

Figure 13.1 PL/SQL mutating trigger.

In the vast majority of cases, a *mutating table problem* is the result of a row-level trigger attempting to read or update the table that is the subject of the triggering event. In Figure 13.1, an attempt is made to read the contents of the *contracts* table from within a row-level trigger. This trigger is itself activated via inserts or updates to that table. Such an operation is forcibly aborted by the DBMS in an attempt to maintain data integrity.

The reason for such an apparently over-restrictive exclusion is that DML operations often affect more than a single row of a table, and, as such, require an exclusive

```
update contracts
set salary=salary*1.1;

update contracts
        *
ERROR at line 1:
ORA-04091: table SB.CONTRACTS is mutating, trigger/function may not
see it
ORA-06512: at "SB.CONTRACTS_BIU_TRIGGER", line 6
ORA-04088: error during execution of trigger
'SB.CONTRACTS_BIU_TRIGGER'
```

Figure 13.2 Mutating trigger refused.

lock on the table until the operation has been fully completed. To read the affected table with a row-level trigger would potentially expose a partially updated view of the table, and in doing so would break the *isolation* requirement of transactional processing.

There is a clash of *operational granularity* between the conflicting parts of the trigger. Statement-level triggers are not affected by such restrictions, in that they either occur before an exclusive lock is taken out by the DML triggering operation, or after all rows have been suitably altered by the operation and the exclusive lock released.

The solution to the *salary* problem is to use a combination of before and after statement-level triggers, a row-level trigger and a package. The syntax of the before-statement-level trigger is given in Figure 13.3. It finds the current highest

```
CREATE OR REPLACE TRIGGER contracts_sbiu_trigger
BEFORE INSERT OR UPDATE OF Salary ON Contracts
DECLARE
   v_contracts Contracts%ROWTYPE;
BEGIN
   SELECT ufa_id, salary INTO v_contracts.ufa_id, v_contracts.salary
   FROM Contracts
   WHERE salary = (SELECT MAX(salary) FROM Contracts
                   WHERE Contracts.left IS NULL);
   mutating_util.putrow(v_contracts);
END contracts_sbiu_trigger;
/
```

Figure 13.3 *Before* statement-level PL/SQL trigger.

paid league player, and, using the *mutating_util* package, records details of that player's current contract in an in-memory PL/SQL table.

The *before* row-level trigger, documented in Figure 13.4, retrieves details of the current highest league player from the PL/SQL table, as saved in the *before* statement-level trigger, and compares that maximum salary with the new updated salary of the player whose contract is currently being processed.

```
CREATE OR REPLACE TRIGGER contracts_rbiu_trigger
BEFORE INSERT OR UPDATE OF Salary ON Contracts
FOR EACH ROW
DECLARE
  v_max_contract Contracts%ROWTYPE;
BEGIN
  v_max_contract := mutating_util.getrow;
  IF :NEW.salary >= v_max_contract.salary
   AND :NEW.ufa_id != v_max_contract.ufa_id THEN
      mutating_util.setflag;
  END IF;
END contracts_rbiu_trigger;
/
```

Figure 13.4 *Before* row-level PL/SQL trigger.

If the previous maximum salary is no longer the maximum, and the player whose salary is in excess of that maximum is not the leading goalscorer whose contract must be honoured, then a flag is set in the PL/SQL package to indicate that an adjustment will be required to the salary of the leading goalscorer.

Figure 13.5 shows the *after* statement-level trigger that will be fired when all associated *inserts* or *updates* have completed. This trigger checks, via a call to the package, whether the previous maximum salary has been exceeded, and if it has, calculates the salary that the leading goal scorer will have to receive if his contract is still to be honoured.

The package used by the various triggers is documented in Figure 13.6. Procedure *putrow* is used by the before-statement trigger to store the salary of the highest paid player prior to the DML update.

The procedure *setflag* is used by the row level trigger to set a Boolean variable if this salary will need adjustment. It uses the after image of the update from the transaction log rather than a separate query to determine this. Because of this, it cannot cause a mutating table error. The after image is available because the trigger is part of the same transaction as the *update*. The transaction isolation principle is not breached, although the user initiating the update may not be aware of the triggers.

```
CREATE OR REPLACE TRIGGER contracts_saiu_trigger
AFTER INSERT OR UPDATE OF Salary ON Contracts
DECLARE
  v_old_contract Contracts%ROWTYPE;
  v_new_max_salary Contracts.salary%TYPE;
  v_star_player_salary Contracts.salary%TYPE;
BEGIN
  IF (mutating_util.getflag) THEN
    v_old_contract := mutating_util.getrow;

    SELECT MAX(salary) INTO v_new_max_salary FROM Contracts
      WHERE Contracts.left IS NULL
      AND Contracts.ufa_id != v_old_contract.ufa_id;

    SELECT salary INTO v_star_player_salary FROM Contracts
      WHERE Contracts.left IS NULL
      AND Contracts.ufa_id = v_old_contract.ufa_id;

    IF v_new_max_salary >= v_star_player_salary THEN
      DBMS_OUTPUT.PUT_LINE('Player ' || v_old_contract.ufa_id ||
        ' requires a salary in excess of ' || v_new_max_salary ||
        ' to ensure his contractual advantage!');
    END IF;
  END IF;
END contracts_saiu_trigger;
/
```

Figure 13.5 *After* statement-level PL/SQL trigger.

The *after* statement-level trigger then uses the function *getflag* to pick up this Boolean and the function *getrow* to return the original highest salary. It finds the new maximum salary and synchronizes the star player's salary.

The output produced by executing the original update request is shown in Figure 13.7. The triggering *update* statement ensures that all players have the same percentage salary rise; therefore there is no change as to which player receives the highest salary, and therefore there is no contractual problem to report to the user.

Figure 13.8 shows the output produced by the *after* statement-level trigger when a contractual problem does occur due to an *update* or *insert* statement changing the highest-paid league player.

Any trigger that causes a mutating table error will normally have to be broken down into this kind of interrelated trigger and package structure.

```
CREATE OR REPLACE PACKAGE mutating_util
IS
  PROCEDURE putrow (i_row IN Contracts%ROWTYPE);
  FUNCTION getrow RETURN Contracts%ROWTYPE;
  PROCEDURE setflag;
  FUNCTION getflag RETURN BOOLEAN;
END mutating_util;
/

CREATE OR REPLACE PACKAGE BODY mutating_util
IS
  TYPE mutating_table_type IS TABLE OF Contracts%ROWTYPE
  INDEX BY BINARY_INTEGER;
  mutating_table mutating_table_type;
  v_update_flag BOOLEAN := FALSE;

  PROCEDURE putrow (i_row IN Contracts%ROWTYPE)
  IS
  BEGIN
    mutating_table(1) := i_row;
    v_update_flag := FALSE;
  END putrow;

  FUNCTION getrow RETURN Contracts%ROWTYPE
  IS
  BEGIN
    RETURN mutating_table(1);
  END getrow;

  PROCEDURE setflag
  IS
  BEGIN
    v_update_flag := TRUE;
  END setflag;

  FUNCTION getflag RETURN BOOLEAN
  IS
  BEGIN
    RETURN v_update_flag;
  END getflag;
END mutating_util;
/
```

Figure 13.6 PL/SQL package used in PL/SQL trigger.

```
SELECT ufa_id, salary
FROM Contracts
WHERE salary = (SELECT MAX(salary) FROM Contracts
        WHERE Contracts.left IS NULL);


UFA_ID          SALARY
---------- ----------
VT432167        998250


1 row selected.

UPDATE contracts
SET salary=salary*1.1;

24 rows updated.

SELECT ufa_id, salary
FROM Contracts
WHERE salary = (SELECT MAX(salary) FROM Contracts
        WHERE Contracts.left IS NULL);


UFA_ID          SALARY
---------- ----------
VT432167       1098075


1 row selected.
```

Figure 13.7 Implicit and transparent.

13.2   PL/SQL PROGRAMMING STRUCTURES

This section considers the remaining basic constructs of the PL/SQL language and describes a number of advanced features that have recently been introduced into the language.

13.2.1   PL/SQL COMMENTS

Like most programming languages, PL/SQL allows for in-line comments in program source code. With such comments not being subject to compilation there is no overhead involved in their use, and as such they should be used to make program code as readable, understandable and maintainable as possible.

PL/SQL offers two different forms of comment syntax: single-line and multiple-line. Single-line comments are initiated with a double hyphen (--) and end with a

```
UPDATE contracts
SET salary=salary*1.1
WHERE ufa_id != 'VT432167';

Player VT432167 requires a salary in excess of 1098075 to ensure his
contractual advantage!

22 rows updated.

SELECT ufa_id, salary
FROM Contracts
WHERE salary = (SELECT MAX(salary) FROM Contracts
        WHERE Contracts.left IS NULL);

UFA_ID          SALARY
----------   ----------
AT245876        1098075
BT46286         1098075
UT236965        1098075
VT432167        1098075

4 rows selected.
```

Figure 13.8 Enforcing complex business rules.

carriage return/line feed. Figure 13.9 shows an example of the use of single-line comments.

Multiple-line comment blocks begin with a slash-asterisk (/*) and end with an asterisk-slash (*/). All lines appearing between these, whether valid PL/SQL syntax or not, will be treat as comments, and as such will not be passed to the compiler. Figure 13.10 shows an example of the use of multiple-line comments in a PL/SQL program.

```
-- This Function returns the highest earning player
FUNCTION getrow RETURN Contracts%ROWTYPE
IS
BEGIN
  RETURN mutating_table(1); -- return 1st row
END getrow;
```

Figure 13.9 PL/SQL single-line comments.

```
/* This Function returns the first (and only) row
from a PL/SQL Table that contains contract
details of the player who is currently earning
the highest salary */
FUNCTION getrow RETURN Contracts%ROWTYPE
IS
BEGIN
  RETURN mutating_table(1);
END getrow;
```

Figure 13.10 PL/SQL multiple-line comments.

13.2.2 *CASE, WHILE-LOOP,* NULL STATEMENTS

In addition to the *if...then...elsif...else...end if* statement described earlier, PL/SQL also offers the *case* conditional statement. This statement should be used instead of a complex set of *if...elsif* conditions, as it increases code readability and maintainability. Figure 13.11 shows an example of a complex *if...elsif* condition and its equivalent *case* condition.

```
IF v_position = 'GOALKEEPER' THEN
        v_g_count = v_g_count + 1;
ELSIF v_position = 'DEFENDER' THEN
        v_d_count = v_d_count + 1;
ELSIF v_position = 'MIDFIELD' THEN
        v_m_count = v_m_count + 1;
ELSIF v_position = 'FORWARD' THEN
        v_f_count = v_f_count + 1;
ELSE
        DBMS_OUTPUT.PUT_LINE('No such position allowed');
END IF;

CASE v_position
   WHEN 'GOALKEEPER' THEN v_g_count = v_g_count + 1;
   WHEN 'DEFENDER' THEN v_d_count = v_d_count + 1;
   WHEN 'MIDFIELD' THEN v_m_count = v_m_count + 1;
   WHEN 'FORWARD' THEN v_f_count = v_f_count + 1;
   ELSE DBMS_OUTPUT.PUT_LINE('No such position allowed');
END CASE;
```

Figure 13.11 PL/SQL – making choices.

The variable following the *case* keyword is referred to as a 'selector', and it is the value of the selector that is matched against the various *when* constants. Once a match is made, the statements following the related *then* are carried out and control is then passed to the statement following the *end case*. If *when* constants are mistakenly duplicated, only the first is executed. There is no fall through, as is sometimes the situation with similar expressions in other programming languages.

An alternative format for the *case* statement is the one shown in Figure 13.12, where the selector is replaced with a Boolean evaluating expression replacing the *when* constants.

```
CASE
   WHEN v_position = 'GOALKEEPER' THEN v_g_count = v_g_count + 1;
   WHEN v_position = 'DEFENDER' THEN v_d_count = v_d_count + 1;
   WHEN v_position = 'MIDFIELD' THEN v_m_count = v_m_count + 1;
   WHEN v_position = 'FORWARD' THEN v_f_count = v_f_count + 1;
   ELSE DBMS_OUTPUT.PUT_LINE('No such position allowed');
END CASE;
```

Figure 13.12 PL/SQL *case* statement – alternative syntax.

PL/SQL also allows the use of a modified *case* statement as an assignment expression. Figure 13.13 illustrates the use of such a *case* assignment.

```
v_position :=
  CASE i_selection
       WHEN 1 THEN 'GOALKEEPER'
       WHEN 2 THEN 'DEFENDER'
       WHEN 3 THEN 'MIDFIELD'
       WHEN 4 THEN 'FORWARD'
       ELSE 'NOT ASSIGNED')
  END CASE;
```

Figure 13.13 PL/SQL *case* assignment.

PL/SQL offers the *for-loop* and the *while-loop* as alternatives to the more basic *loop* iteration expression.

The *for-loop* allows for a fixed number of iterations as opposed to the infinite iterations of the standard *loop* construct. An example of the *for-loop* statement was used in the procedure *matchdates* in Figure 10.55, an extract of which is shown in Figure 13.14.

```
FOR v_week IN 1..38 LOOP
  matchdates_table(v_week):= v_date;
  v_date := v_date + 7;
END LOOP;
```

Figure 13.14 PL/SQL *for-loop*.

A *for-loop* iterates sequentially through a range of integers, carrying out the loop's instructions once per iteration. The range of integers is defined as part of the *for-loop* syntax, with the double dot (..) acting as the range operator.

In Figure 13.14, the range of integer values that will be assigned to the integer variable, *v_week*, is 1 to 38. If the range needs to be processed in reverse order, then the keyword *reverse* needs to follow the keyword *in* immediately. The *exit* statement, as in the case of the basic *loop*, allows the exiting of the *for-loop*. However, an *exit* condition is only required in those circumstances where premature termination of the loop may be required.

The *while-loop* enables a loop to be iterated while a given expression evaluates to *true*. Such semantics allows for the possibility that the loop will not be entered at all. An example of a *while-loop* expression is given in Figure 13.15.

```
WHILE v_week < 39 LOOP
  matchdates_table(v_week):= v_date;
  v_date := v_date + 7;
  v_week := v_week + 1;
END LOOP;
```

Figure 13.15 PL/SQL *while-loop*.

An advantage of the *while-loop* is that there is no requirement to initialize an integer variable for its use, as in the case of the *for-loop*.

The *null* statement performs no program functionality, its main purpose being to allow incomplete conditional statements to compile cleanly. Figure 13.16 provides an example of such a statement. The example shows that although a *goalkeeper* is a valid position, it requires no processing, as there will only ever be one on the pitch at any point in time, regardless of the team's formation.

13.3 PL/SQL COLLECTIONS

PL/SQL offers three constructs that can contain and manipulate single-dimensioned collections of data. The first of these is known as an **associative**

```
CASE v_position
  WHEN 'goalkeeper' THEN NULL;
  WHEN 'defender' THEN v_d_count = v_d_count + 1;
  WHEN 'midfield' THEN v_m_count = v_m_count + 1;
  WHEN 'forward' THEN v_f_count = v_f_count + 1;
  ELSE DBMS_OUTPUT.PUT_LINE('No such position allowed');
END CASE;
```

Figure 13.16 PL/SQL *null* statement.

array, although these have previously been referred to as both PL/SQL *tables* and *index-by tables*. The second collection type is a **nested table**, and the third is called a **variable-size array**, although this name is commonly shortened to **varrays**. This section will present a brief description of each of these three collection types.

13.3.1   ASSOCIATIVE ARRAYS

Figure 10.52 first introduced the concept of a PL/SQL table as a variable used to hold an indexed set of elements in memory. An associative array is a simple extension of the PL/SQL table structure with the addition of two new types of indexing.

```
DECLARE
  TYPE associative_array_type1 IS TABLE OF DATE
    INDEX BY PLS_INTEGER;
  matchdates_table associative_array_type1;
  TYPE associative_array_type2 IS TABLE OF Clubs%ROWTYPE
    INDEX BY VARCHAR2(25);
  club_table associative_array_type2;
  v_date DATE := '14-AUG-2003';

BEGIN
 Select * INTO club_table('Beauty United')
FROM Clubs WHERE Clubs.name = 'Beauty United';
  FOR v_week IN 1..38 LOOP
    matchdates_table(v_week):= v_date;
    v_date := v_date + 7;
  END LOOP;
END;
```

Figure 13.17 PL/SQL associative arrays.

Originally, a PL/SQL table had only the option to index by *binary_integer*; this is now extended to include indexing by *pls_integer* and *varchar2*.

A *pls_integer* is a more efficient implementation of a signed integer type, and in general, acts as a substitute for the *binary_integer* type. A *varchar2* index allows PL/SQL tables to be referenced by character data, particularly useful if creating a virtual collection based on a character-keyed SQL table. Associative arrays are sparse collections; elements are created as necessary without maintaining any pre-defined order between elements. They are specific to PL/SQL, and cannot be used as column data in an SQL table. Figure 13.17 shows examples of the definition and population of two separate associative arrays.

13.3.2   NESTED TABLES

PL/SQL *nested tables* are similar to associative arrays except that they can be used as column data within SQL tables and can thus be made permanent. However, unlike associative arrays, the indexing of nested tables is non-definable, and uses a fixed sequential integer index. *Nested tables* require the use of special constructor operations in order to be given an initial set of elements. Accessing an element is also invariably sequential, as direct access would rely on the element's subscript having a direct equivalence to the element's data values.

A *nested table*, even though it is initially constructed as a dense set of elements, is, in fact, also a sparse collection. Individual elements can be physically deleted without regaining space or index keys. Figure 13.18 shows an example of a PL/SQL anonymous block that defines, populates and accesses a nested table collection.

The constructor of a nested table is a function based on the declared type of that table. In the declaration section of Figure 13.18, *bankhols* is constructed using its type, *dates_table_type*, as its constructor. As there is not an element list associated with this declaration statement, *bankhols* will initially be constructed as a *null* element nested table. That initial declaration is then overridden in the execution section of the PL/SQL block.

The *bankhols* collection is *reconstructed* using the *dates_table_type* constructor with a fully populated set of DATE elements as its input parameters. An element (i.e. a row) of a PL/SQL nested table is accessed via its subscript within the collection set. In Figure 13.18, *bankhols(i)* refers to element *i* of the collection set *bankhols*.

PL/SQL collections have a set of predefined methods associated with them. These methods are used to query the collection set and to extract specific elements or information pertaining to the collection as a whole. Section A.8 presents a list of these methods together with a brief description of their purpose.

The Figure 13.18 example uses the *COUNT* method in order to find the maximum number of elements that need to be processed.

```
DECLARE
  TYPE dates_table_type IS TABLE OF DATE;
  bankhols dates_table_type; -- nested table is NULL
  v_club VARCHAR2(25);
  v_match_date DATE;
  v_count NUMBER := 0;
  CURSOR c_clubs IS
    SELECT name FROM CLUBS;
  CURSOR c_matches IS
    SELECT matchdate FROM MATCHES
    WHERE homeclub = v_club or awayclub = v_club;

BEGIN
  -- Constructor used to populate nested table with elements
  bankhols := dates_table_type ('01-JAN-2004', '09-APR-2004',
         '12-APR-2004', '03-MAY-2004', '31-MAY-2004', '30-AUG-2004',
         '25-DEC-2004', '26-DEC-2004', '27-DEC-2004');
  OPEN c_clubs;
  LOOP
     FETCH c_clubs INTO v_club;
     EXIT WHEN c_clubs%NOTFOUND;
     OPEN c_matches;
     LOOP
        FETCH c_matches INTO v_match_date;
        EXIT WHEN c_matches%NOTFOUND;
        FOR i IN 1..bankhols.COUNT LOOP  -- COUNT is a collection method
           IF v_match_date = bankhols(i) THEN  -- elements are accessed
              v_count := v_count + 1;        -- via their subscripts
              EXIT;
           END IF;
        END LOOP;
     END LOOP;
     CLOSE c_matches;
     DBMS_OUTPUT.PUT_LINE
         (v_club || ' plays matches on ' || v_count || ' bank holidays');
  END LOOP;
  CLOSE c_clubs;
END;
```

Figure 13.18 PL/SQL nested tables.

13.3.3   *VARRAYS*

PL/SQL *varrays* are somewhat similar to PL/SQL *nested tables* in that: they both can be used as elements within an SQL table; require constructors; and elements of each are referenced by their positional subscripts. However, *varrays* differ in several important aspects from *nested tables*: they always contain a dense set of elements. A *nested table* can have any of its elements deleted; *varrays* are stored directly as in-line objects within an SQL table, whereas nested tables are stored indirectly via an association to a system generated *store table*. *Varrays*, unlike nested tables, maintain their element order when transferred between PL/SQL and SQL. In essence, *varrays* operate like *arrays* and *nested tables* operate like *sets*.

Figure 13.19 shows the simple change necessary to convert the PL/SQL nested table example of Figure 13.18 into a working PL/SQL *varray* example.

```
DECLARE
  TYPE dates_table_type IS VARRAY(10) OF DATE;
  bankhols dates_table_type; -- VARRAY is NULL
  ...
BEGIN
  ...
END;
```

Figure 13.19 PL/SQL *varray.*

The major change to the collection type declaration is that it now requires a dimension to indicate the initial maximum number of elements that can be held within it. In the example, the *dates_table_type* is declared as holding a maximum of 10 elements. Each element of the *bankhols* varray is then initiated to *null*. If the size of the *varray* had been set to less than eight (the number of dates actually assigned), then the error shown in Figure 13.20 would occur.

```
DECLARE
*
ERROR at line 1:
ORA-06532: Subscript outside of limit
ORA-06512: at line 8
```

Figure 13.20 PL/SQL *varray* – insufficient elements.

13.4 ⊨ ADVANCED CURSORS

The PL/SQL cursors introduced earlier in this chapter are generally all that are required for most simple PL/SQL applications. There are a number of extensions that have been created to enable the construction of more complex applications. These include: the ability to simplify the sequential processing of table rows retrieved from SQL; the use of run-time definable cursors, known as **cursor variables**; and the ability to retrieve cursors as part of an attribute list of another PL/SQL cursor, known as a **cursor expression**.

13.4.1 CURSOR *FOR-LOOPS*

Figure 13.21 demonstrates the declaration and usage of a simple cursor. The cursor is statically defined to represent a memory structure that will contain the result set of a predetermined *select* statement. To process this result set it is first necessary to *open* the cursor, then serially *fetch* each row, and finally to remove the cursor from memory by issuing a *close* statement against it.

```
DECLARE
        CURSOR c_club IS
            SELECT * FROM clubs;
        v_club Clubs%ROWTYPE;
BEGIN
    OPEN c_club;
    LOOP
            FETCH c_club INTO v_club;
            EXIT WHEN c_club%NOTFOUND;
            DBMS_OUTPUT.PUT_LINE(v_club.name);
        END LOOP;
END;
/
```

Figure 13.21 PL/SQL cursor – standard loop.

Open, fetch until end and *close* can be considered a standard pattern of cursor operation, and is indeed all that is required of many cursors. Based on this knowledge a simpler mechanism for the serial processing of a cursor has been created, and this is demonstrated in Figure 13.22.

The return type of the *fetch* is implicitly declared to be a record structure that will contain attributes equivalent to those found in the cursor's select clause. This cursor record is automatically assigned the name immediately following the *for* clause of the *cursor for-loop*. By using the name of the attribute scoped by the cursor record's name, e.g. *c_club_rec.name*, it is possible to access attributes of the fetched

```
DECLARE
    CURSOR c_club IS
        SELECT * FROM clubs;
BEGIN
    FOR c_club_rec IN c_club LOOP -- Cursor FOR Loop
        DBMS_OUTPUT.PUT_LINE(c_club_rec.name);
    END LOOP;
END;
```

Figure 13.22 PL/SQL cursor *for-loop*.

row. However, such row attributes can only be referenced within the limited scope of the loop.

Cursor for-loops can be used with *implicit cursors* as well as *explicit cursors*. This ability further reduces the amount of coding required to handle simple serial processing of *select* statement result sets. Figure 13.23 shows the previous example rewritten as an implicit cursor.

```
BEGIN
    FOR c_rec IN (SELECT * FROM clubs) LOOP
        DBMS_OUTPUT.PUT_LINE(c_rec.name);
    END LOOP;
END;
/
```

Figure 13.23 PL/SQL implicit cursor *for-loop*.

13.4.2   CURSOR VARIABLES

A cursor is an in-line memory structure that holds the result set of a *select* operation. A *cursor variable* contains a pointer to an area of memory that contains a memory structure that holds such a result set. Such a *reference variable* is a highly flexible construct as it can be easily altered to point to any suitable result set. Figure 13.24 shows the use of a cursor variable to process each row of the *Clubs* table.

A cursor variable type is declared using *ref cursor* and an optional *return* type. A cursor variable is declared as an instance of such a type. The cursor variable is then assigned to point to a result set generated via an implicit cursor attached to an *open-for* statement.

Figure 13.25 shows how easy it is to change the *cv_clubs* cursor variable to point to the memory location of different result sets, and then to process those result sets accordingly. The two *FETCH* statements in the example use the *cv_clubs* cursor

```
DECLARE
   TYPE cursor_ref_type IS REF CURSOR RETURN Clubs%ROWTYPE;
   cv_clubs cursor_ref_type; -- Cursor Variable
   v_club Clubs%ROWTYPE;
BEGIN
   OPEN cv_clubs FOR SELECT * FROM Clubs;
   LOOP
      FETCH cv_clubs INTO v_club;
      EXIT WHEN cv_clubs%NOTFOUND;
      DBMS_OUTPUT.PUT_LINE(v_club.name);
   END LOOP;
   CLOSE cv_clubs;
END;
```

Figure 13.24 PL/SQL cursor variable.

variable to access indirectly the memory location of each result set created by the two implicit cursors.

As *cv_clubs* is an instance of *cursor_ref_type*, itself defined as a *cursor ref* with a *return* type of *clubs%rowtype*, it can be associated with any cursor (*implicit or explicit*) that contains a set of *Clubs* records. This type of cursor variable is referred to as *strongly typed* in that it can only reference result sets that match a specific *return* type. Cursor variables may based upon *cursor ref* types that do not have explicit *return* types. This allows greater flexibility, but they are considered *weakly typed* as they permit the possibility of type mismatch exceptions occurring at run-time.

Cursor variables are primarily of use as in–out parameters to procedures contained within packages. They can be generically defined in the block that calls the procedure, dynamically associated with an appropriate *select* statement in the procedure's body, and passed back in the calling block.

13.4.3   CURSOR EXPRESSIONS

A **cursor expression** allows cursors to be used as attributes of another cursor's select statement. In this way, nested cursors can be created that enable the processing of master/detail (1:N) related SQL tables. Figure 13.26 shows the use of a cursor expression to enable the processing of *Clubs* and *Players*, so as to list each club's name followed by a list of the club's players.

The outer cursor on *Clubs* retrieves rows whether players are associated with the club or not. It is only when the *Clubs* row has been fetched that the inner cursor is reopened and the presence or not of players for that club is tested. The output of the anonymous block seems analogous to an outer join between clubs and players (without the null padding). It gives an insight into the nested loops processing of joins in the database server (Section 15.3.1).

```
DECLARE
   TYPE cursor_ref_type IS REF CURSOR RETURN Clubs%ROWTYPE;
   cv_clubs cursor_ref_type;
   v_club Clubs%ROWTYPE;
BEGIN
   OPEN cv_clubs FOR SELECT * FROM Clubs;
   LOOP
        FETCH cv_clubs INTO v_club;
        EXIT WHEN cv_clubs%NOTFOUND;
        DBMS_OUTPUT.PUT_LINE(v_club.name);
   END LOOP;
   CLOSE cv_clubs;
   OPEN cv_clubs FOR SELECT DISTINCT C.*
                 FROM Clubs C, Players P
             WHERE C.name = P.club
             AND EXISTS (SELECT COUNT(*)
                    FROM Players
                    WHERE Players.club = C.name
                    AND Players.nationality = 'UTOPIA'
                    HAVING COUNT(*) >4);
   LOOP
        FETCH cv_clubs INTO v_club;
        EXIT WHEN cv_clubs%NOTFOUND;
        DBMS_OUTPUT.PUT_LINE(v_club.name);
   END LOOP;
   CLOSE cv_clubs;
END;
```

Figure 13.25 PL/SQL cursor variable.

```
set serveroutput on
DECLARE
   TYPE cursor_ref_type IS REF CURSOR;
   cv_players cursor_ref_type;
   v_club Clubs.name%TYPE;
   v_player Players.surname%TYPE;
```

Figure 13.26 PL/SQL cursor expression (*continued overleaf*).

```
        -- selection attribute is itself a CURSOR
        CURSOR c_clubs IS
                SELECT C.name, CURSOR(SELECT P.surname
                                FROM Players P
                                WHERE P.club = C.name
                                ORDER BY P.surname)
                FROM Clubs C;
BEGIN
    OPEN c_clubs;
    LOOP
        FETCH c_clubs INTO v_club, cv_players;
        EXIT WHEN c_clubs%NOTFOUND;
        DBMS_OUTPUT.PUT_LINE(v_club);
        LOOP  -- The CURSOR is automatically opened and closed
            FETCH cv_players INTO v_player;
            EXIT WHEN cv_players%NOTFOUND;
            DBMS_OUTPUT.PUT_LINE('----' || v_player);
        END LOOP;
    END LOOP;
CLOSE c_clubs;
END;


AC Compassion
Beauty United
----CONSTANTINE
----DICKENS
----DIOCLETIAN
----GREGORY
----HEGEL
----KANT
----MORE
----PAUL
----PLATO
----SOCRATES
----THACKERAY
Bountiful Athletic
Forgiveness FC
Freedom United
Grace Town
...
```

Figure 13.26 (*Continued*)

13.5 ⊂ ADVANCED PL/SQL TRIGGERS

Triggers, based on DML statements, were introduced in Section 10.8; this section briefly examines four additional categories of PL/SQL triggers. **View-level triggers** substitute alternative, user-defined, processing in place of DML events on views. **Nested table triggers** permit the replacement of DML events on individual collection set elements that form part of an SQL view. **Schema-level triggers** allow DDL statements to act as triggering events. **Database-level triggers** respond to certain database-level control events.

13.5.1 VIEW-LEVEL TRIGGERS

SQL views are logical representations of a subset of the underlying relational schema that materialize the external view of the database from the perspective of a set of end-users. However, as previously explained, problems can arise when attempting to update a view that is based on the join of two or more SQL tables. Figure 13.27 demonstrates the impossibility of directly updating a non key-preserved base table via DML operations on its associated SQL view. Figure 9.21 provides the SQL definition of *players_v*.

```
SELECT ufa_id, surname, forename, squad_no NO, position, club, joined
FROM players_v
WHERE ufa_id = 'ED24659';


UFA_ID    SURNAME     FORENAME NO POSITION CLUB          JOINED
--------  ----------  -------  -- -------- ------------- ---------
ED24659   SOCRATES    VICTOR   12 midfield Beauty United 12-JUL-80


UPDATE players_v SET squad_no = 14
WHERE ufa_id = 'ED24659';


SET squad_no = 14
    *
ERROR at line 2:
ORA-01779: cannot modify a column which maps to a non key-
preserved table
```

Figure 13.27 Non-updatable join views.

PL/SQL view-level triggers, known as *Instead Of triggers*, are used to handle the problems associated with issuing DML statements against SQL views.

As explained in Section 13.1, the reason why DML statements are illegal on a view's non key-preserved base table(s) is that the intention as to which of the base table's rows should be updated is *potentially* ambiguous, or could lead to inconsistencies with other view rows based on the same underlying base row. In order to avoid such *possible* ambiguity, Oracle prohibits *any* updates on non key-preserved base tables via views.

However, the expected outcome of a large percentage of such update requests is perfectly clear and unambiguous from the perspective of the database designer. Therefore Oracle provides triggers that are notified of attempted DML events on registered views. The DML operations themselves are intercepted and *discarded prior to execution:* the trigger takes over the intended operation.

Figure 13.28 shows an example of such a view-level trigger that is used to allow the update of the non key-preserved base table of Figure 13.27.

```
CREATE OR REPLACE TRIGGER players_v_iou_trigger
INSTEAD OF UPDATE ON players_v -- UPDATE columns cannot be
BEGIN                          -- individually specified.
  IF :OLD.squad_no != :NEW.squad_no THEN -- WHEN clause not allowed in
    UPDATE Players   -- INSTEAD OF Triggers.
    SET squad_no = :NEW.squad_no
    WHERE ufa_id = :NEW.ufa_id;
  END IF;
END;


UPDATE players_v SET squad_no = 14
WHERE ufa_id = 'ED24659';


1 row updated.


SELECT ufa_id, surname, forename, squad_no NO, position, club, joined
FROM players_v
WHERE ufa_id = 'ED24659';


UFA_ID   SURNAME     FORENAME NO POSITION CLUB          JOINED
-------- ----------  ------- -- -------- ------------- ---------
ED24659  SOCRATES    VICTOR   14 midfield Beauty United 12-JUL-80
```

Figure 13.28 View-level PL/SQL trigger.

13.5.2 NESTED TABLE TRIGGERS

Under the object relational extension contained in SQL:1999 a view can contain a nested table as a virtual, non-atomic column type, and it is possible to construct a trigger that responds to DML events at the row-level of that nested table.

As an example, rather than only holding details of a single contract associated with a particular player, as in the *players_v* view of Figure 13.28, it is possible to hold details of all the contracts associated with a player in a single view attribute. Figure 13.29 shows the definition of such a view, and Figure 13.30 the *contracts_t* nested table type definition it is based upon.

```
CREATE OR REPLACE VIEW players_v
AS
  SELECT P.ufa_id, P.surname, P.forename, P.dateofbirth,
         P.squad_no, P.position, P.nationality, P.club,
         CAST (MULTISET (SELECT C.club, C.joined, C.left, C.salary
                         FROM Contracts C
                         WHERE C.ufa_id = P.ufa_id)
         AS contracts_t) contracts
  FROM Players P;
```

Figure 13.29 Nested table view I.

```
CREATE OR REPLACE TYPE contract_t AS OBJECT (
   club    VARCHAR2(25),
   joined  DATE,
   left    DATE,
   salary  NUMBER(9,2))

CREATE OR REPLACE TYPE contracts_t AS TABLE OF contract_t;
```

Figure 13.30 Nested table view II.

To reference rows of a nested table, in order to carry out DML operations upon them, it is necessary to create a temporary table structure in memory to map its contents. SQL provides the *TABLE* construct for this purpose. Figure 13.31 shows the use of such a structure in order to insert a new contract element into the *players_v* nested table view.

```
INSERT INTO TABLE (SELECT pv.contracts
                   FROM players_v pv
                   WHERE pv.ufa_id = 'VT432167')
VALUES ('Pity City', '01-AUG-1998', '31-JUL-1999', 20000);
```

Figure 13.31 Nested table – insert.

However, as the contents of a view's nested tables are not directly updatable via DML operations on that view, PL/SQL *Instead Of* triggers have to be constructed to enable such nested table updates to take place.

Figure 13.32 shows the result of trying to execute the *insert* of Figure 13.31 directly without a trigger.

```
INSERT INTO TABLE (SELECT pv.contracts
*
ERROR at line 1:
ORA-25015: cannot perform DML on this nested table view column
```

Figure 13.32 Nested table view insert (invalid).

Figure 13.33 shows the required PL/SQL trigger.

```
CREATE OR REPLACE TRIGGER players_contracts_trigger
INSTEAD OF INSERT ON
  NESTED TABLE contracts OF players_v
BEGIN
    INSERT INTO Contracts (ufa_id, club, joined, left, salary)
    VALUES (:PARENT.ufa_id, :NEW.club, :NEW.joined, :NEW.left,
          :NEW.salary);
END;
/
```

Figure 13.33 PL/SQL trigger – nested table view.

Figure 13.34 shows the *insert* now being intercepted by the new trigger that successfully carries out the insert on the view's *contracts* attribute.

```
INSERT INTO TABLE (SELECT pv.contracts
                   FROM players_v pv
                   WHERE pv.ufa_id = 'VT432167')
VALUES ('Pity City', '01-AUG-1998', '31-JUL-1999', 20000);

1 row created.
```

Figure 13.34 Nested table view *insert* (valid).

Figure 13.35 shows that a *select* on the view, *players_v* yields 1 row. The nested table, *contacts_t* is an attribute of the view and has a set of two values for Diocletian. A more orthodox *select* on the base table, *contracts* shows that Diocletian has two rows in the table.

```
SELECT surname, contracts from players_v where ufa_id = 'VT432167';

SURNAME
-------------------------
CONTRACTS(CLUB, JOINED, LEFT, SALARY)

DIOCLETIAN
CONTRACTS_T(CONTRACT_T('Beauty United', '01-AUG-01',  NULL, 650000),
  CONTRACT_T('Pity City', '01-AUG-98', '31-JUL-99', 20000))

1 row selected.

SELECT * from Contracts where ufa_id = 'VT432167';

UFA_ID      CLUB                        JOINED     LEFT        SALARY
---------   -------------------------   ---------  ---------   ----------
VT432167    Beauty United               01-AUG-03              650000
VT432167    Pity City                   01-AUG-98  31-JUL-99    20000

3 rows selected.
```

Figure 13.35 Nested table view – consistent update.

13.5.3 SCHEMA-LEVEL TRIGGERS

Oracle provides the facilities to monitor database-level events and schema-level events, as well as the more usual SQL table/view DML events.

Schema-level events are those operations that either result in a change to a particular database user's schema, or are concerned with accessing or monitoring a particular schema (Table 13.1).

Table 13.1 DDL schema events.

create table	create type	create view	grant and revoke
alter table	alter type	alter view	analyze
drop table	drop type	drop view	rename

Events include all of the standard SQL DDL statements: a catch-all schema event, DDL, can also be subscribed to, and is fired whenever any DDL command is issued against its associated schema.

Figure 13.36 shows a schema-level trigger that prevents the dropping of any tables associated with Liga Utopia by anyone other than the DBA.

```
CREATE OR REPLACE TRIGGER protecttables_trigger
BEFORE DROP ON sb.schema   -- schema event notification can occur
 BEGIN                     -- before or after the DDL command.
  IF DICTIONARY_OBJ_OWNER = 'SB' AND
     DICTIONARY_OBJ_TYPE = 'TABLE' THEN
       RAISE_APPLICATION_ERROR(-20000, 'Cannot drop Liga Utopia Tables');
  END IF;
END;
```

Figure 13.36 PL/SQL schema-level trigger.

```
CREATE OR REPLACE TRIGGER logger_trigger_on
AFTER LOGON ON SB.SCHEMA   -- schema needs to be named
DECLARE
  v_userid VARCHAR2(30);
BEGIN
  v_userid := LOGIN_USER;
  INSERT INTO AuditLog (event, userid, datetime)
  VALUES ('LOGON', v_userid, LOCALTIMESTAMP);
END;
/

CREATE OR REPLACE TRIGGER logger_trigger_off
BEFORE LOGOFF ON SB.SCHEMA
DECLARE
  v_userid VARCHAR2(30);
BEGIN
  v_userid := LOGIN_USER;
  INSERT INTO AuditLog (event, userid, datetime)
  VALUES ('LOGOFF', v_userid, LOCALTIMESTAMP);
END;
```

Figure 13.37 PL/SQL schema-level logging triggers.

Additional events associated with schema-level triggers are *logon, logoff, suspend* and *servererror*. These events allow the monitoring of schema access and the logging of any failed attempts at SQL operations against a schema's data objects.

Figure 13.37 shows the trigger required to record all logons/logoffs from a particular database schema. A *logon* trigger can only fire *after* the user has logged on, and the *logoff* trigger can only be fired just *before* the user has logged out. Figure 13.38 provides the code for a trigger that records all attempts to insert rows with duplicate primary keys into any SQL table belonging to a particular schema.

```
CREATE OR REPLACE TRIGGER error_handling_trigger
AFTER SERVERERROR ON SB.SCHEMA
WHEN (SYS.SERVER_ERROR(1) = 00001) - limit to specific errors
DECLARE
  v_userid VARCHAR2(30);
BEGIN
  v_userid := LOGIN_USER;
  INSERT INTO AuditLog (event, userid, datetime)
  VALUES ('ERROR 1001', v_userid, LOCALTIMESTAMP);
END;
/

INSERT INTO CLUBS VALUES (
'Beauty United' 'Somewhere', 'First', 'Someone');


ORA-00001: unique constraint (SB.PK_CLUBS) violated


SELECT * FROM AuditLog;

EVENT       USERID      DATETIME
----------  ----------- --------------------------
ERROR 1001 SB           01-JAN-03 13.12.23.738000
```

Figure 13.38 PL/SQL schema-level error handling trigger.

13.5.4   DATABASE-LEVEL TRIGGERS

Database-level triggers are those that are concerned with the whole of the database rather than just a specific schema belonging to that database. Events associated with database-level triggers are *logon, logoff, servererror, startup* and *shutdown*. The first three event types are the same as their schema-level counterparts, except that they are not restricted to the event occurring on a particular schema of the database.

The last two database event types occur *after* the database has been successfully started, or just *before* the database is shutdown. Database-level triggers facilitate the monitoring of database access and allow for the logging of any failed attempts at SQL operations against any of a database's objects. Figure 13.39 shows an example of a pair of startup and shutdown database-level triggers, together with some test output.

```
CREATE OR REPLACE TRIGGER logger_db_trigger_on
AFTER STARTUP ON DATABASE   -- no schema needed
DECLARE
  v_userid VARCHAR2(30);
BEGIN
  v_userid := LOGIN_USER;
  INSERT INTO SB.AuditLog (event, userid, datetime)
  VALUES ('STARTUP', v_userid, LOCALTIMESTAMP);
END;
/

CREATE OR REPLACE TRIGGER logger_db_trigger_off
BEFORE SHUTDOWN ON DATABASE
DECLARE
  v_userid VARCHAR2(30);
BEGIN
  v_userid := LOGIN_USER;
  INSERT INTO SB.AuditLog (event, userid, datetime)
  VALUES ('SHUTDOWN', v_userid, LOCALTIMESTAMP);
END;
/

SHUTDOWN the database, STARTUP the database again,
and then LOGON to schema SB.

SELECT * FROM AuditLog;

EVENT       USERID       DATETIME
----------  -----------  -------------------------
SHUTDOWN    SYS          01-DEC-03 14.11.15.457000
STARTUP     SYS          01-DEC-03 14.11.56.526000
LOGON       SB           01-DEC-03 14.12.33.839000
```

Figure 13.39 PL/SQL database-level start/stop triggers.

13.6 ⊝ KEY TERMS

Mutating tables	Problem associated with row-level triggers attempting table access rather than before or after images of rows
Collections	Multi-valued structures with associated methods. Associative arrays; nested tables; varrays
Cursors	Inline memory structures holding the result of an SQL query
Cursor *for-loop*	Language structure allowing iterative processing of an explicit or implied cursor with implied *open*, *fetch* and *close*
Cursor variable	Pointer to an explicit or implicit cursor
Cursor expression	Cursor becomes an attribute of another cursor; equivalent to nested loop processing
Triggers	PL/SQL code fired by notified events
View-level triggers	Substitute direct base table updates for interceptions of non key-preserved table updates through views
Nested table triggers	Substitute direct base table updates for intercepted nested table updates
Schema level triggers	Allow interception or recording of schema events
Database level triggers	Allow interception or recording of database events

13.7 ⊝ EXERCISE

(i) Implement the PL/SQL examples shown in this chapter. Create alternative examples to illustrate your understanding of these PL/SQL features.

CHAPTER 14

IMPLEMENTING IN JAVA

All I know most surely about morality and obligations, I owe to football.

Albert Camus

The initial requirements analysis for the Liga Utopia, using UseCase diagrams, was introduced in Chapter 2. As well as the UseCases, a class diagram was developed that was converted to an entity–relationship diagram (ERD). In subsequent chapters, the UFL case study has been used to develop a normalized database implementation and to illustrate the SQL language, including PL/SQL.

All of this can now be brought together in the development of a first-cut solution for the UFL. This will be done using an integrated development environment (IDE) called JBuilder. This tool has been developed by Borland[1] and is aimed specifically at software engineering for the Java language. This chapter illustrates the use of JBuilder Version 7, Enterprise Edition. This version offers a large number of additional classes to those supplied with the basic Java Development Kit (JDK), available from the original developers of the Java language, Sun Microsystems Inc.[2]

An IDE provides facilities for the automatic grouping of program source files in directories, the generation of code using a visual designer and the maintenance of relationships between source files, ensuring internal consistency to the project. There is a *make* system that ensures that the project is recompiled if a source file has been changed since the last compilation, a run-time environment and provision for the configuration of a deployment package when the developed software is released.

The UseCase diagrams indicated the requirement for a number of interactive screen forms where UFL staff can enter and maintain data in the database. These are divided into three main types.

---

1 http://www.borland.co.uk/
2 http://www.sun.com/ and http://www.java.com/

The simplest type is for the input or update of data in a single table. This may be done with checks on foreign keys, but there is generally only one row displayed in the form.

More complex is the need to display and maintain a one-to-many relationship in a form. This would be necessary, for example, in a form to enter results for matches, noting the goal scorers and the time and nature of their goals. The same would hold true for a form to record the team selection for each club in a match.

Finally, there are reports that need to generated, often in response to user-supplied parameters that will affect the output of the report. The report forms may need complex SQL statements and formatted output to printers.

Figure 14.1 shows a structure diagram of the screen forms resulting from inspection of the UseCase diagrams. The user must first pass through a login form and establish a valid connection to the database. Thereafter each of the three form types, Tables, Relationships and Reports, is available for use. Within each category, detailed forms are provided for the individual tasks required in the specification. This will form the basis for the design of the UFL application.

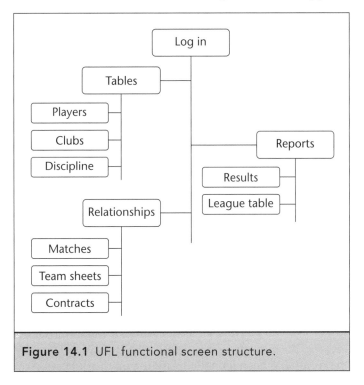

Figure 14.1 UFL functional screen structure.

In order to give an insight into the programming requirements for JDBC objects, the simplest forms will be designed in JBuilder using interface components that are not data-aware. The database connection and the various SQL statements will be added manually to the Java code generated by the interface designer. The more complex relationship forms and the report forms will be created using the data-aware components available in the Enterprise Edition.

14.1 ⊜ THE JBUILDER PROJECT

The first task in the construction of the UFL application is to create a project. Selecting *File |New Project* on the JBuilder menu starts the Project Wizard. Its first screen is illustrated in Figure 14.2. The project name is *ufl* and this has been translated into a directory under the user's home where all the subdirectories belonging to the project will be kept. The next screen allows the user to set project paths; the default values are normally accepted. The third screen allows the insertion of project text such as the author's name, project description and copyright notice that will be embedded in all generated code.

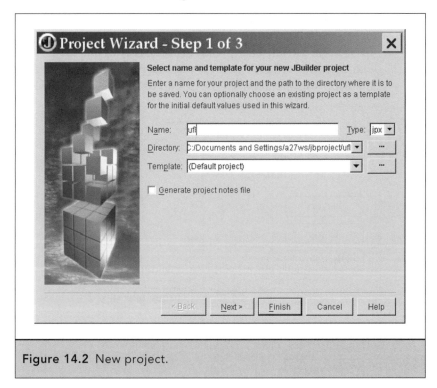

Figure 14.2 New project.

Once the project has been created, the application wizard can be used to generate the outline Java code for the *ufl* application. Select *File |New* and choose the application icon. The wizard's first screen is illustrated in Figure 14.3. The package (or class hierarchy) has been named *ufl* and the main application class will be *UFLApp*.

The next screen (Figure 14.4) shows how to specify the principal frame within the application. When *UFLApp* is run, it will instantiate this frame class. *UFLFrame1* will automatically register with the Windows system, taking the display properties set by the user and adding standard frame components (glyphs) allowing for minimizing, maximizing and closing the window. Registering with Windows will also allow events from the keyboard or the mouse to be communicated to the frame. Check the boxes to generate a menu bar, a status bar and an about box.

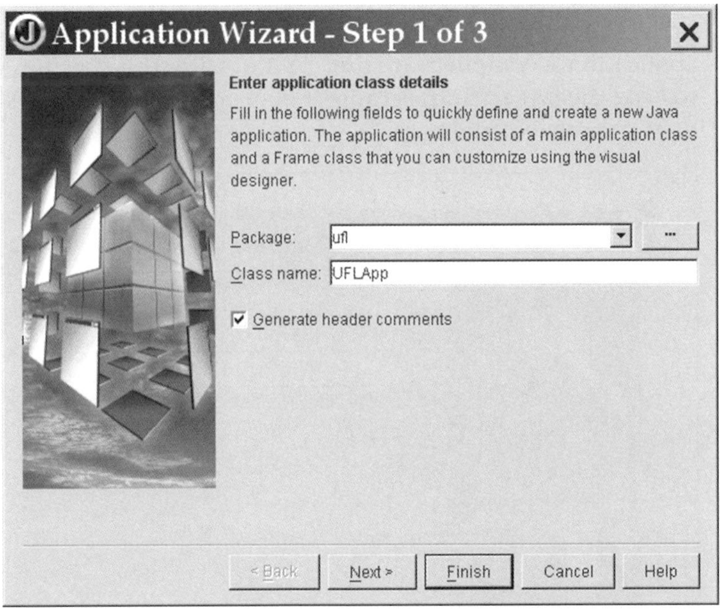

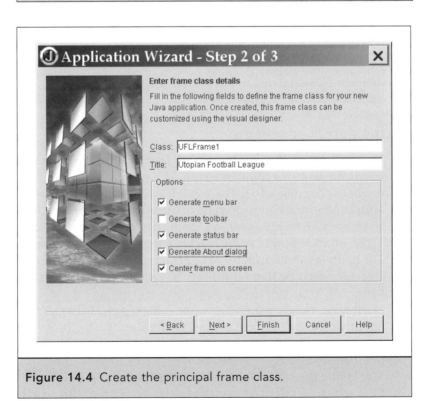

Figure 14.3 Create the application class.

Figure 14.4 Create the principal frame class.

The third step is to create a run-time configuration (Figure 14.5). This will eventually contain a detailed specification for any special conditions required when the application is compiled and run. To start with, this specifies the source files needed to *make* the project and, because it is an application, that it should be run in a standard Java Virtual Machine.

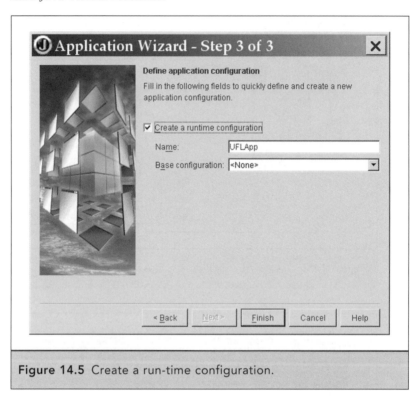

Figure 14.5 Create a run-time configuration.

14.1.1 THE JBUILDER ENVIRONMENT

The application wizard generates the Java code for the classes specified. Figure 14.6 shows the resulting JBuilder screen. The window is divided into three panes with a toolbar and a menu bar. The top left pane is the *project pane* and shows the files associated with the project. Each of the three classes created by the wizard, *UFLApp*, *UFLFrame1* and *UFLFrame1_AboutBox*, has a separate Java file.

The *structure pane* is at the bottom left and shows details of the *UFLFrame1* class. The methods and attributes of *UFLFrame1* are listed here. If the code is edited, any errors revealed by JBuider's interactive syntax checker will also be shown in this pane.

The large pane on the right is the *content pane*. It has six tabs that enable a different type of editor to be applied to the class. Each editor shows a different view. The figure shows the *Source* editor, and the Java code generated by the wizard for the *UFLFrame1* class is displayed.

Selecting the *UML* tab reveals a class diagram for *UFLFrame1*, showing the class from which it is derived and the classes associated with its attributes. Figure 14.7

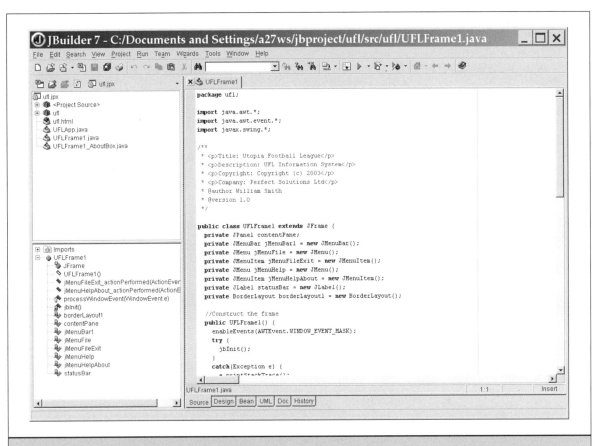

Figure 14.6 The generated *ufl* application.

shows this diagram and also that the *structure pane* has changed to show the class inheritance, associations and dependencies of the components that go to make up *UFLFrame1*

The *Design* tab reveals the visual designer. At its centre is the current *UFLFrame1*. Above this is a tabbed palette of the various components that can be added to the design.

To the right is the *property inspector*, which allows values for the visual or event properties for a selected component to be inserted or amended. Again, the *structure pane* changes to show a tree diagram of the components of the frame

The code generated for the frame and its corresponding visual design are very basic. The status bar is there but is barely distinguishable because it contains no default text and has the same background colours as the surrounding frame. The menu bar is not shown in this diagram since it has a specialist editor.

Figure 14.8 shows the Design view and the result of selecting the status bar and using its property inspector to add default text and to change the font of that text and its foreground and background colours. Any component can be selected either by clicking the mouse button directly on it in the Design editor or by clicking on

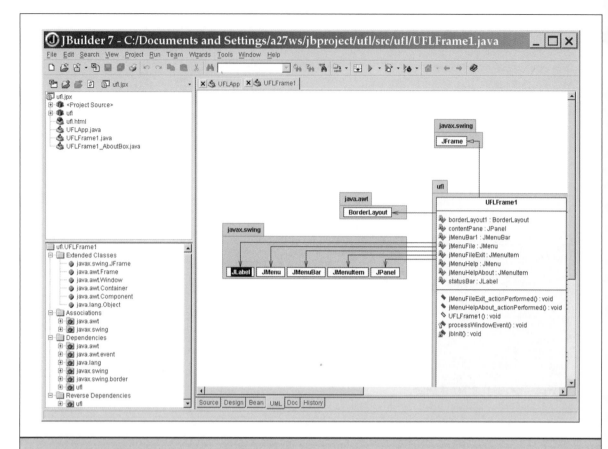

Figure 14.7 UML view.

the component in the structure diagram on the left. The values in the property inspector are changed by typing the value, by selecting it from a drop-down list or by choosing values from a pop-up dialog. Type the word *Status:* in the text field of the status bar's property inspector; choose a background and a foreground colour from the drop-down lists in those fields; and specify the font from the pop-up dialog which appears when the mouse is clicked in the *font* field.

Selecting *Run|Run Project* from the JBuilder menu causes all the Java files to be compiled and the resulting class files to be stored in the correct subdirectory as specified in the project. The *UFLApp* class is then launched in a Java Virtual Machine. *UFLApp* immediately instantiates *UFLFrame1*.

Figure 14.9 shows the running application. *UFLFrame1* has registered with the Windows system and has the normal minimize, maximize and close *glyphs*. The frame can be resized by dragging the edges with the mouse. The status bar with its default text is now clearly visible and the menu bar with two options, *File* and *Help* is displayed.

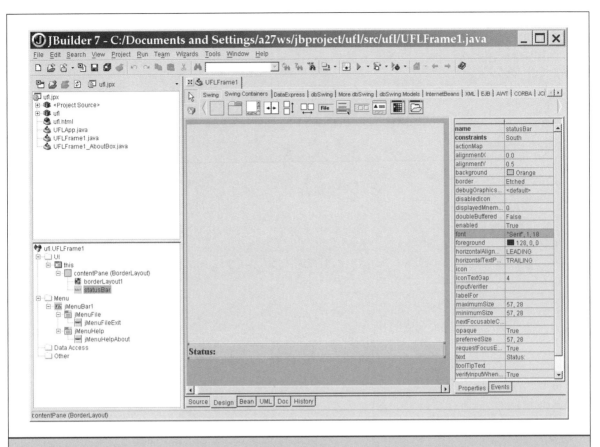

Figure 14.8 The status bar and the property inspector.

The menu bar works. Select *Help|About*. The *About* box pops up with information about the application, copied from the project setup. Select *File |Exit*: the application closes.

Notice that a fourth pane has opened in the main JBuilder screen. This is the *message pane*. It displays error messages from the compiler, run-time errors from the JVM and so on. Once the application has exited and messages have been reviewed, it can be closed with the X glyph (the close box) to give more screen space to the content pane. Closing it while the application is active kills the running application.

14.1.2 CONTAINERS, COMPONENTS AND LAYOUTS

The process of adding the screen forms detailed in Figure 14.1 can now begin. Each of these forms will consist of a number of basic components, such as labels, textfields, comboboxes and buttons.

A label is used to place some text on the form to indicate the purpose of an interactive component. A textfield is an interactive component that allows the user or the program to enter and edit text. A button component is capable of detecting a

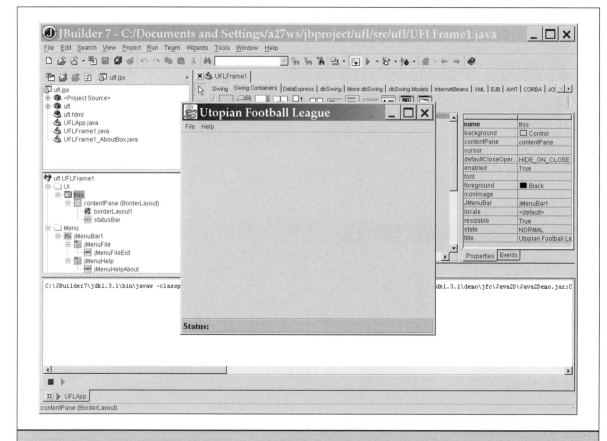

Figure 14.9 The running application.

mouse click and then performing some action that has been programmed into it. A combobox has a drop-down list of available choices and allows the user to select one of them by clicking with the mouse. The selected item is placed in the selection textfield. The combobox is a combination of a button, a listbox and a textfield.

Figure 14.10 illustrates these four types of components taken from the *Swing* palette in JBuilder's design editor.

In order to present an orderly user interface, these components must be grouped and some form of layout imposed. A Java *container* is capable of holding these simple components and has a layout manager associated with it.

Placing the components for the *Login* form in a container will segregate them from the components of the *Players* form, which can also be placed in a separate container, and so on for each of the forms. Each of the containers can have a different layout manager.

There are several classes in the *Swing Containers* tab of the palette. The UFL application will use two of them. The simplest is the *JPanel*. This is a simple rectangle. The *contentPane*, which was added automatically to the application when it was

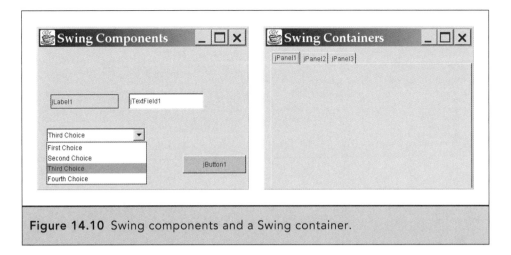

Figure 14.10 Swing components and a Swing container.

generated, is an instance of a *JPanel*. It contains the generated status bar, which is an instance of the *JLabel* class.

The *JTabbedPane* is the second type of container that will be used in the UFL application. This can contain a number of *JPanels*, each one headed by a tab. Selecting the tab brings the panel to the front. This kind of container will be used to group the Table, Relationships and Reports forms. Figure 14.10 also shows a tabbed panel that contains three JPanels. If this were the Table group of forms, each of the tabs might represent the Players, Club and Discipline forms.

Each of these containers also provides a method of laying out the components within it. This is done through a layout manager. There are about eight different types of standard layout manager. *contentPane* is using a *BorderLayout* manager. This organizes its components along its edges; each component can be assigned one of five different positions or constraints: *North*, *East*, *South*, *West* or *Center*. The *BorderLayout* manager will then automatically adjust the size and position of each contained component according to its contents and its constraint. A *JTabbedPanel* has a fixed layout manager that gives the tabbed effect.

In order to build up the layout needed for the UFL application it will be necessary to use layers of panels. Put a *JPanel* into *contentPane*. Click on *JPanel* in the *Swing Containers* palette at the top of the design editor. The cursor changes to a cross hair. Click in the area above the status bar or on the *contentPane* entry in the component tree. The component *JPanel1* is added to *contentPane*. Because *contentPane* is using a *BorderLayout* manager, the new *JPanel* is resized to fill the area of *contentPane* above the status bar.

Rename *JPanel1* as *appPanel*. Eventually it will hold all of the user forms. In its property inspector set the background colour, set its layout to *CardLayout* and the constraint to *Center*. The *appPanel* is important because it reserves the space in *contentPane* between *statusBar* and *jmenuBar1* for all of the panels that will hold the user forms. Its position is *Center* within *contentPane*, but any container it holds will be managed by *CardLayout*.

CardLayout manages any components in *appPanel* like a deck of cards. The top component hides the others. Figure 14.11 shows the JBuilder screen after *appPanel*

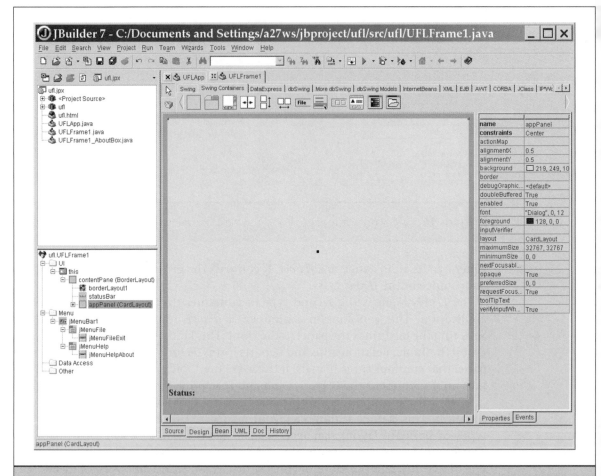

Figure 14.11 The first JPanel.

has been added. Using a stack of containers in this way allows a variation in layouts as different functions of the program are activated.

Add a *JPanel* to *appPanel* and rename it *Login*. Add three *JTabbedPanes* to *appPanel* and rename them *Tables*, *Relationships* and *Reports* respectively. Select *Tables* in the component tree add three *JPanels* to it. Rename them Players, Clubs and Discipline respectively. Select *Relationships* and add three *JPanels*. Rename them *matchResults*, *Teamsheets* and *Contracts*. Select *Reports* and add two *JPanels*. Rename them *Results* and *leagueTables*.

For all theses added components use the property inspector to set *opaque* to *True,* their layout to *null* and their constraint (the tab entry) the same as their *Name*. The main display framework of the UFL application is now complete and the current design is shown in Figure 14.12.

Notice the component tree. Make sure that *Login*, *Tables*, *Relationships* and *Reports* are at the same level and directly connected to *appPanel*. The property

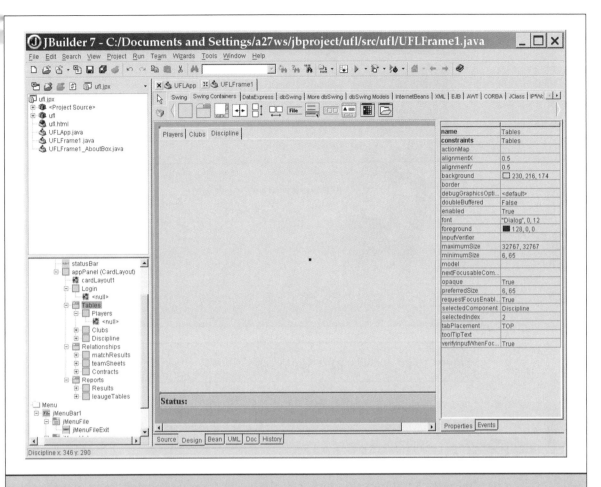

Figure 14.12 A tabbed panel.

inspector for *Tables* is also shown. Attributes for *Name*, constraints, layout and opaque have been set. The constraints appear as the titles of the tabs.

14.1.3   REQUIRED LIBRARIES

Before the detailed design of the forms can begin, there is an important task to perform. The JDBC libraries must be made available to JBuilder. The file *classes12.zip* is part of the Oracle installation and contains the JDBC version 1.2 class library. Find the path to this file in your installation or else download a copy from the Oracle web site. Select *Tools|Configure Libraries* from the JBuilder menu and the library wizard is started. Select the Add button at the bottom of the left pane and use the *New Library* dialog to install the fully qualified path to *classes12.zip* as a library entry called *OracleJDBC* in the JBuilder library path. Figure 14.13 shows this dialog.

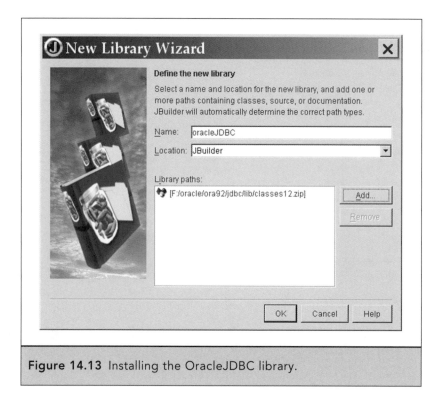

Figure 14.13 Installing the OracleJDBC library.

14.2 THE LOGIN USER FORM

Figure 14.14 shows the design of the *Login* form. It consists of four *JLabels* that contain string constants set in the text attribute of their property inspectors.

There are two *JTextfields*, where the user will enter a user name and a service, and a *JPasswordField*, where the password will be entered. This latter component is a special form of the *JTextField*; whatever is entered is masked with asterisks for added security. There are two *JButtons*: *Clear* and *Connect*.

The components have had their foreground colours, default text, font sizes, styles and text alignments set in the property inspectors. Their position and sizes on the panel can be set by dragging with the mouse. Selecting more than one component at a time can be done by holding the space key and left-clicking. The property inspector for multiple selections shows the common attributes that can be set for the selection. Right-clicking the selection exposes the alignment pop-up. The selection can be lined up vertically and horizontally, spaced evenly and made the same size.

Once the connection to Oracle has been made, the user has no way to expose the Players form and get on with some work. Additional menu items must be placed in the menu bar to permit this.

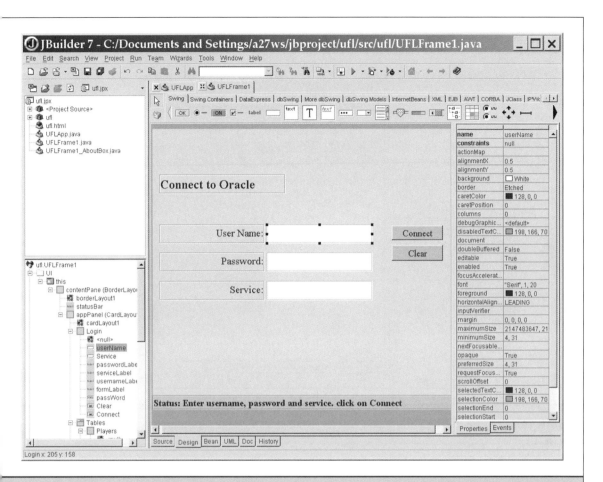

Figure 14.14 The Login screen.

14.2.1   MORE MENUS

Menus have a special design editor (Figure 14.15). Click on the design tab in JBuilder's editor pane and then double click on JMenuBar1 in the component tree. The menu designer is opened.

There is a placeholder for an additional item at the end of the existing menu items. Double click on this and give it the name *Database*. Use the down arrow to enter sub-menu items: *Tables*, *Relationships* and *Reports*.

Each of these will be used to activate the appropriate *JTabbedPanel*. Drag and drop the *Database* item to place it next to the *File* item. Set its enabled attribute to *false*. Until the connection to Oracle is made, the user is prevented from accessing this menu item.

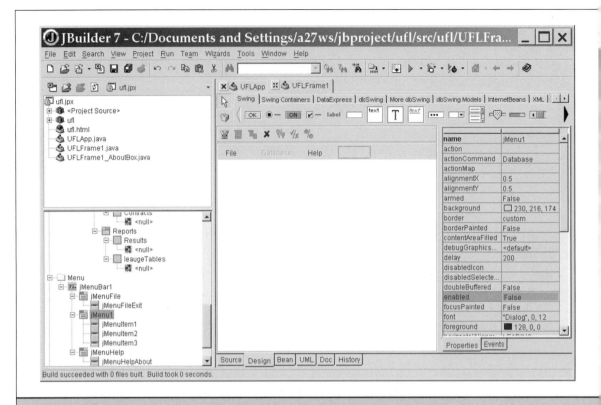

Figure 14.15 More menus.

14.2.2 EVENTS AND ACTIONS

Clicking on the *Login* form's *Connect* button in the running application has absolutely no effect, as the button cannot detect the click and has no response programmed into it. In order to detect events like mouse clicks and key presses, the component must have a listener installed in it. Fortunately, this is relatively simple and involves using the events tab of the button's property inspector. Select the *Connect* button in the design editor and the event tab in the property inspector. Double-click in the *mouseClicked* attribute. The editor moves automatically to the *Source* pane, revealing the Java code it has generated (Figure 14.16). In fact, it has created two code fragments. One creates a *mouseClicked* listener and the second an empty action method called *ConnectmouseClicked*. The listener is specific to the mouse click event and does not, for example detect the mouse cursor passing over the button. The action method is installed in the listener, and whenever the *Connect* button is clicked the action method will be called.

There are two things to do before Java code to create a connection to Oracle can be written in the action method. First, although JBuilder has been made aware of

```
action method
Connect.addMouseListener(new java.awt.event.MouseAdapter() {
     public void mouseClicked(MouseEvent e) {
       Connect_mouseClicked(e);
     }
   });

...

  void Connect_mouseClicked(MouseEvent e) {

  }
```

Figure 14.16 Listener installed; action method.

the location of the JDBC class library, the program must be made aware of those classes. Add a line to the *import* statements at the top of the file (Figure 14.17).

```
import java.awt.*;
import java.awt.event.*;
import javax.swing.*;
import com.borland.jbcl.layout.*;
// add a line to import the JDBC classes
import java.sql.*;
```

Figure 14.17 Import the JDBC classes.

Second, a *Connection* object with global scope must be added as an attribute of the *UFLFrame1* class. There are about thirty different component objects declared as attributes of *UFLFrame1*. These have been inserted as components were added in the design editor. Declare the *conn* object at the end of this list (Figure 14.18).

The action method, *Connect_mouseClicked*, can now be coded as shown in Figure 14.19. If the Oracle server is running on the same machine then use *loopback* or *localhost* as the host name in the connect string. Otherwise, use the fully qualified network name of your Oracle host.

Notice how the contents of the *userName* and *Service* textfields are extracted with the *getText* method. The *passWord* field needs special treatment to extract its contents and convert to a string. The contents of the *Service* field are concatenated with *connect_string* to form the URL for the connection.

All of the *JDBC* calls are made within a try/catch structure. This is to protect the program from run-time errors should an exception be raised because of network

```
public class UFLFrame1 extends JFrame {
  private JPanel contentPane;
  private JMenuBar jMenuBar1 = new JMenuBar();
...
  // declare the Connection object
  Connection conn;
```

Figure 14.18 Declare the connection object.

```
void Connect_mouseClicked(MouseEvent e) {
  String connect_string = "jdbc:oracle:thin:@loopback:1521:";
  try {
    Class.forName("oracle.jdbc.driver.OracleDriver");
    conn=DriverManager.getConnection(connect_string
              +Service.getText(),
              userName.getText(),
              String.valueOf(passWord.getPassword())));
    statusBar.setText("Status: Connected to Oracle");
    jMenu1.setEnabled(true);
  }
  catch(Exception f){
    statusBar.setText("Status: Not Connected to Oracle");
    System.out.println(f.getMessage());
  }
}
```

Figure 14.19 Action method for the connect button.

failure or an SQL error. If an exception is raised in the *try* section, control falls straight through to the *catch* section with the exception as a parameter.

If all goes well, *statusBar* will have its contents changed to show that a connection has been made, the *Database* menu item will be enabled and control will jump to the end of the *catch* section. In this case, that is the end of the method.

If an exception is raised, the *catch* section changes *statusBar* to show a warning and the exception's message is printed in the JVM's monitor pane.

The *Clear* button can now have a listener installed and some very simple code can be written for the action method (Figure 14.20).

Figure 14.21 shows the running application. The connect button has been clicked and the status bar confirms that the connection to Oracle has been made. The *Database* menu item is enabled.

```
void Clear_mouseClicked(MouseEvent e) {
    userName.setText("");
    passWord.setText("");
    Service.setText("");
}
```

Figure 14.20 Action method for the clear button.

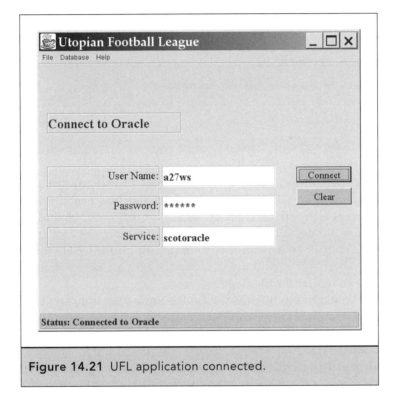

Figure 14.21 UFL application connected.

Listeners must now be installed in the three sub-menu items with action methods to instruct *appPanel*'s layout manager to show the corresponding *Tables*, *Relationships* or *Reports* tabbed panels. For these sub-menu items, the event to be detected is *actionPerformed*.

Figure 14.22 shows the code inserted into the action method created for *jMenuItem1* when the *actionPerformed* event is selected for detection in the property inspector. The *Tables* tabbed panel is brought to the top of the stack of panels by the *CardLayout.show()* method. The *switch* statement detects which of *Tables'* three panels, *Players*, *Clubs* or *Discipline*, is currently selected, and performs setup action accordingly.

```
void jMenuItem1_actionPerformed(ActionEvent e) {
   cardLayout1.show(appPanel,"Tables ");
   switch (Tables.getSelectedIndex()){
      case 0: setupPlayers();
              break;
      case 1:setupClubs();
              break;
      case 2:setupDiscipline();
              break;
      default:break;
   }
}
```

Figure 14.22 Sub-menu action method.

14.3 THE *PLAYERS* FORM

The *Players* form is illustrated in Figure 14.23. It consists of a *JComboBox* called *playerSelect* and seven *JTextFields* called *Surname, Forename, DoB* and so on, with *JLabels* as appropriate. There are three buttons: *Save, New* and *Clear2*. The font sizes, colours and default text content have been set in the property inspector. The *Save* button has its *enabled* property set to *false* and the *Club* textfield has *editable* set *false*. There will be nothing to save until edits are detected, and changing a player's club is a matter for the *Contracts* form.

If the action method for the Tables menu item indicates that, within the Tables panel, *Players* is currently selected, the *setupPlayers()* method (Figure 14.24) loads all the *ufa_id* values from the *Players* table in the database into the *selectPlayer* *JComboBox*.

This same *setupPlayers* method can also be called when the Players tab is selected over *Clubs* or *Discipline* by installing it in the action method of *Tables' stateChanged* listener. Simply double click on the *stateChanged* event in *Tables'* property inspector and then insert the code in the action method as shown in Figure 14.25.

Every time the selected item in the combobox is changed, the attribute fields in the *Players* form must be kept synchronized with it. An *actionPerformed* listener is installed in *selectPlayer* and the action method is coded as shown in Figure 14.26. The *actionPerformed* event will also be triggered when *selectPlayer* has items added to it during *setupPlayers*, so there is no need to call it explicitly there.

The method uses a *PreparedStatement* to find the attributes of the player whose *ufa_id* is current in *playerSelect*. The query string has a '?' placeholder in it. The statement's *setString* method sets the placeholder to the contents of *playerSelect*'s selection field.

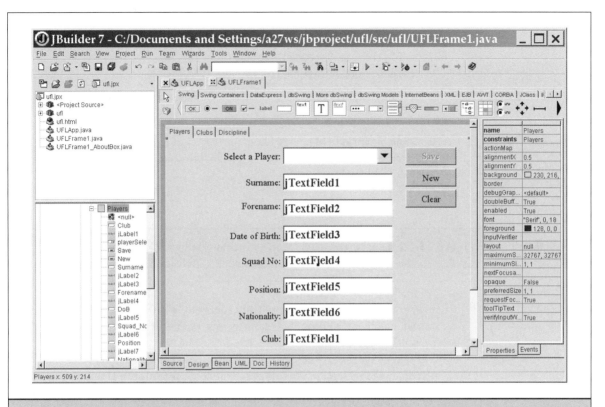

Figure 14.23 The *Players* form.

```
void setupPlayers(){
  statusBar.setText("Status: Maintain Players Table ");
  Save.setEnabled(false);
  String query= "select ufa_id from players";
  try {
   Statement stmt1=conn.createStatement();
   ResultSet rs=stmt1.executeQuery(query);
   playerSelect.removeAllItems();
   while (rs.next())
     playerSelect.addItem(rs.getString(1));
  }
  catch(Exception f){
    System.out.println(f.getMessage());
  }
}
```

Figure 14.24 *setupPlayers* method.

```
void Tables_stateChanged(ChangeEvent e) {
    switch (Tables.getSelectedIndex()){
        case 0: setupPlayers();
                break;
        case 1:setupClubs();
                break;
        case 2:setupDiscipline();
                break;
        default:break;
    }
}
```

Figure 14.25 *Tables' stateChanged* event handler.

```
void playerSelect_actionPerformed(ActionEvent e) {
    String query1=" select * from players where ufa_id =?";
    try {
    PreparedStatement stmt2=conn.prepareStatement(query1);
    stmt2.setString(1,(String)playerSelect.getSelectedItem());
    ResultSet rs=stmt2.executeQuery();
    if (rs.next()){
     Surname.setText(rs.getString(2));
     Forename.setText(rs.getString(3));
     DoB.setText(rs.getDate(4).toString());
     Squad_No.setText(rs.getString(5));
     Position.setText(rs.getString(6));
     Nationality.setText(rs.getString(7));
     Club.setText(rs.getString(8));
     statusBar.setText("Status: Player selected. Edit fields ");
     Save.setEnabled(false);
     }
    }
    catch(Exception f){
      System.out.println(f.getMessage());
    }
}
```

Figure 14.26 *playerSelect* event handler.

The statement is then executed, assigning its returned row to the *ResultSet*, *rs*. If *rs* holds a row, its columns are assigned to the textfields in the *Players* panel. The date of birth needs special processing. It is extracted from *rs* as a *Date* object. The *Date* class has a method *toString* that converts a *Date* into a *String* and formats it as *yyyy-mm-dd*.

The Clear2 button re-establishes the Players form. If the user gets into a tangle whilst editing a player's attributes, clicking on the button triggers a *mouseClicked* event. Add the event listener for the Clear2 button and call *setupPlayers* from the action method (Figure 14.27). This reinitializes the form.

```
void Clear2_mouseClicked(MouseEvent e) {
    setupPlayers();
}
```

Figure 14.27 *Clear2* button's action method.

The *Save* button must be enabled when editing activity is detected in any of the textfields. Install a *keyPressed* event listener in each of the *editable* fields. A sample of the single line of code for each of the action methods is shown in Figure 14.28.

```
void Surname_keyPressed(KeyEvent e) {
    Save.setEnabled(true);
}
```

Figure 14.28 Detecting editing of fields.

With the Save button enabled, code must be written for its *mouseClicked* event handler. Install the appropriate event listener – the code for its action method is shown in Figure 14.29.

The only thing left to do now in the *Players* form is to implement the *New* button to create a new player. The intention is that clicking this button will create a pop-up dialog where the new player's attributes may be edited. Inserting a new player also means that an initial contract must be created.

The *newPlayer* dialog will also demonstrate further use of the combobox to validate user inputs and a method of creating a randomized *ufa_id* that is guaranteed to be unique.

14.4 ⊨ THE *NEWPLAYER* DIALOG

The *newPlayer* dialog will be a separate class from *UFLFrame* and will be created using the dialog wizard. Click *File |New* on the main JBuilder menu and double-click the dialog icon. The wizard is started. Change the class name to *newPlayer* and click *Next*. The outline Java program for the dialog is created and added as a project file.

```
void Save_mouseClicked(MouseEvent e) {
   String query= "update players set surname=?,
                   forename=?,dateofbirth=?,squad_no=?,
                   position=?,nationality=? where ufa_id=?";
      try {
         PreparedStatement stmt=conn.prepareStatement(query);
         stmt.setString(1,Surname.getText());
         stmt.setString(2,Forename.getText());
         stmt.setDate(3,java.sql.Date.valueOf(DoB.getText()));
         stmt.setString(4,Squad_No.getText());
         stmt.setString(5,Position.getText());
         stmt.setString(6,Nationality.getText());
         stmt.setString(7,(String) playerSelect.getSelectedItem());
         stmt.executeQuery();
         Save.setEnabled(false);
      }
      catch(Exception f){System.out.println(f.getMessage());}
}
```

Figure 14.29 Saving the edits.

The design process for the dialog is similar to that followed for the various forms in *UFLFrame1*. The layout is shown in Figure 14.30.

Double click on the file *newPlayer.java* in the project pane. The design tab shows a blank rectangle. Add a *JPanel* to *UI-this* in the component tree. Set its layout manager to *null* or to *XYLayout*. This panel will be the principal container for the dialog. Start by copying all the components; labels, buttons, textfields and comboboxes from the *Players* form to *panel1* in the dialog. Use a multi-select copy and paste. The components will be copied with the same names and visual properties. These will be reflected in the source code for the dialog. Duplicated component names can be used because the dialog is a different class from *UFLFrame1*.

Delete the *Position*, *Nationality* and *Club* textfields. Replace them with *JComboBoxes* and rename the new components accordingly. Delete the *playerSelect* combobox and replace it with a JTextField. Rename this to *Ufa_ID*. Add text fields *startDate* and *Salary* with labels. Add labels for the two sections of the form. The two etched border boxes that group the components are two overlaying transparent panels. There are three buttons: *Save*, *Generate* and *Cancel*.

The source code generated by the dialog wizard now needs several amendments to integrate *newPlayer* into the UFL application. First, two *import* statement must be added so that the dialog can use JDBC and the random number generator in the java.util library (Figure 14.31).

Second, the constructors generated for the dialog must be changed. Because *newPlayer* is a separate class, the connection to Oracle will not automatically be available in the scope of the class. It can, however, be passed as an additional

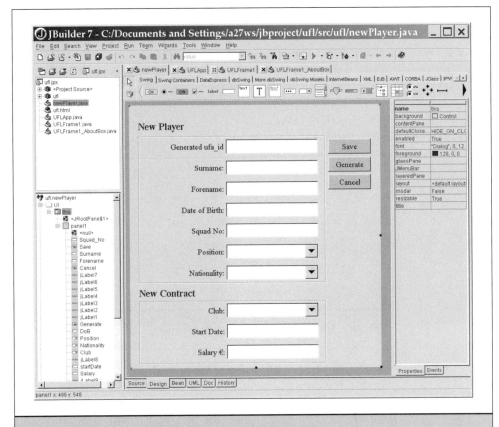

Figure 14.30 The *newPlayer* dialog.

```
// add imports for JDBC and random number generator
import java.sql.*;
import java.util.*;
```

Figure 14.31 Added *import* statements.

parameter to the constructor. There are two constructors for *newPlayer*, following the inheritance rules for the *JDialog* class.

The first takes three parameters, the dialog's parent, its title and whether it is modal[3] or not. The constructor then goes on to call the constructor for its super-class, passing on the parameters it has received. Add a fourth parameter, as shown

---

3 Modal: the frame or dialog must be closed before any other window in the application can be made active. User focus is captured.

```
public newPlayer(Frame frame, String title, boolean modal,
                      Connection conn) {
   super(frame, title, modal);
   try {
     conn1=conn;
     jbInit();
     pack();
   }
   catch(Exception ex) {
     ex.printStackTrace();
   }
}

public newPlayer() {
   this(null, "", false, null);
}
```

Figure 14.32 *newPlayer* constructors.

in Figure 14.32. This will not be passed on to the superclass and has scope only within the constructor.

The secondary constructor allows the dialog to be created with no parameter values. Default values are sent in a call to the primary constructor. Add a *null* default, to harmonize with the signature of the prime constructor, which now requires four input parameters. The prime constructor will be called from *UFLFrame1*, passing the value of the existing connection object.

Because the scope of the parameter is limited to the constructor, its value is immediately transferred to *conn1*, a global *Connection* class attribute in *newPlayer*. Add the declaration for *conn1* to the attributes of *newPlayer*, it will later be used to create SQL statements in the dialog.

In fact, the connection is used almost immediately. Code the *fillFields* method (Figure 14.33) and issue a call to it at the end of the dialog's *jbInit* method. The *fillFields* method populates the *Position, Nationality* and *Club* comboboxes. Using comboboxes restricts the user to choosing only valid entries for these fields. The *DoB* and *startDate* field are initialized to today's date. This gives the user a template to enter these data fields in the correct format. The other textfields on the form are set to blanks.

The method *generateUfa_ID* should also be coded (Figure 14.34) and a call to it inserted just after the *fillFields* call in *jbInit*. This method generates the new player's *ufa_id* using a random number generator. There are two *for-loops*. The first generates two random alphabetic uppercase characters as the prefix of the *ufa_id*. The second generates five numeric characters as the suffix. Each of these characters is concatenated with the initially empty string, *test*, in each round of the loops.

```
void fillFields(){
  Position.removeAllItems();
  Nationality.removeAllItems();
  Club.removeAllItems();
  try {
  Statement stmt=conn1.createStatement();
  String query="select allowed from positions";
  ResultSet rs=stmt.executeQuery(query);
  while (rs.next()) Position.addItem(rs.getString(1));
  query="select distinct nationality from players";
  rs=stmt.executeQuery(query);
  while (rs.next()) Nationality.addItem(rs.getString(1));
  query="select name from clubs";
  rs=stmt.executeQuery(query);
  while (rs.next()) Club.addItem(rs.getString(1));
  query="select SYSDATE from dual ";
  rs=stmt.executeQuery(query);
  if (rs.next()){
  DoB.setText(rs.getDate(1).toString());
  startDate.setText(rs.getDate(1).toString());
  Surname.setText("");
  Forename.setText("");
  Squad_No.setText("");
  Salary.setText("");
  }
 }
 catch(Exception f){ System.out.println(f.getMessage());
 }
}
```

Figure 14.33 Initializing the form.

The first loop, which iterates twice, uses *rand*, the random number generator, through its *nextInt* method, to give a positive number between 0 and 65,000. The generated numbers should be evenly distributed within the range. The modulus operator, %, gives the remainder after its first operand is divided by the second (Figure 14.35).

So, the modulus 26 of the initial random number is calculated. This yields an even distribution of numbers in the range 0 to 25. The character 'A' is 65 in the ASCII coding scheme; adding 65 to the result of the modulus will give a number between 65 and 90. This corresponds to the letters 'A' to 'Z'. Casting the number to a *char* type, converting it to a *String* and concatenating it to the *test* string builds the prefix of the *ufa_id*.

```
void generateUfa_ID(){
  String test="";
  String query="select surname from players where ufa_id=?";
  boolean success=false;
  int x;
  char c;
  Random rand= new Random();
  PreparedStatement stmt;
  ResultSet rs;
  while (!success){
    test="";
  for (x=0;x<2;x++)
    test=test +
          String.valueOf((char)((rand.nextInt(65000)%26)+65));
  for (x=0;x<5;x++)
    test=test +
          String.valueOf((char)((rand.nextInt(65000)%10)+48));
  try {
    stmt=conn1.prepareStatement(query);
    stmt.setString(1,test);
    rs=stmt.executeQuery();
    if(!rs.next())
      success=true;
  }
  catch(Exception f){
    System.out.println(f.getMessage()); }
  }
  Ufa_ID.setText(test);
}
```

Figure 14.34 Generate the *ufa_id*.

```
29%3=2
28%3=1
27 %3=0
```

Figure 14.35 Modulus arithmetic.

A similar thing is done in the second loop, except that the second modulus operand is 10 and the added number is 48. This gives a number in the range 48 to 57: the ASCII characters '0' to '9'. This loop iterates five times, building the *ufa_id*'s numeric suffix.

The string *test* is then used as a parameter to the SQL query. If the ResultSet is empty the generated *ufa_id* does not exist in the database, the variable *success* is turned to *true* and the outer *while-loop* ends. If the result returns a row, the generated *ufa_id* is already assigned to another player. Another key is generated until the Boolean variable *success* can be turned to *true*. The generated *ufa_id* is then guaranteed unique, placed in the textfield and the method ends.

Figure 14.36 shows the dialog running. The size of the pop-up frame can be adjusted with the *preferred size* (in pixels) property of the container, *pane l1*. The next task is to code action methods for the three buttons on the form.

The *Cancel* button closes the dialog, returning control to its parent, *UFLFrame1*. Create a *mouseClicked* listener for *Cancel* (Figure 14.37).

The *Generate* button calls *fillFields* and *GenerateUfa_ID* to reinitialize the form for a second or subsequent new player, and re-enables the *Save* button. Install a *mouseClicked* listener for *Generate* (Figure 14.38).

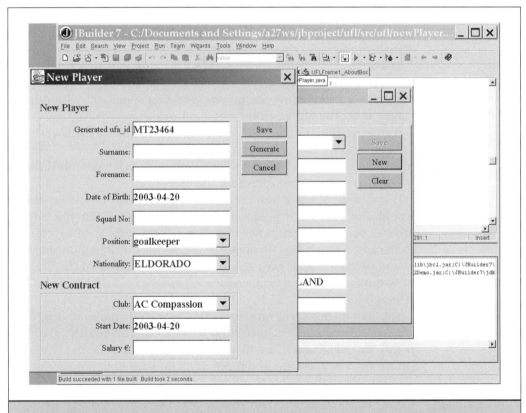

Figure 14.36 *newPlayer* dialog running.

```
void Cancel_mouseClicked(MouseEvent e) {
  this.dispose();
}
```

Figure 14.37 The *Cancel* button's action method.

```
void Generate_mouseClicked(MouseEvent e) {
  fillFields();
  generateUfa_ID();
  Save.setEnabled(true);
}
```

Figure 14.38 The *Generate* button's action method.

The *Save* button must initiate two SQL insert statements: one to add a row to the *Players* table and one to add a row in the *Contracts* table (Figure 14.39). It is essential that if one of them fails, so does the other. There cannot be a player without an initial contract and there cannot be a contract without a corresponding player.

The answer, of course, is to place both statements in a single transaction. The connection object, *conn1*, has a method, *setAutocommit(boolean)*. It is used here to set Oracle's autocommit feature off. The first statement will implicitly open the transaction. There is an explicit commit to end it.

If an exception is raised, control drops through to the *catch* section. Notice that a second, nested *try/catch* structure is needed here to call *conn1.rollback()*. JDBC statements that have the potential to raise remote or SQL exceptions can only be called inside a *try* section that can catch the exceptions.

If the original exception were caused by a network failure, then the rollback would also fail, raising another remote exception, but the transaction is lost anyway since the session has ended and *autocommit* is off. If the original failure were caused by an SQL error, such as a constraint being disobeyed, the rollback would succeed. Either way, the integrity of the database is secure.

Return to the *Players* form and install a *mouseClicked* listener for the *New* button (Figure 14.40).

The action consists of only two lines. First, an instance of *newPlayer* called *dlg* is created. Notice that the connection is supplied as the fourth parameter. The parent is *this*, the *UFLFrame1*, the title is "New Player" and modal is *true*. The next line shows *dlg*. The *show* method is blocked and does not complete until the dialog is closed because the dialog is modal.

The *Players* form and its associated dialog, *newPlayer*, are now complete.

```
void Save_mouseClicked(MouseEvent e) {
  String query= "insert into players(ufa_id, surname, forename,"+
  "dateofbirth, squad_no, position, nationality, club) "+
  "values(?,?,?,?,?,?,?,?)";
  try {
    conn1.setAutoCommit(false);
    PreparedStatement stmt=conn1.prepareStatement(query);
    stmt.setString(1,Ufa_ID.getText());
    stmt.setString(2,Surname.getText());
    stmt.setString(3,Forename.getText());
    stmt.setDate(4,java.sql.Date.valueOf(DoB.getText()));
    stmt.setString(5,Squad_No.getText());
    stmt.setString(6,(String) Position.getSelectedItem());
    stmt.setString(7,(String) Nationality.getSelectedItem());
    stmt.setString(8,(String) Club.getSelectedItem());
    stmt.executeQuery();
    query= "insert into contracts(ufa_id, club, joined, salary)"+
    "values(?,?,?,?)";
    PreparedStatement stmt1=conn1.prepareStatement(query);
    stmt1.setString(1,Ufa_ID.getText());
    stmt1.setString(2,(String) Club.getSelectedItem());
    stmt1.setDate(3,java.sql.Date.valueOf(startDate.getText()));
    stmt1.setString(4,Salary.getText());
    stmt1.executeQuery();
    conn1.commit();
    conn1.setAutoCommit(true);
    Save.setEnabled(false);
  }
  catch(Exception f){
    try {conn1.rollback();     conn1.setAutoCommit(true);
}

    catch(Exception d){
      System.out.println(f.getMessage()); }
    System.out.println(f.getMessage());
  }
}
```

Figure 14.39 The *Save* button's action method.

```
void New_mouseClicked(MouseEvent e) {
  newPlayer dlg=new newPlayer(this, "New Player", true, conn);
  dlg.show();
}
```

Figure 14.40 The *New* button's action method.

14.5 ⊟ THE *MATCHRESULTS* FORM

The *matchResults* form is used to maintain a 1:*N* relationship between the *Matches* and *Goals* tables in the database. The result of a match can be inferred by counting the goals for each team in a match. Because each match will often be associated with more than one goal, the details of each goal (scorer, time of scoring and goal type) must be displayed in a multi-row container. Although it is perfectly possible to program this directly in Java, it is easier to use the data-aware components supplied as part of the JBuilder Enterprise Edition.

The *matchResults* form makes use of components from the *DataExpress* and *dbSwing* tabs in the Design editor's palette. These components rely on a different database connection from that demonstrated in the *Login* and *Players* forms.

Select the *matchResults* panel in the structure tree and click on the design editor tab. Click on the *Database* component. The cursor changes to a crosshair, indicating that the component has been selected. Click anywhere on the editor or structure panes. The *Database* component is added to the structure tree in the Data Access branch. Select the *Database* component and use its property inspector to configure it. Change its name to *uflOracle* and set its connection property as shown in Figure 14.41. Change the values to conform to your local Oracle installation.

You may need to pre-configure automatic access to Oracle.jdbc.driver. OracleDriver through the OracleJDBC library tag. Use the JBuilder menu *Tools|Enterprise Setup* dialog to do this.

Change the settings in the *Database configuration* dialog until clicking on the *Test Connection* button gives a *Success* response.

14.5.1   DATA-AWARE COMPONENTS

The data-aware components are divided into two types: those that access databases or text files directly to retrieve data and those that provide a *viewport* of the retrieved data in a form. Components in the DataExpress tab are largely of the first type and components in the dbSwing tab are of the second type

Components that read the database directly are based on the *DataSet* class. A *tableDataSet* reads a complete database table; a *queryDataSet* reads the rows returned in a single or multi-table SQL query. The dataset copies the data in the

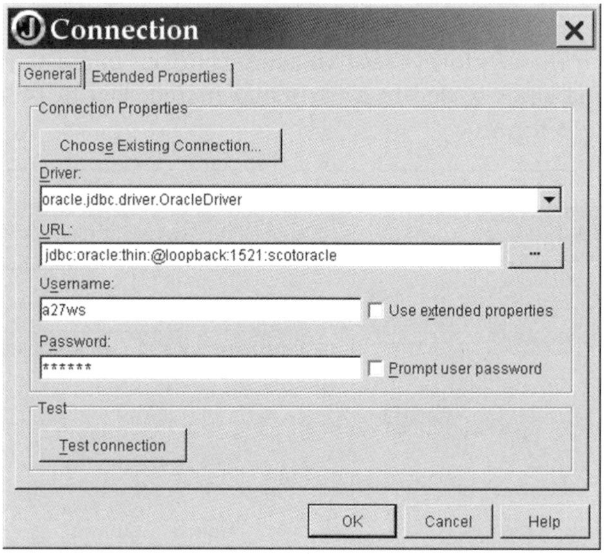

Figure 14.41 Configure the database connection.

returned rows into its structure, which can be thought of as a dynamic two-dimensional array. The columns in the dataset conform to the selection set of the query; each row in the dataset represents a returned row from the query. If the dataset is updatable, read-intending-write locks are left on the rows in the database; if the dataset is read-only then read locks (if supported) are left in the database.

The rows in the dataset can be inspected or changed and new rows added through an appropriate viewport. At some point, the changes and insertions may be saved or, in java-speak, resolved. The rows in the dataset are copied back into the database in write operations that replace previous values or add rows. The dataset identifies the source of each of its cells by its table name, its column name and the *ROWID* of the data in the table. This information is established when the dataset is opened. The dataset can be thought of as a snapshot of the data returned by its query.

Because the dataset is a client-side memory structure it can be manipulated in much the same way as an array. It has a cursor, or pointer to the current row, that has focus through the viewport. The cursor can be moved programmatically to the first row (using the dataset's *first()* method) and each row examined in a loop structure that moves the cursor to the next row until the end of the dataset. The cursor is moved forwards using the dataset's *next()* method or backwards using the *previous()* method. The viewport automates this process to give a visual presentation of the rows without the need for programmer intervention.

Two *Datasets* can be linked together in a Master/Detail relationship. This synchronizes the detail dataset to the master. Whenever a row in the master dataset receives focus, the focus in the detail dataset is moved to a row that matches the row value equality specified in the relationship.

The *matchResults* form uses five datasets linked in master/detail relationships to present the goals scored in a particular match. Figure 14.42 shows the finished *matchResults* form.

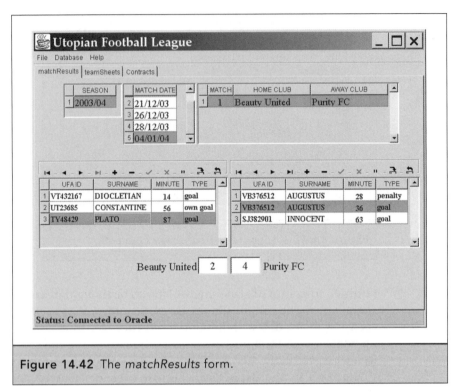

Figure 14.42 The *matchResults* form.

The datasets in the form are connected to visual components or viewports. Each dataset is presented through a *jdbTable* component that shows the rows and columns from the dataset and also marks the current row through a highlight. The *jdbTable* enables each cell to be edited, the changes are reflected in the underlying dataset: its rows are marked as *changed* until the changes are resolved (saved) back to the database.

Each *jdbTable* is contained in a *TableScrollPane* that gives a vertical and horizontal scrollable area to display just a few rows from the *jdbTable*.

In this form, the user selects a particular season from the scroll pane positioned at the top left of the form. Whenever focus in this component changes, a master/detail relationship synchronizes the match dates for that season in the scroll pane to its right (Figure 14.43). Selecting a particular match date in this way triggers a similar response, again synchronized through a master/detail relationship, to show the matches played on that particular date. Selecting a match shows the goals scored by the home team's players in the scroll pane at lower left and the goals scored by the away team players in the scroll pane on the right.

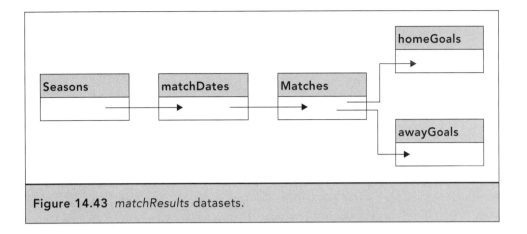

Figure 14.43 *matchResults* datasets.

Every time the data changes in these last two panes, a component event causes the match score to be calculated. This calculation allocates each player's goals or penalties to his team, while own goals are allocated to the opposing side.

The three scroll panes at the top of the form are read-only or *non-resolvable*. Editing fixtures is no business of this form. The two goal panes are fully editable: existing rows can be changed or deleted and new rows can be added.

Each of these panes has a *jdbNavToolBar* linked to it. This automates the editing process. The icons can be clicked to move focus in the pane, add a new row, save changes or refresh the dataset by taking a new snapshot if edits have got into a tangle.

14.5.2   CREATING THE DATASETS

Select the editor pane and click on the *QueryDataSet* component in the *DataExpress* tab. The cursor changes to crosshairs. Drop the *QueryDataSet* on the structure tree. The dataset is added to the Data Access branch.

Double-click on the dataset to expose the dataset design editor. Change its name in the property inspector and click on the ellipsis in the query property to expose the query editor (Figure 14.44).

Specify the *uflOracle* database connection and make sure that the *Execute query immediately* box is checked. The SQL statement can either be typed in directly or it can be built interactively with the SQL Builder tool. Press the Test Query button until it executes successfully. Then press the OK button.

Notice that, instead of just selecting all the *season* values from the *Seasons* table, the query joins the *Seasons* table with the *Matches* table. The query only gives seasons that have corresponding matches in the database. The distinct operator restricts the query so that only one season is returned whether there is only 1 match or 200 matches associated with it.

The dataset editor now shows the columns in the dataset. Set the dataset's *resolvable* property to *false* and clear the *resolve order* property (Figure 14.45).

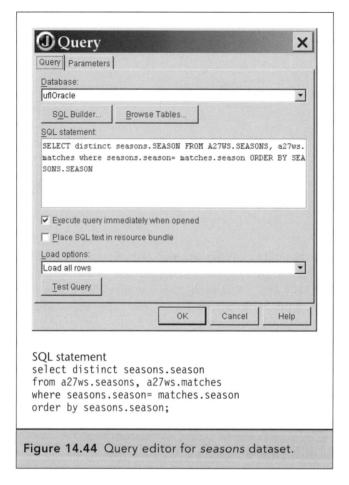

SQL statement
```
select distinct seasons.season
from a27ws.seasons, a27ws.matches
where seasons.season= matches.season
order by seasons.season;
```

Figure 14.44 Query editor for *seasons* dataset.

Column properties are shown in the editor. The list icon enables different column properties to appear in the editor. The caption and width properties can be set later when the dataset is connected to a viewport.

The *matchDates* dataset is established in the same way. Its query is given in Figure 14.46.

The distinct restriction ensure that only one row is returned for each combination of *season* and *matchdate*. Set the other properties for *matchDates* as for *Seasons*, to ensure that it is read-only. The one difference here is that a master/detail relationship with the *Seasons* dataset will be set up to synchronize the rows displayed in *matchDates'* viewport (Figure 14.47).

Click on the ellipsis in the *MasterLink* property of *matchDates* and the *MasterLink* editor pops up. Specify *Seasons* as the master dataset and the *season* column of each dataset as the link columns. Test the link to ensure that it is working and click on *OK*. The *season* column in *matchDates* is needed to make the link, but it will not be displayed in the viewport. The dataset hides detail link columns ensuring they are not editable. All edits and insertions to the detail dataset are kept linked to the master in this way.

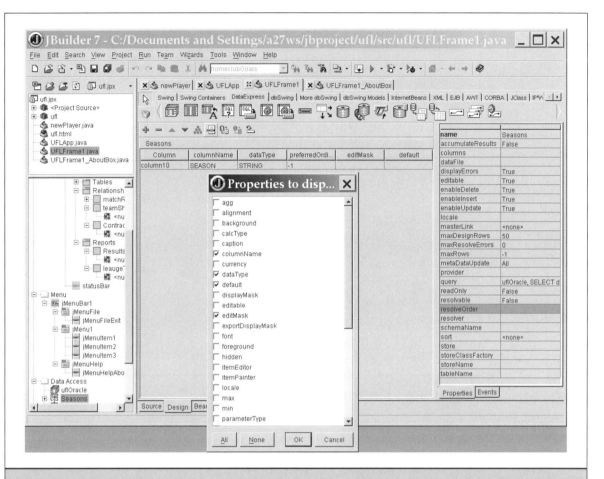

Figure 14.45 Setting the column property inspector.

```
select distinct matches.matchdate, matches.season from a27ws.matches
```

Figure 14.46 *matchDates* query.

The *Matches* dataset has a simple query, shown in Figure 14.48. The master/detail relationship with *matchDates* is created with the *season* and *matchdate* columns as the link. Because *Matches* is the detail dataset, these two columns will not appear in its viewport.

The *homeGoals* dataset has a rather more complex query. This is shown in Figure 14.49. The *Goals* table is joined with *Teamsheets* to retrieve the club that each goalscorer was playing for at the time of the match.

This will also ensure that any inserted goalscorer was actually playing in the match. The join with *Players* is necessary to retrieve the *Surname* column. This is

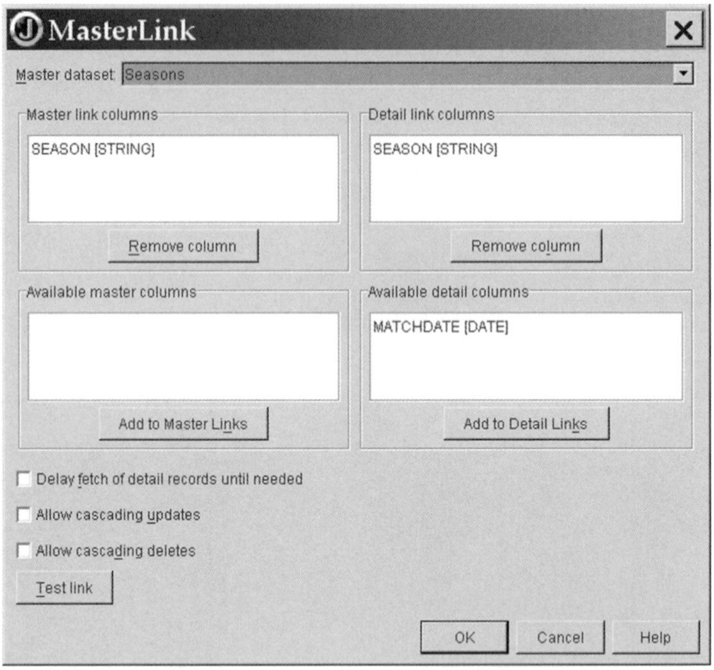

Figure 14.47 Master/detail relationship for *matchDates*.

```
select matches.match_id, matches.homeclub,
           matches.awayclub, matches.matchdate, matches.season
from a27ws.matches
```

Figure 14.48 *Matches'* query.

```
select goals.match_id, goals.ufa_id, teamsheets.club,
         players.surname, goals.minute, goals.type
from a27ws.goals,a27ws.teamsheets,a27ws.players
where goals.match_id=teamsheets.match_id
   and goals.ufa_id=players.ufa_id
   and goals.ufa_id=teamsheets.ufa_id
order by goals.minute
```

Figure 14.49 *homeGoals* query (and *awayGoals*!).

likely to be a better accuracy check for the user than the *ufa_id*. The *awayGoals* dataset has the same query. Two datasets are needed so that edits and insertions can make use of independently positioned current row cursors. The *homeGoals* dataset is linked to *Matches* firstly through *Match_ID* and secondly by a link based on *Matches.HomeClub* and *homeGoals.Club*. Figure 14.50 shows the *MasterLink* dialog for *homeGoals*.

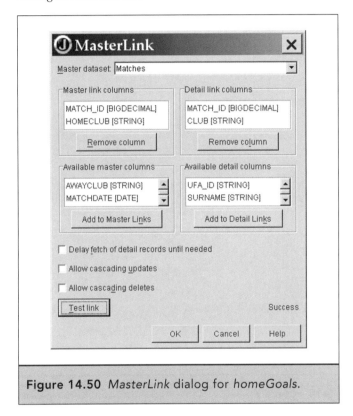

Figure 14.50 *MasterLink* dialog for *homeGoals*.

Although the *awayGoals* dataset has the same underlying query and thus is a snapshot of the same rows in the database, its master/detail relationship is based on *Match_ID* and *Matches.AwayClub* with *awayGoals.Club*.

This ensures that the same row snapshots will never be displayed in their respective viewports and thus updates and insertions will not cause lock conflicts. Since locks are always at the row level and updates are resolved in the dataset through the *ROWID*, this must be the case.

14.5.3   DATASETS AND VIEWPORTS

The tabbed panel, *Relationships*, contains a *JPanel* called *matchResults* and this will be the basis of the results entry form.

Click on the *jdbTableScrollPane* icon in the *dbSwing* palette tab and draw it on the panel. Repeat this four times and arrange the scroll panes as shown in Figure 14.51.

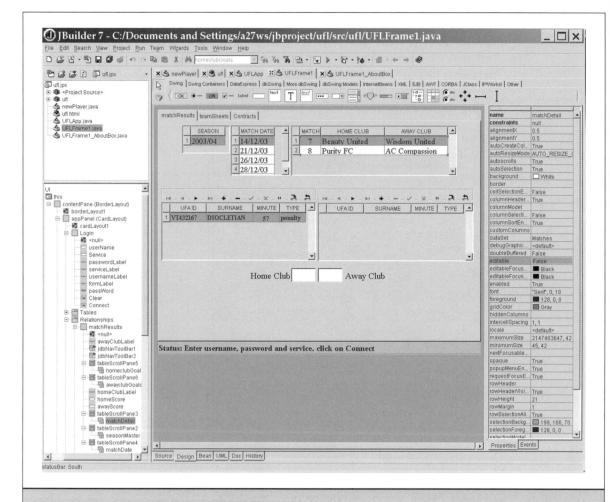

Figure 14.51 Design view with active datasets.

The scroll panes are containers, like *JPanel*. They offer additional functionality, as their name suggests; vertical and horizontal scroll bars appear when their contents fill more than the area set for them in the design editor

Click on the *jdbTable* icon and click inside the first *TableScrollPane*. Rename the *jdbTable* to *seasonMaster*. Initially, *seasonMaster* resembles an empty spreadsheet. It has one column called *A* and one row called *1*. Use the property inspector to assign the dataset *Seasons* to *seasonMaster*. The display changes: *seasonMaster* displays the first row of the dataset assigned to it and *seasonMaster's* column has acquired a name from the dataset. Change *seasonMaster's* foreground font to *serif|18*. The text of the values causes the column to widen, making the column header visible.

The database and dataset components are active in the editor. That is how the data rows have been displayed. The *jdbTable* component is not active. Therefore, the dataset's focus or current row cannot be changed. The viewport to the dataset is static. This display of the data is a handy way of checking that the datasets and the master/detail assignments are working. It also helps in coordinating column width (set in the dataset's properties) with the scroll pane's overall width.

Add four more *jdbTable*s to the remaining scroll panes. Rename them *matchDate, matchDetail, homeclubGoals* and *awayclubGoals* respectively. Assign the datasets *matchDates, Matches, homeGoals* and *awayGoals* to them. The data in the form design should now resemble Figure 14.51. The first row of *Seasons* is linked to the first matching row of *matchDates*. The two rows in the *Matches* dataset, which were played that week, are displayed. Goals scored by players for the home club of the first match and goals scored by players of the away team are displayed in their respective areas.

Notice that the *jdbTable*s have again acquired column headings from the datasets and that master/detail link fields from the detail side are not displayed. Check that the *editable* property of the first three *jdbTable*s is set to false.

Add two *jdbNavToolBar*s to the panel, just above the home and away panes. Assign the left-hand toolbar to the *homeGoals* dataset and the right-hand one to the *awayGoals* dataset. Align and adjust the sizes of these toolbars as shown in the figure. The *jdbNavToolBar* has a number of icons in it which automate the positioning of the dataset's current row (*First, Last Next, Previous*), allow a new row to be added or an existing row to be deleted, saves all pending edits and insertions (resolves) and refreshes the dataset, losing pending updates. When the application is running, all the icons display Tool Tips.

In fact, the *jdbTable* provides these facilities too. Right-clicking on a data cell exposes its default pop-up menu. The sort order of the rows can be specified, rows added or deleted and so on. Figure 14.52 illustrates the running application with pop-up menu.

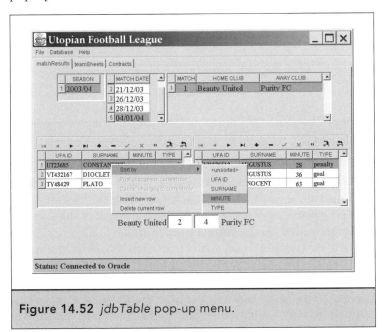

Figure 14.52 *jdbTable* pop-up menu.

The form for the maintenance of the relationship between the *matches* and *Goals* tables in the database is now largely complete. Using data-aware components has greatly simplified the creation of a moderately complex form. So far, there has been no need to change the generated Java code; everything has been accomplished by setting properties within the components.

14.5.4   WHAT'S THE SCORE?

As a final touch and as a vehicle for investigating the programmatic processing of datasets, one more function will be added. This is the calculation of the score. This is a more complicated process than just counting the rows in each of the goals displays, because own goals are credited to the scorer but contribute to the other side's score.

Add two *JLabels* and two *JTextFields* below the goals display. Rename the text fields, *homeScore* and *awayScore* respectively. When the score is calculated, the result is placed in these fields.

The calculation will be triggered by the data changing in either the home goals display or the away goals display. The *calcScores* method will be called from either of these components.

Select the events inspector of the *homeGoals* dataset and double-click in the *dataChanged* event. A *datachange* listener is created for the dataset and its action method is displayed in the source editor (Figure 14.53).

```
void homeGoals_dataChanged(DataChangeEvent e) {
  calcScores();
}

void awayGoals_dataChanged(DataChangeEvent e) {
  calcScores();
}
```

Figure 14.53 *homeGoals* and *awayGoals* action method.

The *calcScores* method is listed in Figure 14.54. Its basic strategy is to loop through all the rows of the *homeGoals* dataset, allocating goals to counters for either the home side or the away side. At the end of the loop the counters contains the score, which can be copied to the form.

There are two problems with this. Firstly, look at the query for the dataset; it contains all the goals for all the matches. The restriction to a particular match is provided, through the master/detail relation, only in its viewport: the *jdbTable*. There will have to be some sort of filter applied to the dataset as the loop progresses through its rows so that only goals for the match in question are processed for the score.

```
void calcScores(){
  int homeCount=0;
  int awayCount=0;
  BigInteger m_id;
  DataRow club = new DataRow(Matches);
Matches.getDataRow(club);
homeClubLabel.setText(club.getString("HOMECLUB"));
awayClubLabel.setText(club.getString("AWAYCLUB"));
m_id=club.getBigDecimal("MATCH_ID").toBigInteger();
DataSetView score=homeGoals.cloneDataSetView();
if (score.rowCount()>0){
 score.first();
 DataRow scoreRow = new DataRow(score);
 do{
 score.getDataRow(scoreRow);
 if(m_id.equals(scoreRow.getBigDecimal("MATCH_ID").toBigInteger()) ){
  if ( club.getString("HOMECLUB").equals(scoreRow.getString("CLUB")))
   if (scoreRow.getString("TYPE").equals("own goal"))
     awayCount++;
   else
     homeCount++;
   else
    if (scoreRow.getString("TYPE")=="own goal"  )
     homeCount++;
    else
     awayCount++;
   }
 }while(score.next());
}
 homeScore.setText(Integer.toString(homeCount));
 awayScore.setText(Integer.toString(awayCount));
 score.close();
}
```

Figure 14.54 The *calcScores* method.

Secondly the dataset's current row will be changed in the viewport if the loop uses the dataset's *first()* and *next()* methods to scan its rows. This will produce a distracting visual ripple on the screen.

The first problem is solved if the *match_id* can be extracted from the current row of the *Matches* dataset. Each of the *homeGoals* rows can be selected if they have the same *match_id*.

In order to do this, a *DataRow* object must be instantiated, using the *Matches* dataset as a parameter to its constructor. The resulting *DataRow*, named, *club* in the program, has a column structure derived from *Matches* and can hold the values from one row of the dataset. The *club* object receives the values from *Matches'* current row as a result of the call to the *getDataRow* method of the *Matches* dataset.

Values from *club* are then used to set text in the *JLabels* on the form indicating the home team and the away team, and to assign the *match_id* to a local variable for later comparison in the dataset loop. The columns of the *club* object are indicated by string parameters to its *getString* or *getBigDecimal* methods.

The answer to the second problem is to make a copy of the *homeGoals* dataset. Moving the current row cursor up and down the copy will have no effect on the viewport. The copy, named *score* in the program, is instantiated from the *DataSetView* class by a call to the dataset's *cloneDataSetView* method. As well as constructing the *score* object, the dataset's rows are copied into it.

The *score* datasetview is tested to make sure there are some goals to assess and, if so, *score's* cursor is positioned at *score's* first row and a *DataRow* called *scoreRow* is derived from the column structure of *score*. The current row is copied into *scoreRow* as the first action of each iteration.

Three nested *if* statements test the values in *scoreRow* for being associated with the particular match, for being a home goal or an away goal and for being an own goal or not. The local variable counters are incremented accordingly in each iteration.

Finally, at the bottom of the datasetview, the *next()* method returns *false* and the loop drops through. The local score counters are used to update the form and the method ends by closing *score* to enable it to be efficiently garbage collected.

The *matchResults* form is now complete.

14.6 THE MATCHRESULTS REPORT

The match results report will list all the fixtures for a given season. Each match listed will show the goalscorers and the final result. The screen design is shown in Figure 14.55.

A *jdbNavComboBox* called *selectSeason* will provide the means for selecting the season for the report. The items in the list portion of the combobox are taken straight from a nominated column of a dataset. Create the *QueryDataSet* called *getSeasons*. It is based on a very simple query (Figure 14.56).

Assigning this dataset to *selectSeason* and nominating the column *season* enables the design editor to show the first row of the dataset in the combobox, just as in the previous section. When the application is active, the combobox is populated automatically and any of the *season* values can be selected to specify the report.

The other components in the *Results* panel are three buttons called *Query*, *Word* and *Clear3*, a label for the combobox and then a *JScrollPane* (a Swing container) holding a *JTextPane* called *reportText*. The *JTextPane* will hold preliminary results from the report query and the *JScrollPane* provides scrollbars when the text contents cannot be displayed in the available area.

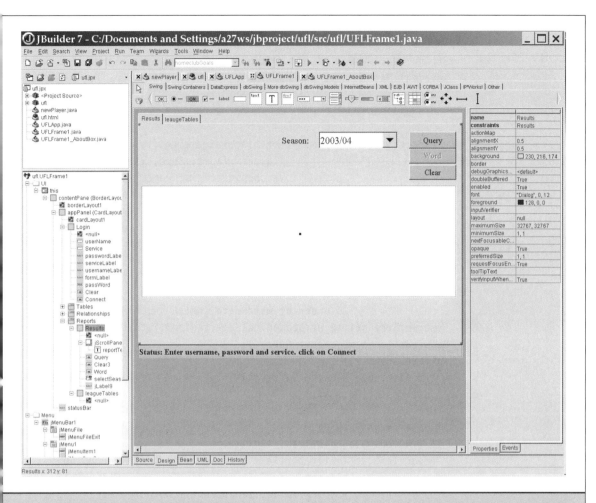

Figure 14.55 Match results report form.

```
select seasons.season from seasons
```

Figure 14.56 *getSeasons* query.

The *Query* button has a *mouseClicked* event listener installed in the events tab of its property inspector. The program code for the listener's action method is shown in Figure 14.57.

This method seems to be long and complicated, but structurally it is really quite simple. A JDBC prepared statement is created with a query string that joins the *players*, *goals*, *matches* and *teamsheets* database tables. The statement has one

```
void Query_mouseClicked(MouseEvent e) {
  String rep;    BigInteger m_id;
  java.sql.Date m_date=java.sql.Date.valueOf("1901-01-01");
  String homeClub="";    String awayClub="";    int homeCount=0;
  int awayCount=0;
 try {
   PreparedStatement stmt =conn.prepareStatement("select surname,
                      players.ufa_id, type, minute,
                      matches.match_id, homeclub, awayclub,
                      teamsheets.club, matchdate
                 from players, goals, matches, teamsheets
                 where players.ufa_id=goals.ufa_id
                 and matches.match_id=goals.match_id
                 and teamsheets.match_id=goals.match_id
                 and teamsheets.ufa_id=goals.ufa_id
                 and matches.season=?
                 order by matchdate, match_id, minute");
   stmt.setString(1,selectSeason.getSelectedItem().toString());
   ResultSet rs=stmt.executeQuery();
   while(rs.next()){
   if (m_date.equals(rs.getDate(9)))
    m_date=rs.getDate(9);
   else{
    m_date=rs.getDate(9);
    if (!homeClub.equals(""))
     reportText.setText(reportText.getText()+"         "+HomeClub
            +" "+String.valueOf(homeCount)+"  "+awayClub +" "
               +String.valueOf(awayCount)+"\n\n");
     homeClub="";
reportText.setText(reportText.getText()+rs.getDate(9).toString()+"\n");
       }
      if (homeClub.equals(rs.getString(6))){
         homeClub=rs.getString(6);
         awayClub=rs.getString(7);}
      else{
        if (!homeClub.equals(""))
         reportText.setText(reportText.getText()+"
           "+homeClub+" "+String.valueOf(homeCount)+"
           "+awayClub +" "+String.valueOf(awayCount)+"\n\n");
        homeClub=rs.getString(6);
        awayClub=rs.getString(7);
```

Figure 14.57 The *Query* button clicked...

```
           homeCount=0;
           awayCount=0;
           reportText.setText(reportText.getText()+"
 "+rs.getString(6)+" vs "+rs.getString(7)+"\n");
         }
       if (homeClub.equals(rs.getString(8))){
           if (rs.getString(3).equals("own goal"))
             awayCount++;
           else
             homeCount++;
           reportText.setText(reportText.getText()+"
 "+rs.getString(1)+" ("+rs.getString(4)+")  "+rs.getString(3)+"\n");
         }
       else{
           if (rs.getString(3).equals("own goal"))
             homeCount++;
           else
             awayCount++;
           reportText.setText(reportText.getText()+"
 "+rs.getString(1)+" ("+rs.getString(4)+")  "+rs.getString(3)+"\n");
         }
     }
   if (!homeClub.equals(""))
     reportText.setText(reportText.getText()+"
       "+homeClub+" "+String.valueOf(homeCount)+"  "+awayClub +"
       "+String.valueOf(awayCount)+"\n\n");
   Word.setEnabled(true);
   Query.setEnabled(false);
    }
   catch(Exception f){
     statusBar.setText("STATUS: "+f.getMessage());
   }
  }
```

Figure 14.57 (*Continued*)

placeholder where the selected item of *selectSeason* is inserted. The statement is executed, placing returned rows into a *ResultSet*. The *ResultSet* is then scanned row by row. Because the query is ordered, local variables detect when the *matchdate* changes in the *ResultSet* or when the *match_id* changes in the *ResultSet*. (This demonstrates the kind of processing necessary to find *breaks* in a report listing or to perform *group by* in an SQL statement.) The code prints headers or sub-headers into the text pane, *reportText*.

Notice that the component does not have a method for appending text, only a *setText()* method. Each text insertion is therefore concatenated with the previous contents to build up the report listing as an insertion rather than a replacement.

Figure 14.58 shows the application running with the *Reports* tabbed pane exposed. The *Results* panel is shown and the *Query* button has just been clicked. The *reportText* pane displays part of the raw report produced by the button's action method. The headers and sub-headers and the summary lines have been produced by the *if* statements in the method.

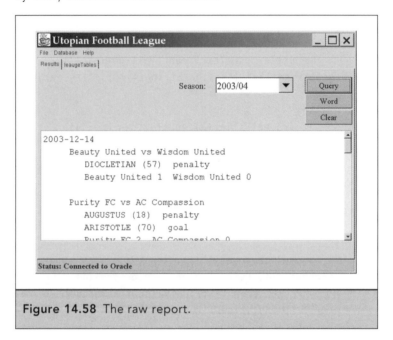

Figure 14.58 The raw report.

In order to enable the fullest formatting and text manipulation for the report text, clicking on the *Word* button will write the report contents to a temporary file and call Microsoft Word with the file as a parameter to the call. The action method for the Word button's action method is shown in Figure 14.59.

This method uses the *File* class, so an additional import statement for *java.io.**
will need to be added at the beginning of the program. The *File* class has a method for creating a temporary file whose filename is guaranteed to be unique. Two parameters are supplied: a *prefix* and a *suffix*. A random number is inserted between these to create the unique filename in the default temp directory associated with the current user.

A common method of inputting or outputting data in Java is through data streams. The streams-based classes inherit from primitives that actually perform very low-level interface management. A *FileOutputStream* is designed specifically for file output and inherits device control from *OutputStream*. It provides a *write()* method which outputs data one byte at a time. A *PrintStream* object is created from an *OutputStream*-related object and provides higher level output methods *print()*

```
void Word_mouseClicked(MouseEvent e) {
  File repFile;
  String rep;
  PrintStream outfile;
  try {
   repFile= File.createTempFile("ufl",".txt");
   outfile= new PrintStream(new FileOutputStream(repFile));
   outfile.println(reportText.getText());
   outfile.close();
   rep=repfile.getCanonicalPath();
   statusBar.setText("STATUS: Report file \
                     "+repfile.getCanonicalPath());
   Runtime.getRuntime().exec("C:\\Program Files \\Microsoft \
          Office\\Office10\\winword.exe /n   \"" + rep +"\"");
  }
  catch (Exception f){
   statusBar.setText("STATUS: "+f.getMessage());
  }
}
```

Figure 14.59 Word button action method.

and *println()* which can more easily send large data objects to the *OutputStream*'s destination.

The method code above shows first how a new *FileOutputStream* is associated with the *File* object, *repFile*, and then used as a parameter for the construction of a *PrintStream* object. This object, *outfile*, has high-level output methods, is associated with file I/O interfaces and, finally, has a guaranteed unique name. The contents of *reportText* are sent to the file in one statement and the file is then closed.

The next line of code copies the name of the temporary file to the status bar as a signal of success. Notice that all of this code is in a *try/catch* structure because the file operation can raise I/O exceptions.

Finally, the file is passed as a parameter to the launching of an external process, the Microsoft Word program. This is achieved by using the *exec* method of the application's Runtime object. Each application has one such object and additional instances cannot be constructed. The call is made via the Class's *getRuntime()* method, which returns the application's Runtime object. This is then use to make the *exec* call.

Notice the rather complicated way in which the parameters to the *exec* method must be manipulated. The call to the Word program must supply a fully qualified pathname to the executable file. This contains several \ characters, which are themselves a special character in Java strings. To enable their presence in the string, a \\ doublet must be used. The file parameter to Word must be enclosed in

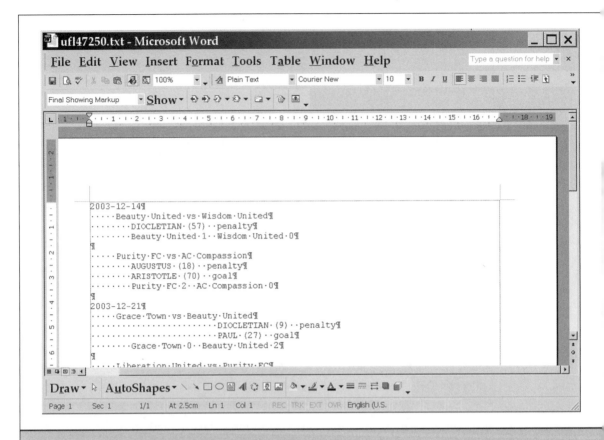

Figure 14.60 The report transferred to Word.

double quotes ("). To enable a " within a string, it must be preceded by a \. Figure 14.60 shows the report in Microsoft Word.

Finally, the *Clear3* button's action is enabled. Install a *mouseClicked* listener in the button's property and write the action method to set *reportText*'s contents to an empty string. Notice that clicking on the *Query* button deactivates it and activates the *Word* button. Clicking on the *Clear* button should activate the *Query* button and deactivate the *Word* button as well as clearing the text in *reportText*.

The *matchResults* report and the UFL application are now complete. Or at least, complete as a demonstration. It is suitable to show as a first-cut solution to a client, but it still has a number of empty panels and there is something wrong with the query underlying the match results report. Can you see what it is? It is connected to the fact that there is no 0–0 draw in the sample results.

14.7 ⊏ EXERCISES

(i) Implement the forms missing from the prototype application:

- Clubs
- Discipline
- Teamsheets
- Contracts
- *leagueTable* report (Hint: Chapter 10 showed the development of a PL/SQL anonymous block to do this. Figure 10.22 shows the code. Convert the block to a packaged procedure or function and call it from the Java program as a *JDBC* callable statement.)

(ii) Correct the query in the *matchReports* form.

PART 4

ADVANCED DATABASE ISSUES

CHAPTER 15

UNDERLYING STRUCTURES

Where the statue stood

Of Newton, with his prism and silent face,

The marble index of a mind forever

Voyaging through strange seas of thought alone.

William Wordsworth, *The Prelude*, Book iii

15.1 INDEXES

Indexes are used to provide fast access paths during the execution of queries. The optimizer will generally choose to use an index in place of a full table scan if the index key is an attribute within the selection restriction or if it is a join attribute. When a primary key constraint is specified on a table, an index is automatically created. Indexes on attributes other than the primary key can be created once the table is populated with data. Each index entry contains the index key value together with a *ROWID* that points directly to the position of the row in the base table that contains the key value.

The index is created, using a data structure which supports fast access to the index entry and thus to the table row, when it is probed with a search value. Oracle provides several such structures that are appropriate for use in different circumstances, taking into account the number of rows in the base table, the distribution of key values, whether the keys are unique or duplicated and whether the base table is subject to constant update and insertion or relatively stable.

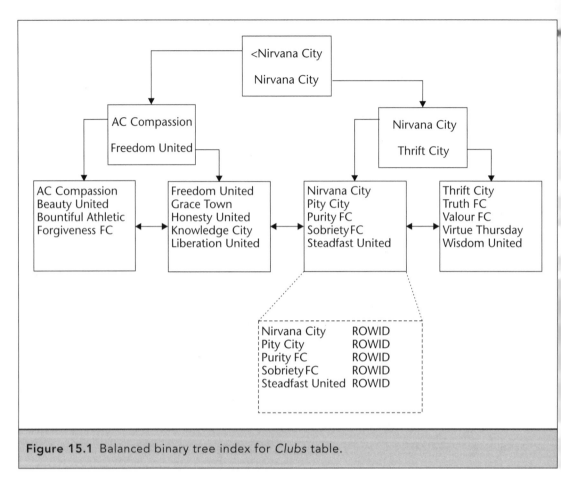

Figure 15.1 Balanced binary tree index for *Clubs* table.

15.1.1   B*-TREE INDEXES

The most commonly used index structure is the balanced binary tree. Section 11.2 illustrated the concept of binary trees in indexes. In fact, Oracle uses a balanced binary tree that equalizes access times to any row.

Figure 15.1 shows that the branch blocks of a B*-tree index contain pointers to lower level branch blocks, enabling a probe for a key value. The actual indexed data values, together with a *ROWID* for the base table, are held in the leaf blocks. The leaf blocks are doubly linked, allowing a descent to the leaf block at the far right or far left and then a range index scan across the leaves.

A unique index will contain only one *ROWID* for each key value. In a non-unique index, the *ROWID* is included with the data value as the sort key. Duplicated key values will thus occupy the same or adjacent leaf nodes. The leaf nodes are of fixed block size. When a leaf block fills up the tree is reorganized, adding a further branch level and doubling the number of leaf nodes.

All leaf blocks of the tree are at the same depth, so retrieval of any record from anywhere in the index takes approximately the same amount of time. B*-tree indexes automatically stay balanced. B*-trees provide excellent retrieval performance for a wide range of queries, including exact match and range searches. Inserts, updates and deletes are efficient, maintaining key order for fast retrieval. B*-tree performance is good for both small and large tables, and does not significantly degrade as the size of a table grows.

15.1.2 REVERSE KEY INDEXES

A reverse key index reverses the bytes of each key value (except the *ROWID*). This can prevent performance degradation in a parallel server environment where modifications to the index are concentrated on a small set of leaf blocks. Contention between CPUs for this concentration of leaf nodes can be reduced by reversing the keys of the index: the insertions become distributed across all leaf keys in the index. This can make some OLTP applications faster if there is a great deal of concurrent update activity.

However, a reverse key arrangement eliminates the ability to run an index range scan. The keys are not ordered lexically, so adjacent keys are not stored in adjacent blocks. Only fetch-by-key or full-index scans can be performed.

15.1.3 BITMAP INDEXES

The purpose of an index is to provide pointers (a *ROWID*) to the rows in a table that contain a given key value. In a bitmap index, a bitmap for each key value is used instead.

Each bit in the bitmap corresponds to a possible *ROWID*. If the table contains 100,000 rows, the bitmap will have 100,000 bits. If a bit is set, then the row with the corresponding position in the table is the key value. A mapping function converts the bit position to an actual *ROWID*, so the bitmap index provides the same functionality as a regular index even though it uses a different representation internally. If the number of different key values is small, bitmap indexes are very space-efficient.

Since there is a bitmap for every distinct key value, this type of index is only efficient where there are a very few unique key values. Bitmap indexes are suitable for decision support systems where the data is relatively stable. Rows that satisfy some, but not all, conditions in a selection predicate are filtered out before the table itself is accessed.

Bitmap indexes are most efficient with low cardinality columns: columns in which the number of distinct values is small compared with the number of rows in the table. If a data warehouse application holds a table with one million rows, of which a column has 10,000 distinct values, this column is a candidate for a bitmap index. The index will have 10,000 entries, and each entry, corresponding to one distinct key value, will have one million bits indicating the presence or otherwise of the particular key value.

Figure 15.2 shows a table containing the results of a customer survey. Four of the attributes have very restricted domains of allowed values. Job has three possible values, Region has three, Gender has only two and Income has four.

Customer	Job	Region	Gender	Income
1010	manual	north	male	bracket_1
1020	professional	south	female	bracket_4
1030	professional	east	female	bracket_2
1040	other	east	male	bracket_4
1050	manual	south	female	bracket_2
1060	professional	south	female	bracket_3

Figure 15.2 Bitmap index candidate.

Creating four indexes on each of these attributes would result in the structures shown in Figure 15.3. Each entry (or 'bit') in the bitmap corresponds to a single row of the customer table. The value of each bit depends upon the values of the corresponding row in the table. The bitmap *region*='north' contains a 1 as its first bit: this is because the region is 'north' in the first row of the *customerSurvey* table. The bitmap *region*='north' has a 0 for its other bits because none of the other rows of the table contain 'north' as their value for *region*.

Since bitmap indexes for the same table will have the same size maps, *AND* and *OR* conditions in the *WHERE* clause of a query can be quickly resolved by performing the corresponding Boolean operations directly on the bitmaps before mapping the result to *ROWIDs*.

An analyst investigating demographic trends of the company's customers might ask, 'How many of our professional customers live in the south or east regions?'.

This query can be processed with great efficiency by merely counting the number of 1s in the resulting bitmap. No table access has been necessary. The logical OR of bitmap 1 with bitmap 2 in Figure 15.4 produces intermediate bitmap 3. This is ANDed with bitmap 4 to give the result, bitmap 5. Count the 1s to give the final result.

15.2 TABLES

It is possible to vary the standard interleaved block structure of table storage. The principal motivation for this will be improve query performance. When table structures are changed to aid one particular query, care must be taken that other queries do not have their execution plans compromised.

Bitmap index on Job

Key	Bitmap					
Professional	0	1	1	0	0	1
Manual	1	0	0	0	1	0
Other	0	0	0	1	0	0

Bitmap index on Region

Key	Bitmap					
north	1	0	0	0	0	0
south	0	1	0	0	1	1
east	0	0	1	1	0	0

Bitmap index on Gender

Key	Bitmap					
female	0	1	1	0	1	1
male	1	0	0	1	0	0

Bitmap index on Income

Key	Bitmap					
bracket 1	1	0	0	0	0	0
bracket 2	0	0	1	0	1	0
bracket 3	0	0	0	0	0	1
bracket 4	0	1	0	1	0	0

Figure 15.3 Bitmap indexes.

15.2.1   INDEX-ORGANIZED TABLES

An index-organized table differs from an ordinary table in that the data for the table is held in its associated index. Changes to the table data, such as adding new rows, updating rows or deleting rows, result only in updating the index.

Instead of maintaining two separate storages for the table and the B*-tree index, the database system only maintains a single B*-tree index which contains both the

```
select count(*) from customer
where Job = 'professional'
and region in ('south', 'east');
```

	Operation	Map					
1	Region='south'	0	1	0	0	1	1
2	Region ='east'	0	0	1	1	0	0
3	1 OR 2	0	1	1	1	1	1
4	Job ='professional'	0	1	1	0	0	1
5	3 AND 4	0	1	1	0	0	1

```
Count(*)
--------
3
```

Figure 15.4

key value and the associated column values for each row. The actual data is stored in the B*-tree index rather than a *ROWID* pointer.

Index-organized tables are suitable for accessing data by the primary key. Secondary indexes can still be built to provide efficient access by non-key attributes.

Index-organized tables provide faster key-based access to table data for queries that involve exact match or range search, or both. The storage requirements are reduced because key columns are not duplicated as they are in an ordinary table and its index.

15.2.2   CLUSTERS

Clusters are an optional method of storing table data. A cluster is a group of tables that share the same data blocks because they share common columns and are often used together.

Players and *Contracts* share the *ufa_id* column. If these two tables were clustered, Oracle would physically store all rows for each *ufa_id* from both the *Players* and *Contracts* tables in the same data blocks.

Disk I/O is reduced and access time improves for joins of clustered tables. In a cluster, a cluster key value is the value of the cluster key columns for a particular row. Each cluster key value is stored only once each in the cluster and the cluster index, no matter how many rows of different tables contain the value. Therefore less storage might be required to store related table and index data in a cluster than is necessary in the non-clustered table format.

To identify data that would be better stored in clustered form, look for tables that are related via referential integrity constraints and tables that are frequently accessed together using a join. There is a reduction in the number of data blocks that must be accessed to process such joins.

The cluster key is the column that the clustered tables have in common. This key is specified when creating the cluster. Tables that are subsequently added to the cluster must share this key. A cluster index must be created on the cluster key after the cluster has been created. To locate a row in a cluster, the cluster index is used to find the cluster key value, which points to the data block associated with that cluster key value.

15.2.3   HASH CLUSTERS

Hash clusters combine the efficiencies of index-organized tables and clustered tables. Rows from a single table or two or more tables that share a common key are stored in the same block (clustered). There is no cluster index. Instead, the position of clustered rows is determined by applying a mathematical transformation to the key value. This transformation is called a hash function and results in a hash key. It provides a direct mapping between the key value and the block position of the data. The full column data of rows sharing the key value is stored in the hash cluster. There is no intermediate cluster index to be maintained.

Figure 15.5 shows that to find or store a row in an indexed table or cluster at least two I/Os must be performed (usually more): the index must be traversed to find or

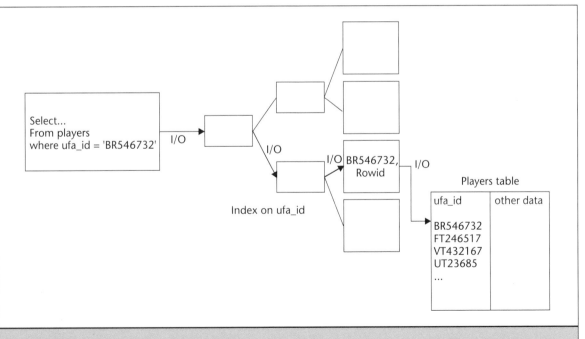

Figure 15.5 Table access by index.

store the key value, and another I/O performed to read or write the row in the table or cluster. An index-organized table would not require the final I/O, since the full row data is kept in the leaf nodes of the index (Figure 15.6).

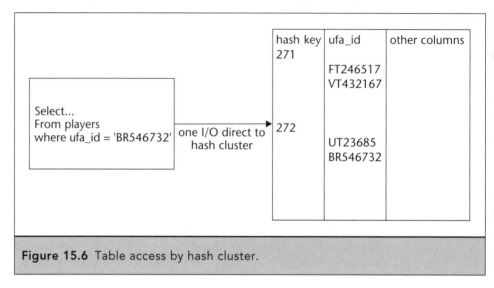

Figure 15.6 Table access by hash cluster.

The mathematical transformation used in hash cluster ing is called a hash function. This is chosen to generate an even distribution of numeric values, called hash values, based on the shared key values of the clustered tables, which may not be evenly distributed. To find or store a row in a hash cluster, Oracle applies the hash function to the row's cluster key value; the resulting hash value corresponds to a data block in the cluster. Oracle then reads or writes the block directly. Usually only one I/O operation is necessary to read or write a row in a hash cluster.

The hash function must be chosen so that under normal conditions two rows with different key values do not produce the same hash key. If they do, a collision is said to have occurred.

The most common technique is to use modulus arithmetic on a prime number with the key value as the denominator. A prime number has no factors, so dividing it by a key value (or a number derived from an alphanumeric key value) always leaves a remainder. That remainder is the result of a modulus operator (Figure 15.7).

```
17 mod 3=2
101 mod 4 =1
```

Figure 15.7 Modulus arithmetic.

The prime number must be larger than the number of key values (the number of rows in the table) so as to allow the possibility of each key value hashing to a different result. The storage space for the table is pre-allocated with the number of blocks equal to the prime number minus 1. The remainder cannot be 0 and it cannot equal the prime number. The job of a hash function is to provide the optimum even distribution of rows among the available hash values of the cluster. To achieve this goal, a hash function must minimize the number of collisions.

If a collision occurs and there is no space in the original block allocated for the hash key, an overflow block must be allocated to hold the new row. The likelihood of this happening is largely dependent on the average size of each hash key value and corresponding data.

A single-table hash cluster can provide fast access to individual rows in a table, as shown in Figure 15.6. If more than one table is clustered on a shared key, a hash cluster will give improved performance for joins between those tables, provided the join predicate is the shared key. A hash-clustered table may exhibit worsened performance for queries requiring sort-ordered access since the rows are kept in random order with respect to the key. Such access would require a full table scan and a sort operation in buffers.

15.3 ⊆ JOIN OPERATIONS

All join operations take place between two relations, since the relational algebra's join is a binary operator. The two relations remain unchanged and a third (joined) relation is the result. If there are more than two tables in the selection domain then the resulting third relation is joined with the next table until join operations are complete (Figure 15.8).

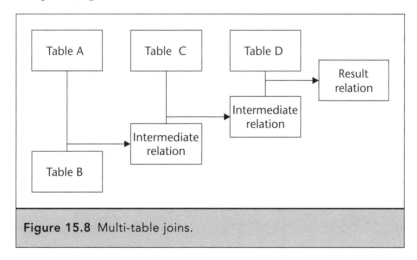

Figure 15.8 Multi-table joins.

The method of joining the relations depends on the selection made by the query optimizer. Oracle has four principal methods available and they are used in different situations. The decision will be based on the underlying storage structure of the tables involved in the selection domain; whether indexes have been specified for attributes involved in the join condition; the statistical distribution of keys in the tables; and the numbers of rows in the participating tables.

15.3.1 NESTED LOOPS

The simplest method of joining two relations is arbitrarily to pick one of them, usually the largest, as the outer or driving table. The other is known as the inner relation. These names refer to their position in the loops.

The outer relation, or a projection of it, is read into an SGA buffer and a projection of the join attribute and *ROWID* from the inner table is read into a separate SGA buffer. For each row of the outer relation, a scan is made of the entire inner relation, searching for a match on the join condition. If a match is found then attributes from the outer relation and attributes from the inner relation, found using the *ROWID*, are placed in the intermediate relation. Which attributes are thus projected will depend on which are required for subsequent joins or which are required for the final selection set.

```
read table A into buffer
read index of Table B (join attribute and ROWID) into buffer
for each row in Table A buffer do
    for each row of Table B buffer do
        if join condition match then
            project appropriate attributes from A and B (using ROWID to
            get attribute from the base table B) into result
    end do;
end do;
```

Figure 15.9 Nested loops: pseudo-code.

The smaller relation is chosen for the inner loop because it is scanned in full for each of the outer loop iterations. Using an index to read the inner table rows is only possible if the index already exists and if its key is the join attribute. Otherwise, a full table scan of the inner table is necessary. Projecting just the join attribute and *ROWID* of the inner table into buffers reduces memory usage in the SGA.

Nested loops can be used for equijoins or theta join s where the join attributes are tested for any of the comparison operators.

15.3.2 SORT MERGE

A sort merge consists of a two-stage operation. First, a full table scan of each table is performed, projecting into separate buffers at least the join attributes, together with any other attributes that will be needed in subsequent operations.

The two buffers are then sorted by the join attribute and the two sorted buffers are scanned in one pass. If the join attributes satisfy the join condition, attributes are projected into the result. If they do not match then the buffer whose sort attribute has the lowest value least is scanned until a match occurs. The scan therefore progresses through the two buffers, advancing its position in each according to the relative values of the join attribute.

A sort merge can only be performed for an equijoin, where the two join attributes are being tested for equality. Figure 15.10 gives sample pseudo-code for a sort merge.

```
read Table A into buffer
sort Table A buffer on join attribute
read Table B into buffer
sort Table B buffer on join attribute
set scan positions at the top of each buffer
while not end of Table A buffer and not end of Table B buffer
if join match then
    project appropriate attributes from A and B into result
    advance Table B scan position
    (Table B may contain duplicate join attribute values)
else
    if Table A join attribute < Table B join attribute
        advance Table A scan position until match or end
    else
        advance Table B scan position until match or end
    endif
endif
endwhile;
```

Figure 15.10 Sort merge: pseudo-code.

15.3.3 CLUSTER JOIN

Oracle can perform a cluster join only for an equijoin that equates the cluster key columns of two tables in the same cluster. In a cluster, rows from both tables with the same cluster key values are stored in the same blocks, so Oracle only accesses those blocks.

Figure 15.11 shows the execution plan for a simple select query in which the *Players* and *Contracts* tables are stored together in the same cluster: Step 2 accesses the outer table (*Players*) with a full table scan. For each row returned by Step 2, Step 3 uses the *Players.ufa_id* value to find the matching rows in the inner table (*Contracts*) with a cluster scan. A cluster join is nothing more than a nested loop join involving two tables that are stored together in a cluster. Since each row from

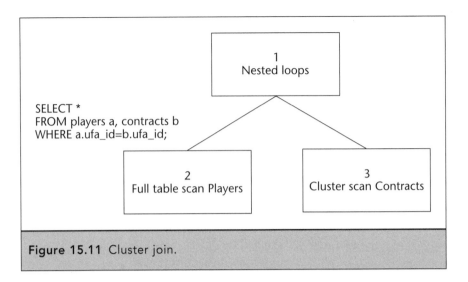

Figure 15.11 Cluster join.

the *Players* table is stored in the same data blocks as the matching rows in the *Contracts* table, Oracle can access matching rows more efficiently.

15.3.4   HASH JOIN

Oracle can only perform a hash join for an equijoin. Oracle performs a full table scan on each of the tables, storing key value and *ROWID* in buffers. A hash structure is then built in memory for the inner table. The hash structure is then probed for each key value in the outer table buffer. Matched key values are placed in the result relation.

The hash structure is constructed in much the same way as a hash cluster. A hash function is applied to the key value. This yields a result that determines that key value's position in the hash structure.

This join method has advantages over a sort merge in that only the smallest buffer needs to be pre-processed to produce the hash structure. The larger, outer table buffer can be processed in serial order. Further, the construction of the hash structure is likely to be more CPU and memory efficient than a sort operation.

Figure 15.12 shows the execution plan for a join between *Players* and *Contracts*. Steps 2 and 3 perform full table scans of the *Players* and *Contracts* tables. Step 1 builds a hash table out of the rows coming from Step 2 and probes it with each row coming from Step 3.

15.3.5   COST-BASED EXECUTION PLANS

With the cost-based approach, the optimizer generates a set of execution plans based on the possible join orders, join operations and available access paths. The optimizer then estimates the cost of each plan and chooses the one with the lowest cost. The optimizer estimates costs for disk, memory and CPU usage.

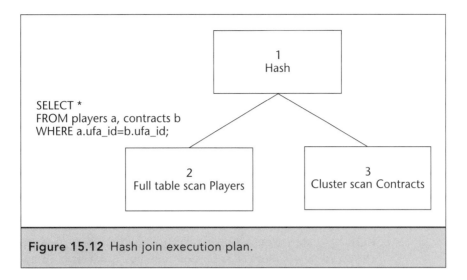

Figure 15.12 Hash join execution plan.

The cost of a nested loops operation is based on the cost of reading each selected row of the outer table and each of the matching rows of the inner table into memory. The optimizer estimates these costs using the statistics in the data dictionary. The cost of a sort –merge join is based largely on the cost of reading all the sources into memory and sorting them.

The optimizer also considers other factors when determining the cost of each operation. A smaller sort area size is likely to increase the cost for a sort–merge join because sorting takes more CPU time and I/O in a smaller sort area.

A larger multi-block read count is likely to decrease the cost for a sort –merge join in relation to a nested loops join. If a large number of sequential blocks can be read from disk in a single I/O, an index on the inner table for the nested loops join is less likely to improve performance over a full table scan.

For join statements with outer join conditions, the table with the outer join operator must come after the other table in the condition in the join order. The optimizer does not consider join orders that violate this rule.

15.4 ⊂ KEY TERMS

Indexes	Key values extracted from a file or table along with a pointer to a source record or row. Keys are organized to provide efficient searches
B*-tree	Balanced binary tree: good general method. Pointers held at leaf nodes; search speed proportional to tree depth; ordered scan performed by traversing the tree
Reverse key indexes	Key values are inserted after reversing the bytes in the value. Randomizes the distribution of clustered values. Useful for range-partitioned parallel searches

Bitmaps	Each row has an entry in the bitmap. The entry is 1 if the row value conforms to the indexing criteria, 0 if not. Predicate (*where* clause) connectors *AND*, *OR* and *NOT* performed using bit-wise operators
Tables	Whole tables can be held in index-like structures
Index organized	Table is stored as a B*-tree organized by primary key. Instead of a *ROWID* pointing to a table row, each entry also contains the non-key attributes
Clustered	Related (equijoin) rows from two or more tables are stored in clustered blocks. Join rows from the tables will always be found in the same block. Blocks allocated sequentially
Hash clustered	Related rows from two or more tables are stored in the same block. Position of the block is determined by applying a hash function to the common attribute(s).
Join methods	Algorithm for joining two relations to form and intermediate or final result
Nested loops	Largest relation read into buffer; smaller relation's join attribute and *ROWID* read into buffer. For each row of large, scan all rows in small; if join condition matched, project necessary attributes into intermediate relation
Sort merge	Project join attribute and *ROWID* for each relation into buffer. Sort each buffer on join attribute. The two buffers are then scanned in tandem. Matching entries are placed in third buffer. Attributes projected, using *ROWID*s in the third buffer, to intermediate result
Cluster join	Only used for already clustered tables. First table is scanned block by block; attributes from second table taken from the same block
Hash join	Both tables scanned; join attribute and *ROWID* projected into two hash structures. Smallest hash structure is scanned. At each entry, larger structure is probed with the hash value to determine match.

15.5 ⊂ EXERCISES

(i) Write a Java program to construct external (to the database) bitmap indexes from a single table. Use your bitmaps to perform count aggregations as described in this chapter.

(ii) Write a Java program to create a new table by joining two large tables or files using an external:

- Sort merge
- Hash join
- Devise a method of quantifying performance.

CHAPTER 16

DECISION SUPPORT SYSTEMS

Where is the wisdom we have lost in knowledge?

Where is the knowledge we have lost in information?

T. S. Eliot, *The Rock*

The majority of database applications process many small concurrent update transactions. A bank's automated teller machine (ATM) system, which must allow for thousands of withdrawal, deposit and transfer transactions to happen concurrently, is a typical example of such an application. This type of processing is known as online transaction processing (OLTP), and databases used to support such processing need to meet the strict ACID properties of transaction processing (see Chapter 8). OLTP is often measured in terms of transaction throughput: the number of committed transactions per second.

16.1 E ONLINE ANALYTICAL PROCESSING

OLAP generally consists of read-only queries that do not require the same level of transactional support. OLAP applications are invariably associated with data warehouses and large collections of data, where they are used to provide easy navigation and investigation of historical data to enable organizations to make informed tactical and strategic decisions (Table 16.1).

At the operational level of business, users are concerned with the finest granularity of data. The highest level of detail is concerned with individual customer accounts, invoices and shipping information. Tactical managers are more interested in aggregated historical data to assist in planning decisions such as customer/ service agent ratios, reorder levels that optimize inventory without compromising delivery and so on. Strategic information has the lowest granularity of data and is

Table 16.1 OLTP and OLAP.

OLTP	OLAP
Updates operational data	Analysis of historical data
Stores detailed data	Stores summarized data
Repetitive processing	Ad hoc complex queries
Predictable usage pattern	Subject oriented
Transaction driven	Fast response time required
Application oriented	Analysis driven
Algorithmic decisions	Supports strategic decisions
Usually small changes	Usually read-only
Large number of transactions	Low transaction throughput
Many operational users	Few 'managerial' users

highly summarized. This can give an overview of a group of companies, identify trends or reveal business opportunities (Table 16.2).

Table 16.2 OLAP applications.

Standard reporting
Ad hoc query and reporting
Multi-dimensional analytical reporting
Predictive analysis and planning

Analytic applications use historical data to answer many questions about enterprise performance. In a group of companies, the information can be analyzed on a company-by-company basis or it can be consolidated for the group.

Planning applications allow organizations to estimate future performance. They generate new data using predictive analytical tools. They use sophisticated statistical methods to identify trends from historical company data and may use external data to assess economic, climate, demographic or other environmental factors on likely organizational performance (Table 16.3).

Financial analysis systems allow organizations to evaluate past performance, forecast revenue and spending, establish profit goals and monitor change effects on the financial plan. Demand planning assists organizations in predicting market demand based on factors such as sales history, special promotions and pricing. Product demand forecasts determine manufacturing goals.

All OLAP systems rely on a consolidated view of transactional data known as a **multi-dimensional conceptual view**. Figure 16.1 shows a simple example from

Table 16.3 Analytic applications.	
Accounting:	Budgeting, cost and profitability analyses
Human resources:	Staff scheduling and optimization
Manufacturing:	Demand planning and forecasting
Retailing:	Site location and demographic analyses
Health care:	Outcomes analysis
Financial services:	Risk assessment and management

the UFL schema. Match statistics over several seasons have been transformed into summaries of each club's goalscoring record, analyzed by type of goal and season. The cube shape shows the three principal dimensions, but there could be further detail. The *Club* dimension, for example, could be subdivided into players.

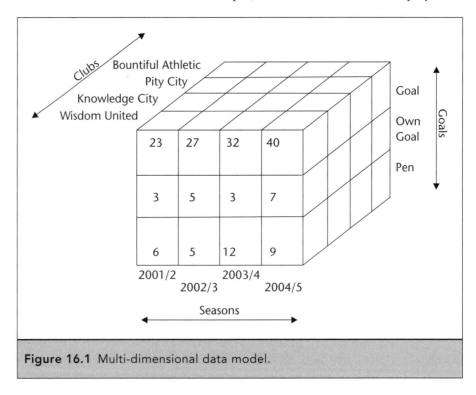

Figure 16.1 Multi-dimensional data model.

The data has been summarized, or pre-calculated. In a relational database, this can be done by using a materialized view extracted from the transactional data. The materialized view is a snapshot and is unaffected by transactional changes in the underlying tables. Only when the view is re-materialized are those changes included.

Each dimension might be capable of further analysis if can be organized in a hierarchy of values or if further dimensions could be added to the model. The *Contracts* dimension might reveal whether there is a relationship between high scoring and salary for forwards or between salary and clean sheets for goalkeepers.

DIMENSION HIERARCHIES	*Clubs → Players* *Season → MatchDates*

Typical OLAP queries might include aggregation: summarizing the data across one or more dimensions.

AGGREGATION	Find total *Goals* (for all clubs, seasons and goal types)

Roll-up is aggregation across different levels of dimension hierarchy.

ROLLUP	Given total goals per player, find total goals per club

Drill down is the disaggregation of summarized data either along the same dimension, using the hierarchy, or across another dimension.

DRILL DOWN	Given total goals per club; find total goals per player Given total goals per club; find total goals per club per season

16.2 DATA WAREHOUSES

A data warehouse is a database that is designed for query and analysis rather than for transaction processing. It often contains historical data derived from transaction data, but it can include data from other sources. A separate OLAP server segregates analysis workload from transaction workload and enables an organization to consolidate data from several sources.

In addition to a database, a data warehouse environment includes an extraction, transformation and loading (ETL) solution, an online analytical processing (OLAP) engine, client analysis tools, and other applications that manage the process of gathering data and responding to user requests.

A common way of introducing data warehousing is to refer to the characteristics of a data warehouse as set out by William Inmon (1996) (Table 16.4).

Data warehouses are designed for data analysis. To learn something specific about a company's performance, a warehouse can be built that concentrates on that aspect, say, manufacturing or customer service. The ability to define a data warehouse by subject matter makes the data warehouse **subject-oriented**.

Table 16.4 Data warehouse characteristics.
Subject-oriented
Integrated
Non-volatile
Time variant

Integration is closely related to subject orientation. Data warehouses must put data from disparate sources into a consistent format. They must resolve such problems as naming conflicts and inconsistencies among units of measure.

Non-volatile means that, once entered into the warehouse, data should not change. This is logical because the principal purpose of a warehouse is to enable analysis of an organization's history. Any user write backs should be concerned only with pre-calculation of new queries: preparations for a new view of the data.

In order to discover trends in business, analysts need large amounts of data. This is very much in contrast to OLTP systems, where performance requirements demand that historical data be removed to an archive. A data warehouse's focus on *cumulative* change over time is what is meant by the term **time variant**.

16.2.1 DATA WAREHOUSING ARCHITECTURES

A typical data warehouse query scans thousands or millions of rows. Data warehouses often use denormalized or partially denormalized schemas to optimize query performance. The process of normalization is designed to protect update, deletion or insertion operations from creating inconsistencies in the data. If the data is static once it is in the data warehouse, the denormalization, or pre-calculation, to prepare the data for lengthy read-only queries is permissible.

Figure 16.2 shows a simple architecture for a data warehouse. End users directly access data derived from several source systems through the data warehouse. Special tools must be used to load the data and create the materialized views before the OLAP tools on the client side may begin to make queries.

A more complex model is shown in Figure 16.3. Data from transactional or external sources is brought together in a staging database. Here the integration process and part of the pre-calculation phase can be carried out by using ETL tools.

The type of database server holding the OLAP data also has architectural implications. A multi-dimensional OLAP (MOLAP) server uses the multi-dimensional data model directly. MOLAP products are specialized database applications, dedicated to serving decision support systems. Client tools query the multi-dimensional database (Figure 16.4).

Considerable conversion work must be carried out during the loading phase, but performance is likely to be enhanced because the data model and the query paradigm have no impedance mismatch. A multi-dimensional database uses the idea of a data cube to represent the dimensions of data available to a user. For example, sales could be viewed in the dimensions of product, model, geography, time, or any

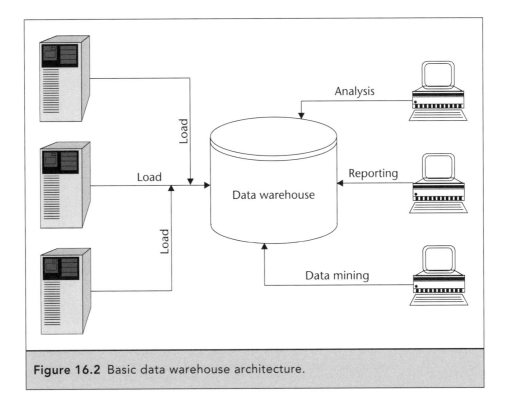

Figure 16.2 Basic data warehouse architecture.

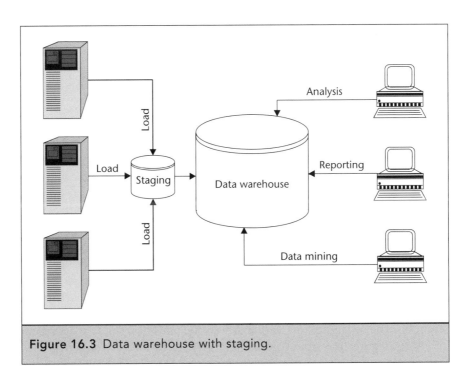

Figure 16.3 Data warehouse with staging.

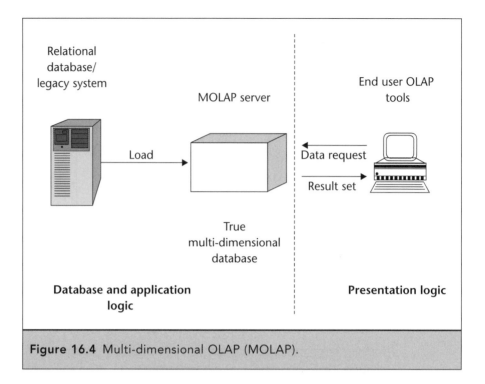

Figure 16.4 Multi-dimensional OLAP (MOLAP).

other additional dimension. In this case, the subject orientation, *sales*, is known as the **measure attribute** of the data cube and the other dimensions are seen as **feature attributes**. Hierarchies and levels can be created within a dimension (for example, city and postcode levels within a regional hierarchy).

If the data warehouse is based on a relational database (ROLAP), the data can still be viewed multi-dimensionally and the SQL language can be embedded in client tools (Figure 16.5). Processing the materialized views or other schema constructs will be less efficient.

Proprietary MOLAP servers naturally use proprietary schema constructs and each vendor's model is different. Multi-dimensional schemas based on relational technology have common cross-product characteristics and there are several alternative designs

16.2.2 DATA MARTS

Data warehouses and data marts are conceptually different – in scope. However, they are built using the exact same methods and procedures.

A data warehouse (or mart) is way of storing data for later retrieval. This retrieval is usually used to support decision-making in the organization. That is why data warehousing is considered almost synonymous with decision support systems. It is possible to customize the data warehouse architecture for different groups within the organization. Data marts are systems designed for a particular line of business. Figure 16.6 shows a data mart architecture where data from a main organizational

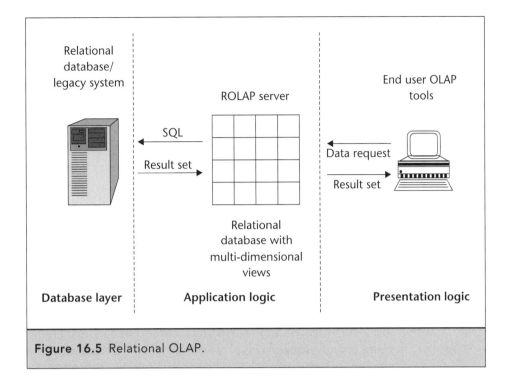

Figure 16.5 Relational OLAP.

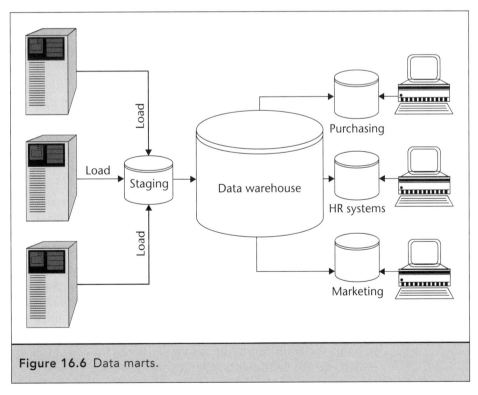

Figure 16.6 Data marts.

data warehouse has been divided into sub-systems for the purchasing, HR and marketing departments. Segregating the data in this way may mean that it can be restructured so that specialist OLAP tools, designed for a particular business function, can be applied to the data.

16.2.3   DATA WAREHOUSING SCHEMAS

The aim is to build a schema that presents a view of transactional data as summaries or aggregations. These data are called measures. Measures are numeric values that are measurable and additive.

Just tracking measures is not enough, however. The measures need to be looked at using *by* conditions: sales by department, goals by club, defects by factory. These *by* conditions are called dimensions. There is almost always a time dimension, but there may be any number of other dimensions.

Therefore, in designing a star schema (defined in Figure 16.8), the first order of business is usually to determine the measure and how it should be seen.

When mapping dimensions into tables, there are a few rules to keep in mind. First, all dimension tables should have a single-field primary key. This key is often just an identity column, consisting of an automatically incrementing number. The value of the primary key is meaningless; the information is stored in the other attributes. These other fields contain the full descriptions of the desired view. For example, if there is a product dimension (which is common) there should be attributes in it that contain the product description, the category name, the sub-category name etc. These fields do not contain codes that link to other tables. Because the fields are the full descriptions, the dimension tables are often fat; they contain many large fields.

The product dimension, for example, contains individual products. Products are normally grouped into categories, and these categories may well contain sub-categories. For instance, a product with a product number of X12JC may actually be a refrigerator. Therefore, it falls into the category of major appliance, and the sub-category of refrigerator. There may be more levels of sub-categories where this product could be classified.

The example in Figure 16.7 shows a hierarchy in a dimension table. This is how the dimension tables are built in a star schema; the hierarchies are contained in the individual dimension tables. No additional tables are needed to hold hierarchical information.

Storing the hierarchy in a dimension table allows for the easiest browsing of the dimensional data. In the above example, choosing a Product could hardly be simpler. Drilling down into the Product dimension schema could be done by choosing a Product and examining the Categories or Sub-Categories. There is no need to join to an external table for any of the hierarchical information.

A star schema consists of a fact table and dimension tables for each of the dimensions in the multi-dimensional view. Hierarchies for each dimension are represented within the dimension table as its attributes.

Product Dimension
Product ID
Product Code
Product Name
Category
Sub-Category

Figure 16.7 Dimension hierarchy.

The dimension tables are linked to the *SalesFact* table through a foreign key. In the simplified example in Figure 16.8, there are three dimension tables related to the fact table. The star schema gets it name from the grouping of the dimension tables around a single fact table like the points of a star (Figure 16.8).

Drilling down *Sales* for the product and time dimensions needs a simple join between three of the tables in the star schema (Figure 16.9).

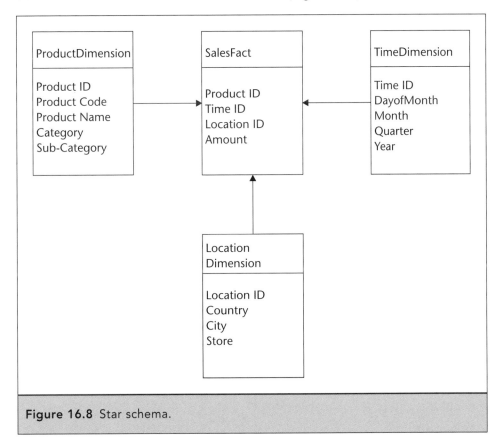

Figure 16.8 Star schema.

```
select sum(SalesFact.Amount)
from TimeDimension, ProductDimension SalesFact
where ProductDimension.ProductID = SalesFact.ProductID
      and TimeDimension.TimeID = SalesFact.TimeID
      and ProductDimension.Category='Beachwear'
      and TimeDimension.Month=3
      and TimeDimension.Year=2003;
```

Figure 16.9 Drill down *Sales* on time and category.

To drill down to a sub-category, merely change the statement (Figure 16.10).

```
select sum(SalesFact.Amount)
from TimeDimension, ProductDimension SalesFact
where ProductDimension.ProductID = SalesFact.ProductID
      andTimeDimension.TimeID = SalesFact.TimeID
      and ProductDimension.Sub-Category='Bermudas'
      and TimeDimension.Month=3
      and TimeDimension.Year=2003;
```

Figure 16.10 Drill down *Sales* on time and sub-category.

A **snowflake** schema breaks the hierarchies in the dimension table into separate more normalized structures. Each point of the star takes on a more complex shape. This leads to more complex and slower response times. Figure 16.11 represents the beginning of the snowflake process. The category hierarchy is being broken out of the *ProductDimension* table. Sub-categories are represented by a recursive relationship. Since the purpose of OLAP is to speed queries, snowflaking is usually not advisable. It may be justified if the data is subject to update.

The **fact table** holds the measures, or facts. The measures are numeric and additive across some or all of the dimensions. The fact table is potentially very large. If sales data has been collected on a daily basis for ten years and there are 500 different products and 200 different locations, then the fact table could be holding 365,000,000 records.

One of the most important decisions in building a star schema is the **granularity** of the fact table. The granularity, or frequency, of the data is usually determined by the time dimension. The finer the granularity, the more records will be in the fact table. Changing from storing daily to monthly receipts will reduce the size of the fact table by a factor of 30, but it will also reduce the scope of the drill down operations.

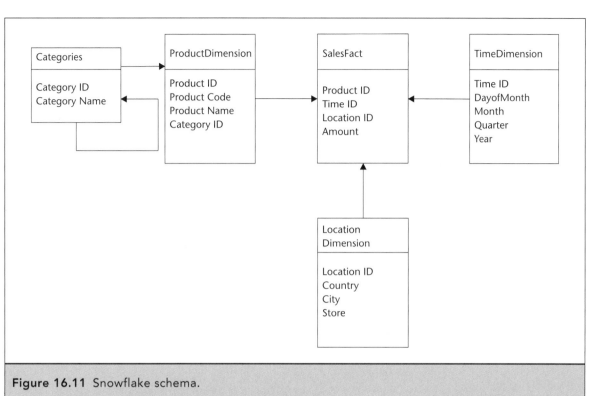

Figure 16.11 Snowflake schema.

One of the major benefits of the star schema is that the low-level transactions are summarized to the fact table grain. This greatly speeds the queries that are performed as part of the decision support.

The calculation above results in an estimate for the maximum size of the fact table. Experience shows that not every product sells on every day at every store. Where there is missing data, adding in zero values would not add anything to the useful aggregations for this OLAP system. The fact table is left **sparsely populated**.

16.2.4   EXTRACTION, TRANSFORMATION, AND LOADING

A data warehouse must be loaded regularly so that it can serve its purpose. The data must consist of timely data so that the queries and analysis reflect the most accurate and appropriate information.

Data from one or more operational systems needs to be extracted and copied into the warehouse. The process of extracting data from source systems and bringing it into the data warehouse is commonly called ETL, which stands for extraction, transformation and loading. ETL refers to a broad process, and not three well-defined steps.

Data warehouse environments have an additional burden in that they have not only to exchange but also to integrate, rearrange and consolidate data from many systems, thereby providing a new unified information base for business intelligence.

Additionally, the data volume in data warehouse environments tends to be very large.

During extraction, the desired data is identified and extracted from many different sources, including database systems and applications. Very often, it is not possible to identify the specific subset of interest; therefore more data than necessary has to be extracted, so the identification of the relevant data will be done at a later point in time.

Depending on the source system's capabilities (for example, operating system resources), some transformations may take place during this extraction process. The size of the extracted data varies from hundreds of kilobytes up to gigabytes, depending on the source system and the business situation. The same is true for the time delta between two (logically) identical extractions: the time span may vary between days/hours and minutes to near real-time. Web server log files for example can easily become hundreds of megabytes in a very short period.

After extracting data, it has to be physically transported to the target system or an intermediate system for further processing. Depending on the chosen method of transportation, some transformations can be done during this process, too. For example, a SQL statement that directly accesses a remote target through a gateway can concatenate two columns as part of the *select* statement.

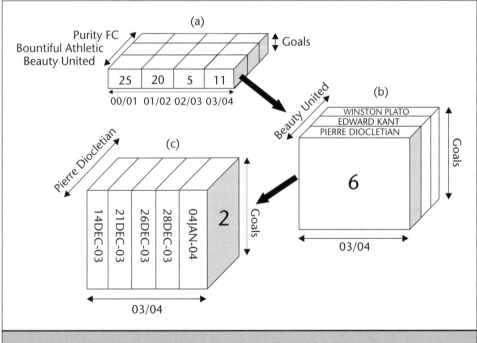

Figure 16.12 OLAP aggregrations.

16.3 ⊜ OLAP AGGREGATIONS

A major requirement of any OLAP application is to provide users with the ability to visualize data at different levels of aggregation. For example, in the UFL system it may be necessary to view a total count of goals scored by each club over a particular season, a count of goals scored by each of the club's players within that season, and details of the matches in which those goals were scored. An example of such aggregation is shown in Figure 16.12.

Figure 16.12(a) shows the highest level of aggregation required: the total number of goals scored by each club per season. Beauty United scored a total of 11 goals in the 2003/04 season. Figure 16.12(b) shows Beauty United's goal scorers in the 2003/04 season, together with the total number of goals each of them scored. Figure 16.12(c) shows the matches in the 2003/04 season in which the Beauty United player Pierre Diocletian scored, together with the number of goals he scored in each of those matches. It is easy to see that of Pierre's six goals in Beauty United's total of eleven in the 2003/04 season, two were scored in the match played on 4 January 2004. The base data upon which the aggregations of Figure 16.12 are built are the individual tuples of the *Goals* table (Figure 16.13).

```
goals { match_id, ufa_id, minute, type }
```

Figure 16.13 Goals table.

```
select matches.season, clubs.name, count (*) goals
from matches, clubs, contracts, players, goals
where matches.match_id = goals.match_id
and goals.ufa_id = players.ufa_id
and players.ufa_id = contracts.ufa_id
and contracts.club = clubs.name
and matches.matchdate
between contracts.joined and NVL(contracts.left, sysdate)
group by matches.season, clubs.name;

SEASON    NAME                             GOALS
--------  ------------------------- ----------
2003/04   Purity FC                          12
2003/04   Beauty United                      11

2 rows selected.
```

Figure 16.14 Goals by club.

The *select* statement in Figure 16.14 returns the total count of goals scored, summarized by club and season. It is important to check which club a player was playing for when he scored a goal. If this were not done, all goals scored by that player would mistakenly accrue to their current club!

```
select matches.season, clubs.name,
players.forename || ' ' || players.surname player, count (*) goals
from matches, clubs, contracts, players, goals
where matches.match_id = goals.match_id
and goals.ufa_id = players.ufa_id
and players.ufa_id = contracts.ufa_id
and contracts.club = clubs.name
and matches.matchdate
between contracts.joined and NVL(contracts.left, sysdate)
group by matches.season, clubs.name,
players.forename || ' ' || players.surname;

SEASON   NAME                  PLAYER                GOALS
-------- --------------------- --------------------- -------
2003/04  Purity FC             DEREK MARX                2
2003/04  Purity FC             JOHN INNOCENT             1
2003/04  Purity FC             LUCIUS AUGUSTUS           5
2003/04  Purity FC             NIKOS ARISTOTLE           2
2003/04  Purity FC             LUIGI SHAKESPEARE         2
2003/04  Beauty United         EDWARD KANT               1
2003/04  Beauty United         CHARLES PAUL              1
2003/04  Beauty United         WINSTON PLATO             2
2003/04  Beauty United         PIERRE DIOCLETIAN         6
2003/04  Beauty United         GEORGE CONSTANTINE        1

10 rows selected.
```

Figure 16.15 Goals by club and player.

Figure 16.15 shows the SQL statement that will yield the total count of goals scored, summarized by player, club and season.

In order to show the player's full name it is necessary to concatenate their forename and surname in the *group by* clause as well as in the selection set.

To view the total count of goals scored, summarized by match, player, club and season, the select statement shown in Figure 16.16 is required.

To display both the total number of goals per player per club per season, and the total number of goals per club, per season, it is necessary to merge the results of the first two select statements. This can be achieved through the *union* construct. Figure 16.17 shows an example of how this mechanism enables different levels of aggregation to be handled within a single SQL query.

Remember, in a *union* operation the structure of each result set has to be identical. Therefore, in the example shown in Figure 16.17 it is necessary to add a 'NULL' column in the club-level aggregation select in order to represent the concatenated player name and thus ensure compatibility with the player-level aggregation select.

```
select matches.season, clubs.name,
players.forename || ' ' || players.surname  player,
matches.matchdate, count(*) goals
from matches, clubs, contracts, players, goals
where matches.match_id = goals.match_id
and goals.ufa_id = players.ufa_id
and players.ufa_id = contracts.ufa_id
and contracts.club = clubs.name
and matches.matchdate
between contracts.joined and NVL(contracts.left, sysdate)
group by matches.season, clubs.name,
players.forename || ' ' || players.surname, matches.matchdate;


SEASON    NAME              PLAYER              MATCHDATE     GOALS
--------  --------------    ------------------  ---------     -----
2002/03   Purity FC         PIERRE DIOCLETIAN   07-SEP-02         1
2002/03   Purity FC         PIERRE DIOCLETIAN   14-SEP-02         1
2002/03   Purity FC         PIERRE DIOCLETIAN   21-SEP-02         2
2002/03   Beauty United     CHARLES PAUL        14-SEP-02         1
2002/03   Beauty United     CHARLES PAUL        21-SEP-02         1
2002/03   Beauty United     CHARLES PAUL        28-SEP-02         2
2002/03   Beauty United     LUCIUS AUGUSTUS     21-SEP-02         1
2003/04   Purity FC         DEREK MARX          21-DEC-03         1
2003/04   Purity FC         DEREK MARX          28-DEC-03         1
2003/04   Purity FC         JOHN INNOCENT       04-JAN-04         1
2003/04   Purity FC         LUCIUS AUGUSTUS     14-DEC-03         1
2003/04   Purity FC         LUCIUS AUGUSTUS     26-DEC-03         2
2003/04   Purity FC         LUCIUS AUGUSTUS     04-JAN-04         2
2003/04   Purity FC         NIKOS ARISTOTLE     14-DEC-03         1
2003/04   Purity FC         NIKOS ARISTOTLE     21-DEC-03         1
2003/04   Purity FC         LUIGI SHAKESPEARE   26-DEC-03         1
2003/04   Purity FC         LUIGI SHAKESPEARE   28-DEC-03         1
2003/04   Beauty United     EDWARD KANT         28-DEC-03         1
2003/04   Beauty United     CHARLES PAUL        21-DEC-03         1
2003/04   Beauty United     WINSTON PLATO       28-DEC-03         1
```

Figure 16.16 Goals by club, player and match.

```
2003/04  Beauty United  WINSTON PLATO      04-JAN-04         1
2003/04  Beauty United  PIERRE DIOCLETIAN  14-DEC-03         1
2003/04  Beauty United  PIERRE DIOCLETIAN  21-DEC-03         1
2003/04  Beauty United  PIERRE DIOCLETIAN  26-DEC-03         1
2003/04  Beauty United  PIERRE DIOCLETIAN  28-DEC-03         1
2003/04  Beauty United  PIERRE DIOCLETIAN  04-JAN-04         2
2003/04  Beauty United  GEORGE CONSTANTINE 04-JAN-04         1

27 rows selected.
```

Figure 16.16 (*Continued*)

```
select matches.season, clubs.name, NULL player, count (*) goals
from matches, clubs, contracts, players, goals
where matches.match_id = goals.match_id
and goals.ufa_id = players.ufa_id
and players.ufa_id = contracts.ufa_id
and contracts.club = clubs.name
and matches.matchdate
between contracts.joined and NVL(contracts.left, sysdate)
group by matches.season, clubs.name
UNION
select matches.season, clubs.name,
players.forename || ' ' || players.surname  player,  count (*) goals
from matches, clubs, contracts, players, goals
where matches.match_id = goals.match_id
and goals.ufa_id = players.ufa_id
and players.ufa_id = contracts.ufa_id
and contracts.club = clubs.name
and matches.matchdate
between contracts.joined and NVL(contracts.left, sysdate)
group by matches.season, clubs.name,
players.forename || ' ' || players.surname;

SEASON   NAME              PLAYER                    GOALS
-------- ----------------- ------------------------- --------

2003/04  Beauty United     CHARLES PAUL                    1
2003/04  Beauty United     EDWARD KANT                     1
```

Figure 16.17 Aggregating across a union.

```
2003/04   Beauty United        GEORGE CONSTANTINE              1
2003/04   Beauty United        PIERRE DIOCLETIAN              6
2003/04   Beauty United        WINSTON PLATO                  2
2003/04   Beauty United                                      11
2003/04   Purity FC            DEREK MARX                     2
2003/04   Purity FC            JOHN INNOCENT                  1
2003/04   Purity FC            LUCIUS AUGUSTUS                5
2003/04   Purity FC            LUIGI SHAKESPEARE              2
2003/04   Purity FC            NIKOS ARISTOTLE               2
2003/04   Purity FC                                         12

12 rows selected.
```

Figure 16.17 (*Continued*)

Until SQL:1999, this rather complicated use of the union construct was the only way in which to achieve multiple levels of aggregation within a single SQL query.

SQL:1999 introduced new aggregating clauses and operations, among which was the **rollup** clause. This clause is an extension of the *group by* clause and is used to produce varying levels of summary information. Figure 16.18 shows how the use of the *rollup* clause greatly simplifies the previous statement, yet still manages to produce equivalent levels of aggregation.

The *rollup* clause is an optional part of the *group by* syntax and takes a bracketed list of *grouping columns* as a parameter. The grouping columns must appear in the selection set. All non-aggregated columns in the selection set must appear somewhere in the *group by* section of a statement.

Its purpose is to cause the output of additional levels of aggregation. Figure 16.18 shows a statement where all the non-aggregated columns from the selection set appear in the *rollup* clause. As well as the usual *group by* aggregated rows being output, there is summary information provided for the total of goals per club per season, the total of all goals per season, and the total of all goals across all seasons.

Each grouping column placed within the *rollup* clause will generate an additional **level** of summary information. The statement in Figure 16.18 has three grouping columns in the *rollup* clause and so produces three additional levels of aggregation on top of the standard aggregation associated with the *group by* clause. Level three summarizes total goals per club, per season. Level two summarizes total goals per season. Level one shows the grand total of all goals for all clubs, across all seasons.

There may be occasions when fewer levels of aggregation are needed. It may be desirable to remove the level one grand total of goals across all seasons. To do this, it is necessary to carry out two levels of aggregation, rather than the previous three, in the *rollup* clause. This is achieved by removing the level one aggregation column, *matches.season*, from the *rollup* clause, and placing it back in the standard *group by* clause, as shown in Figure 16.19. The *group by* clause, with its *rollup* option, still contains all non-aggregated columns.

```
select matches.season, clubs.name,
players.forename || ' ' || players.surname player, count (*) goals
from matches, clubs, contracts, players, goals
where matches.match_id = goals.match_id
and goals.ufa_id = players.ufa_id
and players.ufa_id = contracts.ufa_id
and contracts.club = clubs.name
and matches.matchdate
between contracts.joined and NVL(contracts.left, sysdate)
group by rollup (matches.season, clubs.name,
players.forename || ' ' || players.surname);


SEASON   NAME                PLAYER                       GOALS
-------- ------------------- -------------------------- --------
2003/04  Beauty United       CHARLES PAUL                      1
2003/04  Beauty United       EDWARD KANT                       1
2003/04  Beauty United       GEORGE CONSTANTINE                1
2003/04  Beauty United       PIERRE DIOCLETIAN                 6
2003/04  Beauty United       WINSTON PLATO                     2
2003/04  Beauty United                                        11 level 1
2003/04  Purity FC           DEREK MARX                        2
2003/04  Purity FC           JOHN INNOCENT                     1
2003/04  Purity FC           LUCIUS AUGUSTUS                   5
2003/04  Purity FC           LUIGI SHAKESPEARE                 2
2003/04  Purity FC           NIKOS ARISTOTLE                   2
2003/04  Purity FC                                            12 level 2
2003/04                                                       23 level 1
                                                             23

14 rows selected.
```

Figure 16.18 Goals rolled up by season, club and player.

This statement calculates total goals per season per club per player, total goals per season per club and total goals per season, across all clubs. However, total goals across all clubs and all seasons are no longer calculated.

Rollup provides varying levels of aggregation across a single dimension of multidimensional data. In the previous example, totals were calculated for the number of goals scored per team, and per team-player per season. What if the total number of goals per player were also required? Remember, players can transfer between clubs. The total numbers of goals that they score per season, and across their career, will not necessarily match the totals they score for a particular club.

What is required is a way of aggregating the base data across all possible dimensions. SQL:1999 provides the **cube** extension to the *group by* clause precisely for

```
select matches.season, clubs.name,
players.forename || ' ' || players.surname player, count (*) goals
from matches, clubs, contracts, players, goals
where matches.match_id = goals.match_id
and goals.ufa_id = players.ufa_id
and players.ufa_id = contracts.ufa_id
and contracts.club = clubs.name
and matches.matchdate
between contracts.joined and NVL(contracts.left, sysdate)
group by matches.season rollup (clubs.name,
players.forename || ' ' || players.surname);


SEASON   NAME               PLAYER                     GOALS
-------- ------------------ -------------------------- --------
2003/04  Beauty United      CHARLES PAUL                      1
2003/04  Beauty United      EDWARD KANT                       1
2003/04  Beauty United      GEORGE CONSTANTINE                1
2003/04  Beauty United      PIERRE DIOCLETIAN                 6
2003/04  Beauty United      WINSTON PLATO                     2
2003/04  Beauty United                                       11
2003/04  Purity FC          DEREK MARX                        2
2003/04  Purity FC          JOHN INNOCENT                     1
2003/04  Purity FC          LUCIUS AUGUSTUS                   5
2003/04  Purity FC          LUIGI SHAKESPEARE                 2
2003/04  Purity FC          NIKOS ARISTOTLE                   2
2003/04  Purity FC                                           12
2003/04                                                      23

13 rows selected.
```

Figure 16.19 Goals rolled up by club and player.

this purpose. Figure 16.20 shows the SQL statement required to calculate total goals across all permutations of seasons, clubs and players.

Figure 16.21 presents the various aggregations resulting from the use of the cube option with all dimensions of the three non-aggregated columns. Pierre Diocletian appears seven times in this output.

Each entry shows a different analysis of his scoring record: across all seasons, across all seasons by club, for a particular season, for a particular season by club.

He has scored 10 goals while playing in the Utopia League: four goals for Purity FC and six goals for Beauty United. In the 2002/03 season he scored four goals, all for Purity FC. In 2003/04 he scored six goals, all for Beauty United.

```
select matches.season, clubs.name,
players.forename || ' ' || players.surname player, count(*) goals
from matches, clubs, contracts, players, goals
where matches.match_id = goals.match_id
and goals.ufa_id = players.ufa_id
and players.ufa_id = contracts.ufa_id
and contracts.club = clubs.name
and matches.matchdate
between contracts.joined and NVL(contracts.left, sysdate)
group by cube (matches.season, clubs.name, players.forename || ' ' ||
players.surname);
```

Figure 16.20 Cube aggregation on three dimensions.

SEASON	NAME	PLAYER	GOALS
			30
		DEREK MARX	2
		EDWARD KANT	1
		CHARLES PAUL	5
		JOHN INNOCENT	1
		WINSTON PLATO	2
		LUCIUS AUGUSTUS	6
		NIKOS ARISTOTLE	2
		LUIGI SHAKESPEARE	2
		PIERRE DIOCLETIAN	**10**
		GEORGE CONSTANTINE	1
	Purity FC		15
	Purity FC	DEREK MARX	2
	Purity FC	JOHN INNOCENT	1
	Purity FC	LUCIUS AUGUSTUS	5
	Purity FC	NIKOS ARISTOTLE	2
	Purity FC	LUIGI SHAKESPEARE	2
	Purity FC	**PIERRE DIOCLETIAN**	**4**
	Beauty United		15
	Beauty United	EDWARD KANT	1
	Beauty United	CHARLES PAUL	5
	Beauty United	WINSTON PLATO	2
	Beauty United	LUCIUS AUGUSTUS	1

Figure 16.21 Output from multi-dimension cube option.

Season	Club	Player	Value
	Beauty United	**PIERRE DIOCLETIAN**	6
	Beauty United	GEORGE CONSTANTINE	1
2002/03			9
2002/03		CHARLES PAUL	4
2002/03		LUCIUS AUGUSTUS	1
2002/03		**PIERRE DIOCLETIAN**	4
2002/03	Purity FC		4
2002/03	**Purity FC**	**PIERRE DIOCLETIAN**	4
2002/03	Beauty United		5
2002/03	Beauty United	CHARLES PAUL	4
2002/03	Beauty United	LUCIUS AUGUSTUS	1
2003/04			23
2003/04		DEREK MARX	2
2003/04		EDWARD KANT	1
2003/04		CHARLES PAUL	1
2003/04		JOHN INNOCENT	1
2003/04		WINSTON PLATO	2
2003/04		LUCIUS AUGUSTUS	4
2003/04		NIKOS ARISTOTLE	2
2003/04		LUIGI SHAKESPEARE	2
2003/04		**PIERRE DIOCLETIAN**	6
2003/04		GEORGE CONSTANTINE	1
2003/04	Purity FC		11
2003/04	Purity FC	DEREK MARX	2
2003/04	Purity FC	JOHN INNOCENT	1
2003/04	Purity FC	LUCIUS AUGUSTUS	5
2003/04	Purity FC	NIKOS ARISTOTLE	2
2003/04	Purity FC	LUIGI SHAKESPEARE	2
2003/04	Beauty United		12
2003/04	Beauty United	EDWARD KANT	1
2003/04	Beauty United	CHARLES PAUL	1
2003/04	Beauty United	WINSTON PLATO	2
2003/04	**Beauty United**	**PIERRE DIOCLETIAN**	6
2003/04	Beauty United	GEORGE CONSTANTINE	1

57 rows selected.

Figure 16.21 (*Continued*)

Like the rollup operation, the cube operation can also be partially implemented. Taking a summary column out of the cube clause back into the standard *group by* clause removes levels of summarization. This is shown in Figure 16.22.

The removal of *season* from the cube clause ensures that both players and clubs are always aggregated in relation to a particular season. This results in the dropping

```
select matches.season, clubs.name,
players.forename || ' ' || players.surname  player, count (*) goals
from matches, clubs, contracts, players, goals
where matches.match_id = goals.match_id
and goals.ufa_id = players.ufa_id
and players.ufa_id = contracts.ufa_id
and contracts.club = clubs.name
and matches.matchdate
between contracts.joined and NVL(contracts.left, sysdate)
group by matches.season,
cube (clubs.name, players.forename || ' ' || players.surname);
```

SEASON	NAME	PLAYER	GOALS
2002/03			9
2002/03		CHARLES PAUL	4
2002/03		LUCIUS AUGUSTUS	1
2002/03		PIERRE DIOCLETIAN	4
2002/03	Purity FC		4
2002/03	Purity FC	PIERRE DIOCLETIAN	4
2002/03	Beauty United		5
2002/03	Beauty United	CHARLES PAUL	4
2002/03	Beauty United	LUCIUS AUGUSTUS	1
2003/04			23
2003/04		DEREK MARX	2
2003/04		EDWARD KANT	1
2003/04		CHARLES PAUL	1
2003/04		JOHN INNOCENT	1
2003/04		WINSTON PLATO	2
2003/04		LUCIUS AUGUSTUS	5
2003/04		NIKOS ARISTOTLE	2
2003/04		LUIGI SHAKESPEARE	2
2003/04		PIERRE DIOCLETIAN	6
2003/04		GEORGE CONSTANTINE	1
2003/04	Purity FC		12
2003/04	Purity FC	DEREK MARX	2
2003/04	Purity FC	JOHN INNOCENT	1
2003/04	Purity FC	LUCIUS AUGUSTUS	5
2003/04	Purity FC	NIKOS ARISTOTLE	2
2003/04	Purity FC	LUIGI SHAKESPEARE	2
2003/04	Beauty United		11

Figure 16.22 Cube aggregation on two dimensions.

```
2003/04   Beauty United       EDWARD KANT            1
2003/04   Beauty United       CHARLES PAUL           1
2003/04   Beauty United       WINSTON PLATO          2
2003/04   Beauty United       PIERRE DIOCLETIAN      6
2003/04   Beauty United       GEORGE CONSTANTINE     1
32 rows selected.
```

Figure 16.22 (*Continued*)

```
select matches.season, clubs.name,
players.forename || ' ' || players.surname  player, count(*) goals
from matches, clubs, contracts, players, goals
where matches.match_id = goals.match_id
and goals.ufa_id = players.ufa_id
and players.ufa_id = contracts.ufa_id
and contracts.club = clubs.name
and matches.matchdate
between contracts.joined and NVL(contracts.left, sysdate)
group by grouping sets (matches.season, clubs.name,
players.forename || ' ' || players.surname);


SEASON    NAME                        PLAYER              GOALS
--------  --------------------------  ------------------  --------
2002/03                                                      9
2003/04                                                     23
          Beauty United                                     16
          Purity FC                                         16
                                      CHARLES PAUL            5
                                      DEREK MARX              2
                                      EDWARD KANT             1
                                      GEORGE CONSTANTINE      1
                                      JOHN INNOCENT           1
                                      LUCIUS AUGUSTUS         6
                                      LUIGI SHAKESPEARE       2
                                      NIKOS ARISTOTLE         2
                                      PIERRE DIOCLETIAN      10
                                      WINSTON PLATO           2

14 rows selected.
```

Figure 16.23 Grouping sets (*continued overleaf*).

of aggregated rows showing goals scored per club across all seasons, and goals scored per player across all seasons.

As well as the rollup and cube clauses, SQL:1999 has added a third optional clause to the *group by* operation. **Grouping sets** allows for the output of selected levels of aggregation only. The SQL statement shown in Figure 16.23 calculates the total number of goals scored per season, per club, and per player, only. The detail of such aggregated totals is automatically removed from the statement's output.

16.4 ⊂ DATA MINING

Data mining tools use an automated approach to explore and bring to the surface complex relationships in very large datasets. Data mining tools seek to identify associations between data items, to establish correlation patterns and to make predictions (Table 16.5).

Table 16.5 Data mining applications.	
Retail/marketing:	Identifying buying patterns of customers
	Finding associations among customers' demographic characteristics
	Predicting response to mailing campaigns
Banking:	Detecting patterns of fraudulent credit card use
	Identifying loyal customers
	Predicting customers likely to change their credit card affiliations
	Determining credit card spending by customer groups
Insurance:	Claims analysis
	Predicting which customers will buy new policies
Medicine:	Characterizing patient behaviour to predict surgery visits
	Identifying successful medical therapies for different illnesses

There are two principal aims. A dataset may be queried to discover links in behaviour. Prediction about future behaviour may be deduced from past behaviour (Table 16.6).

There are several kinds of exploratory analysis: association rules, sequential patterns, classification, clustering, Bayesian networks for inferring causality, sequence similarity and visualization. They are all based on well-established mathematical and statistical techniques and rely upon being applied to very large datasets to give meaningful results (Figure 16.24).

Table 16.6 Data mining questions.	
Discovery-oriented (link analysis):	What are the factors that determine sales of Product X
	What are the common factors in aircraft wing failures?
Predictive modelling:	How much profit will this customer generate?
	Where is the best place to build a new road?

Given a collection of customer purchases, is it possible to identify rules of the following form?

{petrol} => {engine oil}

A transaction in which petrol was bought is also likely to have involved the purchase of engine oil.

Figure 16.24 Association rules I.

The rule is tested in the database and produces two measures of how deterministic is the left-hand side over the right-hand side (Figure 16.25).

LHS → RHS

Support:	% of transactions containing all items in LHS and RHS of the rule.
Confidence:	The % of all of the LHS transactions that also contain all RHS items.

Figure 16.25 Association rules II.

Care must be taken when testing a rule. Association tests correlation not causality. Even more caution should be expressed about transitive rules(Figure 16.26).

If {motor insurance] → {petrol}

And {petrol} → {engine oil}

Does it necessarily follow that

{motor insurance} → {engine oil}

Figure 16.26 Correlation not causality.

Unless there is strong support and confidence for the first two rules, they may be dependent on non-overlapping transaction sets. A special promotion on motor insurance would not lead to increased engine oil sales.

SEQUENCING RULES.	Descriptive model that discovers sequence correlations in time-sequenced data. For example, 'People who have purchased a VCR are 300% more likely to purchase a camcorder in the time period 2–4 months after the VCR was purchased'.

Classification and **regression** are perhaps the most popular techniques in data mining at the moment. A predictive model is generated, based on historical data. The model then predicts new cases. The development of the model is known as *data training*. The data used for data training must therefore include a large number of cases where conditions and outcomes are known (Table 16.7).

Table 16.7 Predictive operations.

Classification	Predict class membership. For example, income within one of three categorical values: Low, Middle or High.
Regression	Predict a specific value. For example, estimate future spending.

There are several techniques used in predictive operations. The most notable are decision trees, Bayesian methods and neural networks. They all build their model from the training data. These techniques are used for everything from call centre operators deciding on your telephone loan application to currency speculators coming to a judgement on the future value of the euro.

16.5 SO WHAT EXACTLY IS OLAP?

The entire preceding chapter serves to indicate the type of question that might be answered through OLAP, the kind of systems architectures that might support those question and the extensions to SQL that enable the queries. There is, however, neither a precise definition nor a specification of a minimum OLAP environment nor any universally accepted function or performance benchmark for comparing vendor products. OLAP definitions are anything but exact.

Earlier chapters have indicated that accepted ideas in computing are either founded on mathematical principles, like the relational model and the derived language SQL, or they are defined through an authoritative standard such as the Codasyl database or the many extensions to SQL included in SQL:1999.

Where neither of these conditions exists, the definition is largely in the hands of the marketing departments of the major vendors. Naturally, such definitions vary from vendor to vendor and are often skewed to favour a particular product. OLAP definitions should be approached with some caution and scepticism.

16.5.1   THE CODD RULES AND FEATURES

E. F. Codd published a white paper (Codd and Associates, 1993) which is often quoted as a definition of OLAP and a source of critical features for judging OLAP products. Codd's OLAP rules proved to be controversial due to being vendor-sponsored rather than mathematically based.

The OLAP white paper included 12 rules or tests for OLAP compliance. They were followed by another six rules in 1995 and the rules were restructured into four groups or features (Table 16.8).

The basic features start with the **Multi-dimensional Conceptual View**, which is, perhaps, the most accepted criterion and involves modelling the data, not as two dimensions as in the relational model, but as any number of dimensions as required by the application. This leads to non-normalized data as it clusters associated data together.

Table 16.8 OLAP: Codd's 18 rules (1995 revision).

12 original rules	6 supplemental rules
Multi-dimensional conceptual view	Batch extraction
Transparency	OLAP analysis models
Accessibility	Treatment of Non-normalized data
Consistent reporting performance	Storing OLAP results separate from source data
Client–server architecture	Extraction of missing values
Generic dimensionality	Treatment of missing values
Dynamic sparse matrix handling	
Multi-user support	
Unrestricted cross-dimensional operations	Replaces original rule 7: Automatic adjustment of physical level
Int uitive data manipulation	
Flexible reporting	
Unlimited dimensions and aggregation levels	

Intuitive Data Manipulation would enable direct actions on cells in the view, without recourse to menus or multiple actions. Codd gives no real rationale for this and this feature adds little value to the evaluation process. Perhaps products should give users the choice of how they approach the data.

In proposing **Accessibility** as a basic feature, the OLAP engine takes on the role of middleware, sitting between heterogeneous data sources and the user front-end. Most products can achieve this, but often with more data staging and batching than vendors like to admit.

The **Batch extraction** feature requires that products offer their own staging database for OLAP data as well as offering live access to external data. In effect, this is an endorsement of multi-dimensional data staging plus partial pre-calculation of large multi-dimensional databases and transparent access to underlying detail. Today, this would be regarded as the definition of a hybrid OLAP, which is becoming a popular architecture.

Required support for **OLAP analysis models** specifies that OLAP products should support all four analysis models that were described in the white paper. These models may be characterized as:

- parameterized static reporting
- slicing and dicing with drill down
- 'what if?' analysis
- goal seeking

Including a specific **Client–server architecture** as a basic feature is a rather prescriptive rule. Codd required that the server component of an OLAP product should be sufficiently intelligent that various clients could be attached with minimum effort and programming for integration. This is a much tougher test than simple client–server and relatively few products qualify.

Full compliance with the **Transparency** test means that a user of, say, a spreadsheet should be able to get full value from an OLAP engine and not even be aware of where the data ultimately comes from. Most products fail to give either full spreadsheet access or live access to heterogeneous data sources. Like the previous feature, this is a severe test for open systems.

Not all OLAP applications are read-only. **Multi-user support** means that OLAP tools must provide concurrent access (retrieval and update), integrity and security.

The special features in Codd's revised report consist of four tests. The first is concerned with the **Treatment of Non-Normalized Data**. This is meant to ensure that any data updates performed in the OLAP environment should not be allowed to alter stored denormalized data in feeder systems.

Storing OLAP results separate from source data is really an implementation rather than a product issue, but few would disagree with it. Read--write OLAP applications should not be implemented directly on live transaction data and OLAP data changes should be kept segregated from the base data.

Extraction of missing values may be interpreted to mean that missing values are to be distinguished from zero values.

Treatment of missing values specifies that all missing values are to be ignored by the OLAP analyzer regardless of their source. This relates to the previous test and is probably an almost inevitable consequence of how multi-dimensional engines treat all data.

The reporting features, Codd's third group, starts with a requirement for **Flexible reporting**, ensuring that the dimensions can be laid out in any way that the user requires in reports. Most products are capable of this in their formal report writers, although this is not always the case for interactive viewers.

Uniform reporting performance requires no significantly response degradation resulting from increases in the number of dimensions or the size of the database. Nowhere is it mentioned that the performance must be fast, merely that it be consistent. Experience suggests that merely increasing the number of dimensions or database size does not affect performance significantly in fully pre-calculated databases. However, *ad hoc* reports usually take longer. Performance in good products is almost linearly dependent on the number of cells used to produce the report. In fact, the principal factor that affects performance is the degree to which the calculations are performed in advance and where live calculations are done.

Automatic adjustment of physical level requires that the OLAP system adjust its physical schema automatically to adapt to the type of model, data volumes and sparsity. Most vendors fall far short of this noble ideal.

The final group of features are concerned with dimension control. The **Generic dimensionality** rule takes the purist view that each dimension must be equivalent in both its structure and operational capabilities. The basic data structures, formulae or reporting formats should not be biased towards any one dimension. This has proven to be one of the most controversial of all the original 12 rules. Technology-focused products largely tend to comply with it, so the vendors of such products support it. Application-focused products usually make no effort to comply, and their vendors bitterly attack the rule.

Complying with the **Unlimited dimensions and aggregation levels** rule is technically impossible. There is no such thing as an unlimited entity on a limited computer. Few applications need more than about eight or ten dimensions and few hierarchies have more than about six consolidation levels.

Unrestricted cross-dimensional operations requires that all forms of calculation must be allowed across all dimensions. Products that use relational storage are often weak in this area. Other products with a true multi-dimensional database are strong. These types of calculation are particularly relevant in applications that analyze profitability.

16.2.2   THE FASMI TEST

As an alternative to Codd's highly complex and technical definitions, the authors of an industry newsletter, *The OLAP Report*, devised a much simpler range of criteria. This has the benefit of being easily understood, is not associated with any vendor. The definition is short and easy to remember: Fast Analysis of Shared Multi-dimensional Information (FASMI).

Fast means that the system is targeted to deliver most responses to users within about five seconds, with the simplest analyses taking no more than one second and very few taking more than 20 seconds. Research has shown that end-users are apt to assume that a process has failed if results are not received with 30 seconds. Vendors resort to a wide variety of techniques to achieve this goal, including specialized forms of data storage, extensive pre-calculations and specific hardware requirements.

Analysis means that the system can cope with any business logic and statistical analysis that is relevant for the application and the user. This analysis may be done with the vendor's own tools or in a linked external product such as a spreadsheet. Simply, all the required analysis functionality must be provided in an intuitive manner for the target users. This could include specific features like time series analysis, cost allocations, currency translation, goal seeking, *ad hoc* multi-dimensional structural changes, non-procedural modelling, exception alerting, data mining and other application-dependent features.

Shared means that the system implements all the security requirements for confidentiality (possibly down to cell level) and, if multiple write access is needed, concurrent update locking at an appropriate level. Not all applications need users to write data back, but for the growing numbers that do, the system should be able to handle multiple updates in a timely, secure manner. This is a major area of weakness in many OLAP products, which tend to assume that all OLAP applications will be read-only

Multi-dimensional is a key requirement. The system must provide a multi-dimensional conceptual view of the data, including full support for hierarchies and multiple hierarchies, as this is certainly the most logical way to analyze businesses and organizations. There is no specific minimum number of dimensions that must be handled. The underlying database technology is not specified, providing that the user gets a truly multi-dimensional conceptual view.

Information is all of the data and derived information needed, wherever it is and however much is relevant for the application. The capacity of products is measured in terms of how much input data they can handle, not how many gigabytes they take to store it. The capacities of the products differ greatly – the largest OLAP products can hold at least a thousand times as much data as the smallest.

16.6 KEY TERMS

Architectures	Distinct storage structure for extracting transactional data
Warehouse	Data may be denormalized to support OLAP queries. Depends on data access being read-only
Data mart	Warehouse is split into specialist databases to serve functional components of an organization

Schemas	Dimensional aspects of data represented in star and snowflake models
OLAP aggregations	SQL extensions designed to support OLAP in relational databases
Rollup	Extension of *group by* clause to provide additional levels of aggregation reporting
Cube	Extension of *group by* clause to provide all possible aggregations across all the dimensions of the target
Grouping sets	Extension of *group by* clause to allow for selection of aggregation levels
Data mining	Discovery of patterns or predictions derived from OLAP data.
Patterns	Associations; sequencing
Predictions	Classification; regression

16.7 ⊂ EXERCISES

(i) Use the UFL database to create further examples of Oracle's OLAP aggregations. Illustrate the underlying mechanisms through Explain Plan.

(ii) Search the Internet for *reliable* sources to survey current OLAP products and compare their facilities.

CHAPTER 17

DATABASE PERFORMANCE

"Dear Mr. Churchill, my new play is opening in London and I am enclosing two tickets to the opening night performance. One ticket is for you, and one ticket is for a friend, if you have one."

George Bernard Shaw

"Dear Mr. Shaw, I am very pleased that you sent me the two tickets to the opening night performance of your new play in London, but unfortunately I have another commitment that night and I won't be able to be there, but I would be most pleased if you could send me two tickets to the second night's performance, if there is one."

Winston Churchill

17.1 ⊏ GOALS AND TARGETS

Online transaction processing (OLTP) applications define performance in terms of throughput. These applications must sometimes process millions of very small transactions per day. Decision support systems define performance in terms of response time. Demands on the database that are made by DSS applications vary between a query that fetches only a few records, or a massive query that fetches and sorts hundreds of thousands of records from different tables.

Setting a precise goal for database performance enables a clear recognition of success. Target performance parameters should be formulated in terms of throughput or response time and allow for budgetary constraints.

17.1.1 RESPONSE TIME AND THROUGHPUT

Response time is the sum of service time and wait time. The method of processing jobs has a profound effect on response time. If jobs are queued for sequential processing then the wait time for each job is the response time for all the preceding jobs (Figure 17.1).

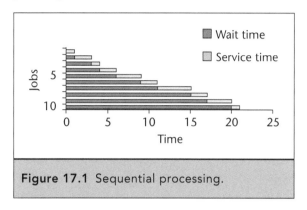

Figure 17.1 Sequential processing.

If more resources are allocated, near parallel concurrent processing of jobs can be achieved. Each independent task executes immediately using its own resources; no wait time is involved (Figure 17.2).

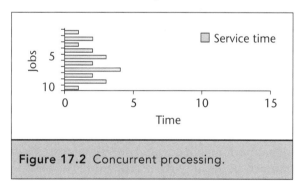

Figure 17.2 Concurrent processing.

17.1.2 SYSTEM THROUGHPUT

System throughput is the amount of work completed in a given time. Reducing service time will get more work done with the same resources. Adding resources for which jobs are contending will reduce wait time bottlenecks and get the work done quicker by reducing overall response time. The service time for a task may stay the same, but wait time increases as contention increases. If many users are waiting for a service that takes 1 second, the tenth user must wait 9 seconds for a service that takes 1 second.

More concurrent jobs bring more contention in the system. It is unlikely that wait time will increase in a linear fashion. The operating system scheduler and the database dispatcher will spend more and more time arbitrating queues, which will add to wait time (Figure 17.3).

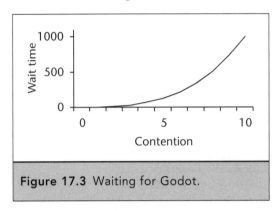

Figure 17.3 Waiting for Godot.

17.1.3 CRITICAL RESOURCES

Resources such as CPUs, memory, I/O capacity and network bandwidth are the key to reducing service time. Adding resources makes higher throughput possible and facilitates swifter response time (Table 17.1).

Table 17.1 Performance factors.	
How many resources are available?	Capacity
How many clients need the resource?	Demand
How long must they wait for the resource?	Wait time; queue length
How long do they hold the resource?	Consumption

Capacity is not just about physical hardware components; the efficiency of the O/S scheduler in maintaining job queues and the database dispatcher in balancing thread contention can be an important influence. The ability to tune the scheduling algorithm or prioritize database jobs over background housekeeping can improve performance without actually adding hardware (Figure 17.4).

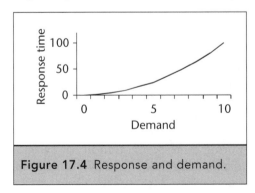

Figure 17.4 Response and demand.

Excessive demand gives rise to greatly increased response time and reduced throughput. Linear increases in demand do not produce proportionate decreases in performance. Often the relationship is exponential because more and more resources are taken off the actual processing tasks to manage incoming jobs (Figure 17.4).

Systems administrators can directly affect demand, consumption and capacity. These are the principal factors in any system of resource utilization. Wait time is simply evidence of a system where these factors are poorly balanced (Table 17.2).

Table 17.2 Performance adjustments.	
Consumption	Use fewer resources per transaction; reduce the number of I/Os per transaction
Demand	Reschedule or redistribute the work
Capacity	Increase or reallocate resources; move to a symmetric multiprocessor, increase main memory

17.1.4 SETTING PERFORMANCE TARGETS

Decisions made during application development have the greatest effect on performance. Once the application is deployed, the database administrator usually has the primary responsibility for performance, but has limited capacity to change fundamental factors.

When designing a system, performance targets should be set. If the application does not meet that specification, the bottleneck should be identified (for example, I/O contention), the cause determined, and corrective action taken. During development, the application should be tested to determine whether it meets the design performance goals before it is deployed.

Tuning is usually a series of trade-offs. Once bottlenecks have been identified, other system resources may have to be sacrificed to achieve the desired results. For example, if I/O is a problem, more memory or more disks may need to be purchased. If a purchase is not possible, the concurrency of the system may have to be limited, by rescheduling when certain user jobs may be submitted, to achieve the desired performance.

With clearly defined performance goals, the decision on what resource to relinquish in exchange for improved performance is simpler.

At no time should achieving performance goals override the ability to recover data. Performance is important, but data recovery and consistency are critical.

17.1.5 SETTING USER EXPECTATIONS

Application developers and database administrators must be careful to set appropriate performance expectations for users. When the system performs a particularly complicated operation, response time may be slower than when it is performing a simple operation. In this case, slower response time is reasonable.

If a DBA promises a 1 second response time, consider how this might be interpreted. The DBA might mean that the operation would take 1 second in the database – and might well be able to achieve this goal. However, users querying over a network might experience a delay of a couple of seconds due to network traffic: they may not receive the response time they expect.

17.1.6   EVALUATING PERFORMANCE

With clearly defined performance goals, success depends on the functional objectives established with the user community, the ability to measure objectively whether the criteria are being met, and the capability to take corrective action to overcome exceptions.

DBAs responsible for solving performance problems must remember all factors that together affect response time. Sometimes what initially seems like the most obvious source of a problem is actually not the problem at all.

Users might conclude that there is a problem with the database, whereas the actual problem is with the network. A DBA must monitor the network, disk, CPU and so on to identify the actual source of the problem rather than simply assume that all performance problems stem from the database.

17.2   PERFORMANCE TUNING METHODS

A well-planned methodology is the key to success in performance tuning. By far the most effective approach to tuning is the proactive technique. The establishment of realistic performance goals and expectations during the requirements analysis predicates this method. During design and development, the application designers can determine which combination of system resources and available database features best meets these needs.

A system which has performance designed in will minimize its implementation and ongoing administration costs. The additional costs in the design phase can save many multiples of those costs in maintenance. The tuning process should not begin when users complain about poor response time. When response time is this poor, it is usually too late to use some of the most effective strategies. At that point, only marginal improvements to performance may be achieved by reallocating memory and tuning I/O.

17.2.1   PRIORITIZED TUNING STEPS

Figure 17.5 shows a series of tuning steps to be undertaken during the development of an application. The steps are prioritized in order of diminishing returns: steps with the greatest effect on performance appear first. For optimal results, therefore,

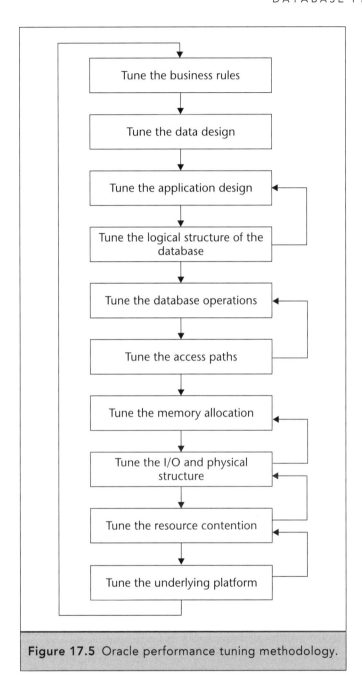

Figure 17.5 Oracle performance tuning methodology.

tuning issues should be resolved in the order listed: from the design and development phases through instance tuning.

Tuning is an iterative process. Performance gains made in later steps may pave the way for further improvements in earlier steps, so additional passes through the tuning process may be useful.

17.2.2 THE BUSINESS RULES

For optimal performance, business rules may have to be adapted. These concern the high-level analysis and design of an entire system. Configuration issues are also considered at this level, such as whether to use a single multi-threaded server system-wide or a cluster of parallel servers.

Performance is directly affected by systems design and implementation, but also by inappropriate business rules.

Designers sometimes provide far greater detail than is needed when they write business functions for an application. They document an implementation, rather than simply the function that must be performed. If managers effectively distil business functions or requirements from the implementation, then designers have more freedom when selecting an appropriate implementation.

Consider, for example, the business function of cheque printing. The actual requirement is to pay money to people; the requirement is not necessarily to print pieces of paper. It would be very difficult to print a million cheques per day, but it would be relatively easy to record that many direct deposit payments and send them over a network to the bank for processing.

Business rules should be consistent with realistic expectations for the number of concurrent users, the transaction response time, and the projected number of records stored online.

For example: a bank employs one loan advisor and one supervisor. There is a business rule that the supervisor must approve loans of over £250. Upon investigation, it is found that there is a long queue of customers. More loan advisors are employed, but the bottleneck moves to the supervisor's function. There is now a queue of loan advisors waiting for the supervisor's approval as well as a queue of customers waiting for the advisors.

A change to the business rule makes the system more scalable. If the supervisor only needs to approve loans exceeding £1000, by changing the scale of the rule more loans can now be dealt with directly by the advisors. Greater concurrency is achieved. Only with the rule change does employing more advisors become effective.

17.2.3 DATA DESIGN

In the data design phase, the data needs of the application must be determined. Identifying relations and their attributes is important. The information must be structured to ensure database consistency, but, where possible, also to meet performance goals.

The database design process undergoes a normalization stage when data is analyzed to eliminate data redundancy. With the exception of primary keys, any one data element should be stored only once in the database. After the data is normalized, however, there may be a need to denormalize it for performance reasons. It might be decided that the database should store frequently used summary values. Rather than forcing an application to recalculate the total price of all the lines in a given order each time it is accessed, it might be more efficient to store the total value for each order in the database.

Another data design consideration is avoiding data contention. Consider a database 1 TByte in size on which one thousand users access only 0.5% of the data. This 'hot spot' in the data could cause performance problems.

17.2.4   APPLICATION DESIGN

Business goals should be translated into an effective system design. Business processes concern a particular application within a system, or a particular part of an application.

An example of good process design is strategically caching data. In retail applications, selecting the VAT rate once at the beginning of each day and caching it within the application avoids retrieving the same information repeatedly during the day.

17.2.5   LOGICAL DATABASE STRUCTURE

This primarily concerns index design, to ensure that the data is neither over- nor under-indexed. In the data design stage the primary and foreign key indexes are determined. In the logical structure design additional indexes may be created to support the application.

Performance problems due to contention often involve inserts into the same block or inappropriate use of sequence numbers. Particular care should be exercised in the design, use and location of indexes, as well as in using the sequence generator and clusters.

17.2.6   DATABASE OPERATIONS

Be certain the application is taking full advantage of the SQL language and the database features designed to enhance application processing. Understanding how the DBMS is executing SQL statements in the application can suggest improvements to those statements.

Enable query-optimizing modes consistent with performance needs. Regular collection of full table statistics ensures that the optimizer makes informed decisions but imposes maintenance overheads.

PL/SQL server-side programming with pre-compiled packages may be more efficient than code kept in the application.

Transaction isolation modes, lock management and transaction options have features and techniques that can promote or hinder throughput.

17.2.7   ACCESS PATHS

Ensure that there is efficient data access. For example, look at the structure of indexes in the light of processing needs. If an application has a low hit rate with only one row from a large table taking part in each transaction, then a hash structure may be appropriate. High hit-rate processing, such as preparing a sorted report from the whole table, would be better served by a B*-tree structure.

Ensuring efficient access may mean adding indexes or adding indexes for a particular routine and then dropping them. It may also mean reanalyzing the design after the database has been built.

If the query planner is consistently building a temporary index on a non-key attribute, it may be advantageous to make this index permanent. This is particularly so if the underlying table data is relatively static. If the table is subject to regular updates or insertions, balance the costs of maintaining the extra index against its advantages in query processing.

17.2.8   MEMORY ALLOCATION

Appropriate allocation of memory resources to Oracle memory structures can have a positive effect on performance. Oracle shared memory is allocated dynamically to the shared pool. Although the total amount of memory available in the shared pool can be explicitly set, the system dynamically manages the allocations to the data dictionary cache, the library cache and the context areas for a multi-threaded server. Memory allocation can be explicitly set for the buffer cache, the log buffer and sequence caches.

Proper allocation of memory resources improves cache performance, reduces parsing of SQL statements and reduces paging and swapping. Care should be taken not to allocate to the system global area (SGA) such a large percentage of the machine's physical memory that it causes unnecessary paging or swapping.

17.2.9   I/O AND PHYSICAL STRUCTURE

Disk I/O tends to reduce the performance of many applications. Most database servers are designed so their performance need not be unduly limited by I/O (Table 17.3).

Table 17.3 Tuning physical structures.

Distribute data across several disks so that I/O is distributed, avoiding disk contention, and use parallel I/O controllers

Store data in data blocks for best access

Create extents large enough for the tables and indexes. Avoid dynamic extension of tables as this adversely affects the performance of high-volume OLTP applications

Evaluate the use of a raw device: a disk without a formatted file system, which the server can access directly without O/S intervention

17.2.10   RESOURCE CONTENTION

Concurrent processing by multiple Oracle users may create contention for resources. Contention may cause processes to wait until resources are available. Take care to reduce the following types of contention: block contention, shared pool contention and lock contention. Evidence of these symptoms can be gained from the various diagnostics tools available to DBAs.

17.2.11   THE UNDERLYING PLATFORM

This will be specific to the implementation hardware, operating system and network configuration. For example, on Unix or Linux-based systems it is possible to tune the size of the buffer cache, which can affect the efficiency of pre-fetch reads: when a file is read, more than is actually requested is read into the cache on the assumption that it will be needed later. The logical volume managers may be optimized and memory and scheduling priority may be tuned for each resident process.

17.3 ⊝ APPLYING THE TUNING METHOD

Never begin tuning without having first established clear objectives. You cannot succeed without a definition of 'success'.

'Just make it go as fast as you can' may sound like an objective, but it is very difficult to determine whether this has been achieved. It is even more difficult to tell whether your results have met the underlying business requirements. A more useful statement of objectives is: 'We need to have as many as 20 operators, each entering 20 orders per hour, and the packing lists must be produced 30 minutes before the of the end of each shift'.

Keep the goals in mind as each tuning measure is considered. Estimate its performance benefits in light of your goals.

Also remember that the goals may conflict. For example, to achieve best performance for a specific SQL statement, it may be necessary to sacrifice the performance of other SQL statements running concurrently on the database.

17.3.1   CREATE REPEATABLE TESTS

Create a series of repeatable tests. If a single SQL statement is identified as causing performance problems, then run both the original and a revised version of that statement in SQL*Plus (with the SQL Trace or Oracle Trace enabled) so that statistical differences in performance may be seen. In many cases, a tuning effort can succeed simply by identifying one SQL statement that was causing the performance problem.

A trial needs to run using a test environment similar to the production environment. This could impose additional restrictive conditions, processing just a subset of the data. The test case should be measured with the trace facility and with timing features.

If the trial tests a variety of changes, such as SQL rewrites, index restructuring or memory reallocations, then be sure to record the effect of each change by reverting to the original scenario and applying one change at a time. Then test the changes in combination. Finally, the trial should be checked for scalability by running against increasing proportions of the full data.

17.3.2 KEEP RECORDS AND AUTOMATE TESTING

Keep records of the effect of each change by incorporating record keeping into the test script. Automated testing with scripts provides a number of advantages.

Cost effectiveness is improved in terms of the ability to conduct multiple trials quickly. It helps ensure that tests are conducted in the same systematic way, using the same instrumentation for each hypothesis being tested. Carefully check test results derived from observations of system performance against the objective data before accepting them.

17.3.3 STOP TUNING WHEN OBJECTIVES ARE MET

One of the great advantages of having targets for tuning is that it becomes possible to define success. Past a certain point, it is no longer cost-effective to continue tuning a system. Although there may be confidence that performance targets have been met, this must nonetheless be demonstrated to two communities: the users affected by the problem and those responsible for the application's success.

17.4 OVERVIEW OF DIAGNOSTIC TOOLS

Oracle provides a number of diagnostic tools, which can be used to track database operations both during the design test phases and into production.

17.4.1 EXPLAIN PLAN AND ORACLE TRACE

Explain plan is a SQL statement listing the access plan selected by the query optimizer. The plan is output via a PL/SQL package and shows an overview of the chosen optimized strategy for executing a submitted SQL statement. When *explain plan* is used, the statement does not proceed to execution.

SQL Trace records SQL statements issued by a connected process and the resources used in executing these statements. It collects all SQL events and Wait events. SQL events include a complete breakdown of SQL statement activity, such as the parse, execute and fetch operations. Data collected for server events include resource usage metrics such as I/O and CPU consumed by a specific event.

Used together, a specific SQL statement can be analyzed by *explain plan* and Oracle Trace. First, the plan reveals the major database operations to be undertaken during the execution phase. These include full table scans, sorting, merge and hash joins. Restriction predicates are linked to the operations as appropriate. If the participating tables have had full histogram statistics collected, then costing in terms of disk I/O and CPU usage can be estimated.

Secondly, the statement can be run with Oracle Trace enabled. Measurements of actual resource utilization during each phase of execution can be taken and compared with the plan estimates. SQL statements should be selected for tuning based on their actual resource consumption. Revised statements or revised strategies such as using pre-parsed queries and materialized views (denormalization) can then be objectively compared on their new plans and actual resource costs.

17.4.2 ORACLE ENTERPRISE MANAGER

This tool provides a common user interface from which administrative tasks and diagnostic applications can be run. Information about the configuration and other management data is itself kept in the database.

Enterprise Manager has access to several diagnostic, testing and advisory packs for investigating various aspects of the system. Recommended changes to the configuration can then be put into effect through its administrative tools (Table 17.4).

Table 17.4 Enterprise Manager.	
Capacity Planner	Collects and analyzes historical performance data for the database and O/S
Performance Manager	Captures, and presents performance data; monitors key metrics for memory, disk I/O
Advanced Event Tests	Memory monitor covers library cache, data dictionary and database buffers, I/O monitoring covers disk and network
Oracle Expert	Analyzes problems detected by diagnostic tools; provides recommendations, implementation scripts and reports
SQL Analyze	Detects resource-intensive SQL, examines execution plans, compares optimizer modes, generates alternative SQL
Tablespace Manager	Reports characteristics of tablespaces; can rebuild specific objects or an entire tablespace for improved space utilization
Index Tuning Wizard	Identifies index changes and additions; determines the best strategy for implementation
Auto-Analyze	Runs at specified times to compute and maintain table statistics

17.5 ⊏ BENCHMARKS AND BENCHMARKING

Most benchmark data should be viewed with healthy scepticism when the purpose is product selection. In any event, performance is only one of many factors influencing an evaluation. Considerations such as the availability of trained DBAs, the vendor's technical support and total cost of ownership are also important determinants.

However, a benchmark constitutes a comprehensive and repeatable test suite that can be applied against a developing database implementation. Adapting benchmark methods to test the implementation as it is tuned can give a reliable estimation of the relative benefits of each change in hardware, operating system and database configuration.

A frequent criticism of benchmarking is that vendors tune their product to perform well in the test rather than produce generally reproducible performance enhancements.

Pre-loading the data into buffers and storing the SQL by pre-parsing and pre-computing the execution plans are two popular methods for saving disk I/O and CPU time. Database storage itself can also be optimized for the test by pre-joining selection domains. Oracle has materialized views that can store the results of a multiple table join, allowing fast data access for the benchmark queries but imposing an overhead on normal table maintenance outside of the test.

Perhaps the biggest issue is the different hardware platforms on which databases run. Comparing two different products running on two different platforms clearly may not permit individual performance factors to be identified. The experiment may lose its objectivity when database and host are a closely tuned and optimized pair.

Benchmark data is cited by virtually every database vendor to claim that its product is the fastest, has the lowest response time or has the greatest throughput. To avoid vendors choosing a test skewed towards their product's characteristics, the Transaction Processing Performance Council (TPC)[1] was created to oversee uniform benchmark tests.

17.5.1 TPC-C – THE ORDER ENTRY BENCHMARK

TPC-C is an online transaction processing (OLTP) benchmark. Its goal is to define a set of functional requirements that can be run on any transaction processing system, regardless of hardware or operating system. It is then up to the test sponsor (usually a hardware supplier or systems integrator) to submit proof, in the form of a full disclosure report, that they have met all the requirements. This methodology allows any vendor to implement the benchmark and guarantees to end-users that they will see a genuine experiment.

TPC-C simulates an environment where a population of simulated operators executes transactions against a database. The benchmark replicates the principal

---

1 The Transaction Processing Performance Council's web site is at `http://www.tpc.org/` (July 2003).

activities of an order-entry environment. The transactions include entering and delivering orders, recording payments, checking order status and warehouse stock monitoring.

The benchmark is designed to scale as new warehouses are created. Each warehouse must supply 10 sales districts, and each district serves 3000 customers. An operator from a sales district can select one of the five operations or transactions offered by the order entry system. The frequency distribution pattern of the transactions is taken from standard industrial work measurement statistics.

The recurrent transactions consist of order entry or payment reconciliation. At irregular intervals, the simulated operators will request order status, process orders for delivery, or query local warehouse stock levels for any of the 100,000 items in the catalogue.

An overall performance metric, tpm-C, measures the number of new order transactions that can be fully processed per minute. This number is achieved in an environment where other types of query are active in a statistically realistic simulation of an actual enterprise.

The objective verification of the benchmark results is achieved by requiring the test sponsor to submit a full disclosure report containing all the information necessary to reproduce the reported performance. This includes the total system cost that should be the true cost of the system to the end-user. It includes the cost of all hardware and software components; maintenance costs; and sufficient storage capacity to hold the data generated over a period of 180 eight-hour days of operation at the reported throughput.

Components of the measured system are stressed by having transactions of different types compete for system resources. Given the mix and the range of complexity and types among the transactions, the tpm-C (transactions per minute, using TPC-C) metric closely simulates a comprehensive business activity. It measures throughput of complete business operations. Because of the requirement for complete documentation, the cost of achieving the throughput can be determined. The top ten reports are available on the TPC web site, having passed through a review process before publication.

A benchmark sponsored by Hewlett-Packard in September 2001 used an extensive array of 272 processors in a clustered database server configuration. The overall system cost was just over US$10.6 million and achieved a little over 700,000 transactions per minute from 576,000 simulated operators. The cost/tpm was US$14.96.

Other benchmarks, reported in the same period, recorded cost/tpm figures between U$13.02 and U$28.58. These represent a whole range of different configurations from various systems suppliers, achieving different throughput results. Factoring for cost gives a comparable measure.

17.5.2 TPC-H AND TPC-R – DECISION SUPPORT BENCHMARKS

TPC-H and TCP-R are decision support benchmarks. They consist of a suite of business-oriented queries and concurrent data updates to a range of standard sized datasets. These benchmarks provide a simulation of decision support systems that are applied against large volumes of data and execute queries with a high degree of complexity.

TPC-H applies *ad hoc* queries for which the test platform may not be pre-optimized. TPC-R allows additional optimizations based on advance knowledge of the queries.

Both benchmarks report a measurement called the Composite Query-per-Hour Performance Metric that reflects multiple aspects of the test system's capability to process queries. These aspects include the selected database size against which the queries are executed, the query processing power when queries are submitted in a single stream, and the query throughput when queries are submitted by multiple concurrent users.

17.5.3   TPC-W – A TRANSACTIONAL WEB BENCHMARK

TPC-W is performed in a controlled Internet environment that simulates the activities of a business oriented transactional web server. The workload exercises a breadth of system components associated with such environments, such as multiple browser sessions, dynamic page generation, transactional updates and complex data structures.

TPC-W reports the number of web interactions processed per second (WIPS). The interactions simulate the activity of a retail store and each interaction is subject to a response time constraint.

Full disclosure reports allow an associated price per WIPS to be derived and the sponsor must provide customer rollout dates for the priced configuration.

17.5.4   THE OPEN SOURCE DATABASE BENCHMARK

OSDB is an international collaborative project that grew out of initial work at Compaq. The test suite has been written by volunteer programmers around the world and the source code is available on the OSDB web site[2]. The code can be downloaded at no cost and the only restriction on its host platform is that the platform must have GNU development tools (also free) and an appropriate C compiler. This generally means that many Unix- and Linux-based hosts are already configured to build the test suite.

The test suite is based on AS3AP, the ANSI SQL Scalable and Portable Benchmark, as documented in *The Benchmark Handbook*, edited by Jim Gray (1998). There are a number of differences, notably in the number of reported results. Benchmarking a standalone Oracle database using OSDB, would be a suitable practical exercise within a student project. There is a wealth of literature that would lead into an academic study of the subject.

---

2 http://osdb.sourceforge.net/ (July 2003)

17.6 ⊏ CASE STUDY

In order to illustrate the use of *explain plan* and Oracle Trace, a simple schema consisting of three tables has been devised. The schema represents an order processing system and has tables for *customers*, *orders* and *lineitems*. A customer may make many orders; each order consists of one or more lineitems.

An SQL batch file and a PL/SQL package, *makeCustomers*, are available on the web site associated with this book. The batch file creates the tables and the package populates the tables with random but consistent data. It allocates primary keys from sequences and ensures foreign key compliance (Figure 17.6). Running the packages creates 50,000 customers, 200,000 orders and 2,000,000 lineitems.

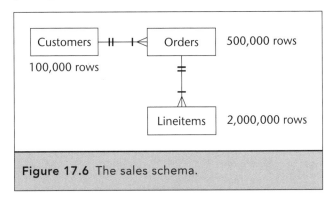

Figure 17.6 The sales schema.

Using large tables makes the results more statistically significant. A single query is needed to illustrate how *explain plan* can help in tuning operations. Figure 17.7 shows the query. It is a three-table join where each of the tables is quite large. Further, the *group by* clause will cause sort operations. This query might be used to create a monthly statement for customers showing their pending or unpaid orders. Each customer might be working on a different 30-day account period, so this

```
explain plan for
select a.cust_id as cust, b.order_no, product, quantity, price,
sum(quantity*price) as tot
   from customers a, orders b, lineitems c
   where a.cust_id=b.cust_id
   and b.order_no=c.order_no
   and a.cust_id=20
   group by a.cust_id, b.order_no, product, quantity, price;

@C:\oracle\ora92\rdbms\admin\utlxpls.sql
```

Figure 17.7 The tuning query.

query would be run at least once every working day. For the sake of this example, the query is restricted to just one customer.

The query is analyzed using the *explain plan* syntax and then formatted output is obtained from *plan_table* using the Oracle-supplied *utlxpls.sql* batch file. This procedure is repeated as schema changes are made to affect the performance of an unchanging query.

The first plan, shown in Figure 17.8, indicates a very high cost for the query. The total is 4491 units. By examining the plan in detail, the root causes can be identified as the full table scans on *lineitems* and *orders* in operations 5 and 6. This leads to high-cost joins, sorts and projects in operations 0, 1 and 2 because the intermediate relations are unrestricted. Further, the size of the buffer required to perform the full table access of *lineitems* is 51 MByte. This will cause considerable buffer contention with other transactions in a multi-user production database.

```
PLAN TABLE OUTPUT
------------------


-----------------------------------------------------------------
| Id  | Operation            | Name        | Rows  | Bytes | Cost |
-----------------------------------------------------------------
|   0 | SELECT STATEMENT     |             |    20 |   840 | 1092|
|   1 |  SORT GROUP BY       |             |    20 |   840 | 1092|
|*  2 |   HASH JOIN          |             |    20 |   840 | 1090|
|   3 |    NESTED LOOPS      |             |     5 |    75 |  159|
|*  4 |     INDEX UNIQUE SCAN| SYS_C003748 |     1 |     5 |    1|
|*  5 |     TABLE ACCESS FULL| ORDERS      |     1 |    10 |  158|
|   6 |    TABLE ACCESS FULL | LINEITEMS   | 2000K|   51M |  899|
-----------------------------------------------------------------


Predicate Information (identified by operation id):

   2 - access("B"."ORDER_NO"="C"."ORDER_NO")
   4 - access("A"."CUST_ID"=20)
   5 - filter("B"."CUST_ID"=20)
```

Figure 17.8 Tuning query plan.

When tuning a query, it is important to make only one change at a time. Whenever full table access appears in the plan prior to that table participating in a join, consider adding an index to the base table.

This is not an index based on a primary key to ensure relational integrity. *Lineitems* does not have a primary key. The cost of operation 6, the full table access of *lineitems*, can be reduced by indexing on the *order_no* attribute. This index will have duplicate keys since there are several line items for each order. This is an index created for performance reasons.

Figure 17.9 shows the SQL command to create this index. The index key is the *order_no* attribute of the table *lineitems*. The index name is *li_ndx*. Once the index is created, the database will automatically maintain it whenever rows are changed in the base table. This will add a small cost to those changes, but the improvement in the test query should compensate for this cost.

```
create index li_ndx on lineitems(order_no);
{re-run explain plan on the query and run utlxpls.sql}


PLAN TABLE OUTPUT
-----------------


---------------------------------------------------------------------
| Id | Operation                     | Name        | Rows |Bytes| Cost |
---------------------------------------------------------------------
|    0|SELECT STATEMENT              |             |   20 | 840 |  171 |
|    1| SORT GROUP BY                |             |   20 | 840 |  171 |
|    2|  TABLE ACCESS BY INDEX ROWID | LINEITEMS   |2000K|  51M|    2 |
|    3|   NESTED LOOPS               |             |   20 | 840 |  169 |
|    4|    NESTED LOOPS              |             |    5 |  75 |  159 |
|*   5|     INDEX UNIQUE SCAN        | SYS_C003748|    1 |   5 |    1 |
|*   6|     TABLE ACCESS FULL        | ORDERS      |    5 |  50 |  158 |
|*   7|     INDEX RANGE SCAN         | LI_NDX      |    4 |     |    1 |
---------------------------------------------------------------------


Predicate Information (identified by operation id):

    5 - access("A"."CUST_ID"=20)
    6 - filter("B"."CUST_ID"=20)
    7 - access("B"."ORDER_NO"="C"."ORDER_NO")
```

Figure 17.9 Index added.

Once the index has been created the *explain plan* command is re-run for the test query and the *utlxpls* utility used to format the plan output. Figure 17.9 shows a dramatic reduction in cost. Just over 81% of the costs of the first test have been wiped out by adding the index. There is an additional operation in this plan, the index range scan of *li_ndx*.

Because statistics have been collected for the underlying table, the optimizer can estimate that only a few rows will need to be scanned. Operation 7 has a corresponding low cost. This operation retrieves *order_no* and *rowid* from the index, allowing a reduced-cost join with the orders table later.

This plan still has a full table access on the *orders* table that can be made more efficient by adding an index on *cust_id*. This index will allow the optimizer to make a better estimate of the number of rows from *orders* that will participate in the join with customers and enable a range index scan of *orders* to produce a much smaller intermediate relation for that join.

Adding the index and re-running the *explain plan* command and the *utlxpls* utility results in the output shown in Figure 17.10. Again, the cost reduction in the estimated plan is spectacular. The second index has resulted in a cumulative saving of almost 99% of the same query optimized under the original conditions.

```
create index ord_ndx on orders(cust_id);
{re-run explain plan on the query and run utlxpls.sql}

PLAN TABLE OUTPUT
-----------------


-----------------------------------------------------------------
| Id| Operation                    | Name       | Rows|Bytes|Cost|
-----------------------------------------------------------------
|  0|SELECT STATEMENT              |            |  20 | 840|  15|
|  1| SORT GROUP BY                |            |  20 | 840|  15|
|  2|  TABLE ACCESS BY INDEX ROWID |LINEITEMS   |2000K| 51M|   2|
|  3|   NESTED LOOPS               |            |  20 | 840|  13|
|  4|    NESTED LOOPS              |            |   5 |  75|   3|
|* 5|     INDEX UNIQUE SCAN        |SYS_C003748 |  1 |   5|   1|
|  6|     TABLE ACCESS BY INDEX ROWID |ORDERS   |   5 |  50|   2|
|* 7|      INDEX RANGE SCAN        |ORD_NDX     |   5 |     |   1|
|* 8|    INDEX RANGE SCAN          |LI_NDX      |   4 |     |   1|
-----------------------------------------------------------------


Predicate Information (identified by operation id):

   5 - access("A"."CUST_ID"=20)
   7 - access("B"."CUST_ID"=20)
   8 - access("B"."ORDER_NO"="C"."ORDER_NO")
```

Figure 17.10 Another index.

Notice that operation 7, the index range scan of *ord_ndx*, has been restricted with the same predicate as the customers table. This has been automatically added by the optimizer to ensure the minimum size possible for the intermediate relations that will participate in the later join.

Remember, these results are estimates from the optimizer based on statistics. Only by running the query, adding the indexes one by one and monitoring actual resource utilization using the *trace* facility can the actual savings be proven.

Figure 17.11 shows a simple experiment with SQL Trace. First, the two indexes, *li_ndx* and *ord_ndx* are dropped and then the trace facility is enabled. The query is then executed three times (Table 17.5), building an index after each run. Disabling the trace facility stops the recording and closes the trace output file. The trace data is recorded in a file in a sub-folder of the instance folder. This default can be changed by a DBA respecifying the value of *USER_DUMP_DEST*.

```
drop index li_ndx;
drop index ord_ndx;
alter session set sql_trace = true;
select a.cust_id as cust, b.order_no,...
create index li_ndx on lineitems(order_no);
select a.cust_id as cust, b.order_no,...
create index ord_ndx on orders(cust_id);
select a.cust_id as cust, b.order_no,...
alter session set sql_trace = false;
```

Figure 17.11 Testing with SQL Trace.

Table 17.5 Query phases.	
Parse	Performs syntactic, semantic and security checks and then produces the execution plan.
Execute	The actual execution of the statement. For insert, update and delete statements, this step modifies the data. For select statements, the step identifies the selected rows.
Fetch	This step retrieves rows returned by a query. Fetches are only performed for select statements.

The data is prepared for presentation by the separate executable *tkprof*. This should run from an OS prompt and takes three parameters: the input file containing the trace data, the sorted and formatted output file and an option specifying no aggregation of data for multiple runs of the same SQL statement.

The, output file (Figure 17.12) can be viewed with any editor or word processor. Each SQL statement has a set of data showing resource utilization during its three phases: parse, execute and fetch. Each of the columns in the *tkprof* output represents a different resource used by the SQL statement. *Count* shows the number of times it was parsed, executed or fetched. Notice that after the statement is first issued, very little resource is used for the parse or execute stages.

```
C:>tk_prof scotoracle_ora_1664.trc   trcoutput.prf aggregate = no

First submission of query...

call    count     cpu   elapsed    disk     query   current    rows
Parse     1      0.05    0.04        0         0        0         0
Execute   1      0.00    0.00        0         0        0         0
Fetch     3      1.58    5.68      10095     10855      0        20
TOTAL     5      1.63    5.73      10095     10855      0        20


Build index li_ndx

Second submission of query...

call    count     cpu   elapsed    disk     query   current    rows
Parse     1      0.01    0.00        0         0        0         0
Execute   1      0.00    0.00        0         0        0         0
Fetch     3      0.12    0.75       888       1650      0        20
TOTAL     5      0.13    0.75       888       1650      0        20


Build index ord_ndx

Third submission of query...

call    count     cpu   elapsed    disk     query   current    rows
Parse     1      0.01    0.00        0         0        0         0
Execute   1      0.00    0.00        0         0        0         0
Fetch     3      0.00    0.08        2        19        0        20
TOTAL     5      0.01    0.08        2        19        0        20
```

Figure 17.12 Run *tkprof*. Formatted output.

The *count* column shows that full parse and full execute for the statement was done only once. Only the fetch phase is performed three times. The database retains the statement in buffers and the syntactic, semantic and security checks are not repeated for multiple runs of the same statement. There is minimal CPU activity associated with the revisions to the execution plan caused by adding the indexes.

This experiment shows the differences in the disk I/O as indexes are added between runs. It confirms the optimizer's estimates and shows how much benefit can be gained by tuning the database structure.

For a fully objective test of all resource utilization, it would be necessary to log out and close the instance between runs so that buffered data did not moderate the results for the second and third repeat queries.

To make similar further efficiency gains in the query it will be necessary to denormalize. Creating a materialized view of the query will enable a new permanent structure in the database (Figure 17.13).

```
create materialized view mv_custorderlines build immediate
refresh complete
start with sysdate
next sysdate +1
as select a.cust_id as cust, b.order_no, product, quantity, price,
(quantity*price) as total
  from customers a, orders b, lineitems c
  where a.cust_id=b.cust_id
  and b.order_no=c.order_no;
```

Figure 17.13 Creating a materialized view.

This will consist of the three table pre-joined for all customers. It can be configured so that changes in the underlying tables such as insertions or deletions are
automatically reflected in the view. The materialized view can be analyzed to
compute statistics in preparation for query optimization. The original query is now
reduced to a simple restriction on the view with a resource utilization of only
0.42% of that under the original conditions.

```
analyze table mv_custorderlines compute statistics;
explain plan for
select * from mv_custorderlines
where cust=20;

PLAN TABLE OUTPUT
-----------------


-------------------------------------------------------------------
| Id |Operation                     |  Name              |Rows|Bytes|Cost|
-------------------------------------------------------------------
|   0|SELECT STATEMENT               |                    | 20| 640 | 8  |
|   1|TABLE ACCESS BY INDEX ROWID |MV_CUSTORDERLINES| 20| 640 | 8  |
|*  2| INDEX RANGE SCAN             | MV_NDX            | 20|      | 3  |
-------------------------------------------------------------------

Predicate Information (identified by operation id):

  2 - access("MV_CUSTORDERLINES"."CUST"=20)
```

Figure 17.14 Materialized view query explained.

The penalty for this improvement is the long query to produce the view and the daily re-establishment of the view to take in any changes to the data. Since this can be scheduled as an overnight job, there will be no real effect on daytime performance. The improvement has been won at very little cost. If the materialized view must be kept in tighter synchronization then a trigger fired by updates to any of the base tables could be created (Figure 17.14).

17.7 ∈ KEY TERMS

Tuning	Changing systems or application parameters to achieve better response or throughput
Oracle method	Iterative tuning procedure that takes ten factors into consideration
Scalability	Application performance may tail off as systems grow. Scalability can be checked through benchmarking with increasing virtual users. Amending business rules may also improve scalability
Benchmarks	A standard test suite designed for reliable comparisons between different hardware/software configurations
TPC	A series of tests now used by most database vendors and systems integrators to publish benchmarks. Relies on full systems disclosure
OSDB	Open Source Database Benchmark: less accepted as a standard but a good introduction to practical benchmarking

17.8 ∈ EXERCISES

(i) Adapt the package *makeCustomers* to produce a different sample schema consisting of a minimum of five entities. Create the tables and populate them with manufactured data. Choose queries that will exercise the optimizer. Produce a report on your experiments.

(ii) Obtain the Open Source Database Benchmark and implement it. Test your own database configuration.

CHAPTER 18

WEB INTERFACES

Out flew the web and floated wide;

The mirror cracked from side to side;

"The curse is come upon me," cried

The Lady of Shalott.

Alfred Tennyson, *The Lady of Shalott*

18.1 ∈ PROGRAMMATIC INTERFACES

The application example in Chapter 14 is designed to reside on a client machine and connect independently to the database server. The application illustrates the use of JBuilder to provide a visual design environment that can be used to generate Java code and compile, test and deploy it.

The UFL application is contained in the various class files produced by the Java compiler. These classes run within a Java Virtual Machine that also finds and loads the JDBC classes when they are needed to connect to the database server. The client host must be correctly configured so that the JDBC classes can be found for the application to run successfully.

This application is suitable for internal use within an organization where the configuration of client machines can be kept under strict control, where data access is restricted to employees and the security and integrity of the data are relatively easy to maintain.

The massive popularity of the Internet has been fuelled by the business opportunities for electronic commerce. This demands that organizations publish data from their database on the World Wide Web and give users access to it through their web browsers. Successful business sites allow interactive use of the database for product information, instant ordering and online payment.

There are three major factors that preclude the use of standalone applications in this context. Firstly, the user interface must be made available through web browsers that do not offer anything more than the ability to interpret code received from a URL. Secondly, there is no control over the run-time configuration of the client computer. Thirdly, the client computer may have any combination of different CPUs and operating systems. All that is common is that the client is running a web browser.

This means that everything necessary for the successful run of an application must be delivered to the browser from the web server and this package must contain all that is necessary to provide a user interface, access to the business logic of the system and facilitate a connection to the database server.

There are several ways to achieve this. They involve a number of different system architectures where components of the overall application may reside and there is a choice of development languages.

A detailed treatment of these development choices is beyond the scope of this book. However, a brief review of some of the principal methods for deploying context-free browser-to-database applications is presented. The source code and JBuilder project files for the case studies in this chapter may be downloaded from the web site associated with this book.

18.2 ⋹ TWO-TIER ARCHITECTURE

The simplest way for the browser to display a user interface and to connect it to a database server is the **two-tier architecture.** The example application in Chapter 14 uses a two-tier architecture. The client program provides both the user interface and the business logic and connects directly to the database server. Portability issues concerning the diversity of browsers and client machines mean that Java is overwhelmingly the language of choice for a web-based two-tier application.

18.2.1 JAVA APPLETS

Nearly all web browsers have a Java Virtual Machine (JVM) that gives an environment for the applet classes to run. Normally this JVM has access to the standard classes that support fundamental user interface components such as those found in the *java.awt* package. If the applet uses any other support classes, these must be downloaded from the server (Figure 18.1). This would apply, for example to the JDBC classes for a type-4 driver to give connection facilities to an Oracle database.

The code for the application in Chapter 14 would be capable of adaptation to an applet. It should be born in mind, however, that it uses a number of GUI support classes that are specific to the JBuilder environment. The deployment configuration would need to take this into account. The necessary classes must be downloaded from the web server along with the applet code. This would place a large Internet traffic overhead on its operation.

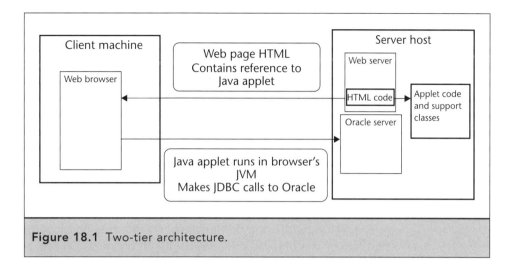

Figure 18.1 Two-tier architecture.

There are also a small number of minor changes that would need to be made. These are related to the way that downloaded Java code runs in a browser's JVM.

Firstly, a browser cannot run code that is designed to run as a standalone application class. It can only run a Java applet. An applet differs from an application in that its principal class extends the Applet class and it does not have a *main* method. When a Java application class is loaded into the JVM, control is passed to the *main* method. This usually has only one line of code: a call to the *init* method that in turn calls the constructor of the class.

A Java applet has only the *init* method and control is passed to this method when an applet is instantiated in a browser's JVM. This restriction is part of the security regime of the browser's JVM. It disallows certain functionality in an environment where code may be downloaded from a web site whose authors may not have totally benign intentions for the user.

Another part of this same security restriction is that the applet may only make a network connection back to the web host from which it was loaded. This means that, for a two-tier architecture, the web server software and the Oracle server must be on the same machine.

The code in the applet can be minimized and simplified by making it responsible only for the user interface and removing the business logic to PL/SQL stored functions and procedures that can kept in the database itself. The applet will then use JDBC calls to these stored programs, which will execute standard SQL queries or updates internally. The results of such queries can then be passed back to the applet for display in the browser window.

There are considerable security drawbacks in using a two-tier architecture to underpin a web interface. The most important is that the database connect information may have to be embedded in the applet. The tokenized code produced by the Java compiler is capable of being reverse engineered to discover this information. Malicious attackers can use this information to write applets that gain access to the database, albeit at a low level of permission, outside of the direct control of the original system's architect.

Such a breach could lead to a significant compromise of the overall database security since the malicious program would have the same permissions as legitimate web users. It might be used to discover order information about these users. If the DBA has not implemented comprehensive security protection, it could be used to originate false product orders.

In order to protect the integrity of the web application and to reduce the deployment complexity, it makes sense to interpose an extra level of access mechanism that abstracts those suspect elements into a centralized service that remains under the direct control of the owners of the system.

18.2.2 TWO-TIER CASE STUDY

This development example illustrates the basic technology of writing an applet that makes uses of JDBC calls and the *applet* tag in HTML that allows a web page to reference such an applet.

The first task is to construct a web page that will reference the applet. This consists of the code shown in Figure 18.2. The *applet* tag provides the link between the web page and the applet. As previously explained, when an applet is loaded into a browser, all of the classes it uses must be available or it will not execute properly. Most browsers have their own JVM that carries support for the basic Java classes, but *jdbcApplet* makes uses of a special set of classes that provide access to

```
<html>
<head>
<title>Systems Building - JDBC Applet</title>
</head>
<body>
<h1>Systems Building - jdbcApplet</h1>

This page contains an example of an applet that uses the Thin JDBC
driver to connect to Oracle and query the players table.
The source code for the applet is in jdbcApplet.java on the <i>Systems
Building</i> web site.<p>

<hr>
<applet codebase ="." archive="classes12.zip"
code="jdbcApplet.class " width=400 height=380>
</applet>

</body>
</html>
```

Figure 18.2 HTML code.

Oracle databases through the *OracleDriver* class. This is not part of the standard browser configuration, so the *codepage* attribute within the *applet* tag indicates where such support classes may be found.

In this case, the *codebase* is the same directory in the web domain from which the web page itself was loaded. The *archive* attribute within the same tag specifies a particular target file where the required classes are to be found and indicates implicitly to the browser that it is a zip file. The *classes12.zip* file is available for download from the Oracle web site.

The *applet* tag then has a *code* attribute that contains the name of the applet class and finally sets up an area in the displayed page of 400 pixels by 380 pixels where the applet will run. The code for *jdbcApplet* is available for download from the web site associated with this book. The user interface consists of simple components from the *java.awt* package, selected for maximum portability.

The applet uses *panels* to divide its display into managed areas (Figure 18.3). These panels can have properties set for background and foreground colours; their positions are regulated by the layout manager of the component that contains them. The applet has a *BorderLayout* manager, which uses the properties *North*, *South*, *Center*, *East* and *West* to determine position.

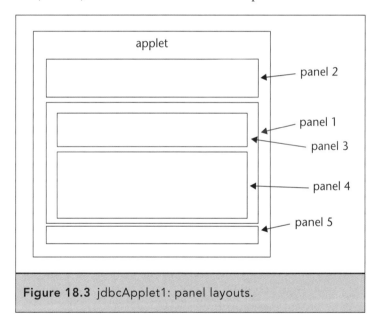

Figure 18.3 jdbcApplet1: panel layouts.

Three panels are added directly to the applet in positions *North*, *Center* and *South*. Two further panels are added to the central panel in position *North* and *Center* relative to their container. The sizes of these panel containers will be adjusted by their layout managers according to sizes of the components they contain and the space available.

Panel 2 contains a *label* component that is assigned the text *JDBC Applet1 Show Players*. *Panel 3* has a *label* with the text *Select a Player* and a Choice component (basic combobox) into which will be loaded the *ufa_ids* of all the rows in the players table of the UFL database.

Panel 4 has a *gridlayout* set to divide the panel into cells, two columns wide and six rows wide. This grid provides a convenient way to position the *labels* and *textfields* that will display the individual details of players selected by *ufa_id* in the *selectPlayer* component.

Any movement or click of the mouse will generate a Java event that can be detected by the program. In this study, the principal interest is in detecting a change in the selected item of the combobox, *selectPlayer*. Figure 18.4 shows a code

```
...
    selectPlayer.addItemListener(new java.awt.event.ItemListener() {
      public void itemStateChanged(ItemEvent e) {
        selectPlayer_itemStateChanged(e);
      }
    });
...
```

Figure 18.4 jdbcApplet: adding a listener.

```
...
  try{
   selectPlayer.removeAll();
   if (conn == null)  {
     DriverManager.registerDriver(new
                      oracle.jdbc.driver.OracleDriver());
     conn=DriverManager.getConnection
     ("jdbc:oracle:thin:@localhost:1521:scotoracle","a27ws","orange");
     }
   Statement stmt = conn.createStatement ();
   ResultSet rset = stmt.executeQuery ("select ufa_id from players");
     while (rset.next ())
       selectPlayer.addItem (rset.getString(1));
   Status.setText("Status: Select a Player");
       getPlayer();
     }
   catch (Exception e)  {
     System.out.println(e.getMessage());
     }
```

Figure 18.5 JDBC: connect and query.

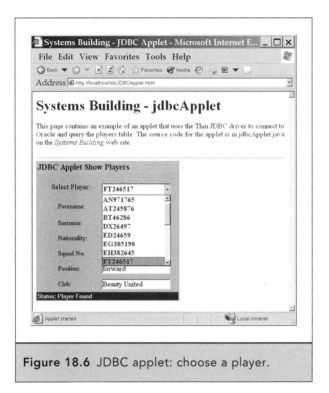

Figure 18.6 JDBC applet: choose a player.

fragment that installs a *listener* in *selectPlayer*, indicating that the method *selectPlayer_itemStateChanged* will be called when the event occurs.

During the initialization phase of the applet, the available values of *ufa_id* in the database must be loaded into the *selectPlayer* component. Restricting user selection in this way ensures that only valid queries are triggered when the items are chosen.

This is done by making the JDBC calls indicated in the code fragment in Figure 18.5. First, the *DriverManager* is informed that the connection will be using the *OracleDriver* and then the connection is created, using a predefined string and an appropriate *username* and *password*. These parameters are specific to the author's Oracle installation and must be changed for other database instances. A statement is created and executed. The rows returned by the query are assigned to a *ResultSet*. The contents of the *ResultSet* are then added, row by row, as items in *selectPlayer*.

The *javac* compiler produces a class file from the Java code. This class file, along with the zip file containing Oracle-specific JDBC classes, is deployed in a subdirectory of the web server's domain. Usually the HTML code for the web page is put in the same place. Any variation must be accounted for in the values of the *codepage* and *code* attributes of the *applet* tag.

A screen capture of the applet running in Internet Explorer is shown in Figure 18.6. The mouse has just been clicked in the *selectPlayer* component; a selection is about to be made.

```
void getPlayer(){
  try {
    PreparedStatement stmt1 = conn.prepareStatement("select * from
                            players where ufa_id=?");
    stmt1.setString(1,selectPlayer.getSelectedItem());
    ResultSet rs = stmt1.executeQuery ();
    if (rs.next ()){
      Forename.setText(rs.getString(3));
      Surname.setText(rs.getString(2));
      Nationality.setText(rs.getString(7));
      Squad_no.setText(rs.getString(5));
      Position.setText(rs.getString(6));
      Club.setText(rs.getString(8));
      Status.setText("Status: Player Found");
    }
  }
  catch (Exception f)  {
      System.out.println(f.getMessage());
  }
}
  void selectPlayer_itemStateChanged(ItemEvent e) {
    getPlayer();
}
```

Figure 18.7

When the selected item changes, the listener ensures that control is passed to the *selectPlayer_itemStateChanged* method. This does nothing more than call another method *getPlayer* where the database query is made. A code fragment for this is shown in Figure 18.7.

Stmt1 is a *PreparedStatement,* initialized with a query string containing a *? placeholder*. The *placeholder* is replaced by the *stmt1.setString* method, taking the actual selected item from *selectPlayer*. The statement is then executed and the returned single row assigned to the *ResultSet*. The various fields of the returned query are then assigned to the appropriate *TextFields* in the applet.

Every time that a new selection is made in the combobox, the action method will ensure that the player's details are shown in the textfields. Figure 18.8 shows the applet display after *selectPlayer*'s selection has changed. The details of player *AK675280* are shown.

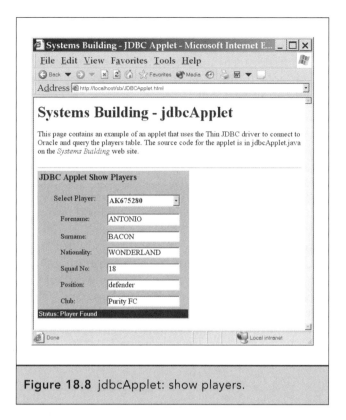

Figure 18.8 jdbcApplet: show players.

18.3 THREE-TIER ARCHITECTURE

The important limitations of the two-tier architecture, as far as Java applets are concerned, are the requirements that the applet can only establish a direct session with an Oracle server on the same machine as the web server and the need for the associated classes to be downloaded with the applet code.

Very often, this might place unnecessary stress on the host machine, where the number of web clients and database clients seeking connections might be numbered in the thousands at any particular time. In any event, the client–server paradigm is meant to offer increased performance through division of the work amongst relatively cheap but increasingly powerful server hosts.

The security restrictions on the Java applet are no bad thing, but most of them are directed at protecting an unwitting client from downloading a malicious applet. There is still scope for attack from those who might seek to damage or undermine the service provision.

18.4 REMOTE METHOD INVOCATION

One solution is to place some kind of intermediary on the web host. This could be an RMI server that would assume responsibility for all the JDBC logic and, perhaps, other application logic. The web-page applet is thus relieved of the requirement to connect directly to the database and need only be responsible for the presentation logic – the user interface. The intermediate RMI server has the business requirements embedded in its code in the form of standard and authenticated connect information, SQL queries or PL/SQL calls.

The deployment configuration problem is simplified since only the RMI server needs access to the JDBC classes. There is therefore no longer any need to download the JDBC classes to the remote web browser. Further, the code running in the server host's JVM is not available for inspection by third parties.

Security is enhanced since the Oracle server is no longer being contacted directly by thousands of unknown users running the applet in their browsers. The applet will be smaller since it has less functionality and will be quicker to download with the web page.

This solution is still complex. It requires additional compilation steps to generate the RMI stub class. Ideally, the Java server program should also be multi-threaded to enable it to respond to more than one concurrent client request. This approach offers great flexibility, since the Java programs – the applet and the server – can be engineered precisely to fulfil the business requirements. This flexibility is paid for in terms of the need for software development time and expertise.

Remote Method Invocation (Figure 18.9) is a Java standard and is specified through a number of standard classes that underpin the communications and data

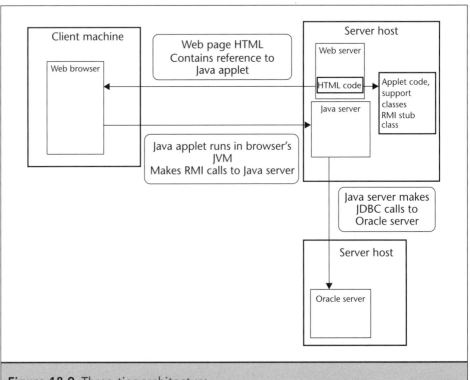

Figure 18.9 Three-tier architecture.

marshalling necessary for a client to make a call to the server. The services are defined in a remote interface. The server implements this interface. It directly implements the service methods in its code body. It indirectly implements the remote nature of the interface by inheritance from one of the standard RMI classes.

18.4.1   THREE-TIER CASE STUDY

Converting the two-tier example into a three-tier client–server system requires that the client applet be divided into two. The new client applet will have responsibility only for the user interface and for detecting user interaction. Figure 18.10 lists the project files required.

queryPlayers.java – RMI interface

rmiappClient.java – RMI client applet

queryPlayersImpl.java – RMI server application

Figure 18.10 Project files.

The JDBC code is taken out and forms the core of a new Java program, the RMI server. The RMI server class contains two functions that can be called by the client. These provide a service firstly to populate the combobox component in the client with the *ufa_id*s of players in the database and secondly to provide the detail of a player when his *ufa_id* is selected in the combobox.

These functions are *wrapped* in a server class that inherits from the *UnicastRemoteObject* class. This latter is a standard Java class that enables the networking connections on the server side.

To preserve type safety and to ensure that the server actually provides the functions that the client will call, a third entity is required in an RMI application. This is the interface class. The interface class simply consists of the signatures of the remote methods. When the client class is compiled, the compiler checks that the remote method calls conform to these signatures. When the server class is compiled, the compiler checks that these methods are actually implemented in the server.

Figure 18.11 show the code for the interface *queryPlayer*. The class contains two methods: *getUfa_IDs* and *getPlayer*. The various class imports provide type definitions for the code used in the interface. The *queryPlayer* class inherits from the *Remote* class. This information will enable the compiler to check that the client calls the methods through a specially obtained remote object reference and not through a local reference. The server will also be checked to ensure that it implements a class compatible with the *Remote* class.

Both *getUfa_IDs* and *getPlayer* return a *Vector* type and may, in case of any networking or database malfunction or error, raise a *RemoteException*. *Exceptions provide a safe way of dealing with* error conditions. Methods that raise exceptions

```
package rmiapp;
import java.rmi.Remote;
import java.rmi.RemoteException;
import java.util.*;
  public interface queryPlayers extends Remote {
    Vector getUfa_IDs() throws RemoteException;
    Vector getPlayer(String p_id)throws RemoteException;
}
```

Figure 18.11 Interface class: *queryPlayers*.

must be called within a *try/catch* structure in the program. If an exception is raised in the *try* section, control is immediately passed to the *catch* section for handling. Program crashes are thus avoided.

The *Vector* type is a flexible, array-like structure that can hold any number of elements. It is used here to transport the contents of the *ResultSets* returned by the server's SQL queries, back to the client. The client does not have access to the *ResultSet* class itself since the whole point of this exercise is to remove all JDBC logic from the client code. In any event, a *ResultSet* is not serializable and thus cannot be directly transported across a network. The *ResultSet* cannot be separated from the query statement that created it.

The server class in this example is called *queryPlayersImpl* because it implements the *queryPlayers* interface. Figure 18.12 shows a code fragment, the class signature, from the file *queryPlayersImpl.java*.

```
...
public class queryPlayersImpl extends UnicastRemoteObject implements
queryPlayers{...
```

Figure 18.12 Implement the *queryPlayers* interface.

The class inherits from *UnicastRemoteObject*, which satisfies the obligation to be compatible with *queryPlayers* as a remote object. The class is defined as implementing *queryPlayers*, which will trigger compiler checks to ensure that it provides full and correct implementations of the defined remote methods in *queryPlayers*.

A final fourth element is required for the RMI application to function properly at run-time. This is a stub class derived from the server class. The stub class is used by the server and the client to perform marshalling and de-marshalling of data and to provide a remote object reference to the client. Remote calls are passed from the client to a stub class on the client machine and networked to the server class via the same stub class resident on the server machine.

In JBuilder, the server's build property can be set to generate the source code for the stub class *queryPlayersImpl_Stub.java*. This simply uses the *rmic* (rmi compiler) program, part of the JDK installation. The *rmic* program can be called from a command window if JBuilder is not in use. The standard Java compiler, *javac*, can the be applied to the other source files.

Java programs do not run directly on the CPU as operating systems processes and therefore cannot make direct network connections. The JVM in which the tokenized compiled server program is interpreted is a process and can make network connections. However in a multi-user or a multi-server host there may be a problem in identifying the particular JVM in which a requested class resides.

A special program, the *rmiregistry*, runs as a process to resolve this difficulty. When the server class, *queryPlayersImpl*, is launched in a JVM, it first registers its presence with the *rmiregistry* and also registers the location of its stub class. It then enters a listening state, waiting for a client request

Figure 18.13 shows the *main* method from the *queryPlayersImpl* class. An object, *server*, is instantiated using the constructor for the *queryPlayersImpl* class. The *Naming.rebind* method registers the object reference for *server* with the *rmiregistry* under the name *//localhost/queryPlayersServer*, the same name that the client method, *Naming.lookup*, will use later in its search. The location of the stub class is also registered. The server object then waits, listening for a client request.

```
 ...
  public static void main(String args[]) {
  try {
   queryPlayersImpl server = new queryPlayersImpl();
   System.out.println("Registering server
                           //localhost/queryPlayersServer");
   //Bind this object instance to the name "queryPlayersServer"
   Naming.rebind("//localhost/queryPlayersServer", server);
   System.out.println("queryPlayersServer bound in registry"); }
  catch (Exception e) {
     System.out.println("queryPlayersImpl err: " + e.getMessage());
     e.printStackTrace();
  }
 }
```

Figure 18.13 Fragment I: player implementation.

The *Naming.lookup* method, when invoked in the client, first contacts the *rmiregistry* on the server host and obtains a remote object reference for the server and a location for the server's stub class file. The stub class is downloaded to run co-resident in the client's JVM. The stub acts as a local proxy for the remote server. From now on, client requests, using the remote object reference, will be passed to the local stub; these will be passed on to the remote stub and thence to the server itself.

Figure 18.14 shows a code fragment from the *rmiappClient* class. The *server* attribute is an instance of the *queryPlayers* class and therefore, by inheritance, *Remote*. The local *Vector* object, *v*, is assigned the return value of *server.getUfa_IDs()*. If the call is successful, *v* has an element for each of the *ufa_ids* found in the database. Mapping the elements of *v* to an *Enumeration* is one way of getting at an unknown (at run-time) number of elements in the vector. A *while* loop assigns each element of the Enumeration to the item list of the *selectPlayer* component.

```
queryPlayers server = null;...
Vector v;
...
 try {
   //bind remote object reference to object in client
   server = (queryPlayers)
             Naming.lookup("//localhost/queryPlayersServer");
   System.out.println("RMI connection successful"); }
 catch (Exception e) {
   System.out.println("Exception occurred: " + e);
   System.exit(0); }
...
    try {
      selectPlayer.removeAll();
      Vector v=server.getUfa_IDs();
      Enumeration e=v.elements();
      while (e.hasMoreElements())
      selectPlayer.addItem (e.nextElement().toString());
      Status.setText("Status: Select a Player");
      v=server.getPlayer((String) selectPlayer.getSelectedItem());
      e=v.elements ();
      Surname.setText(e.nextElement().toString());
      Forename.setText(e.nextElement().toString());
      Nationality.setText(e.nextElement().toString());
      Squad_no.setText(e.nextElement().toString());
      Position.setText(e.nextElement().toString());
      Club.setText(e.nextElement().toString());
      }
    catch (Exception e)  {
      System.out.println(e.getMessage());
      }
```

Figure 8.14 Fragment II: *rmiappClient*.

User interaction is dealt with in the same way as in the two-tier example. A listener is installed in the *selectPlayer* component. When the listener detects that the selected item has changed, control is passed to the action method installed in the listener.

The method *selectPlayer_itemStateChanged* (Figure 18.15) illustrates an alternative way if dealing with a vector when the number of elements is known. The vector's *get()* method is indexed as necessary for each of the display elements. The number of elements is known because *server.getPlayer* returns a vector with six elements, one for each of the attributes of the player whose *ufa_id* was passed as the parameter

```
void selectPlayer_itemStateChanged(ItemEvent f) {
  try {
    Vector v=server.getPlayer(selectPlayer.getSelectedItem());
    Enumeration e = v.elements ();
    Surname.setText(e.nextElement().toString());
    Forename.setText(e.nextElement().toString());
    Nationality.setText(e.nextElement().toString());
    Squad_no.setText(e.nextElement().toString());
    Position.setText(e.nextElement().toString());
    Club.setText(e.nextElement().toString());
    Status.setText("Status: Player found");
  }
  catch(Exception g){    }
}
```

Figure 18.15 Fragment III: *rmiappClient.*

Once the server is running in its JVM and has registered with *rmiregistry*, the client can be launched.

Figure 18.16 shows the client running in JBuilder's applet viewer. The combobox has been loaded and a selection is about to be made.

Figure 18.17 shows the applet after the selection. The player details have been found and synchronized with the combobox.

Table 18.1 summarizes the stages in RMI development.

The RMI client, running as an applet in a browser can only contact the RMI server if it is running on the same machine as the web server from which the page was loaded. The server, because it is running as an application, is not subject to applet security restrictions, and can connect to any host as necessary.

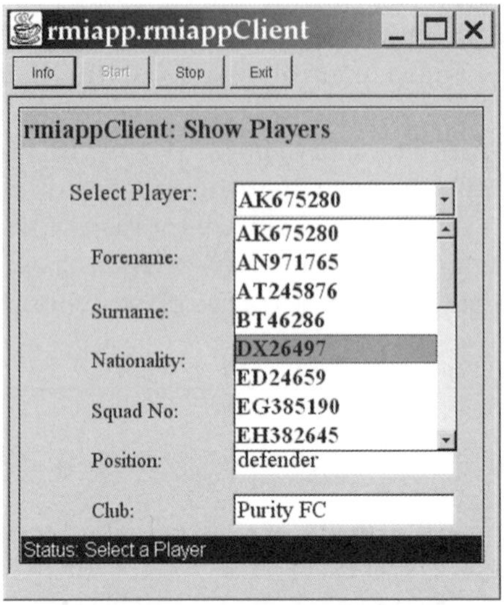

Figure 18.16 Client: making a selection.

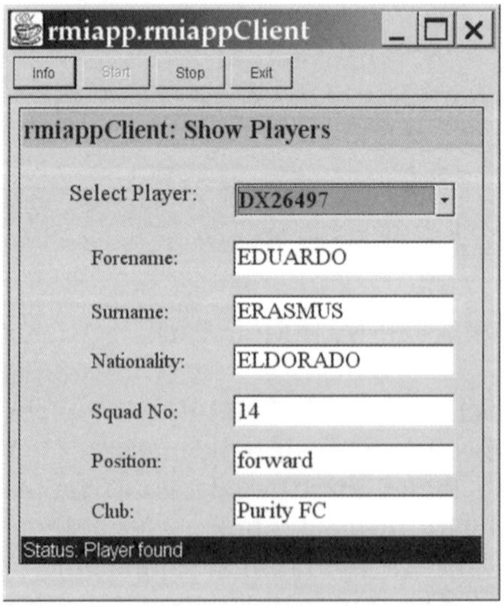

Figure 18.17 Client: selection made.

Create interface definition

Write server implementation of interface

Write client and HTML page

Compile server with rmic to produce stub file

Compile all Java files to produce class files

Move server, interface and stub classes to web server host

Run rmiregistry on web server host

Launch server class on web server host

Move client, stub class and HTML page to web server; position in web domain

Call HTML page from browser with codebase set so stub and any other classes can be downloaded

Table 18.1 Stages in RMI development.

18.5 JAVA SERVLETS

Java servlets have been described as the server-side equivalent of applets. That is to say that they do not run independently as standalone programs. They rely on running inside a servlet engine, usually associated with the web server. Because they run on the server side, they do not themselves have a graphical user interface.

Servlets are written in Java: they are not protocol- or platform-dependent. A servlet need not necessarily be associated with a web server but, since web applications development is the theme of this chapter, it that aspect of their use that will be the focus of this section.

Quite early on in the development of web technology, it was found that there was a need for independent server programs to run on the web host. Their principal purpose was to respond to requests via the web server for dynamically generated HTML code that could be tuned to user demand. If the HTML code can be generated *on the fly*, then *ad hoc* requests could be possible. It would be impossible to create static web pages that answered all the various combinations of user request. The first response was the Common Gateway Interface (CGI). This allowed the web server to call a separate program, passing user supplied parameters to it. The program would respond, embedding its response in HTML tags which would be passed on the user as a dynamic web page.

The most popular CGI mechanism was Perl, an interpreted programming language, but C++, Visual Basic or any other language could be used. The main problems were performance and portability. Each request might mean another copy of the executable or the interpreter being spawned in the memory of the web server. Further, the executable had to be capable of running on the server host and would need to be recompiled to move to another architecture; if there was a compiler or interpreter for that CPU.

Writing a servlet in Java solves the portability problem and because the multi-threaded servlet runs on the web server, one executable can service millions of requests without any need for host spawning or applet downloading.

A client program, usually a browser, accesses the web server and loads a page that makes a request. The request is then processed by the web server's servlet engine, which passes it on to the servlet. The servlet then sends a response through the web server back to the client. One critical advantage for servlet technology is speed. Unlike CGI programs, servlets are loaded into memory once and run from memory after the initial load. Servlets are spawned as a thread, and are by nature multi-threaded. Since they are based on the Java language, they are platform-independent.

18.5.1 SERVLET CASE STUDY

This project will consist of a relatively simple web page that will call a servlet. The servlet will make use of a datamodule class to connect to Oracle and retrieve the contents of the players table in a dataset. The servlet then passes the players data, formatted in HTML, back to the web page

Using JBuilder is convenient because all the configuration data will be organized automatically, and the Tomcat server, which comes with the Enterprise Edition, will host the web page, run the servlet and instantiate the datamodule. Create a new project in JBuilder; give it the name *SBServlet*. Make sure the directory names are correct and press *OK*.

Create a webapp by selecting *File |New* and the *Web* tab. Name it *SBServletwebapp* and click *OK*. The webapp is the configuration tool that will ensure that the Tomcat server has all the necessary resources deployed to its domain.

Create a new servlet. Name it *SBServlet*. Check the *Standard servlet* box in the dialog. Click on *Next*. Check the *doGet* and *doPost* boxes and the *Generate SHTML file* box. Click on Finish. JBuilder creates a simple SHTML file in the webapp and the skeleton of the servlet code

Amend the code for the *SBServlet.shtml* file as shown in Figure 18.18. The code creates a simple form area with a *submit* button in it. When the button is pressed in the rendered web page, a *post* is performed. This is passed by the server to the servlet's *doPost()* method. The servlet tags below will perform a *get* as the page is loaded. This will be passed to the servlet's *doGet()* method. The rest of the HTML is standard.

Figure 18.19 shows the web page in the design view. The two engraved lines across the page are caused by the <hr> tags. The results of the *get* will be shown here because the tags enclose the implied *get* call to the servlet in the <servlet> tags.

The code for the servlet is shown in Figure 18.20. Amend the generated code so that it looks like this. Alternatively, the file can be downloaded from this book's web site.

```
<html>
<head>
<title>
SBServlet
</title>
</head>
<body bgcolor="#c0c0c0">

<form action="/SBServletwebapp/sbservlet" method="post">
<p><H1>Press Submit to post to servlet SBServlet</H1></p>
<p><input type="submit" name="Submit" value="Submit"></p>
</form>
<hr>
<servlet
  codebase =""
  code="sbservlet.SBServlet.class">
</servlet>
<hr>
</body>
</html>
```

Figure 18.18 The SHTML file.

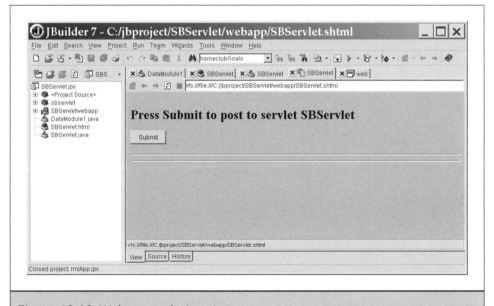

Figure 18.19 Web page: design view.

```
package sbservlet;
import javax.servlet.*;
import javax.servlet.http.*;
import java.io.*;
import java.util.*;
import java.sql.*;
import com.borland.dx.dataset.*;
import com.borland.dx.sql.dataset.*;
import com.borland.datastore.*;
public class SBServlet extends HttpServlet {
  static final private String CONTENT_TYPE = "text/html ";
  DataModule1 dm = sbservlet.DataModule1.getDataModule();
public void init() throws ServletException {}
public void doGet(HttpServletRequest request, HttpServletResponse
response) throws ServletException, IOException {
  response.setContentType(CONTENT_TYPE);
  PrintWriter out = response.getWriter();
  out.println("<H2>The servlet has received a GET. This is the
reply. Press Submit for a list of Players</H2>");
}
public void doPost(HttpServletRequest request, HttpServletResponse
response) throws ServletException, IOException {
    response.setContentType(CONTENT_TYPE);
    PrintWriter out = response.getWriter();
    out.println("<html>");
    out.println("<head><title>SBServlet</title></head>");
    out.println("<H2 bgcolor=\"#c0c0c0\">");
    out.println("<H2>The servlet has received a POST. This is the
reply.</H2>");
  Column [] columns = dm.getQueryDataSet1().getColumns();
  out.println ("<table border = 1><tr>");
  for (int i=1; i < columns.length; i++) {
    out.print("<th>" + columns [i].getCaption() + "</th>");
  }
  out.println("</tr>");
  dm.getQueryDataSet1().first();
  while (dm.getQueryDataSet1().inBounds()) {
    out.print("<tr>");
    for (int i = 1; i < columns.length; i++) {
    out.print ("<td>" + dm.getQueryDataSet1().format(i) + "</td>");
    }
```

Figure 18.20 The servlet class.

```
        out.println("</tr>");
        dm.getQueryDataSet1().next();
    }
    out.println("</table>");
    out.println("</body></html>");
  }
  public void destroy () {}
}
```

Figure 18.20 (*Continued*)

There are several points of note. Firstly, the servlet class extends (inherits from) the *HttpServlet* class: it has no orthodox constructor. The server will perform the instantiation and take over all communication between the web page and the servlet. The *doGet* method writes out just one line of text in HTML tags. This will be displayed in the original calling page. The *doPost()* method writes out several lines of text before processing the dataset. These include the tags for a new page. The method's output will therefore not be displayed in the calling page. A new content page will be created dynamically.

Create a new datamodule for the project. Click *File|New* and select the *datamodule* icon in the *General* tab. Accept the name *datamodule1* and click on *Finish*. Fill in the generated skeleton code as shown in Figure 18.21.

Again, there are some points to note. The *datamodule1* class implements the datamodule interface rather than extending a class. A datamodule acts as a container for other data-aware components. It does not have an orthodox constructor. Instead, it has an attribute, an instance of a *datamodule1*, called *myDM*.

If *myDM* does not already exist, a call to the *getDataModule()* method causes *myDM* to be instantiated by the servlet engine. The constructor does nothing except immediately call *jbInit()*. The object is instantiated in the server and the components it contains are initialized. The calling servlet gets a reference returned to it by which it can address the data-aware components contained within the datamodule.

The datamodule may outlive the servlet that first called it. It then resides in the server awaiting another call from any other servlet whose class definition makes it aware of the *datamodule1* class. Only a specific call to *destroy* or the closure of the server will end the life of the datamodule.

This datamodule has some of the same data-aware components that were seen in Chapter 14. The *database* component makes the connection to Oracle and the *QueryDataSet* contains the queried rows of the players table. The connection string and the SQL query are set in the component property inspectors. The Java code is generated automatically.

When it is instanitiated in the server, *SBServlet* obtains a reference to the datamodule (Figure 18.20). The datamodule either already exists or is immediately

```
package sbservlet;
import com.borland.dx.dataset.*;
import com.borland.dx.sql.dataset.*;
import java.sql.*;
public class DataModule1 implements DataModule {
  static private DataModule1 myDM;
  private Database database1 = new Database();
  private QueryDataSet queryDataSet1 = new QueryDataSet();
  public DataModule1() {
    try {
      jbInit();
    }
    catch(Exception e) {e.printStackTrace();
    }
  }
  private void jbInit() throws Exception {
    database1.setConnection(new com.borland.dx.sql.dataset.
              ConnectionDescriptor("jdbc:oracle:thin:
              @loopback:1521:scotoracle", "a27ws", "orange",
              false, "oracle.jdbc.driver.OracleDriver"));
    queryDataSet1.setQuery(new com.borland.dx.sql.dataset.
              QueryDescriptor(database1,
              "select * from players", null, true, Load.ALL));
    queryDataSet1.open();
  }
  public static DataModule1 getDataModule() {
    if (myDM == null) {
      myDM = new DataModule1();
    }
    return myDM;
  }
  public com.borland.dx.sql.dataset.Database getDatabase1() {
    return database1;
  }
  public com.borland.dx.sql.dataset.QueryDataSet getQueryDataSet1() {
    return queryDataSet1;
  }
}
```

Figure 18.21 The datamodule class.

instantiated by the servlet engine. The returned reference is the object identifier of *myDM* in the datamodule. This is assigned to the *dm* object in the servlet. SBServlet can use a local reference because both it and the datamodule are running in the same address space, the web server's engine. It then processes the dataset through the *dm* reference, getting its column names in an array of the *Column* class and outputting the header row of an *HTML* table. It processes each row of the dataset, getting each of the attribute values, referring to the columns of the current row by number, using the dataset's *format()* method. All of the output is enclosed inside HTML tags, constructing a new page.

Before the project is run, ensure that the webapp has the appropriate configuration information. Figure 18.22 shows the *Run|Configurations* editor. The *Server* tab shows a tree of options. Check all the boxes in the *Command line* and *Libraries* sections.

The running project is shown in Figures 18.23 and 18.24. When the SHTML web page loads, it performs an implied *get* request. This is intercepted by the web server. If the SBServlet does not already exist, it is immediately instantiated by the web server's engine and the *get* request forwarded to its *doGet()* method.

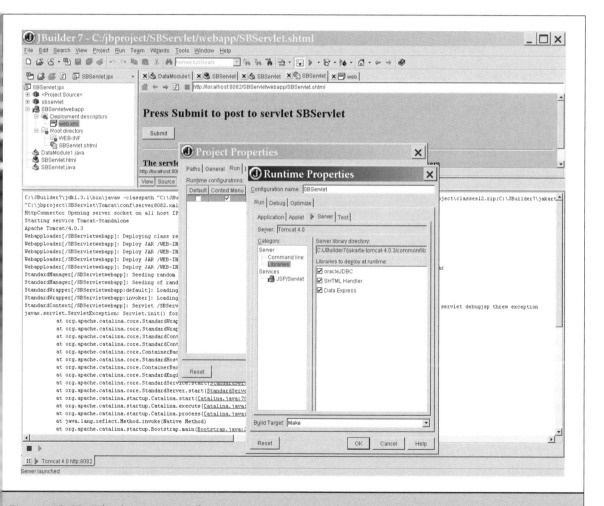

Figure 18.22 Edit the runtime information.

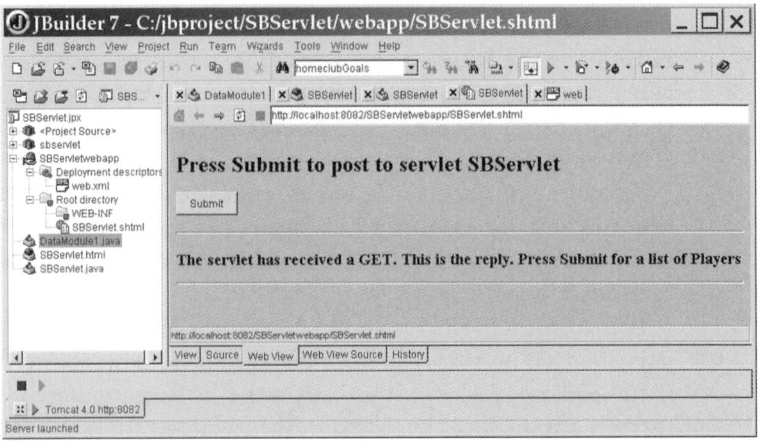

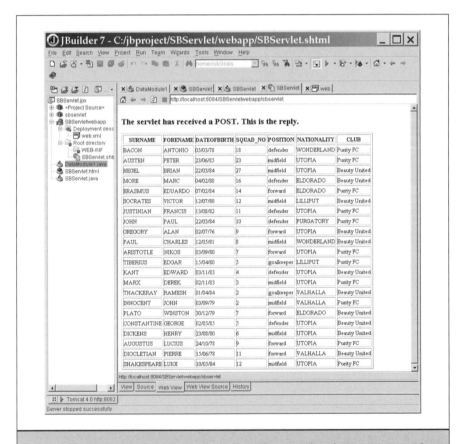

Figure 18.23 SBServlet: the submit form. The *get* has been processed.

Figure 18.24 SBServlet: the players list. The post has been processed.

The output text from the servlet appears between the two engraved lines. Clicking the *Submit* button causes the page to send a *post* request. Again this is passed on, this time to the servlet's *doPost()* method. The database is queried and the results displayed in a new page.

18.6 ⊆ ENTERPRISE JAVABEANS

The *Enterprise JavaBeans* (*EJB*) specification formally defines a Java server-side component model and a programming interface for application servers. Developers build the enterprise beans to contain the business logic of the enterprise. Enterprise beans run on an EJB server that provides services such as transaction management and security.

Developers do not have to worry about programming these low-level and complex services, but can focus on encapsulating the business rules of an organization within the beans, knowing that the services are available to the beans when they are needed.

Two-tier architectures run into difficulties of scale if the number of clients increases markedly. This can be for reasons of configuration if libraries have to be downloaded with applets or it can be because the server cannot cope with load increases.

When the logic of a multi-tier application needs updating, changes are made to the software in the middle tier, greatly simplifying the management of updates. The EJB specification is an attempt to simplify the building of distributed systems by relieving much of the development burden through the provision of standard services. The EJB architecture aims to provide better scalability and easier systems management.

For example, if the application were a logistics system, the enterprise bean developer would need to understand warehousing and transport. The system administrator must know about monitoring a deployed and running application. EJB server and container services, available from several different vendors, handle many of the more difficult but standard tasks. This makes enterprise beans portable. Once a bean is written, it can be deployed on any server that adheres to the EJB standard. Table 18.2 shows the different roles and responsibilities in designing and deploying enterprise beans.

18.6.1   HOW AN ENTERPRISE BEAN WORKS

The bean provider or developer must generate the bean classes that contain the business process logic. In addition, two types of interface must be created. The home interface defines the methods a client uses to create, locate and destroy instances of an enterprise bean. The remote interface defines the business methods implemented in the bean. A client accesses these methods through the remote interface.

Table 18.2 EJB development roles.

Application roles	Bean provider	Writes the bean. Creates the home and remote interfaces.
	Application assembler	Writes the application that uses the beans. The application may include GUI clients, applets, servlets or JSP pages. Assembly instructions are embedded in deployment descriptors.
Infrastructure roles	EJB server provider	Provide a framework in which to run EJB containers. This must have, at a minimum, a naming service and a transaction service.
	EJB container provider	Provide tools to deploy enterprise beans and the runtime support for the beans. A container provides management services to one or more beans..
Deployment roles	Deployer	Adapts the application to the target environment, modifying the properties of the enterprise beans. For example, deployers set transaction and security policies.
	Systems admin	Monitors application execution; takes action if it behaves abnormally. Responsible for administering the enterprise's computing and networking infrastructure.

Once the bean is deployed in the EJB container, the client calls the *create ()* method defined in the home interface to instantiate the bean. The home interface is implemented in the container. Other methods declared in the home interface permit the client to locate an instance of a bean and to remove a bean instance when it is no longer needed.

Once the bean is instantiated, the client can call the business methods within it. The client never calls a method in the bean instance directly, however. The methods available to the client are defined in the remote interface of the bean, and the remote interface is again implemented by the container. When the client calls a method, the container receives the request and delegates it to the bean instance.

The case study at the end of the next section demonstrates how a JavaServer page calls a simple bean to access the UFL database. Table 18.3 describes the different types of enterprise bean.

Table 18.3 Types of enterprise bean.	
Session bean	Session beans can be either stateful or stateless. Stateless beans do not maintain state for a particular client and thus can support multiple clients. A stateful session bean executes on behalf of a single client. Session beans are often short-lived: they are removed at the end of the client's session.
Entity bean	An entity bean provides an object view of data in a database and usually serves more than one client. Entity beans are considered to be long-lived. They maintain a persistent state, living as long as the data remains in the database. The container can manage the bean's persistence, or the bean can manage it itself.
Message-driven bean	Behaves as a Java Message Service (JMS) listener. The EJB container manages the bean's entire environment. They maintain no conversational state and can process messages from multiple clients. The bean is essentially a block of application code that executes when a message arrives at a particular JMS destination.

18.7 JAVASERVER PAGES

JavaServer Pages (JSPs) are also becoming widely used in web applications to provide an alternative to the relatively complicated RMI mechanism described above. They also avoid the need for a static HTML page used to call servlets. JSP uses a technology specified by Sun Microsystems as a convenient way of generating dynamic HTML content that a browser can interpret. The JSP is directly referenced in the browser's calling URL. The generated HTML is the web server's response.

JSPs are closely associated with Java servlet technology and with enterprise beans. They allow the inclusion of Java code snippets and calls to servlets, beans or other external Java components, as well as HTML tags. JSP code is distinct from other Web scripting code, such as JavaScript. Anything that can be included in a normal HTML page can be included in a JSP page.

The JSP *is* the web page. Eventually, all the Java snippets, bean references and HTML code are translated by the compilation process into a single Java-only file. This is compiled to a single class. When the browser calls a JSP in a URL, the web server launches the class in its servlet engine, along with any other dependent servlet or bean classes. The JSP class outputs the necessary HTML to construct the page in the browser. There is no need to download any support libraries, so network traffic is minimized and browser configuration is unnecessary (Table 18.4).

Table 18.4 Deploying a JSP web application.
Create a service context to hold the Web application.
Create and compile each of the servlets, beans and JSP servlets that make up the application.
Make sure that any other external objects called by servlets or called directly, such as Enterprise JavaBeans, are loaded, published and accessible through the service context.
Test the application using a Web browser or other HTTP client.

18.7.1   JSP CASE STUDY

The example application uses the *jspSB.java* server page to output the HTML code that is eventually seen in the web page. The JSP calls a simple bean that makes the Oracle connection, performs a query and returns a *ResultSet* to the JSP. The JSP then formats the contents of the returned *ResultSet*, embedding the columns and rows in HTML table tags. The application is developed in JBuilder in order to use the automated configuration tools that ensure that the web application runs correctly.

Create a new project; name the project *jspSB* and make sure that this name is reflected in the standard directories for the project. Use the *Project|Project Properties* dialog, selecting the *Server* tab to configure a single server for all services. Select *Tomcat 3.3* as the web server.

Add a webapp to the project. Select *File |New* and select the web application icon in the *Web* tab. Name it *jspSBwebapp* and click on *OK*. The web app holds the configuration information, including a list of libraries and servlet or bean classes to deploy to the work domain of the Tomcat server at run-time.

Add a JSP to the project. Select *File |New* and select the *JavaServer Page* icon in the Web tab. Name it *jspSB* and check the *Generate submit form* and *Generate sample bean* buttons. The generated code for the JSP contains a mixture of JSP code and HTML. The important part of this code is the section that identifies the generated bean, *jspSBBean*, in JSP tags. This enables the JSP page to call the bean methods from the server. Edit the code in the JSP page as shown in Figure 18.25. All the source files for this project are on the book's web site, so the code can be downloaded and pasted into this file.

Mixing Java statements and HTML makes the source difficult to read, but it should be clear that the *java.SQL.** library path is imported in the first line. This makes JDBC classes available to the program. Later, a *ResultSet* is assigned to the returned value of the bean's *myPlayers* method. The rather confusing code that follows is caused by having to put the Java statements in JSP tags (<%...%>) and the Table (<TABLE.../TABLE>, Table Header (<TH... /TH) and Table Data (<TD.../TD>) HTML tags around the content of the *ResultSet* fields. Notice also that the *ResultSet* operations are in a *try/catch* structure because of the possibility of raised exceptions.

The *ResultSet* can be passed as a parameter because both the JSP class and the bean will be instantiated in the same address space: Tomcat's servlet engine.

```
<%@ page import="java.sql.*" %>
<html>
<head>
<title>
jspSB
</title>
</head>
<jsp:useBean id="jspSBBeanId" scope ="session" class
="jspsb.jspSBBean" />
<body>
<h1>
Systems Building JSP uses JDBC Bean
</h1>
<p>Today is: <%= jspSBBeanId.myDate() %>.</p>
<%    try {
      ResultSet rset =jspSBBeanId.myPlayers() ;
      if (rset.next()) {%>
        <TABLE BORDER=1 BGCOLOR="COCOC0">
        <TH WIDTH=100 BGCOLOR="white"> <I>UFA ID</I> </TH>
        <TH WIDTH=120 BGCOLOR="white"> <I>SURNAME</I> </TH>
        <TH WIDTH=120 BGCOLOR="white"> <I>FORENAME</I> </TH>
        <TH WIDTH=110 BGCOLOR="white"> <I>POSITION</I> </TH>
        <TH WIDTH=120 BGCOLOR="white"> <I>NATIONALITY</I> </TH>
        <TH WIDTH=120 BGCOLOR="white"> <I>CLUB</I> </TH>
        <TR> <TD ALIGN=CENTER> <%= rset.getString(1) %> </TD>
             <TD ALIGN=CENTER> <%= rset.getString(2) %> </TD>
             <TD ALIGN=CENTER> <%= rset.getString(3) %> </TD>
             <TD ALIGN=CENTER> <%= rset.getString(6) %> </TD>
             <TD ALIGN=CENTER> <%= rset.getString(7) %> </TD>
             <TD ALIGN=CENTER> <%= rset.getString(8) %> </TD>
        </TR>
<%  while (rset.next()) {%>
        <TR> <TD ALIGN=CENTER> <%= rset.getString(1) %> </TD>
             <TD ALIGN=CENTER> <%= rset.getString(2) %> </TD>
             <TD ALIGN=CENTER> <%= rset.getString(3) %> </TD>
             <TD ALIGN=CENTER> <%= rset.getString(6) %> </TD>
             <TD ALIGN=CENTER> <%= rset.getString(7) %> </TD>
             <TD ALIGN=CENTER> <%= rset.getString(8) %> </TD>
        </TR>
<%  }%>
        </TABLE>
```

Figure 18.25 *jspSB.jsp* source code (*continued overleaf*).

```
<%  }
      else {%>
        <P> Sorry, the query returned no rows! </P>
<%      }
      rset.close();
    } catch (SQLException e) {
      out.println("<P>" + "There was an error doing the query:");
      out.println ("<PRE>" + e + "</PRE> \n <P>");
    }%>
</body>
</html>
```

Figure 18.25 (Continued)

The simple bean created along with the JSP needs substantial amendment. Change the code in *jspSBBean.java* to that shown in Figure 18.26. Again, this can be downloaded and pasted into the file. The bean has two methods, *myDate* and *myPlayers*. The first demonstrates how to construct a formatted date string and pass it back to the *JSP*. The second makes the Oracle connection, executes a query and passes a *ResultSet* back to the JSP.

Before the project is compiled, check that the run-time configuration is properly set. Select *Run|Configuration*; in the dialog select the configuration *jspSB* and click on *Edit*. The Server tab should show the tree for Server and Services options. The Command line options *make output path available* and *make libraries available* should both be checked. In the Library options, make sure that the required library, *OracleJDBC*, is checked.

When the project is compiled, the bean source code produces a standard class file in the output directory. The JSP code is used to generate a Java-only source file. This converts the HTML to equivalent Java output statements. The source can be seen in the .../classes/Generated Source directory. The source is copied to the *jspSBwebapp* directory and compiled to a class.

Using the configuration information, the Tomcat server loads the *jspSB* servlet class and the *jspSBBean* class. The resulting interaction is a stream of string outputs that consists only of HTML. This stream is caught and displayed in the browser window. Figure 18.27 shows this output.

If a user tries to determine the source code of the JSP by using *View* |*Source* in the browser's menu, Figure 18.28 shows a listing of what they would see. The browser is only aware of receiving a stream of HTML code from the requested URL. The listing is quite long: there is a block of six lines of <td> tagged attribute formatting for each player in the returned *ResultSet*.

The actual source or class code for the JSP or the bean cannot be downloaded and is secure from those who might wish to reverse engineer it.

```
package jspsb;
import java.text.*;
import java.util.Date ;
import java.sql.*;

public class jspSBBean {
 private String today="";
 private Connection conn;
 private ResultSet rs;

public String myDate(){
 SimpleDateFormat formatter= new SimpleDateFormat
                ("E, dd MM yyyy G 'at' hh:mm:ss a zzz");
 Date currentTime_1 = new Date();
 today = formatter.format(currentTime_1);
 return today;}

public ResultSet myPlayers(){
 try {
  if (conn==null){
   DriverManager.registerDriver(new
           oracle.jdbc.driver.OracleDriver());
   conn=DriverManager.getConnection
   ("jdbc:oracle:thin:@localhost:1521:scotoracle","a27ws","orange");
   }
  Statement stmt = conn.createStatement ();
  rs = stmt.executeQuery ("select * from players order by
                         club,surname");
  return rs;
  }
 catch(Exception e){
  return null; } }
 }
```

Figure 18.26 Source code for *jspSBBean*.

18.8 ⊏ XML

The extensible mark-up language, XML, offers an alternative strategy for connecting relational database content to a web page data presentation.

Like HTML, XML is an application of SGML (Standard Generalized Markup Language). HTML tags elements purely for presentation by a browser, for example <bold>Beauty United</bold>. XML tags elements as data: <club>Beauty United</

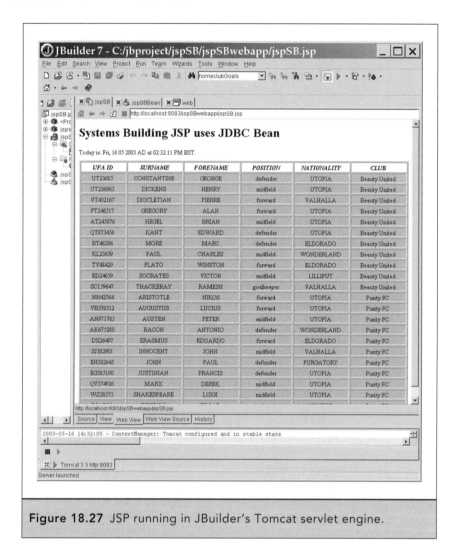

Figure 18.27 JSP running in JBuilder's Tomcat servlet engine.

club>. XML gives context to words and values in web pages, identifying them as data instead of simple textual or numeric elements. An XML document depends upon a stylesheet in order that its data may be rendered as a web page in a browser

Every XML document must have a root or top-level element. This is the outermost element and contains all the other elements. Any name for the root element may be chosen – hence the word *extensible* in XML. XML tags can be user-defined. In HTML, tags are standardized.

A Document Type Definition (DTD) is a set of rules that define the allowable structure of an XML document. DTDs derive their format from SGML and can be either included in an XML document or referenced as an external file. A DTD uses the tag structure to define the names of elements, attributes and entities of a document without specifying their actual values.

```
<html>
<head>
<title>
jspSB
</title>
</head>

<body>
<h1>
Systems Building JSP uses JDBC Bean
</h1>
<p>Today is: Fri, 16 05 2003 AD at 02:32:11 PM BST.</p>

        <TABLE BORDER=1 BGCOLOR="COCOCO">
        <TH WIDTH=100 BGCOLOR="white"> <I>UFA ID</I> </TH>
        <TH WIDTH=120 BGCOLOR="white"> <I>SURNAME</I> </TH>
        <TH WIDTH=120 BGCOLOR="white"> <I>FORENAME</I> </TH>
        <TH WIDTH=110 BGCOLOR="white"> <I>POSITION</I> </TH>
        <TH WIDTH=120 BGCOLOR="white"> <I>NATIONALITY</I> </TH>
        <TH WIDTH=120 BGCOLOR="white"> <I>CLUB</I> </TH>
        <TR> <TD ALIGN=CENTER> UT23685 </TD>
             <TD ALIGN=CENTER> CONSTANTINE </TD>
             <TD ALIGN=CENTER> GEORGE </TD>
             <TD ALIGN=CENTER> defender </TD>
             <TD ALIGN=CENTER> UTOPIA </TD>
             <TD ALIGN=CENTER> Beauty United </TD>
        </TR>

        <TR> <TD ALIGN=CENTER> UT236965 </TD>
             <TD ALIGN=CENTER> DICKENS </TD>
             <TD ALIGN=CENTER> HENRY </TD>
             <TD ALIGN=CENTER> midfield </TD>
             <TD ALIGN=CENTER> UTOPIA </TD>
             <TD ALIGN=CENTER> Beauty United </TD>
        </TR>
```

Figure 18.28 JSP output (fragment).

The file xmlPlayerlist.dtd, shown in Figure 18.29, first defines the *xmlPlayer* tag as an element consisting of eight attributes. Each of those attributes is then defined as a tag containing data. Finally, the *xmlPlayerlist* tag is defined as consisting of any number of *xmlPlayer* tags. The file is named after the root tag, *xmlPlayerlist*.

```
<?xml version ="1.0" encoding="UTF-8">
<!ELEMENT xmlPlayer (ufa_id, surname, forename, dateofbirth,
                     squad_no, position, nationality, club)>
<!ELEMENT ufa_id (#PCDATA)>
<!ELEMENT surname (#PCDATA)>
<!ELEMENT forename (#PCDATA)>
<!ELEMENT dateofbirth (#PCDATA)>
<!ELEMENT squad_no (#PCDATA)>
<!ELEMENT position (#PCDATA)>
<!ELEMENT nationality (#PCDATA)>
<!ELEMENT club (#PCDATA)>
<!ELEMENT xmlPlayerlist (xmlPlayer+)>
```

Figure 18.29 Document Type Definition (DTD).

18.8.1   WELL-FORMED AND VALID XML DOCUMENTS

An XML document that conforms to the structural and notational rules of XML is considered **well-formed**. A well-formed XML document does not have to contain or reference a DTD. A well-formed document is *parsable*, i.e. it is **syntactically** correct although it may not yet have all the information that makes it **semantically** meaningful.

WELL-FORMED XML	Document must start with the XML declaration, <?xml version ="1.0"?>
	All elements must be contained within one root element
	All elements must be nested in a tree structure without overlapping
	All non-empty elements must have start and end tags

A well-formed XML document that also conforms to a DTD is **valid**. When an XML document containing or referencing a DTD is parsed, the parsing application can verify that the XML conforms to the DTD. The application may then proceed with the assurance that all data elements and their content follow rules defined in the DTD.

The XML document in Figure 18.30 conforms to the DTD referenced in it with the *doctype* tags. In fact, it was derived from the DTD by a JBuilder tool.

The XML document in Figure 18.31 was created by extracting data from the *Players* table using an XML data-aware component in JBuilder. Although it contains data, the browser view of this document will simply list the data as a continuous string unless it is rendered in the browser with an associated stylesheet.

```
<?xml version ="1.0" encoding="UTF-8"?>
<!DOCTYPE xmlPlayerlist SYSTEM "xmlPlayerlist.dtd">
<xmlPlayerlist>
    <xmlPlayer>
        <ufa_id>pcdata</ufa_id>
        <surname>pcdata</surname>
        <forename>pcdata</forename>
        <dateofbirth>pcdata</dateofbirth>
        <squad_no>pcdata</squad_no>
        <position>pcdata</position>
        <nationality>pcdata</nationality>
        <club>pcdata</club>
    </xmlPlayer>
</xmlPlayerlist>
```

Figure 18.30 Well formed and valid XML document.

```
<?xml version ="1.0" encoding="UTF-8"?>
<!DOCTYPE xmlPlayerlist SYSTEM "xmlPlayerlist.dtd">
<xmlPlayerlist>
  <xmlPlayer>
    <ufa_id>AK675280</ufa_id>
    <surname>BACON</surname>
    <forename>ANTONIO</forename>
    <dateofbirth>1978-03-05 00:00:00.0</dateofbirth>
    <squad_no>18</squad_no>
    <position>defender</position>
    <nationality>WONDERLAND</nationality>
    <club>Purity FC</club>
  </xmlPlayer>
  <xmlPlayer>
    <ufa_id>AN971765</ufa_id>
    <surname>AUSTEN</surname>
    <forename>PETER</forename>
    <dateofbirth>1985-06-23 00:00:00.0</dateofbirth>
    <squad_no>23</squad_no>
    <position>midfield</position>
    <nationality>UTOPIA</nationality>
```

Figure 18.31 XML document: partial listing (*continued overleaf*).

```
        <club>Purity FC</club>
      </xmlPlayer>
...
```

Figure 18.31 (*Continued*)

Figure 18.32 shows how the XML document would appear in a browser without the benefit of an applied style.

```
AK675280 BACON ANTONIO 1978-03-05 00:00:00.0 18 defender WONDERLAND
Purity FC AN971765 AUSTEN PETER 1985-06-23 00:00:00.0 23 midfield
UTOPIA Purity FC AT245876 HEGEL BRIAN 1984-03-22 00:00:00.0 27
midfield UTOPIA Beauty United BT46286 MORE MARC 1980-02-04 00:00:00.0
16 defender ELDORADO Beauty United DX26497 ERASMUS EDUARDO 1984-02-07
00:00:00.0 14 forward ELDORADO Purity FC ED24659 SOCRATES VICTOR 1980-
07-12 00:00:00.0 12 midfield LILLIPUT Beauty United EG385190 JUSTINIAN
FRANCIS 1982-08-13 00:00:00.0 11 defender UTOPIA Purity FC EH382645
JOHN PAUL 1984-03-22 00:00:00.0 10 defender PURGATORY Purity FC
FT246517 GREGORY ALAN 1976-07-02 00:00:00.0 9 forward UTOPIA Beauty
United KL23659 PAUL CHARLES 1981-05-12 00:00:00.0 8 midfield
WONDERLAND Beauty United NH42764 ARISTOTLE NIKOS 1980-09-03 00:00:00.0
7 forward UTOPIA Purity FC PG46385 TIBERIUS EDGAR 1
...
```

Figure 18.32 XML document: no style.

The player list view stylesheet shown in Figure 18.33 formats the same XML file as a list of selected attributes (Figure 18.34). The player rows are sorted in surname order.

The stylesheet inserts HTML list tags <dl> </dl> around the row data, which is processed in a loop. The *surname* and *forename* values are embedded in a <dt> </dt> pair and the other attributes are embedded in a <dd> </dd> pair.

The players table view derived from the same XML file is shown in Figure 18.35. The same data has been given a completely different appearance by an alternative stylesheet (Figure 18.36).

There are a number of data-aware components in the JBuilder design palette that are specifically tailored either to output dynamic XML documents from SQL queries or to store XML data in database tables. The dynamic output can be formatted with a standard set of stylesheets for a particular application.

```xml
<?xml version ="1.0"?>
<xsl:stylesheet xmlns:xsl="http://www.w3.org/1999/XSL/Transform"
version ="1.0"
xmlns:java="http://xml.apache.org/xslt/java"
exclude-result-prefixes="java">
<xsl:output method="xml" indent="yes"/>
<xsl:output encoding="ISO-8859-1"/>
<xsl:strip-space elements ="*"/>
  <xsl:template match="/">
    <html>
        <head>
           <xsl:element name="title">Players List View </xsl:element>
        </head>
        <body>
          <xsl:element name="h1">ListView of Players:</xsl:element>
          <xsl:element name="h1">xmlPlayerlist.xml Transformed by
                PlayerListView.xsl </xsl:element>
            <dl>
              <xsl:for-each select ="xmlPlayerlist/xmlPlayer">
                 <xsl:sort select ="surname"/>
                   <xsl:element name="dt">
                           <xsl:value-of select ="surname"/>
                           ,
                           <xsl:value-of select ="forename"/>
                   </xsl:element>
                   <xsl:element name="dd">
                   playing for
                           <i><xsl:value-of select ="club"/></i>
                           , Nationality:
                           <xsl:value-of select ="nationality"/>
                           , Position:
                           <xsl:value-of select ="position"/>
                   </xsl:element>
                </xsl:for-each>
            </dl>
         </body>
         </html>
  </xsl:template>
</xsl:stylesheet>
```

Figure 18.33 Player list view stylesheet.

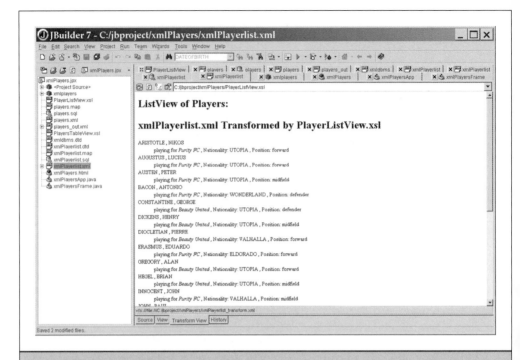

Figure 18.34 List view display.

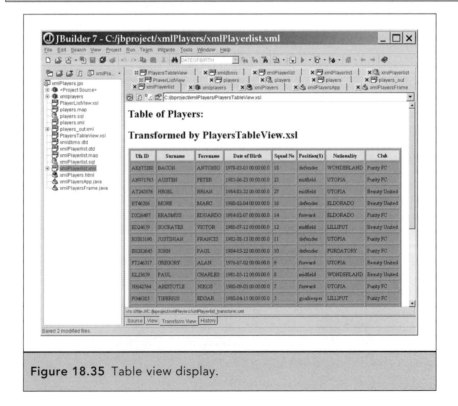

Figure 18.35 Table view display.

```
<?xml version ="1.0"?>
<xsl:stylesheet
xmlns:xsl ="http://www.w3.org/1999/XSL/Transform"
version ="1.0"
xmlns:java="http://xml.apache.org/xslt/java"
exclude-result-prefixes="java">
<xsl:output method="xml" indent="yes"/>
<xsl:output encoding="ISO-8859-1"/>
<xsl:strip-space elements ="*"/>
<xsl:template match="/">
  <html>        <head>
    <xsl:element name="title">Players Table View: xml </xsl:element>
    </head>        <body>
      <xsl:element name="h1">Table of Players: xmlPlayerlist.xml
                 Transformed by PlayersTableList.xsl </xsl:element>
      <xsl:element name = "table">
        <xsl:attribute name="border">2</xsl:attribute>
        <xsl:attribute name="bgColor">#FF8040</xsl:attribute>
        <xsl:attribute name="cellPadding">3</xsl:attribute>
        <xsl:attribute name="cellSpacing">3</xsl:attribute>
        <xsl:attribute name="frame">box</xsl:attribute>
        <xsl:attribute name="bordercolor">black</xsl:attribute>
        <xsl:attribute name="rules">all</xsl:attribute>
        <tr BGCOLOR = "Yellow">
         <th>Ufa ID</th><th>Surname</th><th>Forename</th><th>
            Date of Birth</th><th>Squad No</th><th>Position($)</th>
         <th>Nationality</th><th>Club</th>
        </tr>
        <xsl:for-each select ="xmlPlayerlist/xmlPlayer">
          <xsl:sort select ="ufa_id"/>
            <tr>
            <xsl:element name="td">
                    <xsl:value-of select ="ufa_id"/>
            </xsl:element>
        <xsl:element name="td">
                <xsl:value-of select ="surname"/>
        </xsl:element>
        <xsl:element name="td">
                <xsl:value-of select ="forename"/>
        </xsl:element>
        <xsl:element name="td">
```

Figure 18.36 *Players* table view stylesheet (*continued overleaf*).

```
                    <xsl:value-of select ="dateofbirth"/>
        </xsl:element>
        <xsl:element name="td">
                <xsl:value-of select ="squad_no"/>
        </xsl:element>
        <xsl:element name="td">
                <xsl:value-of select ="position"/>
        </xsl:element>
        <xsl:element name="td">
                <xsl:value-of select ="nationality"/>
        </xsl:element>
        <xsl:element name="td">
                <xsl:value-of select ="club"/>
        </xsl:element>
    </tr>
    </xsl:for-each>
  </xsl:element>
</body>  </html>  </xsl:template>  </xsl:stylesheet>
```

Figure 18.36 (*Continued*)

18.8.2   WHY USE XML?

XML is an Internet standard for information exchange. It facilitates efficient data communication where the data is in many different formats and sourced from different platforms. The data can be sent to many different platforms and separating presentation from content allows it to appear in different formats.

Web-based applications can be built using XML, which helps the interoperation of web, database, networking and middleware. XML provides a structured format for data transmission. It enables the representation of data in a manner that can be self-describing and thus universally used. As an open standard it offers platform and application independence.

18.9   KEY TERMS

Applet	Relatively simple to engineer; needs to be embedded in static web page. Sophisticated functionality may need massive support files downloaded. Subject to stringent security restrictions and attack through reverse engineering
RMI applet/ server	Thin applet responsible only for GUI; may still need support archives and still needs a static web page. Business logic and

	data access in server not easily subject to attack. Server may contact any other host as necessary
Servlet	Simpler architecture to engineer. Restricted to standard HTML events (*Get*, *Post* etc.). Server facilities provided by web host; no restriction on contacting other hosts. More secure than applet. Code is not downloaded, but its name is revealed in the web page.
Enterprise bean	Captures business logic in a class that relies on a server for instantiation. Methods callable from servlets or JSP. Beans can be stateful (have attributes) or stateless. Variable lifetime and user connectivity. Used to assemble large applications from standard bean components
JSP	No static web page; the JSP is the page. Operates with same security rating as the web server. JSP can use all types of bean. No real limitation on functionality. Complicated initial configuration. Easy to maintain complex systems
XML	Markup standard derived from SGML. Data can be extracted from a database or written back to tables. XML documents transformed through styles into HTML. Data-aware components may be used to create dynamic XML documents or to store XML data.

18.10 EXERCISES

(i) Design the *Clubs* form, described in Chapter 14. Implement it as an applet in a web page.

(ii) Adapt the implementation of the *Players* form from Chapter 14 to display in a web page. Use servlet technology to create both the user interface and support the combobox queries.

(iii) Adapt the *matchResults* form in Chapter 14 to display in a web page. Use JSP technology supported by data-aware components in a bean.

(iv) Adapt the *matchResults* report from Chapter 14 to display in a web page. Use XML and a suitable stylesheet to format the report.

CHAPTER 19

PARALLEL DATABASES

There isn't a Parallel of Latitude but thinks it would have been the Equator if it
had had its rights.

Mark Twain, *Following the Equator*

This chapter outlines some performance and reliability issues associated with traditional, single processor, centralized database systems, and describes a number of architectural alternatives devised to alleviate such problems. Specific focus is given to parallel database architectures that enable a single database to distribute its associated query processing across multiple processors and disks.

19.1 ⊆ RELIABILITY, AVAILABILITY AND SCALABILITY

Today, the majority of commercial database systems adopt either a simple client–server architecture or, increasingly less likely, a multi-user mainframe architecture. The rationale for the client–server model over that of the mainframe model is detailed in Chapter 12. Figure 19.1 shows a diagram of the client–server database architecture. The database server is responding to simultaneous client requests.

The number of clients, the network type and topology, the server capacity, and the amount of processing carried out at the client side can all vary. However, the quintessential architecture of a client–server database system remains as shown. That is, independent processors, running client software on physically remote machines, make database requests via a communication network and receive responses from a separate processor running database server software.

A client–server database is an example of distributed processing. Essentially, the database application is split between the client and the database server. The client carries out the so-called presentation logic and provides a user interface that enables an end-user to make database requests and to view the results of such

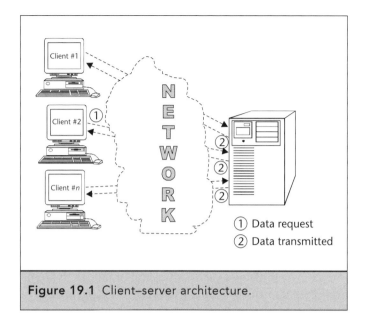

Figure 19.1 Client–server architecture.

requests. The client may also perform some application-specific business logic, such as data validation against entries that the end-user may wish to insert into the database. Client-side data validation helps to limit the amount of network communication between client and server, and so reduces processing of invalid user requests.

The responsibilities of the database server are to accept client requests, to service those requests, and to return the result back to the client. The database server is also responsible for ensuring consistent concurrent access, recovery and security of the database system.

The database systems provided by most university computing labs generally consist of a single database server, with many lab-based client workstations running vendor-specific client software. In the case of Oracle, all client machines would usually require a copy of SQL*Plus to handle user interaction, and a local copy of Oracle Net networking software to communicate with the Oracle server. Figure 19.2 details Oracle's client–server architecture. Full details of Oracle processes are discussed in Chapter 11.

In certain situations, this simple client–server architecture can be problematic. Specific issues of concern are database reliability, data availability, transaction throughput and database scalability.

The standard client–server system involves only a single server. Such systems are referred to as *centralized database systems.* All of the data resides in a single central location. If the database server fails then all of the data located at that central location is unavailable and all client requests will fail.

Centralized database systems have a *single point of failure.* With small, non-mission-critical systems this is not considered a particular handicap. If the server fails, then the users (clients) will just have to wait until it is repaired and back online.

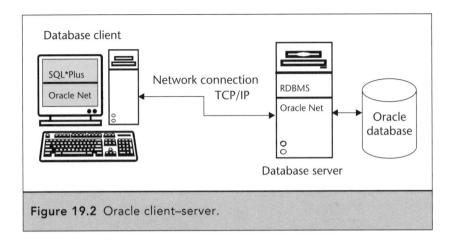

Figure 19.2 Oracle client–server.

In the majority of cases, where data availability is considered essential to the functioning of the business, such a situation of failure has to be avoided. The solution to the problem of restricted availability relies on identifying the potential areas of data server congestion and failure and taking appropriate measures to either prevent them or quickly recover from them.

In terms of hardware failure on the database server, the hard disk(s) could crash or its memory or processor could fail. A simple hardware solution to disk crashes is to have a backup disk that *mirrors* the data on the main, or *master*, disk. If the master disk fails, then processing is immediately switched to the backup, or *slave*, disk, which then becomes the master, allowing the original master disk to be repaired or replaced at a convenient point. Such *fault tolerance* is at the disk level, not the database level, and is an example of *hardware redundancy*. Indeed, from the database server's perspective, it is reading and writing to the same logical local disk, regardless of whether it is physically writing to the master or slave device.

A hardware level solution is also available for processor failure. This relies on hosting the database server on a multiprocessor hardware platform, and running it over a suitable multiprocessor operating system. Unix can theoretically have up to 64 individual CPUs configured for symmetric multiprocessing. Should an individual processor fail, the operating system can automatically bypass the bad CPU and continue processing. This allows for inbuilt, and transparent, *CPU failure tolerance*.

To more reliably avoid memory, disk or processor failure, it is necessary to have access to a **synchronized** backup database operating on a completely separate hardware platform (memory, processor, hard disk and software). To maintain such a replicated database server requires its data, and the data's associated operations, to be duplicated at the database level rather than at the disk level. This is necessary as an incorrectly functioning processor or memory could result in invalid data being written to disk. Making a copy of such incorrect data to the backup disk would merely hide the underlying hardware problem.

By replicating data operations on the backup database server as well as on the main database server, it is possible to validate the outcome of the operation on the original server and identify any subtle, non-catastrophic, server failure that may have occurred. In such an event all processing would be transparently redirected to the backup. This architecture allows for transparent **failover** in the event of any server hardware failure.

The difficulty with such a model is in maintaining synchronicity between the current master server and its mirrored replica. This problem, and the various solutions proposed, is examined in Section 20.6 on replication. That section also explains how replication of data can be used to optimize data availability as well as increase database server accessibility.

The size of the database and the throughput of transactions against it can also affect performance. A database that can handle 1 GByte of data and 100 transactions per second may fail to handle 10 TByte of data with 1000 transactions per second. Such a failure is referred to as a failure of *scalability*. This is a common problem that besets database application systems that are inadequately tested for future growth or throughput prior to rollout. It is also a problem that can lie dormant for some time as the database continues to grow towards its non-documented maximum.

Solutions to problems of scale lie in the realm of parallelism: the ability to take a large problem, break it into small parts, work on each of those parts simultaneously and then merge the part solutions into a single solution to the original problem. Parallel database architectures developed to achieve scalability are discussed in Section 19.4.

Data that is accessed across a network, as in the case of a client–server database system, is of course affected by the availability of the network connection between the client and the server. In a centralized server architecture, if the network connection to the database server is unavailable no client data processing can occur. Once again, a single point of failure exists.

A possible solution to such total failure is to have more than one database server, and to position each server at a different node of the network. In a local area network these would, in all likelihood, be **replication servers**.

It was, until recently, generally thought preferable to partition the database between a number of database servers, and to locate each server next to the group of clients that make most use of that data subset.

This geographical distribution of data is used to achieve high *locality of reference* and to limit the effect of any single database server failure or network inaccessibility. The benefits are primarily to those clients that are collocated with the server. However, increasingly reliable, secure and fast wide area network connections are reducing the range of situations where systems designers would consider data distribution, or fragmentation, as a fundamental requirement for a new information system. Such distributed database architectures, and the various issues associated with them, are discussed in Chapter 20.

19.2 ⊨ PARALLEL DATABASES

As the amount of data in a database increases, or the number of transactions against a database multiplies, it may become necessary to increase the database's physical resources in order to maintain an acceptable level of performance. If an agreed maximum transaction response time is one second, then it should always be one second (or less) regardless of the size of the database. Likewise, if the number of transaction requests increases from 100 per second to 1000 per second, the maximum response time for a single transaction should remain at one second. If a database has these properties, it is said to possess *linear scale-up*.

A related database property to scale-up is that of *speed-up*. A database possessing *linear speed-up* can reduce the time it takes to process a fixed number of transactions, against a fixed sized database, *proportionate* to the amount of resources the database has available to it. A database containing 1 GByte of data, and averaging one hundred transactions per second, achieves a response of one second per transaction. If the database's resources are increased by a factor of 10, the response should decrease to one tenth of a second per transaction.

Database resources include processors (CPUs), memory and data disks. The principal factor in achieving good speed-up and scale-up is essentially the number of processors that are provided in the system. Increases in the computational power of individual CPUs (uniprocessors) only marginally improve the performance of a database system compared with the addition of further CPUs. The reason for this is that individual processors, no matter how fast, operate in a serial manner (one operation at a time).

If a transaction, consisting of 10 individual file and buffer operations, currently takes 1 second to process on a uniprocessor database. Each operation averages 0.1 seconds. If the speed of the processor is improved by 25%, the transaction will (at best, given disk I/O etc.) take 0.75 seconds, with each operation taking 25% less time to complete. However, if instead of purchasing a faster processor, an additional slower processor was installed in the database host, performance could improve by up to 100%. The transaction would take only 0.5 seconds to complete, even though each operation would continue to average 0.1 seconds. Such a significant improvement is achieved because it is possible to perform each of the 10

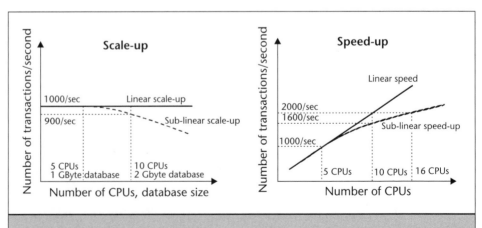

Figure 19.3 Scale-up and speed-up.

operations in parallel. Indeed, in such a situation, with 10 separate processors, transaction throughput could be improved by as much as 1000%.

Figure 19.3 shows examples of scale-up and speed-up graphs. Straight lines identify both linear speed-up and linear scale-up, whereas sub-linear performance is indicated by the graph's reducing curves.

19.3 ⊖ PARALLEL ARCHITECTURES

There are three main architectural models for parallel database servers: **shared memory**, **shared disk** and **shared nothing**.

19.3.1 SHARED MEMORY ARCHITECTURE

The shared memory parallel database model is generally built upon a *symmetrical multiprocessing* (SMP) architecture. This model consists of a host computer with multiple processors (CPUs). All of the host's memory, and each of its attached disks, is accessible by each one of its processors. As both memory and disks are shared, this architecture is also referred to as *shared everything*. A simple SMP shared memory model is outlined in Figure 19.4.

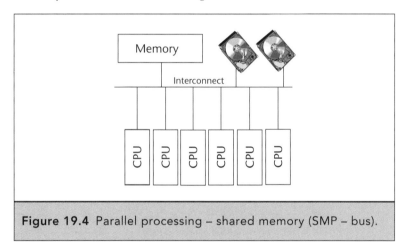

Figure 19.4 Parallel processing – shared memory (SMP – bus).

Even though it is possible for an SMP system to share a single disk, a more usual configuration would include a set of integrated disks. The main drawback with the SMP model is that the CPUs are connected via a shared bus to the same pool of memory. There is a limit to the number of processors that can be effectively accommodated with an acceptable level of memory bandwidth contention. The optimum number of processors is generally between 4 and 16.

A number of recent advances in memory-to-CPU interconnection, such as crossbar switching, as shown in Figure 19.5, and the introduction of large processor cache memories, have reduced memory contention and raised the

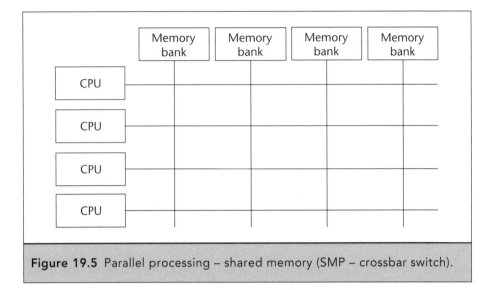

Figure 19.5 Parallel processing – shared memory (SMP – crossbar switch).

number of CPUs that can effectively be accommodated in an SMP implementation to over 32. However, shared memory architectures are also constrained by the necessity to maintain memory consistency through the use of some form of synchronization mechanism (e.g. semaphores or locks) in order to restrict conflicting simultaneous access to the same item of memory. As the processors of a shared memory system share a common set of disk drives, the level of scalability that is achievable is also constrained by the available disk input-output bandwidth. Too small a bandwidth will cause a high level of contention between processors and therefore reduce scalability.

A more recent alternative to the tightly coupled shared memory architecture of SMP is the loosely coupled *non-uniform memory access* architecture (NUMA), shown in Figure 19.6. In this scheme, all interconnected processors have access to all memory. However, unlike SMP, memory access costs are dependent on whether

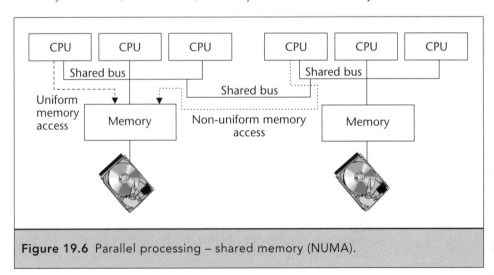

Figure 19.6 Parallel processing – shared memory (NUMA).

the processor is accessing its own *local* memory or making a *remote* access to the local memory of another processor. When a processor requires remote memory, effective *cache coherency* protocols are used to fetch the remote memory into the processor's local memory.

Performance in NUMA systems, as with SMP, is limited by memory bus bandwidth. Contention increases as CPUs are added to the system, and beyond a certain point, performance can start to decrease rather than increase. Such a diminishing return violates both linear scale-up and speed-up. The exact point at which adding CPUs to a system results in minimal (or negative) performance improvement varies with application type and system architecture. It is generally recognized that most typical shared memory systems do not scale well beyond 64 processors. Even though there is little interprocessor communication overhead resulting from using common memory structures, because of memory bus and disk I/O contention, neither SMP nor NUMA shared memory architectures will ever be able to offer true linear scalability beyond a limited number of processors.

Nevertheless, an advantage of these shared memory systems, from the perspective of database vendors and system architects, is that applications currently running on single-processor-based hardware do not have to undergo major rewrites in order to enjoy an incremental performance improvement by being ported to shared memory systems.

19.3.2 SHARED DISK ARCHITECTURE

Unlike the single node shared memory model, the shared disk model consists of multiple processing nodes; each with its own dedicated memory, connected to a set of common disks. Each node can either contain a single CPU or can implement its own SMP or NUMA shared memory architecture.

A shared disk model can be built either on top of a *massively parallel processing* (MPP) distributed memory substructure, or around a cluster of loosely coupled cooperating nodes. In MPP architectures, processing nodes communicate by sending messages to each other over a very fast interconnect network, whereas nodes in a cluster communicate via message passing over a high-speed bus. In a shared disk cluster configuration, each node is connected to a common set of database disks via a high-speed data bus.

In an MPP shared disk architecture, each node is physically connected to its own private disk, but executes a system-level *virtual disk layer* that enables access to the complete set of database disks. Oracle uses the notion of *disk affinity* to enable an MPP shared disk configuration access over its databases. Figure 19.7 gives an example of a clustered SMP shared disk architecture, and Figure 19.8 outlines an MPP shared disk example.

As memory is not shared amongst the nodes of a shared disk parallel database, each node has to have its own instance of the database server process and a data cache. Consequently, given that disks are shared, a *lock manager* is required to maintain *cache consistency* across all the nodes, and locks are used to ensure that each node in the cluster continues to have the same view of the data. The additional

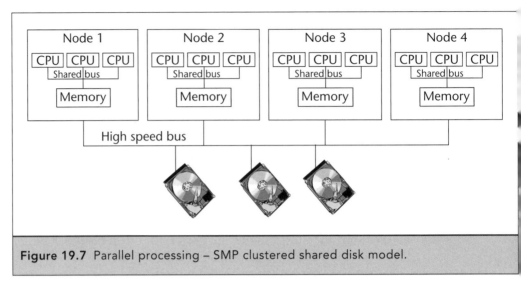

Figure 19.7 Parallel processing – SMP clustered shared disk model.

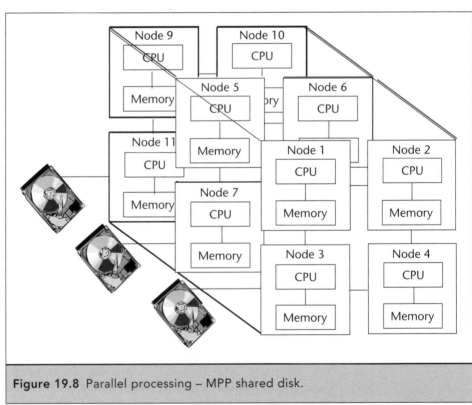

Figure 19.8 Parallel processing – MPP shared disk.

overhead in maintaining such locks and ensuring data cache consistency results in a negative impact on scalability and performance. Also, as the shared disk model uses *data shipping* to move data from disk to node, I/O bandwidth acts as an additional constraint upon achievable levels of scalability. However, as there is no memory contention, the shared disk model generally scales better than a shared memory model.

19.3.3   SHARED NOTHING ARCHITECTURE

As with the shared disk model, a shared nothing parallel database can either be built on top of an MPP environment, or can be constructed over a clustered set of nodes. In either case, each of the nodes will be attached to a dedicated disk (or *disk pool*), with each disk containing a discrete portion of the overall database. Figure 19.9 shows a high-level view of such architecture.

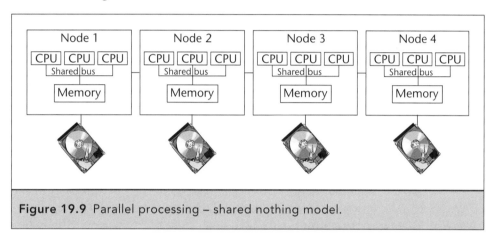

Figure 19.9 Parallel processing – shared nothing model.

Each shared nothing node maintains a separate instance of the database process. In contrast to the shared disk model, a shared nothing node can only directly access the portion of database data contained in its own physically attached disk(s). If the data to be processed by a particular node resides on a disk connected to another node then it needs to send an appropriate processing request message to that node.

The recipient node will then process the requested data operation and return the result set to the requesting node. Such function shipping is costly and should be minimized in order to maximize the scalability of the shared nothing model. Theo-retically, because neither memory nor disk is shared, the shared nothing model could provide linear scalability for an unlimited number of processors. Indeed, shared nothing machines containing many hundreds of processors have already been developed.

However, such a situation is highly dependent on the degree of parallelism supported by the operating system and application software running over such architecture, and the effectiveness with which the database is distributed across the nodes. If an operation performed at a particular node has local access to all the data it requires then it will perform well.

If it does not, a function-shipping request will need to be passed to the node that does posses the data. This can result in node hot spots where the same data is frequently requested, and this in turn can reduce scalability because of the resulting disk I/O and processor bottlenecks.

19.4 DATABASE PARALLELISM

There are four different types of parallelism that can be applied to database applications (Table 19.1).

Table 19.1 Database parallelism.
Inter-transactional parallelism
Intra-transactional (inter-query) parallelism
Intra-query (inter-operator) parallelism
Intra-operator parallelism

19.4.1 INTER-TRANSACTIONAL PARALLELISM

Inter-transactional parallelism is the simultaneous execution of different transactions. All database systems interleave the operations of different transactions in order to achieve acceptable levels of concurrency (see Section 8.4.1 on serializability). However, such *time slicing* does not increase overall transaction throughput, only distributes it more evenly. This is because transaction operations are still performed serially. With inter-transactional parallelism, it is possible to allocate transactions to different processors for simultaneous processing.

19.4.2 INTRA-TRANSACTIONAL PARALLELISM

Intra-transactional parallelism is the parallel execution of different database queries belonging to the same transaction. In many cases, a transaction's queries exhibit *execution-independence*. This enables such queries to be executed in parallel. A transaction to 'swap' a player in one club for a player in another club will contain four update instructions and two inserts. Each player will have their current 'team' attribute updated in the *Players* table, the *left* attribute of their current contract will be updated to the date of transfer and a new row will be inserted for each of the two players' contracts with their new club. All six of these queries are combined into a single, atomic logical unit of work (LUW). However, each individual query has execution independence of the other five. Therefore, all six can be executed in parallel, the only constraint being that the transaction is not committed until all six queries are successfully executed.

19.4.3   INTRA-QUERY PARALLELISM

Intra-query parallelism is the parallel execution of a query's constituent database operations. Every query, transactional or otherwise, consists of a set of discrete database operations derived from the relational algebra.

For example, the SQL query in Figure 19.10 can be broken down into the five relational algebra operations of Figure 19.11. The *Players* restriction and the *Contracts* restriction can be performed in parallel, as they are process-independent of each other.

```
SELECT surname, firstname, salary
FROM Players, Contracts
WHERE Players.ufa_id = Contracts.ufa_id
AND Contracts.left IS NULL
AND Players.club = 'Beauty United';
```

Figure 19.10 Intra-query SQL statement.

```
RESTRICT Contracts ON Contracts.left IS NULL → T1;
PROJECT T1 OVER surname, firstname, ufa_id → T3
RESTRICT Players ON Players.club = 'Beauty United' → T2;
PROJECT T2 OVER salary, ufa_id → T4.
JOIN T3 AND T4 ON T3.ufa_id = T4.ufa_id → ANSWER;
```

Figure 19.11 Parallel processing – multi-operation relational algebra.

The same is true of the two project operations. Both pairs of operations can therefore benefit from intra-query parallelism by executing on separate nodes. This type of intra-query parallelism is known as *independent parallelism.*

It should be noted that the relationship between each of the two restricts, and their corresponding projects, is that of a producer and a consumer. The project operation takes as input the output of the restrict operation.

As there is no requirement for each restrict's output to have been *completed* prior to it being input to the corresponding project operation, it is possible for the two projects to be performed in parallel with the two restricts, consuming each restricted tuple as it is produced. This allows for a type of intra-query parallelism known as *pipelining*. Figure 19.12 shows a high-level overview of both types of intra-query parallelism.

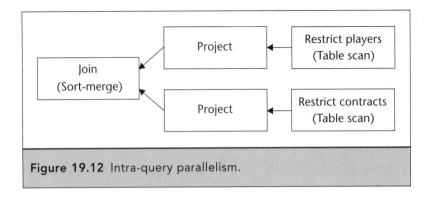

Figure 19.12 Intra-query parallelism.

19.4.4 INTRA-OPERATOR PARALLELISM

Intra-operator parallelism is the parallel execution of a single database operation. This type of parallelism is often referred to as *partition parallelism* as it relies on database tables being partitioned across a number of separate processing nodes.

Ignoring the question of indexing, the *Players* restrict operation of Figure 19.12 will require a full table scan of the *Players* relation. If, however, *Players* data were equally distributed across a number of processing nodes, then it would be possible to scan each section of the relation in parallel, and, using pipelined parallelism, to project each set of results at additional processing nodes.

Figure 19.13 demonstrates how the speed of the restrict and project operations of Figure 19.12 can be proportionally increased in relation to the number of processing nodes used for intra-operator parallelism. Intra-operator parallelism is ideally suited to shared nothing architectures, where each node has a dedicated disk partition.

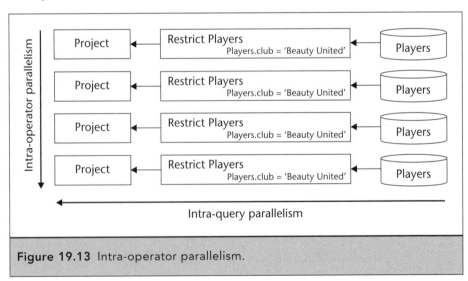

Figure 19.13 Intra-operator parallelism.

In such an architecture, disk blocking (commonly known as interference) is removed and linear speed-up is possible. However, in order to achieve such levels of parallelism it is necessary to use an appropriate horizontal data-partitioning technique.

19.4.5   RANGE PARTITIONING

Range partitioning involves splitting a data relation and assigning each row to a particular disk on the basis of the value of one or more of its attributes. The *Matches* table could be split according to which season the match occurred, with a separate disk partition created for all the matches associated with a particular season. Such a technique would enable all of a season's match data to reside at a single node. This would allow queries involving the *Matches* table to be processed in parallel according to season. Figure 19.14 shows the Oracle SQL (DDL) statement required to split the *Matches* table across four disk partitions.

```
CREATE TABLE Matches (
match_ID NUMBER,
    homeClub VARCHAR2(25),
    awayClub VARCHAR2(25),
    matchDate DATE,
    season VARCHAR2(8))
PARTITION BY RANGE (season)
(PARTITION season_00 VALUES LESS THAN ('2001/02') TABLESPACE node1,
 PARTITION season_01 VALUES LESS THAN ('2002/03') TABLESPACE node2,
 PARTITION season_02 VALUES LESS THAN ('2003/04') TABLESPACE node3,
 PARTITION season_03 VALUES LESS THAN ('2004/05') TABLESPACE node4);
```

Figure 19.14 Creating range partitions in Oracle.

It is important to note that in the given example, a certain amount of house-keeping is required to ensure that the table always has a partition defined for the current season. Therefore, at the end of each season, a new partition will need to be added to the table for the following season's matches. Figure 19.15 provides an Oracle SQL example of such an operation.

```
ALTER TABLE Matches
ADD PARTITION season_04 VALUES LESS THAN ('2005/06')
TABLESPACE node1;
```

Figure 19.15 Creating a new range partition in Oracle.

It is also possible to remove particular partitions from a range-partitioned table, although care will need to be taken to ensure that deleting such data breaks no referential integrity constraints. Figure 19.16 shows how to delete a data partition containing historical data that is no longer required.

```
ALTER TABLE Matches
DROP PARTITION season_00;
```

Figure 19.16 Removing a range partition in Oracle.

Range partitioning is particularly useful when there are distinct logical ranges of data that require storing together and where the resulting partitions are likely to be processed in parallel. In order to achieve maximum intra-operation parallelism, it is essential that data is evenly distributed across all partitions.

19.4.6 HASH PARTITIONING

Hash partitioning involves partitioning a relation's tuples on the basis of a value that is calculated for each of the table's rows through the use of a fixed function applied against one (or more) of the relation's attributes.

Although the hashing function used by the database server is opaque from the perspective of the table's creator, it will always be guaranteed to split the tuples of a relation into a user-defined number of partitions.

Hash partitioning is most appropriate in two specific situations: firstly, where the hashing attribute is a key to the relation and this results in evenly sized partitions that can perform full table scans using intra-operator parallelism; and secondly, where the partitioning attribute is the subject of frequent *point* queries that require the selection of all tuples with a specific value for that attribute. Figure 19.17 gives an example of creating hash partitions using Oracle SQL.

```
CREATE TABLE Goals (
match_ID NUMBER,
    UFA_ID VARCHAR2(10),
    minute NUMBER,
    type VARCHAR2(10))
PARTITION BY HASH (match_ID)
PARTITIONS 4 -- partitions created with system-generated names
STORE IN (node1, node2, node3, node4);
```

Figure 19.17 Creating hash partitions in Oracle.

19.4.7 ROUND ROBIN PARTITIONING

Round robin partitioning involves evenly splitting a data relation between a fixed number of partitions, regardless of attribute values. Therefore, if there are n partitions, the relation's ith tuple will be allocated to partition P on the basis of $(P_i \bmod n)$. Given four partitions, the tenth tuple of a relation would always be placed at the second partition. However, the round robin technique is only optimum in situations where entire relations require processing and intra-operation parallelism can be maximized. In situations where small subsets of a relation's tuples are required, such as frequently occurs when *associatively accessing* tuples on the basis of particular attribute values, or it would usually be more efficient to partition according to the possible values of the operation's predicate attribute. Oracle does not support round robin partitioning.

19.4.8 LIST PARTITIONING

List partitioning is a partitioning technique introduced by Oracle with its Oracle 9i database product. List partitioning works by distributing a relation's tuples across partitions according to discrete attribute values.

Therefore, unlike range partitioning, it is possible to allow the database administrator a finer level of control over the mapping of tuples to partitions.

This is of most benefit in achieving a set of *balanced* partitions where a relation's data distribution follows discrete values of the partitioning attribute. A balanced partition is related to a uniform number of disk accesses across partitions, rather than an even distribution of tuples between partitions. Figure 19.18 provides an example of table creation using list partitioning.

```
CREATE TABLE Goals (
match_ID NUMBER,
   UFA_ID VARCHAR2(10),
   minute NUMBER,
   type VARCHAR2(10))
PARTITION BY LIST (type)
(PARTITION misc VALUES ('own goal', 'disallowed') TABLESPACE node1,
 PARTITION penalty VALUES ('penalty') TABLESPACE node2,
 PARTITION standard VALUES ('goal') TABLESPACE node3);
```

Figure 19.18 Creating list partitions in Oracle.

19.5 PERFORMANCE ISSUES

Obtaining maximum scalability through parallelism depends upon the combination of hardware architecture used and the partitioning strategy adopted for each relation by the database developer. The optimum partitioning of database relations is therefore a physical database design issue that needs to be considered. The best partitioning strategies should attempt to maximize parallelism while minimizing *data skew* and inefficient processing.

Data skew produces an increasing variance in the service times of certain operations executing in parallel. This is a result of an unequal distribution of tuples between nodes. If an operation is divided into 10 parallel sub-tasks, the time taken to perform the whole task will be (ignoring any overheads associated with issuing multiple sub-tasks and collating their results) the time taken to execute the slowest sub-task. Therefore, if the operation is a full table scan and the partitioning strategy adopted is round robin, the scan will take 1/10th of the time it would take with no parallelism.

If the partition strategy adopted were range partitioning, and 80% of the tuples were held at one partition, the scan would take 80% of the time it would with no parallelism. Increasing the number of nodes participating in the parallel scan to 20 would reduce the round robin time to 5%. If the distribution were still 80% at a single node, there would be no speed improvement no matter how many nodes were operating in parallel using unchanged range partitioning.

Inefficient processing can also result from the partitioning strategy adopted. Provided the number of clubs does not change, there will always be the same number of matches played each season. Therefore, given 20 clubs, the *matches* table would contain 760 tuples (38 per club) for each season. If the *Matches* table contained data related to four seasons, and this was partitioned using round robin, or range (over season), or hash (over match date), across four partitions, each partition would have 760 tuples assigned to it (provided the hashing algorithm were optimal).

Performing any full table scan, to list all matches for example, would be equally fast regardless of the partitioning technique adopted. Performing an associative access, selecting all matches played in a particular season, would also be equally fast regardless of the partitioning technique, as each node would have to access each of its 760 tuples. However, the resulting 400% speed increase over a single processor system only requires processing to be performed at a single node if the range partitioning technique is used.

Round robin and hash partitioning would require all four nodes to perform the same operation. Range partitioning in this situation therefore enables other processors to participate in inter-query parallelism, and so increases overall system parallelism.

The response time for sequential scans reduces because more processors are used to execute the query, whereas for associative scans the response time improves because the size of the task decreases, as there are fewer tuples stored at each node.

Maximizing performance therefore relies on each relation having an appropriate partitioning strategy for the types of queries that are likely to be asked of it, and the degree of parallelism being optimal for the size and throughput of the particular database. The optimal amount of parallelism for a database system is affected by the cost associated with initiating an operation across a number of nodes. For instance, overall query response time will increase with additional parallelism if the operation initiation time becomes a significant fraction of the operation's total execution time.

If it takes 0.1 seconds to initiate an operation request at a node, and one second for a node to process 100 tuples, one node (i.e. no parallelism) would take 100.1 seconds to process 10,000 tuples. Ten nodes processing 1000 tuples each would take 11 seconds $((0.1 \times 10) + 10)$. One hundred nodes processing 100 tuples each would also take 11 seconds $((0.1 \times 100) + 1)$. One thousand nodes processing 10 tuples each would take 100.1 seconds $((0.1 \times 1000) + 0.1)$. In reality, the cost of using a large number of nodes is even higher than this as it would include the time taken to collate the results of each of the separate sub-tasks.

19.6 KEY TERMS

Centralized database	Simplest form of distributed processing; single point of failure
Hardware redundancy	Mirrored storage; synchronized backup; failure tolerance; transparent failover
Replication servers	Copy subset of data to several remote servers. Defence against host failure or network partition; locality of reference for remote users. Raises problems of synchronization
Parallel architectures	Using more than one CPU to access a single physical database
Shared memory or shared everything	Symmetrical multiprocessing, shared bus; bandwidth limits CPU numbers. Crossbar switching or NUMA increases bandwith
Shared disk	Built on multi-node, massively parallel processing (MPP) or a cluster of loosely coupled cooperating nodes. Each CPU has an Oracle instance; locking and data shipping consume resources and bandwidth: limits to scalability
Shared nothing	Database is partitioned across MPP nodes. Function shipping is costly but can be limited by partition design. Scalability good
Parallel databases	Four characteristic modes
Inter-transactional	Simultaneous execution of transactions allocated to different CPUs
Intra-transactional	Simultaneous execution of statements with independent execution allocated to CPUs

Intra-query	Parallel execution of a single query's constituent operations (file and buffer ops)
Intra-operator	Parallel execution of single query operation. Data must be partitioned
Partitioning	Range; round robin; hash; list

19.7 ⊝ EXERCISES

(i) Investigate the similarities and the difference between concurrency control schemes for parallel databases and distributed databases.

(ii) Investigate the current application of parallelism to object databases.

CHAPTER 20

DISTRIBUTED DATABASES

Good sense is of all things in the world the most equally distributed, for everyone thinks himself so abundantly provided with it

René Descartes, *Discourse on Method*, part I

A distributed database is a collection of independent database installations, situated on different nodes of a local or wide area network. Each of the individual participating databases offers a part of the overall dataset of the distributed database. Any type of database can participate. They could be relational, object or Codasyl, or adhere to any other data model.

The aims of a distributed database are to give a seamless view of the data, hiding the disparities of the underlying host's data model to provide a unified method of accessing the data, to preserve the consistency of the distributed view of the data, and to improve the availability of the dataset.

Distributed databases are most often superimposed on existing local databases. The reasons for doing so are usually more to do with the organization of the business environment than any technical computing factor.

Acquisitions or mergers of companies may bring together several companies that have their own separate information systems. While these individual systems may serve their local businesses, the headquarters of such a group will have a need for correlated reports that represent the trading data of each of the group members (Figure 20.1).

Ownership of the data may also be a factor. Industry associations share data for mutual benefit. The members of such associations would be insistent on retaining overall control of their own systems, but might allow read-only access to certain parts of the data. Insurance companies, for example, share data on accident claims to prevent fraud.

During early research into the problems of distributed databases, it was thought that performance might be a reason for positioning data close to the principal

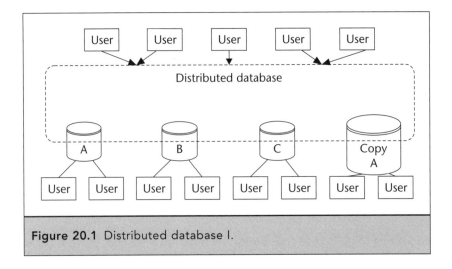

Figure 20.1 Distributed database I.

users. If the groups of users were spread across a wide geographical area, this might once have been a reason for designing data distribution into a new development. The development of fast, secure networks has undermined this rationale and very few distributed databases are designed from the ground up.

Keeping live copies of the data at different sites is another important and current motivation for the use of distributed databases. This has implications for maintaining high availability of the data and for disaster recovery.

20.1.1 COMPLEXITY MODELS

Figure 20.1 shows a typical distributed database. It consists of a partial view of each the participants' datasets. The individual nodes have their own local users who issue local queries. Other users connect to the distributed database. They are global users who issue global queries. The diagram says nothing about the kinds of database servers contributing to the distributed view or how much each node contributes to that view.

A model of the complexity of a distributed database will give an insight into the difficulty or otherwise of providing a satisfactory systems solution to any proposition. Three main factors have to be taken into account: autonomy, distribution and heterogeneity (Figure 20.2).

Autonomy measures the degree to which individual nodes are susceptible to outside control. Clearly, in an array of database servers, each one has its own transaction and recovery mechanism. In a situation where there are local users submitting queries in addition to remote queries against the allowed portion of the schema, it is unlikely that there could be any relaxation or delegation of these controls.

Site autonomy means that each server participating in a distributed database is administered independently from all other databases. Although several databases can work together, each database is a separate repository of data that is managed individually.

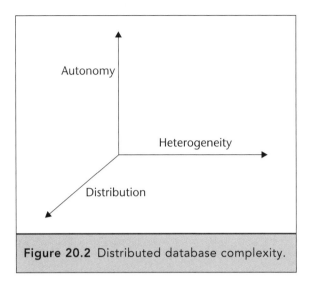

Figure 20.2 Distributed database complexity.

Autonomy represents the level of control that an individual database site has over the data that it holds. It is therefore only of relevance to sites that have local as well as global users. If all users of a distributed database are global users of its collective data then there is no local autonomy.

Heterogeneity is a measure not only of the variety of different vendors' products, but also of the presence of different data models and query languages in the distributed database. The more diverse this factor becomes, the more problematic is the acquisition of a unified view and the provision of a single query mechanism. Most distributed database implementations, especially those necessitated by business acquisition or serving industry associations, will have high heterogeneity ratings.

Distribution measures the degree to which distributed queries will need to take data from more than one site. In a situation where a centralized database is replicated across a series of other nodes, each node is capable of completing any query. Provided updates, insertions and deletions are propagated to each replica, they continue to offer a low distribution rating and offer high availability. If the distributed view has tables spread across many sites or if tables from many sites are required to be joined in most queries, the distribution rating will be high.

However, the three axes of this model give a slightly misleading view. First, the three dimensions are not of equal importance in assessing complexity; nor can they be precisely measured. Further, they not as orthogonal (mutually independent) as the diagram makes them appear.

Perhaps a more realistic model is the taxonomy outlined in Figure 20.3, which classifies distributed databases according to their architecture.

Database heterogeneity is considered the major dimension when classifying distributed database architectures. Such heterogeneity is usually assumed to indicate different DBMSs (such as Oracle and SQL Server) with a similar data model (e.g. relational). However, it could also mean different operating systems, different data models or even different versions of the same DBMS.

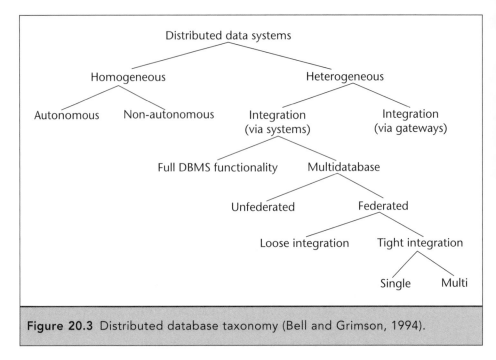

Figure 20.3 Distributed database taxonomy (Bell and Grimson, 1994).

In the case of a multi-site homogeneous network of loosely integrated pre-existing databases, or a federated multi-database made up of pre-existing heterogeneous databases, autonomy is related to how much of each site's databases implies that each constituent database site has complete control over what data is, and more importantly, is not, made available to other sites.

The level of data integration of federated multi-databases can be classified as either *tight* or *loose*. These separate classifications indicate whether (a) there is a global view of the entire distributed database that global users can access; (b) a set of distinct user views can be built directly over the local schemas of the local databases; or (c) export schemas (essentially predefined views of the local conceptual schema) are provided by each local database node in order to exercise its autonomy over local access rights.

Tightly integrated federated multi-databases generally exhibit only a single global conceptual schema. However, it is possible, although rare, and difficult in practice, to enable multiple global conceptual schemas to be constructed over the same component local databases.

The remaining categories of distributed database are heterogeneous databases integrated via the use of software gateways and unfederated multi-databases. With gateway integration, simple low-level network connections are built between component database systems without any of the higher-level system integration that would be necessary to provide the benefits of a single logical database. Unfederated multi-databases provide a single global view of a collection of non-autonomous local databases, and require data queries to be presented via a central coordinating site.

20.1.2   TRANSPARENCIES

If the complexity model provides a guide to the difficulty of providing a system solution, then what is really needed is a guide to how that solution might best be achieved. As with most large-scale problems in computing, the way forward is made clearer by breaking down the overall objective into smaller, more manageable tasks.

The ultimate aim is to provide a mechanism that transforms the complexity of the distributed database into a user view of a single data source that responds in the same way as a local database. This mechanism must also, as far as is possible, be kept hidden from the user so that its presence is **transparent** in the user's view of the data. The key word here is *transparent*.

All distributed systems, of which the distributed database is one example, have similar aims: to raise the level of abstraction, or to generalize the user view of the system so that underlying complexity is hidden (Figure 20.4).

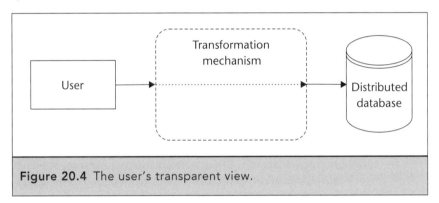

Figure 20.4 The user's transparent view.

The overall transparent view can be described in terms of eight types of transparency that can be linked in a dependency hierarchy. Figure 20.5 shows these dependencies. From the diagram, it can be seen, for example, that scalability transparency is dependent on migration and replication transparencies, which, in turn, are dependent on access and location transparencies.

Access transparency means that a mechanism is provided whereby the user accesses a remote resource in much the same way as a local resource. Mapping a local drive letter in Windows to a subdirectory of a network file server is an example of this. The actual mechanism is hidden: the remote resource is not actually a drive but the head of a directory tree below the remote drive root. Nevertheless, Windows Explorer presents exactly the same file manipulation operations for the mapped drive as for a local drive: directory listings, file copies, cut and paste and so on are all done in the same way.

This same drive mapping is also an example of **location transparency**. The precise location of the remote subdirectory in the map is hidden. If the network administrator had provided the subdirectory on the remote machine as a link to yet another machine, the user accessing files on the mapped drive would be

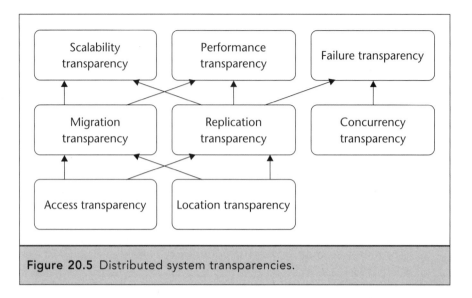

Figure 20.5 Distributed system transparencies.

unaware of the complex chain of network operation required to open a file for editing.

Concurrency transparency means that if remote resources are accessed, and possibly updated, by more than one user at the same time then each user process will be unaware of any interference from the others. Transactions in a local database have their isolation maintained through a lock manager, but extensions to this are required for a distributed transaction. Remote print queues, established so that users may share a high-capacity printing resource, are another instance where user manipulation of their own jobs in the queue needs segregation. The detailed process by which this is achieved is hidden from public view.

When a remote resource changes location, the change is hidden from the user by **migration transparency**. The test for this whether the same SQL statement works before and after the location change, whether the same drive map needs no amendment after the change and so on. Certainly, the DBA or the network administrator will be aware of any such changes and may have to make appropriate alterations. The transparency of the location change is, however, a matter for the user view and if this is preserved, the transparency is maintained.

Network file servers may be mirrored or datasets in databases may be replicated to provide assured availability or better performance. **Replication transparency** means that the user is unaware of which precise copy is being used as a result of an access request. The selection of a particular copy may be made based on optimized response or availability, but that selection is made without the knowledge of the user. In fact, the user should not even be aware of the existence of any copies of the requested resource. Whether there are two or twenty replicas available, the requesting process accesses them in the same way as a local resource (access transparency) and is unaware of which host which is meeting the request (location transparency).

At the highest level of abstraction in the transparency diagram are three related transparencies. **Scalability transparency** attempts to ensure that users are kept unaware of additional resources (service providers) or additional users (service consumers). **Performance transparency** aims to provide the same level of *response* or *throughput* despite fluctuations in demand. **Failure transparency** masks system crashes in individual nodes, partitions (breaks) in the network or software malfunctions. Looking at the dependencies of these transparencies gives a clue as to how they might be realized.

These eight transparencies are not particular to distributed databases. They are essential for many types of distributed systems: network file systems, loosely coupled CPU clusters, process migration schemes and shared memory arrays are other examples.

Distributed databases, however, are among the most complex of distributed system problems and often need solutions for every transparency.

20.2 DISTRIBUTED DATA

Clearly, any approach to providing transparencies for a distributed database must start with the two foundational properties: access and locational transparency. The most important resource in the system is the data in the individual node databases, and it is here that the process of reconciling underlying data models starts. A means must be found of exporting a vision of the data in each of the databases that supports harmonization of the access method, gives a unified view of the data structures and offers scope for hiding the location.

20.2.1 DISTRIBUTED SCHEMAS

Each of the participating databases will have its own data dictionary kept inside the databases. This data dictionary is crucial for maintaining the storage structures and the structural and behavioural rules applied to the data, and for supporting queries from existing local users who may or may not be destined to issue distributed queries. The data dictionary cannot be used directly as it contains all the local definitions.

However, a flexible mechanism for superimposing a different way of looking at the data was described in Chapter 9: the database view. Database views can be constructed to offer maps of internal storage names and common naming conventions that may be required for the distributed queries.

At the simplest level, if one database has an *employee* table with a *surname* attribute and another has a *payroll* table with a *familyname* attribute, these differences can be resolved by views. It may even be possible to construct a view within, say, a Codasyl database, that bridges its normal navigational query language with SQL. Even if it is not possible to do this with the Codasyl database manager, it would surely be possible to build a relatively simple software bridge.

Reference architectures for databases were proposed as long ago as 1972. The American National Standards Institute established the Standards Planning and

Requirements Committee, ANSI/SPARC, which first reported in 1977[1] on a standard architecture for centralized databases. No single model has resulted since different degrees of complexity might or might not support any proposal. However, there are common threads in the various propositions that lead the distributed database designer through this process of matching the disparate data storage (Figure 20.6).

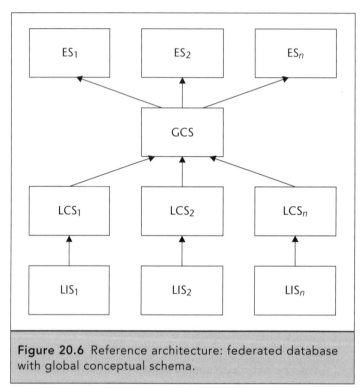

Figure 20.6 Reference architecture: federated database with global conceptual schema.

Each contributing database has its own Local Internal Schema (LIS) related directly to the stored data. A conceptual (or virtual) schema can be constructed at each site using views or external software as appropriate. This is known as the Local Conceptual Schema (LCS); conceptual because it does not refer directly to stored data..

A coordinating host then collects the local conceptual schemas together into a Global Conceptual Schema (GCS). The GCS is the union of the local conceptual schemas. At this stage, the preparations for access transparency are well under way, since the local conceptual schema should conform to a common data model and hence a common query mechanism. The GCS has knowledge of the position of each part of the schema, but not necessarily the way in which access transparency was achieved in the individual site mappings between LIS and LCS.

---

1 This work led on to the establishment of the SQL:1999 and SQL3 standards for relational databases.

A subset of the GCS, the Export Schema (ES), can then be exported to serve the needs of each group of users at the remote query hosts. This subset can vary between just one table and the whole GCS depending on user query requirements. Each of these export schemas is thus configured and customized to serve its user population. The export schemas do not contain location details beyond the location of the GCS, so this architecture supports a high degree of both access and location transparency.

Consider a simple example: two companies within a group independently maintain relational databases. One company is a manufacturer; the other manages private health care.

The *Manufacturer* database has an *Employee* table with attributes as shown in Figure 20.7. The *HealthCare* database, on another site, has a *Doctor* table with different attributes. These two tables can be made to appear **congruent** using views. The differences in attribute names are masked by allocating pseudonyms in the view. If there were also differences in attribute size or format, these could also be hidden with SQL functions in the view creation (Figure 20.8).

```
Manufacturer      Employee {emp_ID, surname ...}

HealthCare        Doctor {doctor_ID, familyname ...}
```

Figure 20.7 Local internal schemas.

```
Manufacturer DBA     Create view payroll as select emp_ID
                     ID, surname name from customers;

HealthCare DBA       Create view payroll as select doctor_ID
                     ID, familyname name from doctors;
```

Figure 20.8 Local conceptual schema.

```
Coordinator DBA      Create view payroll as
                     select * from [Manufacturer].payroll
                     Union
                     Select * from [HealthCare].payroll;
```

Figure 20.9 Global conceptual schema.

```
Headquarters DBA    Create synonym payroll for [Co-ordinator ].payroll;
```

Figure 20.10 Export schema.

```
Headquarters user    Select * from payroll;
```

Figure 20.11 Local or remote?

A central coordinator has access to these views granted to it and combines them into one view with a union operation (Figure 20.9).

Access to the global payroll view is granted to the headquarters site and the coordinator location further masked by use of a synonym (Figure 20.10).

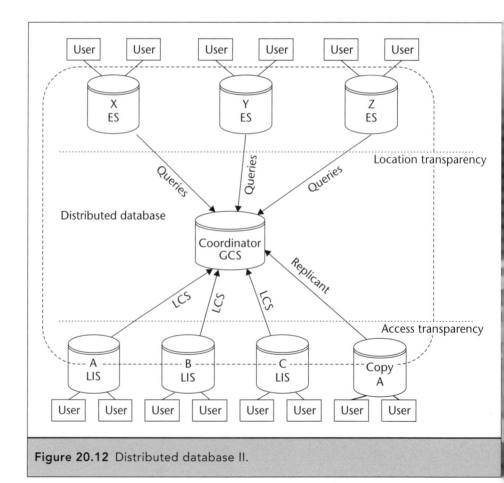

Figure 20.12 Distributed database II.

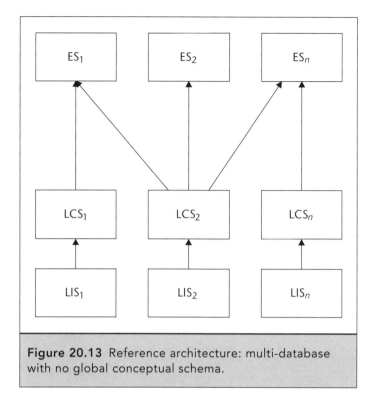

Figure 20.13 Reference architecture: multi-database with no global conceptual schema.

Users at headquarters can now issue a query against the local synonym without any necessary knowledge of the location of the data sources or the nature of the database types (Figure 20.11).

Because both of the example databases are relational, standard SQL is enough to harmonize the differences in the local data dictionaries. There is no requirement for both databases to come from the same vendor. If one of them were a Codasyl database then more complex local processing might be necessary to produce the desired effect. This might involve an additional purpose-built software layer for the local conceptual schema to convert from a navigational to a relational view of the data. Most vendors of modern network and hierarchical database software provide a form of SQL that reduces the need for such specialist software.

Finally, in practical terms, the coordinator host and each remote query host need a method of implementing the *[Host].object* notation. This will generally involve a client–server connection. The ES host will assume the role of client to the GCS host for the schema to be exported and for queries to be submitted (Figure 20.12).

The coordinator will assume the role of client to the individual node servers for the construction of the global conceptual schema. Where the database servers are all Oracle installations this is relatively easily achieved through a **database link**. If the nodes are relational and support SQL:1999 then communication can be achieved through ODBC or JDBC since the databases will have common Call Level Interfaces (see Sections 12.5 and 12.6). Special gateway products are available to provide the connection in more complex situations.

A variation of the reference architecture described above is the multi-database model, which, because of its high autonomy requirement, admits of no central coordination. Customized subsets of each local conceptual schema are taken directly into each export schema, which are therefore responsible individually for providing final location transparency and may use differing techniques for achieving this. This lack of central coordination also has implications for distributed transaction management (Figure 20.13).

20.2.2   HORIZONTAL FRAGMENTATION

A global conceptual schema brings together a unified view of the distributed data. Its principal functions are to hide precise locational detail from the export schema and to resolve the data into the *appearance* of single entity sets. In a situation where one node contains a complete entity set, this task is simplified and the GCS need do no more than create a synonym for the view represented in a single local conceptual schema.

Manufacturer.payroll (view)

ID	name
DF1547	Jones
BK1675	Brown

HealthCare.payroll (view)

ID	name
234876	Morecombe
456987	Wise

Coordinator.payroll (union view)

ID	name
DF1547	Jones
BK1675	Brown
234876	Morecombe
456987	Wise

Figure 20.14 Horizontal fragmentation.

However, when the individual local entity sets provide only a part of the desired view, the data is said to be fragmented. In the case where each local conceptual schema supplies only some of the rows of the view, the data is **horizontally fragmented**.

Horizontal fragmentation can be resolved through a union in the global conceptual schema. This is demonstrated in Figure 20.14. The local conceptual schemas must be **union compatible**: they must have the same attribute names and types.

20.2.3 VERTICAL FRAGMENTATION

When each of the local conceptual schemas provides only some of the attributes for the desired view, the data is **vertically fragmented**. A third company in the distribution example provides in-house training for the group.

It maintains a database that contains the *courses* table along with appropriate attributes. The Training Company's DBA creates a view for this table and makes it available to the coordinator (Figure 20.15).

A view of the training records for the *HealthCare* doctors can now be constructed in the GCS host by means of a join operation between two remote sites (Figure 20.16).

Vertical fragmentation is always resolved through a join. Creating the *medicaltraining* view merely saves the view definition in the *Coordinator*'s data dictionary. Should a query involving this view be received, it will have to be materialized. This can only happen at one site, since ultimately the join takes place in file and buffer operations. The join can take place at the *Training* site, the *HealthCare* site or at the *Coordinator* site. Whichever one is chosen is a matter for the distributed query optimizer (Figure 20.17).

```
(a) Training          Courses {course ID, delegate_ID, date, cost}

(b) Training DBA      Create view groupcourses as select * from courses;
```

Figure 20.15 (a) Local internal schema; (b) Local conceptual schema.

```
Coordinator     create view medicaltraining as
                select ID, name, course_ID, date, cost
                from [HealthCare].payroll, [Training].groupcourses
                where ID=delegate_ID;
```

Figure 20.16 Global conceptual schema.

HealthCare.payroll (view)

ID	name
234876	Morecombe
456987	Wise

Training.groupcourses (view)

course_ID	delegate_ID	date	cost
AC34	234876	...	...
AD45	456987	...	...
MF23	234876	...	...
MX34	234876	...	...
FD25	DF1547	...	...
FD25	BK1675	...	...

Coordinator.medicaltraining (join view)

ID	name	course_ID	date	cost
234876	Morecombe	AC34	...	...
456987	Wise	AD45	...	...
234876	Morecombe	MF23	...	...
234876	Morecombe	MX34	...	...

Figure 20.17 Vertical fragmentation.

20.2.4   HYBRID FRAGMENTATION

The most complex case occurs when there is both horizontal and vertical fragmentation. This is call hybrid fragmentation and must be resolved in the global conceptual schema by the use of both union and join views.

All of the schema solutions so far have involved unmaterialized views. Only the view definition is kept in the GCS. It is, of course possible to keep a materialized view in the coordinator's database. However, even if this is worth doing for performance reasons, care must be taken to ensure that the view does not go out of date with respect to its base views or tables.

When a distributed query is issued from an export schema host, it will be directed to the *Coordinator* host. The database there will be responsible for materializing the views taken from the various local conceptual schemas, correlating the result and passing it back to the originator of the query (Figure 20.18).

Taking into account the fragmentation effects in a distributed database and recording the allocation of fragments to participants leads to a redrawing of the ANSI/SPARC three-level model into a five-level diagram where the role of the central coordinator in providing location transparency is made more clear (Figure 20.19).

Coordinator.payroll
(union view)

ID	name
DF1547	Jones
BK1675	Brown
234876	Morecombe
456987	Wise

Training.groupcourses (view)

course_ID	delegate_ID	date	cost
AC34	234876	...	...
AD45	456987	...	...
MF23	234876	...	...
MX34	234876	...	...
FD25	DF1547	...	...
FD25	BK1675	...	...

Coordinator.medicaltraining (join view)

ID	name	course_ID	date	cost
234876	Morecombe	AC34	...	...
456987	Wise	AD45	...	...
234876	Morecombe	MF23	...	...
234876	Morecombe	MX34	...	...
DF1547	Jones	FD25	...	...
BK1675	Brown	FD25	...	...

Figure 20.18 Hybrid fragmentation.

20.3 DISTRIBUTED QUERY PROCESSING

A distributed query needs to have the same checks and operations applied to it as a local query. The differences are mainly to do with where those checks and operations happen. Figure 7.9 shows what happens to a local SQL query to transform it from the high-level SQL language into a series of file reads or writes, buffer sorts or sort merges.

In principal, distributed query processing is very similar (Figure 20.20). When the user query is issued at the export schema site it can only be checked syntactically and semantically against the export schema. When this is done, the query is passed to the *Coordinator* site.

Here, the query can be checked semantically against the global conceptual schema. The query is then passed for optimization where a distributed execution plan is devised. Remember, the *Coordinator* has the precise stored data details hidden from it because access transparency is provided at the local sites. The *Coordinator*

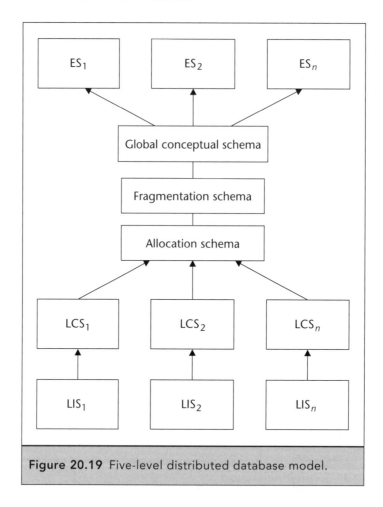

Figure 20.19 Five-level distributed database model.

does have location information and it has information about view objects. In effect, the distributed query is decomposed into a number of sub-queries, optimized for locational efficiency, which can be satisfied by each local site. There may be some processing of intermediate results by the *Coordinator* and the final result will certainly be correlated here and passed back to the user. Figure 20.20 shows a diagram of a general scheme for processing distributed queries.

When the queries are received at participating sites, they are subject to all the normal processes of a local query. In fact, because of autonomy considerations, the local site does not distinguish between a query from a local user and one from the *Coordinator*. The received query is subject to further syntactic and semantic checking and optimized to produce a local execution plan. This is put into effect through the recovery manager, which maintains the transactional logging and locking systems and the query executive, which performs the necessary file and buffer operations to satisfy the query.

The results of the local query are passed back to the *Coordinator*. Only the *Coordinator* is aware that it is an intermediate result in the global query. The local site has no knowledge of the global query, only the local query that it has completed. Each

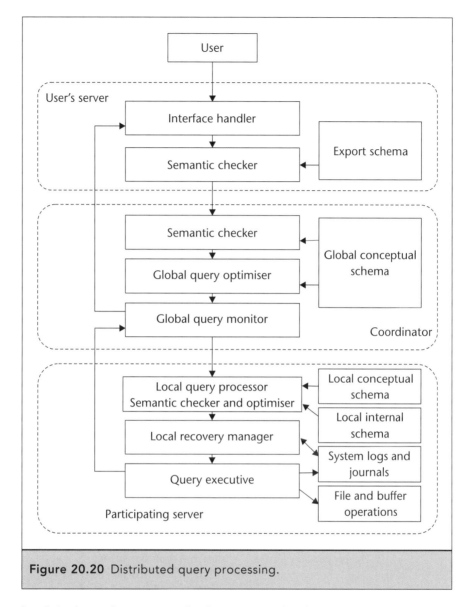

Figure 20.20 Distributed query processing.

local site has information only about its own local schemas. It has no knowledge of the other local sites in the distributed database. Only if it also receives a copy of an export schema and thus becomes both a local site and a remote query site can it have an inkling of remote data beyond its realm. In this case, it would still only be aware of the *Coordinator* as a source of that external data and the detailed location information would continue to be hidden from it.

Access and location transparencies in the distributed database keep every node on a *need to know* basis.

The purpose of the query optimizer in a centralized database is to construct the optimum execution plan based on information about the size, organization and key value distribution of schema objects in the query. The distributed query optimizer, based in the *Coordinator*, has similar aims but, because of local schema autonomy, it cannot impose a plan on the local server. Further, because the global conceptual schema, from which it must construct the plan, is based on information about views, not all of the necessary information is present to produce a fully detailed execution plan.

The *Coordinator*, through the GCS, is the only repository of locational information in the distributed database. Therefore the principal aim of distributed query optimization is an execution plan optimized for locational efficiency. The distributed query is decomposed into local queries that can be submitted to the local databases. The order of submission is crucial. Clearly, the components of a distributed join must exist before the join is executed. The global query must be serialized.

In addition, for efficient operation this decomposition must be based not only on knowledge of the location of each object in the GCS but also on where best to process the intermediate results of the query.

Figure 20.21 shows an example of how a distributed query might be decomposed. The query, received from an export schema host, requests a materialization of the GCS view, *medicaltraining*. The *Coordinator* decides to use its own database as the location for the join which it knows is implicit in the definition of *medicaltraining*. A temporary table, *tempA*, is constructed as the result of a local query to the *Training* site. A second temporary table, *tempB*, is established with returned materialized rows of a query to the *HealthCare* site. A join between the two temporary tables is then performed and the result returned to the source of the query (Figure 20.21).

```
Distributed query        select * from medicaltraining;

Decomposed queries       create tempA as select *
                             from [Training].courses;
                         create tempB as select *
                             from [HealthCare].payroll;
                         select ID, name, course_ID, data, cost
                             from tempA, tempB
                             where ID=delegate_ID;
```

Figure 20.21 Distributed query decomposition I.

The costs of this query are the sum of the two local queries, network transfers of their results to the *Coordinator* and the join at the Coordinator site.

There are at least two alternatives to this strategy (Figure 20.22). The materialized payroll view could be transferred to the *Training* site, the join performed there and the results transferred back to the *Coordinator*.

Distributed query   `select * from medicaltraining;`

Decomposed queries   `create [Training].tempA as select *`
                              `from [HealthCare].payroll;`
                        `select ID, name, course_ID, data, cost`
                              `from [Training].courses, [Training].tempA`
                              `where ID=delegate_ID;`

Figure 20.22 Distributed query decomposition II.

Notice that although the transfer of the payroll rows from *HealthCare* to *Training* seems to be done in one statement, it will involve an implicit temporary table on the *Coordinator* since *HealthCare* is unaware of *Training*'s existence and cannot perform the transfer directly. A third strategy would be to transfer the *courses* rows to *HealthCare* and to perform the join there.

As far as the global query is concerned, the most efficient plan is the one that restricts network traffic the most. If *payroll* is small compared to *courses* then the second strategy might be best. The transfer of *payroll* to *Training* would have little network cost and the join result would be small because only a restricted number of rows from *courses* would match the transferred *payroll* rows.

No rational decision about this can be made without some information about the relative sizes of the materialization of *payroll* and *courses*. In Section 7.3, the *analyze* command was demonstrated as a means of collecting table statistics which the local optimizer uses. The *Coordinator* could, from time to time, collect similar statistics by materializing the views in the GCS and analyzing them.

Once the global query has been decomposed and the local queries dispatched to the local nodes, the local query optimizer assumes responsibility for the final transformation of the received query into optimum file and buffer operations. Not only are statistics taken into account, but also information about table storage structure, indexes and so on.

20.5 ⋲ DISTRIBUTED TRANSACTIONS

The transaction mechanism for assuring the data security of a centralized database was discussed at length in Chapter 8. The properties of atomicity, consistency, isolation and durability are just as important for a distributed database

A database must guarantee that all statements in a transaction, distributed or non-distributed, either commit or roll back as a unit. The effects of an ongoing transaction should be invisible to all other transactions at all nodes; this transparency should be true for transactions that include any type of operation, including queries, updates, insertions or deletions.

In a distributed database, transaction control must be coordinated with the same characteristics over a network to maintain data consistency, even if a network or system failure occurs.

The particular problem for distributed transactions is that the global query is decomposed into a serialized set of local transactions that are submitted to autonomous local servers. If one of these should fail for any reason and the others succeed, the distributed view will be compromised. Each local server will maintain local consistency through its transaction mechanism, but there must be some form of transaction control exercised through the *Coordinator*.

20.5.1 TWO-PHASED COMMIT

The atomicity and consistency of a distributed database can only be guaranteed if all of the local transactions succeed or, if one fails, the others are rolled back. In order to achieve this situation, a voting system is superimposed on the distributed transaction. Essentially, this divides the end of the transaction into two parts or phases. The system is known as the **two-phased commit** or 2PC (Figure 20.23).

At the end of each local transaction, the transaction is either in a pre-commit state or a failed state (see Figure 8.1). A voting coordinator asks each participating server to vote according to its state. If there is **unanimity** for a global commit, the voting coordinator issues a global commit command and each participating server

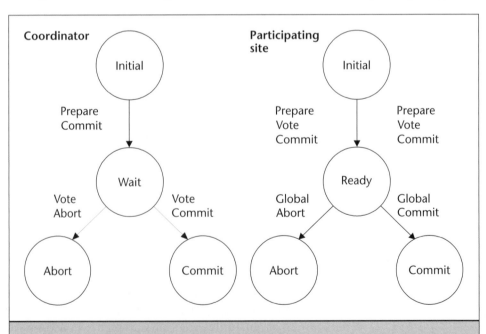

Figure 20.23 Two-phased commit state transitions.

commits its local transaction and acknowledges the command to the voting coordinator.

If there is so much as one vote against a global commit then the voting coordinator issues a global abort command. Servers that were in a pre-commit state perform a rollback, servers that were in a failed state move to the abort state. In each case an acknowledgement is again sent back to the coordinator.

The two-phase commit mechanism attempts to guarantee that either all participating servers in a distributed transaction commit or all roll back. A two-phase commit mechanism also protects implicit local DML operations performed by integrity constraints or triggers.

Most mainstream database packages implement 2PC. There are many articles in the research literature that propose the strengthening of the 2PC mechanism to take into account its perceived limitations, such as failure of the voting coordinator during either of the phases or failure of a participant after voting. Any extensions to 2PC, such as those that allow for compensating (reverse) transactions to be issued if atomicity were compromised or for the election of a replacement voting coordinator, would have to be included in specially constructed software.

20.5.2   DISTRIBUTED CONCURRENCY

The two-phase commit guarantees atomicity, durability and consistency. There is still a need to preserve the isolation principle through concurrency control.

The global transaction manager, as part of its function, dispatches the optimized and decomposed global query as discrete local queries. While each of these local queries is securely isolated within the local server by that server's lock and log managers, a problem arises from the fact that the local server has no knowledge of the part that each local query is playing in a global query.

Consider two global queries received and passed through the global transaction process. The first reads a table at one site as a precursor to updating matching rows at another site. The second updates rows in the table at the first site. If the local database is operating according the SQL92 transaction principles (see Section 8.8), the first transaction could experience non-repeatable reads or phantom reads.

Some form of concurrency control at the global query level is required to avoid this situation by imposing a serializable level of concurrency. A taxonomy of the various concurrency control schemes proposed by researchers, investigated in experimental installations or adopted by vendors is given in Figure 20.24.

As with centralized databases, the first division is between optimistic and pessimistic methods.

Optimistic methods, whether lock-based or using timestamps, postpone conflict resolution or validation, until the time that a transaction enters the pre-commit phase. Reads are taken from committed data; writes are made to so-called shadow files and kept private from other transactions. The validation phase determines whether the execution of the transaction was serializable. If it was, the transaction is committed. If it was not, the transaction is rolled back and restarted after a random time delay. Sections 8.6.3 and 8.6.4 discuss the tests for validation.

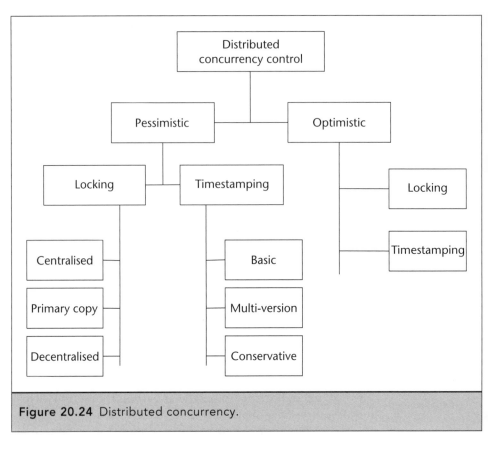

Figure 20.24 Distributed concurrency.

Optimistic control does not produce wait states or mutual exclusion. Therefore deadlocks will not arise. Not having to maintain and check lock acquisition reduces the transaction manager's overhead. This favours throughput, but may result in a large number of restarts if its use is not matched to the type of processing in the distributed database (Table 20.1).

Table 20.1 Conditions for optimism.
All transactions are read-only
Many transactions, each accessing/modifying only a small amount of a very large dataset
Fraction of transaction executions in which conflicts take place is small compared to total

Pessimistic methods validate the acquisition of locks or the sequence of timestamps at the moment of request. A lock manager grants locks based on lock compatibility, as shown in Table 8.3. In a distributed database, the lock manager, which may not necessarily be collocated with the global transaction manager (if, indeed, there is one), maintains a lock table on global schema objects. Local schema objects are under the control of the local database.

If the distributed database has only one repository for the lock table and only one lock manager then this is a centralized system.

There are two ways of distributing the work of a centralized lock manager. The Primary Copy method identifies a primary site for each item in the GCS. Each lock request is made to that site. Several sites may thus assume responsibility for the management of all of the global schema objects. Each one is responsible not only for a particular schema object, but also for any replicas of that object that may exist. This reduces the susceptibility of the overall distributed database to a single point of failure in the locking system, but there is still a single point of failure, and perhaps a bottleneck, for each schema object.

A distributed locking system copies the entire locking information to every node that originates global queries. Each node is capable of updating this information either to grant lock acquisition or to reclaim relinquished locks. However, permission to update the locks is restricted to the current holder of a token or baton which circulates among the nodes.

Changes made by the baton-holder are broadcast as update messages before the baton is passed on. Lock requests or releases are made at the node originating the transaction and thus involve no network traffic, but are delayed until the node receives the baton. The total number of messages is reduced, but response time is increased because transactions are held at each node until the baton arrives. Similarly, the baton cannot be passed on until acknowledgements of the broadcast changes have been received.

Distributed timestamps and multi-versioning follow similar lines to their centralized cousins. One major difficulty is obtaining accurate timestamps across the network where each CPUs clock is drifting at a different rate. One proposed solution to this problem is a ticket server that would issue sequentially ordered tickets to transactions as they started. Transaction ordering in the validation phase would then be based on ticket ordering.

20.6 ⊆ REPLICATION

Replication is the process of copying and maintaining database objects, such as tables, in multiple databases that make up a distributed database system. Changes applied at one site are captured and stored locally before being forwarded and applied at each of the remote locations. This is called update propagation and it is a central requirement in keeping all the replicas consistent with each other.

Replication can bring a number of advantages to a distributed database system, but it also brings an additional set of problems that are principally concerned with the maintenance of consistency between the replicated data.

If copies of database objects are made, the overall database will become more resilient to individual node failure or to breaks in the network. The failure transparency is enhanced if a transaction can proceed by using an alternative replica, although the failed site's replica will be inconsistent with any updates.

Distributed database systems may collocate replica tables that are frequently the subject of global queries, with the users responsible for such queries. Having copies of heavily accessed database may avoid repeatedly sending the full dataset across a network to support global joins. Performance may be enhanced through this technique, but any gains may be mitigated by network costs in propagating updates.

In order to make the information about replicas available to the distributed database it is clearly necessary to extend the scope of the model that has been used so far. The inclusion of a replication schema at the coordinator level is one way to do this. Figure 20.25 shows a model for a heterogenous, distributed multi-database with limitations on the autonomy of local databases: a federated multi-database.

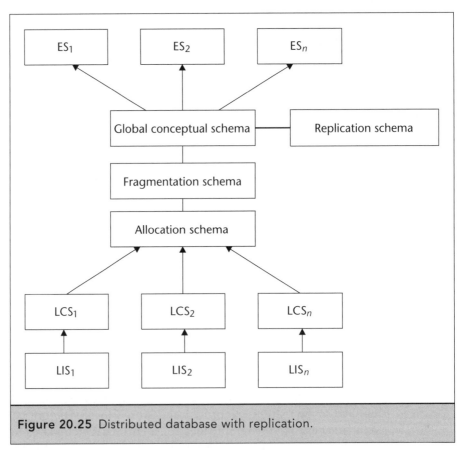

Figure 20.25 Distributed database with replication.

Data can be replicated using updatable materialized views of global schema objects created under the control of the coordinator at selected local sites. An updatable materialized view allows inserts, updates and deletions of rows in the view.

One of the sites holding the replicated materialized views will be the master or originating site. This site holds the base tables that support the view. Depending on the autonomy of local sites within the distributed database, it might be desirable that these tables remain directly accessible for local transactions. If the base tables are updated directly, the local materialized view will be inconsistent with its base tables, as will the replicas of it that are distributed around the nodes of the distributed database. Such autonomous local updates will have been made outside of any global query.

The only solution is that autonomy must be reduced to disallow direct updates to the base tables of replicated materialized views. The introduction of replication into a distributed database has implications for the autonomy of local sites. Conversely, if local sites must remain fully autonomous then replication of data from those sites becomes problematic.

Replication within a distributed database also has implications for distributed query optimization, for transaction control and for concurrency control.

20.6.1 QUERY MANAGEMENT WITH REPLICATION

If a replicated object is to participate in a query, the distributed query optimizer must now make use of the replication schema to select which of the replicas will be used directly. The selection criteria will be based on whether replicas are collocated with other global schema objects in the query. This will be particularly relevant if localized joins can be achieved. If a replica is to be updated in the query, then the inclusion of propagation updates in the closing phase of the query will be included in the transaction execution plan produced by the optimizer.

The global transaction manager receives the execution plan and submits its components as queries to the local databases. Normally, two-phased commit procedures would be instituted either by the global transaction manager or by the temporary appointment of a commit point server. There are several voting protocols that can be used when a distributed database has replicated elements. These involve a relaxation of 2PC's consensus (commit needs a unanimous vote) rule to a **quorum** or majority rule.

If a network failure partitions the distributed database into two sections that cannot communicate, one of them will consist of more nodes than the other. This is called the **primary partition**. Only nodes in the primary partition can now participate in the voting decision. If the primary partition contains all the unreplicated nodes or enough replicas to ensure that the entire updated dataset is present, voting can proceed. The secondary partition must, by this definition, contain only replicas or the originating sites of replicas now found in the primary partition. If the commit point server is not in the primary partition, a replacement can be elected.

If the sites in the primary partition that vote to commit contain all of the updated dataset, the commit request is issued. All of the replica sites in the secondary partition and those replicas in the primary partition not voting to commit are marked as inconsistent. When the inconsistent sites are restored to the distributed database, the commit point server for the transaction issues propagation updates to bring them back into consistency.

Because of the replicas in the distributed database, the transaction has survived a catastrophic network event. All of this has been hidden from the user issuing the original global query. Failure transparency is enhanced when replication is present at a cost of rather complicated procedures. There are several variations of this simplified account of quorum voting protocols in the research literature. These are concerned with multiple network partitions, identification of primary partitions, failures of voters or coordinators.

20.7 ⊝ DISTRIBUTED DATABASE CASE STUDY

The Utopian Professional Players Association (UPPA) is the trade union for players in the UFL. It has a small budget and cannot afford the same kind of expensive computing and software systems that the UFL has invested in.

Surprisingly, the UFL has agreed that it can have limited access to the main Oracle system for taking players' personal details into its membership system. The membership system runs in Microsoft Access and one of its functions is to record the monthly membership subscription paid by each of the players.

Access has a way of making the connection to Oracle based on the ODBC standard. Before the Access program can make the connection, the local ODBC driver manager must have a data source configured for its use.

In Windows XP this is done through the Administrative Tools folder of the Control Panel. Figure 20.26 shows the Data Source configurator screen. An Oracle ODBC driver is added to the driver manager when Oracle is installed. The driver configuration specifies which Oracle instance the data source will use and its ODBC name. Fill in the form as shown, with suitable amendments, and click on *Test Connection* until the *success* message appears.

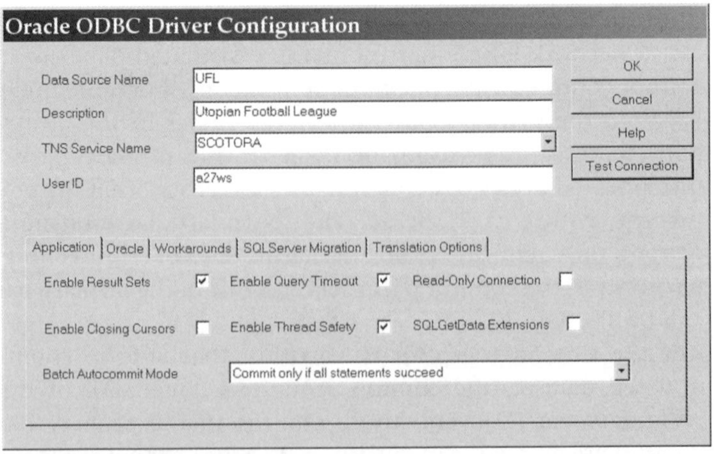

Figure 20.26 ODBC DSN configuration.

After clicking on OK, the new data source, UFL, is listed in the Machine Data Source tab (Figure 20.27).

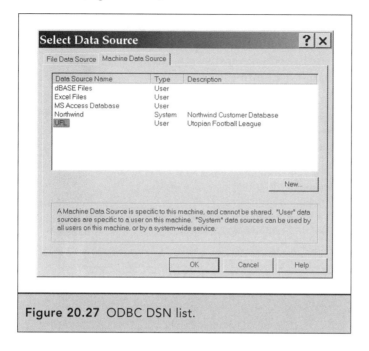

Figure 20.27 ODBC DSN list.

This data source can be used to connect to the UFL database from any ODBC-compliant program. As well as MS Access this includes Excel, PowerPoint or Word and any user program, written in (say) C++ with the ODBC API.

Launch the MS Access program and create a blank database called *ufltest*. Select *File |Get External Data|Link Table* from the Access main menu. The file selector dialog appears. Select *ODBC Databases ()* from the *Files of Type* drop down. The DSN selector appears.

Select the UFL data source and supply the password for the Oracle user name configured in it (Figure 20.28).

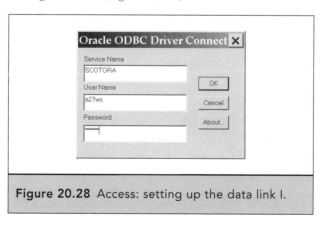

Figure 20.28 Access: setting up the data link I.

The tables in the user schema are displayed. Choose the *Players* table and check the *Save Password* box. Click on *OK*.

The Oracle table is now installed in Access as an updatable view called *A27WS_PLAYERS* (Figure 20.29). It is updatable because the password was saved with the view definition and Access is free to connect with the data source to synchronize data whenever the view changes. Opening the view in Access will also bring the latest data into the view.

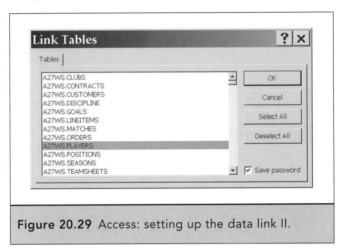

Figure 20.29 Access: setting up the data link II.

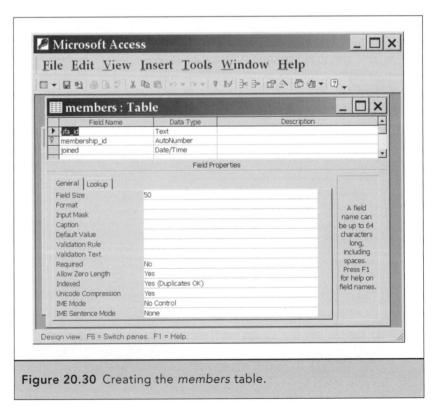

Figure 20.30 Creating the *members* table.

If the password were not saved with the view definition, a read-only view would be created and a snapshot of the data would be taken. Any changes in the data on the Oracle side would need a new snapshot to be taken manually.

A simple Access application that uses this table view can now be constructed. The members table has just three fields. Figure 20.30 gives the details.

The query shown in Figure 20.31 appends rows into members. It takes the *ufa_id* from each player and today's date as the date of joining. Because the *membership_id* is a primary key and is an autonumber type, it is automatically incremented for each row inserted. Access calls this an *append query*. It is stored in the database a query *insert members*.

```
INSERT INTO members ( ufa_id, joined )
SELECT A27WS_PLAYERS.UFA_ID, Date () AS Expr1
FROM A27WS_PLAYERS;
```

Figure 20.31 Insert rows into *members.*

A join view can now be created between members and *A27WS_PLAYERS*. The join is made on the common field, *ufa_id*. This is a *select* query and is stored as *members and players* (Figure 20.32).

```
SELECT members.ufa_id, A27WS_PLAYERS.SURNAME, A27WS_PLAYERS.FORENAME,
A27WS_PLAYERS.DATEOFBIRTH, A27WS_PLAYERS.NATIONALITY,
A27WS_PLAYERS.CLUB, members.membership_id, members.joined
FROM A27WS_PLAYERS RIGHT JOIN members ON A27WS_PLAYERS.UFA_ID =
members.ufa_id;
```

Figure 20.32 The join view: *members and players.*

The subscriptions table has a simple structure, shown in Figure 20.33. This table can be populated with the append query *insert subs*, shown in Figure 20.34.

The *members* form can now be created using the forms wizard (Figure 20.35). The main form is based on the *members and players* view and contains a sub-form based on *subscriptions*. The form and its sub-form are linked in a master/detail relationship, based on *membership_id*. The Access database, *ufltest.mdb*, is available on the book's web site. The datalink to Oracle will need localizing.

The data link to the *Players* table is providing all of the transparencies described earlier in the chapter. Once the link is configured, it behaves just like a local table with no special processing or knowledge about location required. Any changes to players' data are recorded in the Oracle base table. Changes made directly to the table show up in the view. Concurrent access is provided by normal lock management on the Oracle side.

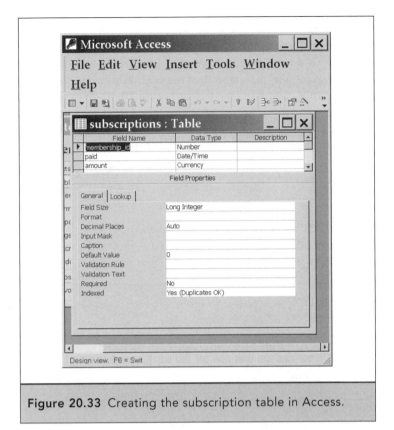

Figure 20.33 Creating the subscription table in Access.

```
INSERT INTO subscriptions ( membership_id, amount, paid )
SELECT [members ].membership_id, 25.76 AS Expr1, DateAdd("m",5,Date
()) AS Expr2
FROM members;
```

Figure 20.34 *Insert subs.*

20.8 KEY TERMS

Distributed systems	Shareable system resources are distributed across a network
Transparencies	The use of remote resources is made as similar to local access through software layers that perform transformations without user awareness
Distributed databases	A single or multiple view of data residing in independent databases distributed across a network

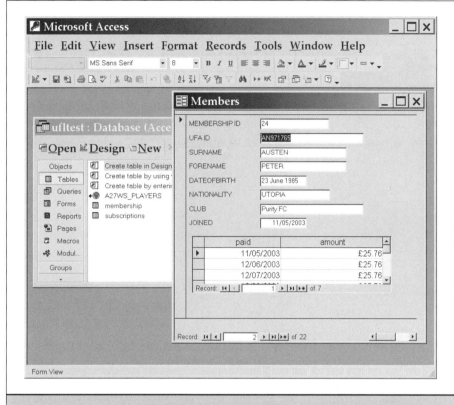

Figure 20.35 Populate the subscriptions table with an append query.

Schemas	Local schemas are exported and consolidated, often in a global conceptual schema. The whole or part is then re-exported to global query users
Processing	The system for processing global queries may be distributed or centralized. Needs similar functionality as for a single database
Optimization	Global queries may be optimized for locational efficiency
Transactions	Global queries need ACID properties. Distribute concurrency controls; two-phase commit
Replication	Selected local databases are replicated on remote hosts. Aid to reliability and availability. Replication transparency need facilities for update propagation and defence against network partitions

20.9 ⊨ EXERCISES

(i) Research the various proposals in the literature for centralized and distributed deadlock detection and resolution. Write a simulation of deadlock detection in a language of your choice.

(ii) *As network speeds and reliability increase, any benefits of distributing data for performance improvement have long since disappeared.* Discuss this statement in relation to what you can find in the research literature and in reliable sources on the Internet.

CHAPTER 21

TEXT AND DOCUMENT MANAGEMENT

There's a great text in Galatians,

Once you trip on it, entails

Twenty-nine distinct damnations,

One sure, if another fails.

Robert Browning, *Soliloquy of the Spanish Cloister*

21.1 ∈ INFORMATION OVERLOAD

Documentation for businesses, governments, news media, universities, libraries and practically every organization plays an increasingly critical role. It is fundamental to their ability to provide public and private services based on knowledge assets and even to sustain their existence.

And yet, the amount of information in the form of text, diagrams, pictures, sound and video kept on electronic media is expanding at a phenomenal rate and is seemingly out of control. It becomes more difficult to manage and, most importantly for the user, to navigate.

Since the mid-1970s, attempts have been made to integrate text and other media into the general range of information systems available to public and private organizations of all sizes. In this chapter, we shall look at some of the underlying principles of document management and some simple solutions (Table 21.1). The final section reviews Oracle's interMedia Text package and illustrates its use.

Table 21.1 Information retrieval – development phases.

Text load and indexing	Recognize file format, convert to common format for presentation; establish word string pattern; word location analysis (inversion); suffix stemming
Text analysis	Document signatures; automated thesaurus
Issue queries	Adaptive query feedback

21.2 HOW LONG IS A STRING?

The problems with text are both syntactic and semantic. Text is written in human languages and humans are still generally better at interpreting and understanding language than computers. The syntactic problem relates to structural uncertainty; the semantic problems relates to the meaning of words and their contexts.

English has a grammar that sometimes seems more often defined by the exceptions rather than by the rules of usage. The structure of a language can sometimes be defined only in the simplest terms. English language consists of words, which make up sentences. One or more sentences make paragraphs and one or more paragraphs make up documents. Sentences should contain a verb but not always. There should be a subject, but this is sometimes inferred. Subject: verb: object. That last sentence passed Microsoft Word's grammar check with flying colours! (Without the colons, Word objects to it.)

Most information retrieval systems take words as the basic building block of their databases. Different file formats from text processors or HTML from Internet sources can be read directly and are usually converted into a common presentational format in order to display the context of searches.

Divining the meaning of words within sentences, paragraphs and documents is a critical factor in ensuring that queries bring back results that are relevant to the searcher's purpose. Many documents, even formal reports and manuals, contain colloquialisms, ambiguities, analogies and other figures of speech, which make it difficult to interpret. Establishing semantic linkage between documents which are about the same subject but do not necessarily contain the same words will enhance the search for relevant, pertinent and timely information.

Dealing with the syntactic and semantic problems associated with language takes place during the three phases of an information retrieval (IR) system's development.

21.2.1 WHAT IS A WORD?

A definition of a word is needed before bulk loading of documents can begin. The simplest definition is a string of alphabetic characters separated by spaces or punctuation. However, some words contain punctuation. *It's* is a word and so is £50.00.

Three groups of characters can be defined within the English ASCII character set (Table 21.2). The word *concordable* refers to the concordances long maintained and created manually by librarians and which are, essentially, inversions of important documents.

Table 21.2 Character actors.

Concordable	A...Z 0...9 £ These characters can always contribute to word strings. A word always starts with one of these characters.
Optionally concordable	'/.@ These characters may contribute to word strings if they are followed immediately by a concordable character. If this is not the case, they must be considered as a word terminator.
Non-concordable	,<>?!()*& These characters never contribute to word strings and must be considered word terminators.

21.2.2 INVERTED INDEXES

The simplest structural definition of a language in terms of words, sentences, paragraphs and documents gives a clue to the easiest way to convert the flow of text into something that a database might be able to store. To create a table in a database it is necessary to formulate an entity which has a fixed number of attributes, each one with a known type and domain.

A word is the best choice as the basic entity in a text database. It can easily be stored as a string type. A word has a size of between 1 and, say, 30 characters[1] and data about its position in a sentence, a paragraph and a document can easily be collected.

Figure 21.1 shows an inversion of a single document into an un-normalized relation. The occurrence of each word is characterized by four numbers, which indicate the document, the paragraph, the sentence and the position in the sentence. This a lossless decomposition because the original document can be reconstituted from the list. The word *the* occurs twice: at positions 1 and 5; *cat* at position 2; *sat* at position 3; *on* at position 4 and *mat* at position 6.

When normalizing this relation, it will be more efficient to allocate an integer key taking up 64 bits than to use the word itself as the primary and foreign keys. The number is allocated to a word from a sequence in the order that the word is discovered. A simple SQL query reveals the sentence (Figure 21.2).

---

1 Outside of chemical names, one of the longest words in English is antidisestablishmentarianism (28 characters). Welsh is another matter entirely!

Word	Occurrence
CAT	1,1,1,2;
MAT	1,1,1,6;
ON	1,1,1,4;
SAT	1,1,1,3;
THE	1,1,1,1; 1,1,1,5

Figure 21.1 Inverted index.

Word	Word_No
CAT	2
MAT	5
ON	4
SAT	3
THE	1
Words relation	

Word_No	Doc	Para	Sentence	Position
1	1	1	1	1
2	1	1	1	2
3	1	1	1	3
4	1	1	1	4
1	1	1	1	5
5	1	1	1	6
Occurrences relation				

```
Select word from words, occurrences
Where words.word_no=occurrences.word_no
and doc=1 and para=1 and sentence=1
order by position;

WORD
-------
THE
CAT
SAT
ON
THE
MAT

6 rows selected.
```

Figure 21.2 In the beginning was the word... and then the occurrence.

21.2.3 STOP THAT

Small connecting words like *if*, *and* and *but* take up a large proportion of English language text. Just 48 conjunctions, prepositions and other words contribute more than 50% of any normal document. Filtering these words out with a stop list is another good method for ensuring that the word list contains entries with a rich information content.

21.2.4 ROOT AND BRANCH

Queries will be enhanced if distinct forms of words are not filed as different words in the database. Regular verb tenses: play, playing, played; adjectives: national, nationally, sufficient; adverbs: systematically, successfully; and plurals should all be filed as occurrences of their root, which is generally a noun or a verb. Removal of suffixes such as *ally*, *ient*, *ness* and *fully* is relatively easy in English. Even double suffixes, such as in *hopefulness*, can be filtered out.

This results in a smaller word list and allows a semantic link to be established between the variously suffixed word roots. Plurals, adjectives and adverbs generally describe similar concepts to their roots.

Filtering prefixes would also reduce words to their root, but is generally not a good idea nor so easily achieved. Prefixes are often negations of the root: helpful, unhelpful, theist, atheist. Removing the prefix would mean that opposing concepts were being joined in the database.

Text inversion, identification of words as patterns of character classes, stopped words and suffix stemming are the major algorithmic techniques that can be applied to the syntactic analysis of documents during the loading phase. Other techniques exist, but suffer from the law of diminishing returns. The computing and programming efforts that must be employed do not render corresponding improvements in query efficiency.

21.2.5 NEAR TO YOU

Much can be discovered about the meaning and context of words by the company they keep. The data in the occurrences table gives a number of possibilities for measuring **proximity** (Table 21.3).

If a word occurs in the same document as another, they may have a semantic connection. If the word *analysis* occurs in the same sentence as *systems* then it probably has a different association than if it were in the same sentence as *inorganic*.

Early text retrieval systems developed a similar syntax for queries based on logical connectors, illustrated in Figure 21.3. Although results based on binary logical or proximity operators could be ranked in terms of the number of 'hits' returned, the query relied on the *presence* or *absence* of the actual search terms in the document.

Table 21.3 Proximity searches.	

`systems AND analysis`
`systems AND analysis NOT`
`inorganic`
	Returns documents where both terms occur at least once. The second query excludes those documents that also contain the word inorganic.

`systems /p2 analysis`	Returns documents which contain the two words within 2 paragraphs of each other.
`systems /s3 analysis`	Documents where the two words occur within 3 sentences of each other.
`systems w/4 analysis`	Documents where the words occur within four words of each other

21.2.6   RECALL AND PRECISION

There are number of different measures that attempt to assess a particular IR system's ability to search a document collection effectively and efficiently. They are based on the concept of **relevance**. Whether a document is relevant is subjective. It depends on the individual researcher, on the query formulation and on the researcher's own knowledge and understanding of the subject of the search.

When a query is performed against a document collection, some documents will be retrieved and other rejected (Figure 21.3). Of the retrieved documents, some will be relevant and others not. The rejected documents will also consist of some that would have been relevant and some that were correctly rejected. Consideration of the relative proportions of these four groups of documents leads to measures of the effectiveness of the search.

	Relevant	Not relevant
Retrieved	a: Hits	b: Noise or fallout
Not retrieved	c: Misses	d: Correctly rejected

Recall: $a/(a + c)$: proportion of relevant items retrieved out of the total number of relevant items contained in a database

Precision: $a/(a + b)$: a signal-to-noise ratio – proportion of retrieved materials that are relevant to a query

Figure 21.3 Recall and precision.

Used together, the two ratios express the filtering capacity of the system. Recall and precision tend to be inversely related. Attempts to introduce factors that increase recall may diminish precision, and vice versa.

21.2.7   WIDENING THE SEARCH

Methods to increase recall usually rely on including documents that are relevant to the concepts contained in the search terms, although those precise terms may not actually appear in the document.

There are two principal ways of doing this. One is to process the database looking for words that often appear together in documents. If this correspondence meets certain statistical tests, then it may be possible to generate an automatic search thesaurus of related terms. If the words appear to be about related concepts or topics then perhaps when a search is made for one term its related terms will indicate an additional set of documents which, although they do not contain the actual search term, may be about the same topic.

Automatic thesaurus generation is a problematic task and involves highly complex statistical balances in attempting to produce an objective, calculated relevance factor. Ranking the returned documents on the strength of their *relevance connection* to the original search is one way of limiting the relegation of precision in favour of recall.

A second method involves the characterization of a document as containing certain key concepts or themes. After making an initial query, using normal or expanded word matches, the user marks certain retrieved documents as being particularly relevant. The system attempts to characterize these choices using complex statistics to represent the user feedback. A document signature is produced which is then reapplied to the database to retrieve other documents with similar signatures but which were not included in the original retrieval.

The extended query can then be saved and reapplied against an increasing document collection. The objective is to extend recall without compromising precision.

21.2.8   EVALUATING IR SYSTEMS

Most evaluations of IR systems use recall and precision as one of the quantitative tests of an evaluation of an IR system (Table 21.4). The problem for such evaluations is finding an objective measure for relevance and estimating the relevant documents that are not retrieved (misses) in a search.

21.3 ⊆ ORACLE TEXT

Oracle Text is a package supplied with the Enterprise Edition. It provides specialized tools for managing document collections. Text content is integrated with structured data about the documents and may form part of a general information system for an organization. Applications can access text content through both object or relational interfaces. Text retrieval applications can query and analyze documents from local or Internet sources. Data may be originated in most common formats.

Table 21.4 Evaluating IR systems.

Common criteria

Recall
Precision
User effort
  Amount of time a user spends conducting a search
  Amount of time a user spends negotiating his inquiry and then separating relevant from irrelevant items
  Response time
Benefits
Search costs
Cost effectiveness
Cost benefits

The text services require users to be granted the CTXAPP role, which enables them to create indexes in the context format, create preferences that specify default indexing and query behaviour, make text queries and use the Oracle Text PL/SQL packages

Dynamic text data, where documents are regularly added to the database, require repeated index maintenance. This can be done manually by the user or automatically by the CTXSYS administrator launching the *ctxsrv* server, which performs index updates as documents are added.

21.3.1 LOADING AND INDEXING TEXT

Documents are loaded in a table. Structured information, such as author, publisher and publication date, can be inserted into columns within the table with appropriate data types. Each row of the table thus represents one document in the collection. The text content is loaded into a single column, which can be a *VARCHAR2*, *CLOB*, *BLOB*, *CHAR* or *BFILE* according to the size characteristics of documents in the collection. The document is loaded unchanged into the column. The column, therefore, must be capable of holding the full document. About a page of text can be held in a *VARCHAR2* or a *CHAR* column. 4 GByte can be loaded into a *CLOB*, *BLOB* or *BFILE* column.

The table *fitness_reports* contains summary reports on player injuries that all clubs are required to post in the UFL database (Figure 21.4). In this case, the *text* column can hold a maximum of 200 characters. The column is loaded directly from the insert statements and does not come from a pre-existing document. A special index of type *ctxsys.context* is constructed on the *text* column of *fitness_reports*.

Larger entries could be held in a binary large object (*BLOB*) column (Figure 21.5) and Oracle has facilities to load external files into such a column. These can be originated in a number of common formats, including HTML, Microsoft Word (.doc), and Adobe Acrobat (.pdf). The external file is loaded unchanged into the

| create table | ```
create table fitness_reports (ufa_id varchar2 (10),
                              author varchar2 (20),
                              report_date date,
                              text varchar2 (200));
``` |
| insert rows | ```
insert into fitness_reports
values('AK675280','Mercury', '15-Jan-03','Antonio
has an Achilles tendon strain which is responding
to treatment');
``` |
| | ```
insert into fitness_reports
values('VB376512','Mercury', '01-Dec-02','Lucius
has a knee tendon injury. He is not expected to
play for about six weeks');
``` |
| | ```
insert into fitness_reports
values('AK675280','Mercury', '15-Feb-03','Antonio
is now undertaking light training');
``` |
| | ```
insert into fitness_reports
values('AK675280','Mercury', '01-Mar-03','Antonio
is now match fit');
``` |
| Index text column | ```
create index fitndx on fitness_reports(text)
indextype is ctxsys.context;
``` |

Figure 21.4 Loading and indexing text I.

| create statement | ```
create table contract_details
           (contract_id number primary key,
           ufa_id varchar2 (10),
           club varchar2 (25),
           contract_date date,
           contract_text blob);
``` |
| sql*loader command | ```
sqlldr userid=a27ws/qwerty control=loader1.txt
``` |

Figure 21.5 Loading text II.

column. It is only during the indexing process that the word recognition software strips the formatting for the index entries.

A *BLOB* cannot be copied directly into a row using the standard DDL *insert* statement. The SQL*Loader utility is used to insert or append rows. This utility runs from a DOS prompt. Figure 21.5 shows the command line. There are two parameters: the user's authentication and the name of the control file that contains instructions for the loader program.

The contents of the control file (loader1.txt) are shown in Figure 21.6. This indicates a datafile (loader2.txt) which contains the structured row data and an external file reference for the text data, the table to be loaded and the columns represented in the datafile. The datafile itself contains one row of data, including the name of a Word document containing the full contract details.

loader1.txt

```
LOAD DATA
INFILE 'loader2.txt'
INTO TABLE contract_details
FIELDS TERMINATED BY ','
(contract_id, ufa_id, club, contract_date, ext_fname FILLER CHAR(80),
contract_text LOBFILE(ext_fname)TERMINATED BY EOF)
```

loader2.txt

```
1,VB376512,Purity FC,21-Jul-00, C:\Docs\Contract.doc,
```

Figure 21.6 SQL*Loader files.

Large objects are not stored in the same way as other data. A large object (LOB) is stored near the row and a reference called a lob locator is actually stored in the table column. The locator is used internally by Oracle to reference the actual contents of the LOB.

Once the file has been copied into the database by the SQL*Loader program, the *contract_text* column can be indexed in the same way as previously. The MS Word format is detected automatically when a context index is created and formatting is stripped from words in the index (Figure 21.7).

```
create index conndx on contract_details(contract_text) indextype is
ctxsys.context;
```

Figure 21.7 Indexing text.

The system has defaults for the way in which *context* indexes are created. It detects the column type and uses filtering for binary column types like *long raw*, *BLOB* or *BFILE*. This avoids formatting characters appearing in the index. If English is the language specified when the database was installed a standard stop list is used to eliminate unnecessary words from the index. Fuzzy and stemming queries are enabled and supported by the index.

Index maintenance is necessary after an application inserts, updates or deletes documents in the base table. This can be done manually with *ALTER INDEX*, or an external process, *ctxsrv*, can be made part of the Oracle instance, providing automatic synchronization.

21.3.2 TEXT QUERIES

The *contains* function is used to search the text column; the function appears in the *where* clause, specifying the search condition. Word matches are made by using a context index on the column holding the loaded text.

The *contains* function takes three parameters: the column to be searched, the search term and an optional numeric label (Figure 21.8).

```
SELECT ufa_id, substr(text,1,50) from fitness_reports
        WHERE CONTAINS(text, 'tendon', 1) > 0;


UFA_ID     SUBSTR(TEXT,1,50)
---------- --------------------------------------------------
VB376512   Lucius has a knee tendon injury. He is not expect
AK675280   Antonio has an Achilles tendon strain which is res

2 rows selected
```

Figure 21.8 Searching text I.

The function returns a relevance score based on how many documents contain the search term compared to the total number of documents in the collection. Testing the returned value as greater then zero gives those rows holding the search term (Figure 21.9).

```
select ufa_id, club from contract_details
        where contains(contract_text, 'salary', 1) > 0;

ufa_id     club
---------- ------------
VB376512   Purity FC

1 row selected.
```

Figure 21.9 Searching text II.

When the text is held in a LOB column, it cannot easily be returned directly in an SQL query. The LOB could be holding as much as 4 GByte. The first row of *contract_details* actually holds about 4 MByte.

```
select ufa_id, club score(1)from contract_details
          where contains(contract_text, 'salary', 1) > 0;

UFA_ID      CLUB               SCORE(1)
----------  -----------------  ---------
VB376512    Purity FC              100
```

Figure 21.10 Searching text III.

The relevance score is associated with the label in the *contains* function and can be determined using the *score* operator (Figure 21.10). Since there is only one document in the *contract_details* table, any successful query will have a relevance of 100. As more documents are added, the relevance score will become more meaningful and can be used for ranking the returned rows.

Proximity searching is also enabled, using the *near* operator. This takes as a parameter a list of search words or phrases and a specification of how much separation may occur between words in the list. If the order variable is set to *TRUE*, the terms must occur in the order they appear in the list. Notice in Figure 21.11 that the *near* clause is quoted within the *contains* operator. *Max_span* is set to 50, so the *contains* function will return greater than zero for any row where the three search terms occur within 50 words of each other.

```
NEAR((word_1, word_2,..., word) [, max_span [, order]])

select ufa_id, club score(1)from contract_details
where contains(contract_text, 'near((transfer, fee, agent)',50) 1) > 0
;

UFA_ID      CLUB                             SCORE(1)
----------  -----------------------------    ---------
VB376512    Purity FC                            100

1 row selected.
```

Figure 21.11 Proximity search.

The normal Boolean operators (AND, OR, NOT) can also be applied to search terms as well as stemming and fuzzy searches. Thesaurus searches are also available and a special thesaurus may be loaded for technical applications

All of the context features can be used by an external program such as a Java application using JDBC. The user may then be presented with a graphical user interface that constructs the *select* statement from user responses. The query returns a *hitlist* that may be ordered by relevance. The document contents can then be delivered to the application and displayed in a variety of ways.

Typically, a text query application allows the user to view the documents returned by a query. The user selects a document from the hitlist and then the application presents the document in some form. With interMedia Text, the document can be rendered in different ways. For example, documents can be presented with query terms highlighted.

Oracle Text provides most, if not all, of the standard indexing and querying mechanisms and operators found in a typical IR system. In addition, it offers structured data describing the text data and seamless integration with a general organizational information system. All queries, for whatever type of data, use SQL.

These advantages are won at a cost. The loading of documents into the database where they will be subject to transactional control is complicated, and the tools provided have not been made easier to use in several generations of Oracle release versions. The administration of specialized thesauri to underpin theme searching and expanded and constricted term searching is similarly confusing and non-instinctive.

Enhancing the text retrieval facilities beyond the functions provided to incorporate sophisticated user relevance feedback systems or applications using artificial intelligence involves the same stages of systems development as for any major information system. Easy production of a graphical user interface can be accomplished using, for example, the Java language with access to the database through JDBC. In addition to the text management facilities, such a system would have built-in reliability and data safety stemming from the standard transactional control mechanisms of Oracle.

21.4 ⊂ KEY TERMS

Unstructured data	Documents do not have a fixed structure. They consist of sentences that contain a variable number of words. Words also have a variable length but a reasonable maximum
Inversion	Analyzing a document using words as the basic entity but retaining positional information so that the document can be reconstructed and so proximity searching is possible. Referred to as indexing because the word and its position are analogous to a database index

Stopping	Removing common words that are necessary connectors in the language but do not convey a high degree of semantic content (if, and, but)
Stemming	Removing (for English) word endings so that verbs, adjectives and adverbs are reduced to a common root which conveys common semantics. (run*ning*, run*able*, run*ability* = run)
Recall	A measure of search efficiency: compares result set with total documents in collection
Precision	A measure of search efficiency: compares result set with total number of relevant documents
Query feedback	System learns user preferences for selecting relevance. This can be based on document signatures: a statistic that records when a word has the preferred meaning and is accompanied by certain other words

21.5 ⋲ EXERCISE

(i) Design a schema for a large-scale document collection. Sample collections are available for download from the Internet. One example is the RFC (Request for Comment) archive[2]. Load the sample collection into the database.

Alternative tracks:

- Design and implement a user interface using a Java application to make queries and display results.
- Perform interactive queries with explain plan to analyze performance.
- Analyze recall and precision with the sample data.

---

2 http://www.rfc-editor.org/download.html

BIBLIOGRAPHY

Aho, A. V., Beeri, C. and Ullman, J. D. (1979) The theory of joins in relational databases. *ACM Transactions on Computer Systems*, **4**(3), 297–314.

Armstrong, W. (1974) Dependency structures of database relationships. In *Proc. IFIP Congress*, Geneva, pp. 580–583.

Armstrong, W. W. and Delobel, C. (1980) Decomposition and functional dependencies in relations. *ACM Transactions on Database Systems* **5**(4), 404–430.

Bayardo, R. J. Jr and Agrawal, R. (1999) Mining the most interesting rules. In *Proc. 5th ACM SIGKDD Conference on Knowledge Discovery and Data Mining*, pp. 145–154.

Bernstein, P. A. (1976) Synthesizing Third Normal Form relations from functional dependencies. *ACM Transactions on Database Systems*, **1**(4), 277–298.

Birrell, A. and Nelson, B. J. (1984) Implementing Remote Procedure Calls. *ACM Transactions on Computer Systems*, **2**(1), 39–59.

Booch, G., Jacobson, I. and Rumbaugh, J. (1998) *The Unified Modeling Language User Guide*. Reading, MA: Addison-Wesley.

Burns, T., Fong, E. N., Jefferson, D., Knox, R., Mark, L., Reedy, C., Reich, L., Roussopoulos, N. and Truszkowski, W. (1986) Reference Model for DBMS Standardization, Database Architecture Framework Task Group (DAFTG) of the ANSI/X3/SPARC Database System Study Group. *ACM SIGMOD Record*, **15**(1), 19–58.

Camps, R. (1996) Domains, relations and religious wars. *ACM SIGMOD Record*, **25**(3), 3–5.

Carey, M. J. (1994) Parallel Database Systems in the 1990s. In *Proceedings of the 1994 ACM SIGMOD International Conference on Management of Data*. ACM Press. p. 466.

Carey, M. J. and Livny, M. (1989) Parallelism and concurrency control performance in distributed database machines. In *Proceedings of the 1989 ACM SIGMOD International Conference on Management of Data*. ACM Press. pp. 122–133.

Carey, M. J. and Stonebraker, M. (1984) The performance of concurrency control algorithms for database management systems. In *VLDB 1984, Proc. Tenth International Conference on Very Large Data Bases*, Singapore. San Francisco, CA: Morgan Kaufmann. pp. 107–118.

Carey, M. J., Mattos, N. M. and Nori, A. (1997) Object–relational database systems: principles, products and challenges (Tutorial). *Proceedings of the ACM SIGMOD International Conference on Management of Data*.

Chamberlin, D. D. (1976) Relational Data-Base Management Systems. *ACM Computing Surveys*, **8**(1), 43–66.

Chaudhuri, S. and Dayal, U. (1997) An overview of data warehousing and OLAP technology. *ACM SIGMOD Record*, 26(1), 65–74.

Chen, P. P. (1976) The entity–relationship model – toward a unified view of data. *ACM Transactions on Database Systems*, **1**(1), 9–36.

Codd, E. (1970) A relational data model for large shared data banks. *Communications of the ACM*, **13**(6), 377–387.

Codd, E. F. (1971) Normalized Data Structure: A Brief Tutorial. *Proceedings of 1971 ACM-SIGFIDET Workshop on Data Description, Access and Control.* ACM Press. pp. 1–17.

Codd, E. F. and Associates (1993) *Providing OLAP (on-line analytical processing) to user-analysts: an IT mandate.* Commissioned by Arbor Software (now Hyperion Solutions).

Colliat, G. (1996) OLAP, relational, and multidimensional database systems. *SIGMOD Record,* **25**(3), 64–69.

Davidson, S. B., Garcia-Molina, H. and Skeen, D. (1985) Consistency in partitioned networks. *ACM Computing Surveys,* **17**(3), 341–370.

Database Task Group (1971) *CODASYL: DBTG Report.* Technical Report, ACM.

Deux, O. (1990). The story of O_2. *IEEE Transactions on Knowledge and Data Engineering,* **2**(1), 91–108.

DeWitt, D. J. and Gray, J. (1990) Parallel database systems: the future of database processing or a passing fad? *SIGMOD Record,* **19**(4), 104–112.

Dobkin, D. P., Jones, A. K. and Lipton, R. J. (1979) Secure databases: protection against user influence. *ACM Transactions on Database Systems,* **4**(1), 97–106.

Elmagarmid, A. K. and Du, W. (1990) A paradigm for concurrency control in heterogeneous distributed database systems. In *Proceedings of the Sixth International Conference on Data Engineering.* IEEE Computer Society Press. pp. 37–46.

Fadous, R. and Forsyth, J. (1975) Finding candidate keys for relational data bases. In *Proceedings of the 1975 ACM SIGMOD International Conference on Management of Data.* ACM Press. pp. 203–210.

Garcia-Molina, H. and Barbará, D. (1985) How to assign votes in a distributed system. *Journal of the ACM,* **32**(4), 841–860.

Garcia-Molina, H. and Kogan, B. (1987) Achieving high availability in distributed databases. In *Proceedings of the Third International Conference on Data Engineering.* IEEE Computer Society. pp. 430–440.

Gotlieb, L. R. (1975) Computing joins of relations. In *Proceedings of the 1975 ACM SIGMOD International Conference on Management of Data.* ACM Press. pp. 55–63.

Gray, J. (ed.) (1998) *The Benchmark Handbook,* 2nd edn. San Francisco: Morgan Kaufmann. Available on-line at: `http://www.benchmarkresources.com/handbook/introduction.html`.

Gray, J. and Graefe, G. (1997) The five-minute rule ten years later, and other computer storage rules of thumb. *ACM SIGMOD Record,* **26**(4), 63–68.

Gray, J., Chaudhuri, S., Bosworth, A., Layman, A., Reichart, D., Venkatrao, M., Pellow, F. and Pirahesh, H. (1997) Data cube: a relational aggregation operator generalizing group-by, cross-tab, and sub totals. *ACM Journal of Data Mining and Knowledge Discovery,* **1**(1), 29–53.

Harman, D. (ed.) (1992) *The First Text REtrieval Conference (TREC1),* National Institute of Standards and Technology, Special Publication 500-207. (The Text REtrieval Conference (TREC) started in 1992 as part of the TIPSTER Text program. Its purpose is to support research within the information retrieval community by providing the infrastructure necessary for large-scale evaluation of text retrieval methodologies. TREC reports are available at http:// trec.nist.gov/.)

Inmon, W. (1996) *Building the Data Warehouse.* New York: John Wiley & Sons.

Jarke, M. and Koch, J. (1984) Query optimization in database systems. *ACM Computing Surveys,* 16(2), 111–152.

Khoshafian, S. and Valduriez, P. (1987) Sharing, persistence, and object-orientation: a database perspective. In *Advances in Database Programming Languages.* ACM Press/Addison-Wesley. pp. 221–240.

Khoshafian, S., Valduriez, P. and Copeland, G. P. (1988) Parallel query processing for complex objects. In *Proceedings of the Fourth International Conference on Data Engineering.* IEEE Computer Society. pp. 210–217.

Kimball, K. (1996) *The Data Warehouse Toolkit.* New York: John Wiley & Sons.

Kung, H. T. and Robinson, J. T. (1981) On optimistic methods for concurrency control. *ACM Transactions on Database Systems*, **6**(2), 213–226.

Labio, W. and Garcia-Molina, H. (1996) Efficient snapshot differential algorithms for data warehousing. In *Proceedings of 22th International Conference on Very Large Data Bases, VLDB '96*. pp. 63–74.

Martin, J. (1990) *Information Engineering*. Englewood Cliffs, NJ: Prentice Hall (three volumes).

Munz, R. and Krenz, G. (1977) Concurrency in database systems – a simulation study. In *Proceedings of the 1977 ACM SIGMOD International Conference on Management of Data*. ACM Press. pp. 111–120.

Ng, W. and Yau, J. (2002) Adapting web interfaces by WHAT. In *International Conference on Adaptive Hypermedia and Adaptive Web Based System AH'2002*. Lecture Notes in Computer Science Vol. 2347. Berlin: Springer-Verlag. pp. 551–555.

Oracle Corp. (2002) *Oracle9i Application Developer's Guide – Object-Relational Features. Chapter 1, Introduction to Oracle Objects*. Release 2 (9.2).

Ries, D. R. and Stonebraker, M. (1977) Effects of locking granularity in a database management system. *ACM Transactions on Database Systems*, **2**(3), 233–246.

Roussopoulos, N. (1998) Materialized views and data warehouses. *ACM SIGMOD Record*, **27**(1), 21–26.

Sakai, H. (1980) Entity–relationship approach to the conceptual schema design. In *Proceedings of the 1980 ACM SIGMOD International Conference on Management of Data*. ACM Press. pp. 1–8.

Salton, G. (1968) *Automatic Information Organization and Retrieval*. New York: McGraw-Hill.

Sharman, G. C. H. (1976) A constructive definition of Third Normal Form. In *Proceedings of the 1976 ACM SIGMOD International Conference on Management of Data*. ACM Press. pp. 91–99.

Simsion, G. (1994) *Data Modelling Essentials*. New York: Van Nostrand Reinhold.

Skeen, D. (1981) Nonblocking commit protocols. In *Proceedings of the 1981 ACM SIGMOD International Conference on Management of Data*. ACM Press. pp. 133–142.

Spertus, E. and Stein, L. A. (1999) A relational databases interface to the World-Wide Web. In *Proceedings of the Fourth ACM conference on Digital Libraries*. ACM Press. pp. 248–249.

Stonebraker, M., Wong, E., Kreps, P. and Held, G. (1976) The design and implementation of INGRES. *ACM Transactions on Database Systems*, **1**(3), 189–222.

Thomas, R. H. (1979) A majority consensus approach to concurrency control for multiple copy databases. *ACM Transactions on Database Systems*, **4**(2), 180–209.

Tomasic, A., Garcia-Molina, H. and Shoens, K. A. (1994) Incremental updates of inverted lists for text document retrieval. In *Proceedings of the 1994 ACM SIGMOD International Conference on Management of Data*. ACM Press. pp. 289–300.

Van Rijsbergen, C. J. (1979) *Information Retrieval*. London: Butterworths. Available at http://www.dcs.gla.ac.uk/Keith/Preface.html.

Welty, C. and Stemple, D. W. (1981) Human factors comparison of a procedural and a nonprocedural query language. *ACM Transactions on Database Systems*, **6**(4), 626–649.

Yourdon, E. (1989) *Modern Structured Analysis*. Englewood Cliffs, NJ: Prentice Hall/Yourdon Press.

Zhang, A. and Elmagarmid, A. K. (1993) A theory of global concurrency control in multidatabase systems. *VLDB Journal*, **2**(3), 331–360.

APPENDIX

I am Sir Oracle,

And when I ope my lips let no dog bark!

William Shakespeare, *The Merchant of Venice*

A.1 INSTALLING ORACLE

The Oracle software can be downloaded from the Oracle web site (warning: 1.5 GByte) or purchased for minimal cost on a set of three CDs. Install the complete software on the hard drive of your PC. Follow the install instructions, choosing the Enterprise Edition install and select all the software components available. Your will need about 3.5 GByte of free space on your disk. There are a few choices to be made during installation:

- Select the standard example database without replication
- Specify a name for the Oracle instance (e.g. SCOTORA). This is the name of the Oracle process.
- Specify the communications protocols that will be configured for use (normally TCP/IP).
- Specify a different name for the SID (System Identifier), e.g. SCOTORACLE. This is the name of the database to which the process will connect.
- Specify passwords for the SYS and SYSTEM users. These are two DBA accounts that own the data dictionary structures. Write down the passwords.

If you have shared access to a network host running the full version of Oracle 9i then refer to your systems administrator for information on using the Oracle Enterprise Manager, passwords, connect strings and so on.

This book uses the standard configuration choices made for a local Enterprise Edition installed on a single PC running Windows XP Professional Edition; you may not see precisely the same screens if you are using any other configuration.

You will find that shortcuts to the main components of Oracle will make using the various packages easier. Using Windows Explorer, go to the directory `C:\Documents and Settings\All Users\Start Menu\Programs\Oracle - OraHome92`. Create a shortcut for this folder and drag it to your desktop.

The standard installation configures the Oracle server to start when the machine is switched on. When the machine is shut down the Oracle server will also be shut down. This is normally safe, as Oracle will recover automatically from an unscheduled shutdown. To be absolutely safe, use the Enterprise Manager to dismount the database and shut down the Oracle instance before shutting down the PC.

A.2 USING ORACLE ENTERPRISE MANAGER

Use the Enterprise Manager to perform routine maintenance and SQL*Plus to create user data structures and investigate the SQL language.

After starting the Enterprise Manager, select a database with which to connect. Login as the SYS user, give the password and select the role of SYSDBA.

Figure A.1 shows the Enterprise Manager after logging in. The connection to the database instance is highlighted. All of the object types in this database are shown as folders in a tree.

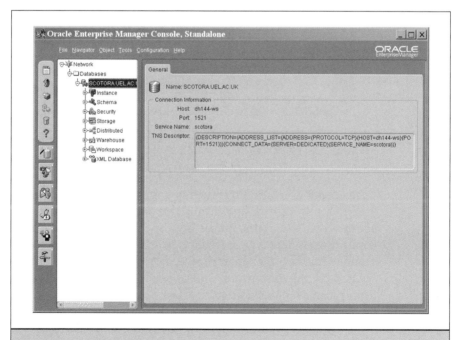

Figure A.1 Oracle Enterprise Manager.

Warning: the Enterprise Manager is a very powerful tool, especially when you are logged in as a DBA. You can ruin the database and make it inoperable if you make mistakes. If in doubt, cancel any operation about which you are not sure.

The user who will develop the UFL application must now be created. Click on the Security folder and then on the Users folder. Right click on the Users folder and select Create from the dropdown menu. The Create User Dialog appears. Specify a user name and a password in the General tab of the dialog (Figure A.2); click on the Role tab and from the list of different roles available, allocate the Connect and Resource roles to this new user. To do this simply select the CONNECT role and use the arrow symbol to copy it to the bottom section. Do the same with the RESOURCE role. These will allow the new user to connect to the instance and create tables, indexes and other structures.

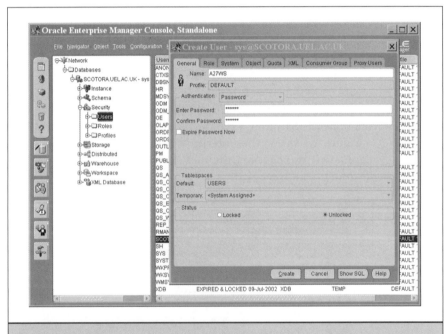

Figure A.2 Oracle Enterprise Manager: create user.

Developer users should generally have the same rights and privileges as operator users. This prevents a situation where parts of the application work for developers because of their higher status and operators cannot use the facility. When the application is deployed, parts of it can be segregated between users based on their group membership or their profile, not their rights.

Click on the System tab and allocate the UNLIMITED TABLESPACE privilege from those available using the arrow symbol. The new user will be able to create tables, indexes and other structures and populate them with data. The *SHOW SQL* button opens a frame containing the SQL commands that will be executed when the Create button is clicked.

The Enterprise Manager can also be used to inspect the properties of tables. Select the Schema folder and then select the folder SCOTT. A list of SCOTT's tables and indexes appears. Right clicking on the EMP table displays a pop-up menu; selecting *View|Edit* shows the structural definitions (attributes) of the table (Figure A.3).

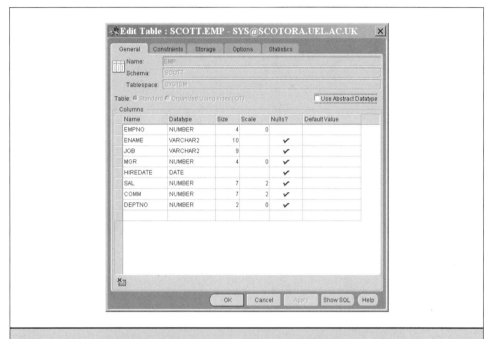

Figure A.3 Oracle Enterprise Manager: View/Edit table. The attributes (column definitions) of the EMP table.

Clicking on the tabs reveals other kinds of information about the selected table (Figure A.4).

The structure of the index can be examined by selecting it in the SCOTT schema, right-clicking and choosing *View|Edit* (Figure A.5).

Right-clicking on the *EMP* table and selecting *View|Edit Contents* from the pop-up shows the that the table has 14 rows (Figure A.6).

Nothing is private from the SYS user acting as SYSDBA. Allocating this role to anyone for a production database creates a position of great trust and responsibility.

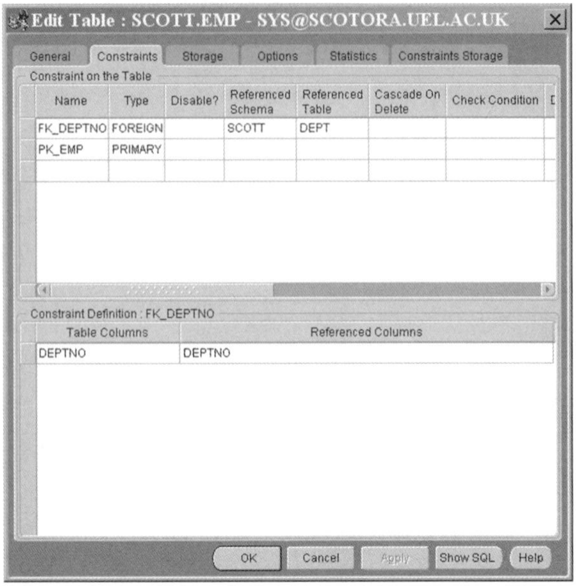

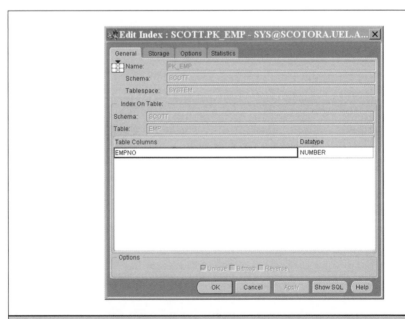

Figure A.4 Oracle Enterprise Manager: Constraints tab. SCOTT has defined two constraints for this table. *PK_EMP* defines a primary key that has resulted in an index called *PK_EMP* being established.

Figure A.5 Oracle Enterprise Manager. Details of the *PK_EMP* index. It is associated with the table *EMP* and has one attribute, *EMPNO*.

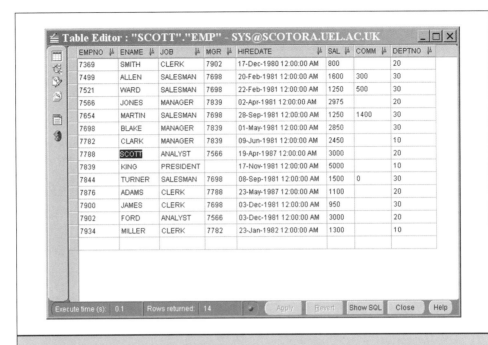

Figure A.6 Oracle Enterprise Manager: View|Edit Contents. Contents of the *EMP* table.

A.3 ⊆ USING SQL*PLUS

SQL*Plus is an interactive tool provide by Oracle. It emulates a remote terminal and enables the user to enter SQL statements and view the results. The SQL*Plus Worksheet is a Windows-aware version and is contained in the Enterprise Manager suite of programs. Launch the program from the *Oracle 9i Tools/Applications Development* folder.

Enter username, password and the Oracle service to which you wish to connect in the Login screen (Figure A.7).

The worksheet window is divided into four areas. There is a menu of options at the top and a command sidebar. The input pane is above the output pane. Enter the SQL statement in the input pane. Make sure it is terminated with a semi-colon. Click on Execute (the Lightning icon in the command side-bar) and the result of your query (or an error message) is shown in the output pane (Figure A.8).

Local script files can be run from the worksheet using the Worksheet drop-down menu item (Figure A.9). Browse the folders until you find the script you want.

Oracle supplied scripts are in `C:\Oracle\ora92\rdbms\admin`, or similar. Here you will find the scripts need to set up the explain table and format explain plan output. Most of the other scripts in this directory are restricted to DBA use.

Any scripts for establishing the UFL tables or the performance testing schema can be downloaded and run from your own folder.

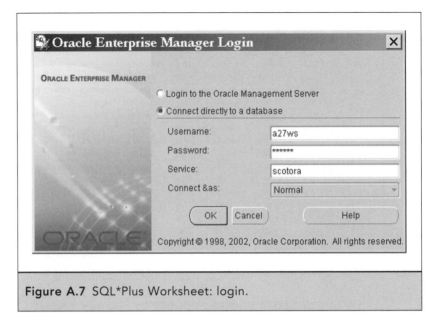

Figure A.7 SQL*Plus Worksheet: login.

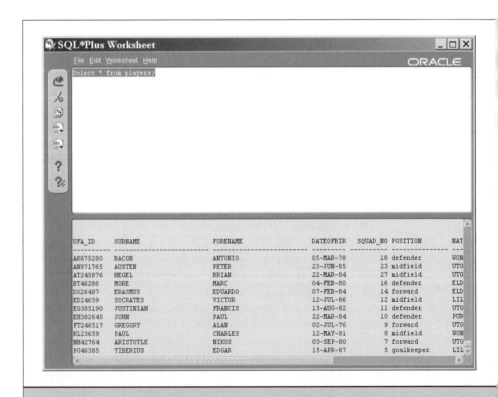

Figure A.8 SQL*Plus worksheet.

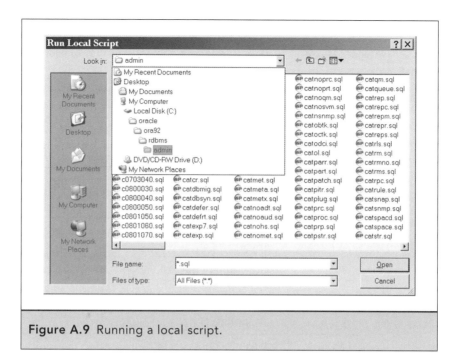

Figure A.9 Running a local script.

A.4 DATA TYPES, CLASSES AND EXCEPTIONS

Table A.1 Java primitive data types.

byte	8 bit integer	From −128 to 127
char	16 bit character	Unicode character set
short	16 bit integer	From −32768 to 32767
int	32 bit integer	From −2,147,483,648 to 2,147,483,647
long	64 bit integer	8 byte (64 bit) integer
float	32 bit floating point	A floating point type that takes a 4 byte number to about 7 decimal places ($\pm 2.0 \times 10^{9}$)
double	64 bit floating point	A floating point type that takes an 8 byte number to about 15 decimal places ($\pm 9.0 \times 10^{18}$)
boolean	True or false	T/F, Y/N, 0/1

Table A.2 Oracle data types.	
varchar2 (size)	Variable-length character string. Maximum size is 4000, and minimum is 1.
nvarchar2(size)	Variable-length character string having maximum size 4000 bytes.
number(p,s)	Number having precision p and scale s. The precision p can range from 1 to 38. The scale s can range from –84 to 127.
long	Character data of variable length up to 2 GByte
date	Valid date range from 1 January 4712 BC to AD 31 December 9999.
raw(size)	Raw binary data of length size bytes. Maximum size is 2000 bytes.
long raw	Raw binary data of variable length up to 2 GByte.
rowid	Hexadecimal string representing the unique address of a row in its table. This data type is primarily for values returned by the ROWID pseudocolumn.
urowid [(size)]	Hexadecimal string representing the logical address of a row of an index-organized table. The maximum size and default is 4000 bytes.
char (size)	Fixed-length character data of length size bytes. Maximum size is 2000 bytes.
nchar(size)	Fixed-length character data of length size characters or bytes, depending on the choice of national character set. Maximum size is 2000 bytes.
clob	Character large object containing single-byte characters. Maximum size is 4 GByte.
nclob	A character large object containing multibyte characters. Maximum size is 4 GByte.
blob	A binary large object. Maximum size is 4 GByte.
bfile	Contains a locator to a large binary file stored outside the database. Maximum size is 4 GByte.

Table A.3 Java/JDBC type mapping and methods.

Java type	SQL type	Access method
boolean	BIT	getBoolean(...)
byte	TINYINT	getByte(...)
short	SMALLINT	getShort(...)
int	INTEGER	getInt(...)
long	BIGINT	getLong(...)
float	REAL	getFloat(...)
double	DOUBLE	getDouble(...)
java.math.BigDecimal	NUMERIC	getBigDecimal(...)
java.lang.String	VARCHAR2	getString(...)
byte[]	VARBINARY	getBytes(...)
java.sql.Date	DATE	getDate(...)
java.sql.Time	TIME	getTime(...)
java.sql.Timestamp	TIMESTAMP	getTimestamp(...)
java.sql.Blob	BLOB	getBlob(...)
java.sql.Clob	CLOB	getClob(...)
java.sql.Array	ARRAY	getArray(...)
java.sql.Ref	REF	getRef(...)
java.sql.Struct	STRUCT	getObject(...)

Table A.4 PL/SQL named exception conditions.

ORA-00001	DUP_VAL_ON_INDEX	Attempt made to store duplicate values in a unique index column.
ORA-00051	TIMEOUT_ON_RESOURCE	Time-out occurred at the database while waiting for a resource.
ORA-01001	INVALID_CURSOR	Attempt made to use a cursor that is either not open or does not exist.
ORA-01012	NOT_LOGGED_ON	Attempt to issue a PL/SQL request while not connected to Oracle
ORA-01017	LOGIN_DENIED	Attempt to login to Oracle with an incorrect usernames or password.
ORA-01403	NO_DATA_FOUND	Single row Select returned no rows
ORA-01422	TWO_MANY_ROWS	Single row Select returned multiple rows
ORA-01476	ZERO_DIVIDE	Attempt to divide by zero.
ORA-01722	INVALID_NUMBER	Attempt to convert a character string to a number.
ORA-06500	STORAGE_ERROR	PL/SQL has run out of memory, or memory has become corrupted.
ORA-06501	PROGRAM_ERROR	PL/SQL has an internal problem
ORA-06504	ROWTYPE_MISMATCH	Cursor return type does not match assignment variable type
ORA-06511	CURSOR_ALREADY_OPENED	Attempt to open a cursor that is already open.

A.5 ⊆ PERFORMANCE EXPERIMENTS

```
Drop table customers;Drop sequence neworder;
Drop sequence newcustomer;Drop table orders;
Drop table lineitems;Create sequence neworder;
Create sequence newcustomer;
Create table customers(cust_id number primary key,
                       Surname varchar2 (20),
                       Forename varchar(15));
Create table orders (order_no number primary key,
                     Cust_id number,
                     Order_date date);
Create table lineitems(order_no number,
                       Product varchar2 (15),
                       Quantity number,
                       price number(6,2));
```

Figure A.10 SQL Create statements.

```
Create or replace package makeCustomer AS
    Function getString(x integer) Return varchar2;
    Procedure fillcustomer;
end makeCustomer;

create or replace package body makeCustomer as
    function getString(x integer) return varchar2 is
    cus varchar2 (25);
    y integer;
    BEGIN
    cus:='';
    for y in 1..x loop
       cus := cus||chr(abs(mod(dbms_random.random,26))+65);
    end loop;
    return cus;
    END getstring;
```

Figure A.11 RL/SQL package (*continued opposite*).

```
    procedure fillCustomer is
    a integer;   b integer;
    c integer;   d integer;
    e integer;   f integer;
    g number(6,2);
    BEGIN
    dbms_random.initialize (76835);
    for a in 1..100000 loop
      select newcustomer.nextval into d from dual;
      insert into customers (cust_id,surname,forename)
      values(d,getstring(15), getstring(12));

      for b in 1..5 loop
        select neworder.nextval into e from dual;
        insert into orders (order_no,cust_id,order_date)
        values(e,d,SYSDATE);
        for c in 1..4 loop
          f:=mod(abs(dbms_random.random),97);
          g:=mod(abs(dbms_random.random),1000)/23;
          insert into lineitems (order_no, product, quantity,price)
         values(e,getstring(15), f, g);
        end loop;
      end loop;
    end loop;
    dbms_random.terminate;
    end fillCustomer;
End makeCustomer;
execute makeCustomer.fillCustomer;
```

Figure A.11 (*Continued*)

```
select a.cust_id as cust,b.order_no,product,quantity,price,
sum(quantity*price) as tot
 from customers a, orders b,lineitems c
 where a.cust_id=b.cust_id
 and b.order_no=c.order_no
 and a.cust_id=20
 group by a.cust_id,b.order_no,product,quantity,price;
```

Figure A.12 Performance test query.

A.6 ⊂ ENTITIES AND RELATIONSHIPS

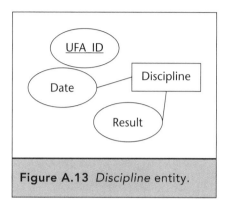

Figure A.13 *Discipline* entity.

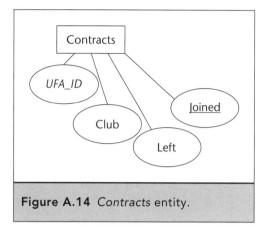

Figure A.14 *Contracts* entity.

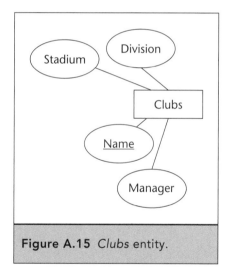

Figure A.15 *Clubs* entity.

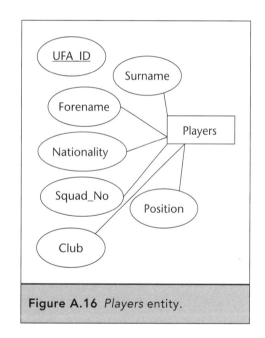

Figure A.16 *Players* entity.

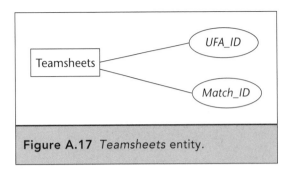

Figure A.17 *Teamsheets* entity.

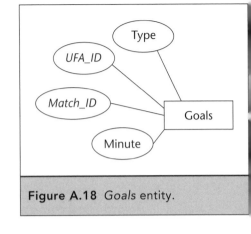

Figure A.18 *Goals* entity.

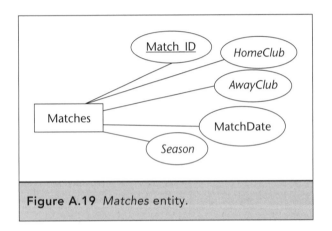

Figure A.19 *Matches* entity.

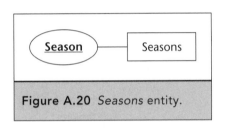

Figure A.20 *Seasons* entity.

A.7 ⊜ PL/SQL COLLECTION METHODS

Table A.5	
COUNT	Returns the number of elements that are contained within the collection.
EXISTS	Checks whether an element has been deleted or not – remember, nested tables can contain sparse elements, i.e. gaps are allowed! It does not work with Varrays, as these are dense collections.
FIRST	Returns the first (existing) element's subscript number (index) in a collection. In general this will be 1 – unless element 1 has been deleted!
LAST	Returns the last (existing) element's subscript number (index) of a collection.
LIMIT	This method is mainly of use to varrays. It returns the maximum number of elements a collection can contain. This method returns NULL with associated arrays and nested tables, as both are unbounded collection types.
PRIOR	Returns the subscript number of the previous (existing) element in the collection class. If there is no preceding element, NULL is returned.
NEXT	Returns the subscript number of the next (existing) element in the collection class. If there is no next element, NULL is returned.
EXTEND [(n)]	Allows the creation of one or more NULL elements in the collection set. This method does not work with associated arrays as they are implicitly extended as elements are added.
TRIM [(n)]	Physically removes one or more elements from the end of a collection set.
DELETE [(i)]	Used to delete specific elements from a collection, where (i) refers to an element's subscript. If no specific element is specified, all elements are deleted. This method does not work with varrays, as these are dense collections that do not allow gaps between elements.

INDEX